Beginnings & Endings

The Best of Beta Sigma Phi's Appetizers and Desserts

EDITORIAL STAFF

Executive Editor	Anita McKay
Managing Editor	Mary Cummings
Project Editor	Anne Lacy Boswell
Editorial Consultant	Georgia Brazil
Editor	Jan Keeling
Award Selection Judge	Charlene Sproles
Art Director	Steve Newman
Book Design	Jim Scott
Production Design	Jessie Anglin, Sara Anglin
Test Kitchen	Charlene Sproles

© Favorite Recipes® Press, A Division of Heritage House, Inc. 2003
   P.O. Box 305141, Nashville, Tennessee 37230

ISBN: 0-87197-511-4

Manufactured in the United States of America

First Printing 2003

Recipes for Cover photographs are on page 111.

Contents

Beta Sigma Phi

Dear Beta Sigma Phis,

This cookbook is dedicated to the many Beta Sigma Phi members around the world. I think you will find the recipes in this book interesting and creative for you to use. We all know what great cooks Beta Sigma Phis are! "Beginnings & Endings" will be a useful tool for you to use for your family or for entertaining.

When purchasing this cookbook, remember that you are helping Beta Sigma Phi chapters with a favorite project. Remember your family and friends with this cookbook. This is one they will enjoy.

With every good wish to you for successful "Beginnings & Endings."

Sincerely yours,

Walter W. Ross, III

Beginnings

Dips & Spreads

ARTICHOKE DIP

All of our sisters as well as our KEGS (Kappa Epsilon Guys) love this dip.

8 ounces cream cheese, softened
1/2 cup mayonnaise
1/2 cup sour cream
1 cup grated Parmesan cheese

1 garlic clove, minced
1 teaspoon dill weed
1/8 teaspoon salt
1 teaspoon Worcestershire sauce
1/2 small onion, chopped

Combine the cream cheese, mayonnaise, sour cream, Parmesan cheese, garlic, dill weed, salt, Worcestershire sauce and onion in a food processor container. Process for 2 minutes or until smooth. Spoon into a baking dish. Bake, uncovered, at 375 degrees for 45 minutes to 1 hour or until top is golden brown. Serve warm with tortilla chips. Yield: 24 servings.

Kim Floyd, Kappa Epsilon
Cartersville, Georgia

HOT ARTICHOKE DIP

You may use the microwave instead of the oven if you desire. Microwave on High for 5 minutes, stir, then microwave for 1 minute longer.

1 cup mayonnaise
1 (4-ounce) can artichokes, drained and chopped
1 cup grated Parmesan cheese

1/8 teaspoon hot red pepper sauce, or to taste
Green chiles or chopped green onions

Combine the mayonnaise, artichokes, Parmesan cheese and hot red pepper sauce in a bowl and mix well. Spoon into a baking dish. Bake, uncovered, at 350 degrees for 30 minutes. Top with green chiles and serve with crackers. Yield: 8 to 10 servings.

Pamela C. Bridger, Preceptor Psi
Sheridan, Wyoming

CHEESY ARTICHOKE DIP

Substitute any type of hot pepper sauce for the Tabasco if you like.

1 cup low-fat mayonnaise
1 cup (4 ounces) shredded mozzarella cheese
1 cup (4 ounces) shredded Cheddar cheese

1/4 cup grated Parmesan cheese
1 garlic clove, minced
Dash of Tabasco sauce
1 (14-ounce) can artichokes, drained and chopped

Combine the mayonnaise, mozzarella cheese, Cheddar cheese and Parmesan cheese in a large bowl and mix well. Stir in the garlic and Tabasco sauce. Stir in the artichokes. Spoon into a 9-inch pie plate. Bake at 350 degrees for 15 minutes or until bubbly. Serve hot with crackers. Yield: 15 servings.

Linda Bertram, Preceptor Zeta
Minnedosa, Manitoba, Canada

HOT ARTICHOKE DIP

2 (14-ounce) cans artichokes, drained and chopped
1 (4-ounce) can mild green chiles, chopped
1/2 cup grated Parmesan cheese

1 cup (4 ounces) shredded mozzarella cheese
1 cup mayonnaise
1/2 teaspoon garlic powder

Combine the artichokes, green chiles, Parmesan cheese, mozzarella cheese, mayonnaise and garlic powder in a large bowl and mix well. Spoon into a small lightly buttered baking dish. Bake, uncovered, at 350 degrees for 20 minutes. Serve warm with assorted crackers. Yield: 6 servings.

Jean Anderson, Preceptor Alpha Beta
Colorado Springs, Colorado

SPICY SPINACH AND ARTICHOKE DIP

1/2 cup (1 stick) butter or margarine	*8 ounces cream cheese, softened*
1 medium onion, chopped (about 1 cup)	*1 cup sour cream*
2 (10-ounce) packages frozen chopped spinach, partially thawed	*1 cup (4 ounces) shredded Monterey Jack cheese*
	1 cup (4 ounces) grated Parmesan cheese
1 (14-ounce) can artichoke hearts, drained and chopped	*2 tablespoons Tabasco sauce*
	Salt to taste

Melt the butter in a large skillet over medium-low heat. Add the onion and sauté for 5 minutes or until soft. Stir in the spinach and artichokes. Add the cream cheese, sour cream, half the Monterey Jack cheese, half the Parmesan cheese, Tabasco sauce and salt. Cook until heated through, stirring constantly. Pour into a baking dish and top with the remaining cheeses. Bake, uncovered, at 350 degrees for 10 to 15 minutes or until hot and bubbly. Serve with your favorite crackers. Yield: 10 to 12 servings.

Chris Van Gelder, Laureate Gamma Nu
Palmdale, California

BROCCOLI DIP

2 (10-ounce) packages frozen chopped broccoli, cooked and drained	*1 (6-ounce) can chopped mushrooms, drained*
	1 (10-ounce) can cream of mushroom soup
1/2 cup (1 stick) butter	*1 (6-ounce) roll garlic cheese or jalapeño cheese, sliced*
1 medium onion, chopped	

Arrange the broccoli in a 1 1/2- to 2-quart baking dish. Melt the butter in a skillet over medium-low heat. Sauté the onion and mushrooms in the butter until tender. Stir in the soup and garlic cheese. Cook until cheese is melted, stirring frequently. Pour the cheese mixture evenly over the broccoli. Bake, uncovered, at 350 degrees for 30 minutes. Serve with butter crackers. Yield: 32 servings.

Carmen Pousson, Eta Kappa
Iota, Louisiana

HOT BROCCOLI CHEESE DIP

8 ounces cream cheese, softened	*1 (10-ounce) package frozen chopped broccoli, thawed and drained*
1 cup sour cream	
1 rounded teaspoon Italian seasoning	
1 cup (4 ounces) shredded Cheddar cheese	

Mix the cream cheese, sour cream and Italian seasoning in a bowl. Stir in the Cheddar cheese and broccoli. Spoon into a 9-inch pie plate. Bake, uncovered, at 350 degrees for 20 minutes. Sprinkle with additional shredded cheese. Bake for 5 minutes longer. Serve with crackers. Yield: 15 to 20 servings.

Mary Prehm, Xi Gamma Eta
Paris, Tennessee

CURRIED CHEESE DIP

2 cups (8 ounces) shredded Cheddar cheese	*1/4 cup chopped scallions*
	1 (2-ounce) can sliced black olives, rinsed and drained
8 ounces cream cheese, softened	*1 1/2 teaspoons Madras curry powder*
1/2 cup milk	

Combine all the ingredients in a 1-quart slow cooker. Cook on High for 45 minutes to 1 hour or until very hot. Stir to mix well. Serve with assorted cut-up fresh vegetables or crackers for dipping. Yield: 25 servings.

Virginia Ann Thomas, Preceptor Gamma Eta
Merritt Island, Florida

DILL PICKLE DIP

2 large dill pickles, drained and shredded	*8 ounces cream cheese, softened*
	Pickle juice

Mix the pickles and cream cheese in a bowl. Stir in enough pickle juice to make dipping consistency. Serve with corn chips. Yield: 12 to 15 servings.

Joyce Homan, Laureate Delta Eta
Abilene, Texas

ONION DIP

3 large onions, chopped	*2 cups mayonnaise*
2 tablespoons butter	*1 garlic clove, minced*
2 cups (8 ounces) shredded Swiss cheese	*1 (8-ounce) can water chestnuts, drained and chopped*
1/2 teaspoon hot red pepper sauce	*1/4 cup water*

Sauté the onions in the butter in a skillet over medium-low heat for 10 minutes or until translucent. Combine the cheese, hot red pepper sauce, mayonnaise, garlic, water chestnuts and water in a bowl and mix well. Stir in the sautéed onions. Spoon into a glass 9×13-inch baking dish. Bake at 375 degrees for 25 to 30 minutes or until hot and bubbly. Serve with chips or crackers. Yield: 40 servings.

Vanette Allen, Laureate Zeta Eta
Bryan, Texas

❖ GARLIC PESTO DIP

8 ounces cream cheese, softened	1/2 cup sun-dried tomatoes in oil, drained and finely chopped
1/4 cup sour cream	
2 tablespoons butter, softened	1/2 cup pesto
4 garlic cloves, minced or pressed	

Combine the cream cheese, sour cream, butter and garlic in a bowl and mix well. Layer the sun-dried tomatoes, half the cream cheese mixture, pesto and the remaining cream cheese mixture in a glass baking dish. Chill, covered, for 24 hours. Invert onto a serving plate. Warm slightly and serve with crackers. Yield: about 2 1/2 cups.

Carol Best, Preceptor Beta Omicron
Westfield, New York

CHILI CON QUESO

If you prefer, you may microwave this dip on Medium for 10 minutes or until the cheese is melted, stirring occasionally.

16 ounces Mexican Velveeta cheese, cubed	1 (15-ounce) can chili without beans

Place the cheese in a 1-quart baking dish. Stir in the chili. Bake, uncovered, at 350 degrees for 1 hour or until cheese is melted. Stir occasionally. Serve hot with tortilla chips. Yield: 32 servings.

Joan Kilgallon, Xi Theta Beta
Ocala, Florida

CORN AND CHEESE SALSA

1 (15-ounce) can white corn, drained	1 cup (4 ounces) shredded Cheddar cheese
1 cup hot salsa	

Combine the corn and salsa in a saucepan over medium-high heat and cook until the mixture begins to bubble, stirring frequently. Add the cheese and heat until melted, stirring frequently. Serve hot over corn chips or tortilla chips. Yield: 10 to 15 servings.

Fay Scordato, Alpha Phi Master
Cantonment, Florida

TEXAS DIP

8 ounces cream cheese, softened	4 cups (16 ounces) shredded Cheddar cheese
1 (15-ounce) can chili	

Spread the cream cheese in a glass pie plate. Spread the chili over the cream cheese layer; layer the Cheddar cheese over the chili. Bake at 350 degrees for 25 minutes. Serve hot with corn chips or other chips. Yield: 24 servings.

Marie G. Smith, Alpha Zeta Master
St. Petersburg, Florida

MEXICAN DIP

Use low-fat cream cheese if you like.

16 ounces cream cheese, softened	1 (16-ounce) jar salsa
1 (16-ounce) can refried beans	2 cups (8 ounces) shredded Cheddar cheese

Spread the cream cheese in a 9x13-inch baking dish. Layer the refried beans, salsa and Cheddar cheese over the cream cheese layer. Bake at 350 degrees for 30 minutes. Serve with tortilla chips. Yield: 12 servings.

Melissa Cooper, Laureate Sigma
Mobile, Alabama

CHILI CHEESECAKE DIP

1 cup crushed tortilla chips	8 ounces Colby or Monterey Jack cheese, shredded
3 tablespoons butter or margarine, melted	1 (4-ounce) can chopped green chiles
16 ounces cream cheese, softened	Dash of Tabasco sauce
2 eggs	1 cup sour cream

Press a mixture of the tortilla chips and butter over the bottom and up the side of a 9-inch springform pan. Bake at 325 degrees for 15 minutes. Combine the cream cheese and eggs in a mixing bowl and beat until smooth. Add the Colby cheese, green chiles and Tabasco sauce and mix well. Pour into the prepared springform pan. Bake at 325 degrees for 30 minutes. Remove from oven. Spread the sour cream evenly over the top while cheesecake is still warm. Cool completely before removing from pan. Chill, covered, until ready to serve. Garnish with olives, salsa and sliced red or yellow bell peppers. Serve with tortilla chips. Yield: 20 servings.

Frances Parks, Alpha Sigma Master
St. Charles, Missouri

TEXAS CON QUESO

1 pound ground beef	2 (6-ounce) cans sliced mushrooms, drained
16 ounces Velveeta cheese	1 (4-ounce) can chopped green chiles
1 (8-ounce) jar picante sauce	
1 (10-ounce) can golden mushroom soup	

Brown the ground beef in a skillet, stirring until crumbly; drain. Add the cheese, picante sauce, soup, mushrooms and green chiles and cook over low heat until cheese is melted and mixture is hot, stirring frequently. Serve with chips. Yield: 12 servings.

Charlotte Backstedt, Xi Beta Xi
El Cajon, California

NACHOS

You may use 4 ounces Monterey Jack cheese plus 4 ounces jalapeño cheese if you prefer.

1 to 1½ pounds ground beef	*8 ounces Monterey Jack cheese, shredded*
2 (16-ounce) cans refried beans	*1 (8-ounce) bottle taco sauce, mild or medium-hot*
1 (4-ounce) can chopped green chiles	*Sour cream (optional)*

Brown the ground beef in a skillet with any desired seasonings such as chopped onion, chopped celery, garlic powder, salt and pepper, stirring until crumbly; drain. Spread the beef mixture in a 9×13-inch baking dish. Layer the refried beans, green chiles and cheese over the beef layer. Pour the taco sauce evenly over the top. Bake at 350 degrees for 30 to 40 minutes or until hot and bubbly. Spoon over tortilla chips. Top with sour cream and serve. Yield: 6 to 8 servings.

Gloria Diffenderfer, Xi Delta Psi
Redford, Michigan

NACHO BEAN DIP

1 pound ground beef	*1 (16-ounce) can spicy refried beans*
1 (6-ounce) bottle mild taco sauce	*8 ounces Cheddar cheese*
1 (4-ounce) can chopped green chiles	*1 (3-ounce) can sliced olives, drained*

Brown the ground beef in a skillet, stirring until crumbly; drain. Stir in the taco sauce and green chiles. Spread the refried beans in an even layer in a 9×13-inch baking dish. Layer the ground beef mixture over the refried bean layer. Shred the cheese and sprinkle evenly over the ground beef layer. Sprinkle olives evenly over the cheese. Bake at 350 degrees for 30 to 45 minutes or until hot and bubbly. Serve over broken regular or spicy tortilla chips. Garnish with chopped lettuce and tomatoes and sour cream. Yield: 8 to 10 servings.

Kay Fairbanks, Eta Xi
Bend, Oregon

REUBEN DIP

2 (3-ounce) packages thin sliced corned beef, chopped	*1 (6-ounce) can sauerkraut, well drained*
2 cups (8 ounces) shredded Swiss cheese	*5 tablespoons mayonnaise*
2 cups (8 ounces) shredded Cheddar cheese	*½ teaspoon prepared or dried mustard*

Mix all the ingredients in a bowl. Spoon into a 9×13-inch baking dish. Bake at 350 degrees for 30 minutes or until bubbly. Yield: 20 to 30 servings.

Norma Shelp, Alpha Iota
St. Louis, Missouri

CHICKEN CHILI DIP

2 boneless skinless chicken breasts, cooked and chopped	*1 (10-ounce) jar salsa*
	3 ounces cream cheese, softened
1 (15-ounce) can chili without beans	*2 cups (8 ounces) shredded Colby cheese*

Spread the chicken in an ungreased 7×11-inch baking dish. Combine the chili, salsa and cream cheese in a mixing bowl and beat at medium speed until well mixed. Spread the chili mixture over the chicken layer. Layer the Colby cheese over the chili layer. Bake at 350 degrees for 35 minutes or until heated through and cheese is melted. Serve with tortilla chips or crackers. Yield: 8 to 12 servings.

Dianne Berthe, Xi Alpha Sigma
Eagan, Minnesota

BUFFALO CHICKEN DIP

¾ to 1 cup chopped celery	*1½ cups (6 ounces) shredded sharp Cheddar cheese*
3 boneless skinless chicken breasts, cooked and shredded	*1 cup ranch salad dressing*
16 ounces cream cheese, softened	*6 to 12 ounces hot red pepper sauce (to taste)*

Sauté the celery in butter in a skillet until translucent. Stir in the chicken and cream cheese and cook over low heat until cream cheese liquefies. Add 1 cup of the shredded Cheddar cheese, the ranch salad dressing and hot red pepper sauce. Simmer until cheese is melted, stirring occasionally. Pour into a 2-quart baking dish. Sprinkle with the remaining Cheddar cheese. Bake at 300 degrees for 25 to 30 minutes. Serve with tortilla chips. Yield: 24 servings.

Darlene Rzodkiewicz, Laureate Zeta Iota
Pittsburgh, Pennsylvania

ANDOUILLE DIP

Andouille is a real touch of home for me. It makes me think of Louisiana and it's good Creole cookery.

1 pound ground beef, pork or chicken	2 pounds andouille or other precooked sausage
1 cup chopped onion	2 (10-ounce) cans cream of mushroom soup
1 cup chopped celery	
1 cup chopped green onions	2 pounds Velveeta cheese
1 cup chopped green bell pepper	Salt and pepper to taste
3 cloves garlic, minced	

Brown the ground beef with the onion, celery, green onions, bell pepper and garlic in a large skillet, stirring until crumbly; drain. Put the andouille through a sausage grinder. Add the ground andouille and soup to the ground beef mixture in the skillet over low heat; stir well. Add the Velveeta cheese; cook and stir until cheese is melted and mixture is blended. Season with salt and pepper. Serve hot with crackers or sturdy chips. Yield: 40 servings.

Page D. Meyer, Laureate Eta
Greenville, South Carolina

ALABAMA DIP

1 pound ground beef	1 (16-ounce) jar picante sauce
1 pound hot sausage	
2 pounds Velveeta cheese	1 (10-ounce) can cream of mushroom soup
1 (10-ounce) can tomatoes with green chiles	

Brown the ground beef and sausage in a skillet, stirring until crumbly; drain. Combine the cheese, tomatoes with green chiles, picante sauce and soup in a slow cooker. Cook on Low for 2 hours or until cheese is melted, stirring occasionally. Stir in the beef mixture. Serve with nacho chips. Yield: 8 cups.

Brandi Maxey, Xi Nu Iota
St. Elmo, Illinois

CHILE SAUSAGE DIP

The use of a slow cooker makes this a simple recipe with no last-minute care.

2 pounds sausage	4 tomatoes, diced, or
2 (4-ounce) cans chopped green chiles, drained	1 (10-ounce) can diced tomatoes, drained
2 (10-ounce) cans cream of mushroom soup	

Brown the sausage in a skillet, stirring until crumbly; drain. Combine the sausage, green chiles, soup and tomatoes in a slow cooker. Cook on Low for 2 to 3 hours or until heated through. Serve with large taco chips or tortilla scoops. Yield: 40 servings.

Doris K. Wilson, Beta Upsilon
Warrensburg, Missouri

PEPPERONI PIZZA DIP

8 ounces cream cheese, softened	1/2 cup chopped pepperoni
1/2 cup sour cream	1/4 cup chopped green onions
1 teaspoon oregano	
1/8 teaspoon garlic powder	1/4 cup chopped green bell pepper
1/8 teaspoon crushed red pepper	1/2 cup (2 ounces) shredded mozzarella cheese
1 cup pizza sauce	

Combine the cream cheese, sour cream, oregano, garlic powder and red pepper in a small bowl and beat until smooth. Spread the cream cheese mixture evenly in a 9- to 10-inch quiche dish or other baking dish. Spread the pizza sauce over the top. Sprinkle with pepperoni, green onions and bell pepper. Bake at 350 degrees for 15 minutes. Sprinkle with mozzarella cheese. Bake for 10 minutes longer or until cheese is melted. Serve with crackers or chips. Yield: 24 servings.

Lenora Kesanen, Preceptor Theta
Virginia, Minnesota

WHITE PIZZA DIP

1 envelope savory herb with garlic soup mix	1 (4-ounce) jar sliced mushrooms, drained
1 cup sour cream	1/4 cup chopped pepperoni
1 cup ricotta cheese	
1 cup (4 ounces) shredded mozzarella cheese	

Combine the soup mix, sour cream, ricotta cheese, 3/4 cup of the mozzarella cheese, mushrooms and pepperoni in a bowl and mix well. Spoon into a shallow 1-quart baking dish. Sprinkle with the remaining 1/4 cup mozzarella cheese. Bake at 350 degrees for 30 minutes or until hot and bubbly. Serve with bread or crackers. Yield: 2 cups.

Jan Meredith, Laureate Beta Gamma
Fredericksburg, Virginia

ZESTY CRAB DIP

1 (14- to 16-ounce) round loaf crusty bread	1 tablespoon Worcestershire sauce
8 ounces cream cheese, softened	2 tablespoons chopped fresh dill weed
1/2 cup mayonnaise	1 (6- or 8-ounce) package flaked crab
1 tablespoon prepared horseradish	

Cut a 1-inch slice from the top of the bread. Scoop out the center of the loaf to leave a 3/4-inch-thick shell. Combine the cream cheese, mayonnaise, horseradish, Worcestershire sauce, dill weed and crab in a bowl and mix well. Spoon into the bread shell. Bake at 375 degrees for 10 minutes. Serve warm with crackers, raw vegetables and the scooped-out bread pieces. May be served cold as well. Yield: 25 servings.

Lesley Nittler, Zeta Rho
Fort Collins, Colorado

CURRY DIP

2 cups mayonnaise	1 garlic clove, minced
5 teaspoons ketchup	5 to 8 teaspoons curry powder, or to taste
1 1/2 teaspoons Worcestershire sauce	Dash of Tabasco sauce
1 tablespoon grated onion	1/2 teaspoon salt

Stir the mayonnaise in a bowl until very creamy. Add the ketchup, Worcestershire sauce, onion, garlic, curry powder, Tabasco sauce and salt; mix well. Chill, covered, for 1 or 2 days to allow flavors and color to develop. Serve with raw vegetables, crackers or boiled shrimp. Yield: 2 cups.

Bonnie O'Bannon, Eta Xi
Birmingham, Alabama

CLASSIC CHEESE FONDUE

1 garlic clove, halved	1 cup (4 ounces) crumbled feta cheese
1 1/2 teaspoons cornstarch	Dash of nutmeg
1 cup dry white wine	Dash of pepper
1 tablespoon fresh lemon juice	French or Italian bread, cubed
12 ounces natural Swiss cheese, shredded	Boiled new potatoes

Rub the inside of a fondue pot with the cut sides of the garlic; discard the garlic. Whisk together the cornstarch, wine and lemon juice in a saucepan over medium heat. Cook until air bubbles rise and cover the surface of the mixture, stirring vigorously and constantly; do not cover or allow the mixture to boil.

Add the Swiss cheese and feta cheese to the wine mixture 1 handful at a time, stirring constantly. Cook until the cheese mixture is bubbling and blended. Stir in the nutmeg and pepper. Remove the cheese mixture quickly to the fondue pot and keep warm over the fondue burner. If the fondue becomes too thick, stir in a little warmed white wine. Instruct guests to spear a bread cube or potato and dip in the cheese mixture, swirling the cheese around to keep the fondue in motion. Yield: 24 servings.

Melody Johnson, Theta Rho
Clarksville, Arkansas

BAKED CHEESE FONDUE

Herbes de Provence is a blend of herbs and spices including marjoram, savory, basil, rosemary, and thyme.

6 ounces cream cheese, softened	2 teaspoons chopped fresh parsley
1/3 cup light mayonnaise	2 cloves fresh garlic, minced
1/3 cup shredded Gruyère cheese	1/4 teaspoon dried herbes de Provence
1/3 cup shredded Swiss cheese	1/4 cup shredded Gruyère cheese

Combine the cream cheese, mayonnaise, 1/3 cup Gruyère cheese, Swiss cheese, parsley, garlic and herbes de Provence in a bowl and mix well. Spread the cheese mixture in a shallow baking dish. Sprinkle with 1/4 cup Gruyère cheese. Bake at 325 degrees for 20 minutes or until hot and bubbly. Serve with slices of French bread. Yield: 12 servings.

Tami Maillet, Mu
Kingston, Nova Scotia, Canada

FRESH VEGETABLE DIP

It is delightful seeing sorority sisters enjoy this dip— and the dip is heart-healthy.

1 cup mayonnaise	1 teaspoon prepared horseradish
1 teaspoon garlic salt	
1 teaspoon curry powder	1 teaspoon grated onion
1 teaspoon tarragon vinegar	1/4 teaspoon garlic powder

Combine the mayonnaise, garlic salt, curry powder, tarragon vinegar, horseradish, onion and garlic powder in a bowl. Whisk until smooth. Serve with fresh vegetables such as cauliflower, celery, carrots, bell peppers, broccoli and radishes. Yield: 10 to 12 servings.

Nora Susan Wilson, Preceptor Alpha Pi
Manchester, Tennessee

QUICK RANCH DIP

1 envelope dry ranch
   dressing mix
2 cups sour cream
1/2 cup bacon bits

1 cup (4 ounces) finely
   shredded sharp
   Cheddar cheese

Combine the ranch dressing mix, sour cream, bacon bits and cheese in a bowl and mix well. Chill, covered, for 8 to 10 hours. Serve with corn chips or crackers. Yield: 3 cups.

Nadine Hitt, Theta Master
Rogers, Arkansas

SWEET MUSTARD SAUCE

This sauce keeps well in the refrigerator, so the recipe may be doubled.

1 1/2 tablespoons dry
   mustard
2 eggs
1 tablespoon flour

1/2 cup sugar
1/2 cup white vinegar
1 tablespoon butter

Combine the dry mustard, eggs, flour, sugar and vinegar in a saucepan over low heat. Whisk until smooth. Cook until bubbly, stirring constantly. Stir in the butter and remove from heat. If too thick, stir in a little hot water. Pour into a jar and chill. Serve as a dip for pretzels. Yield: 1 cup.

Laura Schultes, Xi Gamma Kappa
Bowling Green, Ohio

HONEY DILL DIP

This dip is great for chicken fingers or chicken nuggets.

1 cup mayonnaise
1 tablespoon honey

1 teaspoon dill weed

Combine the mayonnaise, honey and dill weed in a small bowl and whisk until smooth. Chill and serve. Yield: 1 cup.

Rina Cumberland, Mu Theta
Kenora, Ontario, Canada

HORSERADISH DIPPING SAUCE

1/2 cup mayonnaise
2 teaspoons lemon juice
2 teaspoons prepared
   horseradish

1 teaspoon Dijon
   mustard

Combine the mayonnaise, lemon juice, horseradish and Dijon mustard in a small bowl and mix well. Chill and serve with assorted crackers and raw vegetables. Yield: 1/2 cup.

Joanne Hamilton, Preceptor Omicron
Fruitvale, British Columbia, Canada

FRIENDSHIP BREAD DIPPING OIL

This is great with French bread, dill bread, cheese bread, and rosemary garlic bread. Keep refrigerated, but let it stand at room temperature for 30 minutes to 1 hour before serving. A bottle of dipping oil with a loaf of bread makes a great gift.

2 cups light olive oil
1/2 to 1 teaspoon crushed
   red pepper
1/4 teaspoon freshly
   ground black pepper
1 1/2 teaspoons capers
1 teaspoon fennel
1 teaspoon chopped
   fresh oregano

1 teaspoon chopped
   fresh basil
1 teaspoon minced fresh
   garlic
3/4 cup grated Parmesan
   cheese
1/4 cup chopped fresh
   parsley (optional)

Pour the olive oil into a clean empty wine bottle. Add the crushed red pepper, black pepper, capers, fennel, oregano, basil, garlic, Parmesan cheese and parsley. Replace the cork in the bottle and shake vigorously to combine. Let stand 1 hour at room temperature to develop the flavors. To serve, shake and then pour a small amount in a flat dish. Serve with warm bread either sliced or torn into bite-size pieces for dipping. Yield: 2 1/2 cups.

Gina Dixon, Omega Sigma
Jamesport, Missouri

BLEU CHEESE DIP

8 ounces cream cheese,
   softened
1 envelope Italian salad
   dressing mix
1 cup sour cream

1/4 cup crumbled bleu
   cheese
3 tablespoons dried
   chopped chives

Combine the cream cheese, salad dressing mix and sour cream and blend until smooth. Stir in the bleu cheese and chives. Serve with crackers and raw vegetables. Yield: 2 1/2 cups.

Elena E. Bennett, Alpha Phi Master
Bakersfield, California

ALMOND ORANGE DIP

1 cup chopped blanched
   almonds
2 tablespoons butter
1/3 cup fresh orange juice
1 cup firm plain yogurt
Pinch of ginger
2 tablespoons chopped
   parsley

2 tablespoons chopped
   chives
1/4 teaspoon grated
   orange zest
Salt and black pepper
   to taste
Dash of cayenne pepper

Sauté the almonds in the butter until lightly browned. Combine the sautéed almonds and orange juice in a blender container and purée. Combine the almond mixture and remaining ingredients in a bowl and whisk well to blend. Chill, covered, until serving time. Serve with raw vegetables, crackers or chips. Yield: 2½ cups.

Jackie Vanderspoel, Beta Beta
Ft. Myers Beach, Florida

SPICY CORN DIP

1 cup sour cream
1 cup mayonnaise
2 (11-ounce) cans
   Mexicorn, drained
3 jalapeño peppers,
   seeded and minced

1 (7-ounce) can chopped
   green chiles
4 green onions, chopped
1¼ cups (5 ounces)
   shredded Cheddar
   cheese

Combine the sour cream, mayonnaise, Mexicorn, jalapeño peppers, green chiles, green onions and cheese in a bowl and mix well. Serve with tortilla chips or fresh vegetables or both. Yield: 32 servings.

Peggy S. Hill, Xi Alpha Nu
Natchez, Mississippi

CUCUMBER DIP

8 ounces cream cheese,
   softened
⅓ cup mayonnaise
1 teaspoon salt
¼ teaspoon garlic
   powder
⅛ teaspoon pepper

2 medium cucumbers,
   peeled and grated
1½ teaspoons onion,
   grated or finely
   chopped
1 cup sour cream

Mix the cream cheese, mayonnaise, salt, garlic powder, pepper, cucumbers, onion and sour cream in a bowl. Serve with crackers. Yield: 2½ cups.

Joyce Boor, Theta Master
Great Bend, Kansas

LEEK SOUP DIP

1 (10-ounce) package
   frozen chopped
   spinach, thawed
1 cup mayonnaise
2 cups sour cream

1 package leek soup mix
½ carrot, grated
¼ cup chopped water
   chestnuts

Drain the spinach, pressing out the excess moisture. Combine the spinach, mayonnaise, sour cream, leek soup mix, carrot and water chestnuts in a bowl and mix well. Serve in a hollowed-out round sourdough loaf with bread chunks and assorted crackers. Yield: 3½ cups.

LaNae Franklin, Laureate Gamma Xi
Lacey, Washington

OLIVE DIP

8 ounces cream cheese,
   softened
¾ cup mayonnaise
¾ cup chopped green
   olives

2 tablespoons olive juice
Pepper to taste
½ cup chopped pecans

Combine the cream cheese, mayonnaise, olives, olive juice and pepper in a bowl and mix well. Stir in the pecans. Chill, covered, for 1 to 2 hours and serve. Yield: 3 cups.

LaRue Odenbach, Xi Eta
Pingree, North Dakota

FESTIVE RED PEPPER DIP

8 ounces fat-free cream
   cheese, softened
1 (7-ounce) jar roasted
   red peppers, drained
   and chopped

⅔ cup reduced-fat
   mayonnaise
1 garlic clove, minced
4 green onions, sliced
1 teaspoon dill weed

Stir the cream cheese in a bowl until smooth. Stir in the roasted red peppers, mayonnaise, garlic, green onions and dill weed. Chill, covered, for at least 1 hour before serving. Serve with raw vegetables, chips or multi-grain crackers. Yield: 3 cups.

Marian Erdman, Laureate Rho
Merriill, Wisconsin

HUMMUS WITH PITA CHIPS

2 garlic cloves
½ teaspoon salt
1 (15-ounce) can
   chick-peas, drained
⅓ cup well-stirred
   tahini
2 tablespoons fresh
   lemon juice

2 tablespoons olive oil
1 teaspoon cumin
3 tablespoons water
3 tablespoons minced
   parsley leaves
Salt and pepper to taste
1 (6-count) package pita
   bread

Mince and mash the garlic with ½ teaspoon salt to form a paste. Combine the garlic paste, chick-peas, tahini, lemon juice, olive oil and cumin in a food processor container and process until smooth, scraping down the side once or twice. Add the water, parsley, salt and pepper and pulse just until combined. Split the pita bread by cutting along the outer edge. Brush lightly with olive oil. Cut into wedges and arrange on an ungreased baking sheet. Bake at 425 degrees for 10 minutes or until lightly toasted, watching carefully to prevent burning.
Yield: about 2 cups hummus.

Linda Brunski, Laureate Iota
Carlisle, Pennsylvania

SPINACH DIP

1 cup sour cream	1 (10-ounce) package
1 cup real mayonnaise	frozen chopped
1 envelope dry ranch	spinach, thawed
dressing mix	1 loaf French bread,
1 bunch green onions,	cut into bite-size
chopped	pieces

Combine the sour cream and mayonnaise in a bowl. Stir in the ranch dressing mix and green onions. Squeeze out the excess moisture from the spinach, a handful at a time. Stir the spinach into the sour cream mixture. Serve with bread pieces. Yield: 2½ cups.

Marcy Knotwell, Xi Beta Delta
Encampment, Wyoming

CHEESY ZUCCHINI DIP

3 cups shredded	1½ cups light
zucchini	mayonnaise
2 cups (8 ounces)	¼ cup reduced-fat sour
shredded Cheddar	cream
cheese	1 cup chopped pecans
⅓ cup shredded part-	¼ cup thinly sliced red
skim mozzarella	bell pepper
cheese	Salt and pepper to taste

Mix the zucchini, Cheddar cheese, mozzarella cheese, mayonnaise, sour cream, pecans, bell pepper, salt and pepper in a medium bowl. Chill, covered, for at least 1 hour before serving. Yield: 8 cups.

JoAn Pidd, Alpha Mu Master
Gold River, California

AVOCADO CHEESE DIP

2 avocados, mashed	1 cup (4 ounces)
Pinch of salt	shredded Cheddar
½ teaspoon lemon juice	cheese
½ envelope or 1½	1 (4-ounce) can sliced
tablespoons taco	black olives, drained
seasoning mix	1 large ripe tomato,
1 tablespoon hot red	diced
pepper sauce	¼ cup chopped green
1 cup (4 ounces) shredded	onions
Monterey Jack cheese	

Combine the avocados, salt and lemon juice in a bowl and mix well. Stir in the taco seasoning mix and hot red pepper sauce. Spread on a 10-inch plate. Layer the Monterey Jack cheese, Cheddar cheese, olives, tomato and green onions in the order listed over the avocado layer. Serve with taco chips. Yield: 6 to 8 servings.

Rita Hart, Xi Iota
Sidney, Nebraska

GUACAMOLE

2 ripe avocados, peeled	Juice of ½ lemon
and mashed	1 tablespoon olive oil
2 tablespoons finely	Salt and pepper to taste
chopped onion	

Combine the avocados, onion, lemon juice, olive oil, salt and pepper in a bowl and stir to blend. Chill, covered, for 1 hour before serving. Serve with chips and crackers. Yield: 10 servings.

Kaye W. Stykes, Xi Delta Eta
Somerset, Kentucky

GUACAMOLE PIE

3 (6-ounce) tubs frozen	2 tomatoes, chopped
guacamole, thawed	4 or 5 slices bacon,
1 (4-ounce) can chopped	crisp-cooked,
green chiles	crumbled
1 or 2 onions, chopped	4 ounces Cheddar
½ cup sliced or chopped	cheese, shredded
black olives	

Combine the guacamole and green chiles in a bowl and mix well; spoon onto the center of a serving plate. Arrange the onions, olives, tomatoes, bacon and cheese in layers around the dip. Eat with tortilla chips, scooping through all the layers.
Yield: 12 servings.

Mary A. Storey, Laureate Theta Nu
San Antonio, Texas

ASPARAGUS GUACAMOLE

Don't tell your guests this delectable dip is asparagus until after they've tasted it!

1 pound fresh	1 tablespoon lemon
asparagus, cut in 1-	juice
inch pieces	½ teaspoon salt
⅓ cup chopped onion	¾ teaspoon minced
1 garlic clove, minced	fresh cilantro
2 tablespoons low-fat	Hot red pepper sauce
mayonnaise	to taste

Bring ½ inch of water to boil in a saucepan over medium-high heat. Add the asparagus. Reduce heat and simmer for 5 minutes or until tender. Drain well. Combine the asparagus, onion and garlic in a food processor container. Process until smooth. Spoon into a bowl. Let cool, covered, in the refrigerator. Add the mayonnaise, lemon juice, salt, cilantro and hot red pepper sauce and stir to blend. Serve with tortilla chips. Yield: 2 cups.

Charlene Gonzalez, Xi Beta Lambda
Derby, Kansas

GREEN PEA GUACAMOLE

2 cups frozen peas
3 tablespoons low-fat
    mayonnaise
2 teaspoons lemon juice
1/2 teaspoon chili
    powder

1 teaspoon cumin
1 garlic clove, minced
1/2 cup mild or medium
    low-sodium salsa
Salt to taste

Bring 1/4 cup of water to a boil in a small saucepan. Add the peas and return to a boil. Reduce the heat and simmer, covered, for 2 minutes. Cool under cold running water. Drain well. Place in a food processor container. Add the mayonnaise, lemon juice, chili powder, cumin and garlic and process until almost smooth, scraping the side once or twice as necessary. Pour into a bowl. Stir in the salsa and salt. Chill, covered, for 1 to 2 hours to allow flavors to develop. Will keep in the refrigerator for 4 to 5 days. Serve with corn chips. Yield: about 12 servings.

Kathryn Wilson, Laureate Alpha Lambda
Manhattan, Kansas

GUACAMOLE MOUNTAIN DIP

1 onion, chopped
2 tomatoes, chopped
1 (4-ounce) can chopped
    olives, drained
2 cups (8 ounces)
    shredded Cheddar
    cheese
2 cups (8 ounces)
    shredded Monterey
    Jack cheese

1 (4-ounce) can chopped
    green chiles
3 avocados
1 teaspoon lemon juice
Salt and pepper to taste
2 cups sour cream
1 envelope dry ranch
    dressing mix

Combine the onion, tomatoes and olives in a bowl and mix well; mound in the center of a serving plate. Sprinkle with a mixture of the Cheddar cheese and Monterey Jack cheese. Sprinkle with the green chiles. Mash the avocados with the lemon juice, salt and pepper and spread over the mound. Drizzle with a mixture of the sour cream and ranch dressing mix. Serve with tortilla chips. Yield: 12 to 18 servings.

Christine Soard, Theta Psi
Cookeville, Tennessee

MEXICAN TACO DIP

1 (16-ounce) can refried
    beans
1 to 2 tablespoons
    mayonnaise
2 cups sour cream
1 envelope taco
    seasoning mix
1 onion, chopped

2 tomatoes, chopped
1 (6-ounce) can pitted
    black olives, thinly
    sliced
1 or 2 green bell peppers,
    chopped
16 ounces Cheddar
    cheese, shredded

Spread the refried beans on a serving plate. Combine the mayonnaise, sour cream and taco seasoning mix in a bowl and mix well. Spread the sour cream mixture evenly over the refried beans layer. Sprinkle the onion, tomatoes, olives, bell peppers and cheese over the sour cream mixture. Serve with nacho chips. Yield: 40 servings.

Ruth Snyder, Preceptor Upsilon
S. Windsor, Connecticut

NACHO RICE AND BEANS

May also be served hot as a side dish.

2 teaspoons olive oil
3/4 cup sliced mushrooms
2 bell peppers, chopped
1 large onion, chopped
2 garlic cloves, minced
1 (16-ounce) can crushed
    tomatoes
1 (15- or 16-ounce) can
    black or kidney beans

1/2 teaspoon salt
1/2 teaspoon chili
    powder
3/4 teaspoon cumin
1/8 teaspoon cayenne
    pepper
1 to 2 tablespoons sugar
5 to 6 cups cooked
    brown rice

Heat the olive oil in a Dutch oven. Add the mushrooms, bell peppers, onion and garlic. Stir in the tomatoes, beans, salt, chili powder, cumin, cayenne pepper and sugar; simmer until hot and bubbly. Stir in the rice. Serve cold as a dip for chips.
Yield: 12 or more servings.

Shirley Whitman, Omega Master
Ithaca, Michigan

LAYERED MEXICAN BEAN DIP

1 (16-ounce) can refried
    beans
3 ounces Monterey Jack
    cheese
3 medium avocados,
    mashed
1 tablespoon lemon
    juice

1/2 teaspoon salt
1/4 teaspoon pepper
1 cup sour cream
1/2 cup mayonnaise
1 envelope taco
    seasoning mix
3/4 cup salsa

Combine the refried beans and cheese in a saucepan over medium heat. Heat until the cheese is melted, stirring frequently. Spread in a shallow bowl and let cool. Spread a mixture of the avocados, lemon juice, salt and pepper over the refried beans mixture. Spread a mixture of the sour cream, mayonnaise and taco seasoning mix over the avocado layer. Spread the salsa over the top and garnish with green onions, tomatoes, olives and shredded sharp cheese. Serve with corn chips. Yield: 15 or more servings.

Doris Evans, Delta Delta Master
Eureka, California

WHIPPED SALSA DIP

8 ounces cream cheese,   3/4 cup thick picante
    softened   sauce

Combine the cream cheese and picante sauce in a
mixing bowl and beat at high speed until light and
fluffy. Serve with corn chips or tortilla chips.
Yield: 8 to 12 servings.

Walda Weaver, Xi Gamma Omicron
Pryor, Oklahoma

FIESTA DIP

It takes 15 minutes or less to make this dip. You can
prepare it just before serving time or hours ahead
of time.

1 (15-ounce) can black   1 (15-ounce) can niblet
    beans, rinsed and   corn, drained
    drained
1 medium to large red
    bell pepper, chopped

Combine the black beans, bell pepper and corn in a
bowl and mix well. Spoon into an attractive bowl and
serve with scoop-style corn chips.
Yield: 8 to 10 servings.

Cheryl Houchen, Laureate Tau
Mission, Kansas

EASY SALSA

The longer it stands, the better it tastes! You may
substitute an extra-large can of tomatoes for the fresh
tomatoes if you like.

4 to 6 fresh tomatoes,   1 teaspoon salt
    cut up   1 teaspoon oregano
2 jalapeño peppers   Cilantro to taste
1/4 onion   2 or 3 large garlic cloves

Combine the tomatoes, jalapeño peppers, onion, salt,
oregano, cilantro and garlic in a blender container.
Process until desired consistency. Yield: 3 to 4 cups.

Mary Skipworth, Zeta Iota
Loveland, Colorado

BLACK BEAN AND CORN SALSA

1 (15-ounce) can black   1 garlic clove, minced
    beans, drained   2 tablespoons minced
1 (11-ounce) can   fresh cilantro
    Mexicorn, rinsed and   Juice of 1/2 lime
    drained   1/2 cup canola oil
2 tomatoes, diced   1/4 cup balsamic vinegar
2 avocados, cut up   1 envelope Italian salad
3 green onions, chopped   dressing mix

Combine the black beans, Mexicorn, tomatoes, avocados, green onions, garlic, cilantro, lime juice,
canola oil, vinegar and salad dressing mix in a bowl;
mix well. Chill, covered, for at least 4 hours before
serving. Serve with tortilla chips or dip chips.
Yield: 10 to 12 servings.

Jane Taylor, Gamma Master
Menomonee Falls, Wisconsin

VEGETABLE AND SHRIMP SALSA

1 teaspoon salt   1/2 cup chopped green
1/4 cup olive oil   onions
6 tablespoons fresh lime   2 tablespoons minced
    juice   garlic
2 tablespoons sugar   2 jalapeño peppers,
1 pound cooked shrimp,   seeded and chopped
    coarsely chopped   2 tablespoons chopped
1 cup chopped red bell   fresh cilantro, or to
    peppers   taste (optional)
1 cup chopped yellow   2 avocados, chopped
    bell peppers

Combine the salt, olive oil, lime juice and sugar in a
covered jar and shake vigorously. Combine the
shrimp, bell peppers, green onions, garlic, jalapeño
peppers and cilantro in a bowl; mix lightly. Pour the
lime mixture over the vegetable mixture and toss to
combine. Chill, covered, for at least 1 hour. Add the
avocados just before serving and toss gently. Serve
with lime-flavored taco chips. Yield: 8 to 10 cups.

Jane Slater, Xi Beta Delta
Brooklyn Park, Minnesota

PICO DE GALLO

This spicy dip will keep for at least 2 weeks in the
refrigerator. Jalapeño peppers may be substituted for
the yellow chiles.

8 long green chiles,   1/4 cup chopped fresh
    roasted   cilantro leaves
2 small yellow chiles,   2 tablespoons vegetable
    roasted   oil
5 green onions,   1 teaspoon white vinegar
    including tops   1/2 teaspoon garlic
5 medium tomatoes,   powder
    peeled and chopped   Salt to taste

Peel, devein and chop the green chiles. Peel and chop
the yellow chiles. Chop the green onions. Combine
the chiles, green onions, tomatoes, cilantro, oil, vinegar, garlic powder and salt in a bowl; mix well. Chill,
covered, until serving time. Serve with tortilla chips
or corn chips. Yield: 2 to 3 cups.

Judy McMillie and Shirley Pearce, Laureate Alpha Beta
El Paso, Texas

✦ LIME CUCUMBER SALSA

1 large cucumber, peeled, seeded, finely chopped
1 or 2 garlic cloves, minced
1 jalapeño pepper, chopped
3 green onions, chopped
2 tablespoons minced fresh cilantro
2 tablespoons fresh lime juice
2 tablespoons olive oil
1/2 teaspoon salt
1/4 teaspoon pepper

Combine the cucumber, garlic, jalapeño pepper, green onions, cilantro, lime juice, olive oil, salt and pepper in a bowl and mix well. Chill, covered, for at least 2 hours. Yield: about 1 1/2 cups.

Cindi Dryden, Beta Omega
Richmond, Kansas

PEACH SALSA

8 cups finely chopped unpeeled tomatoes
4 green jalapeño peppers, finely chopped
3 cups chopped onions
3 cups chopped green bell peppers
2 tablespoons salt
1/2 cup white vinegar
1 tablespoon brown sugar
1 (12-ounce) can tomato paste
5 peaches, chopped

Combine the tomatoes, jalapeño peppers, onions, bell peppers, salt, vinegar, brown sugar, tomato paste and peaches in a large kettle over medium-high heat. Bring to a boil. Reduce heat and simmer, uncovered, for 3 hours. Serve cold with corn chips.
Yield: 1 to 2 quarts.

Joyce B. DeCrocker, Xi Zeta Epsilon
Kalamazoo, Michigan

FRUIT SALSA

6 to 8 flour tortillas, cut into eighths
Cinnamon-sugar mixture to taste
2 Granny Smith apples, peeled and sliced
1 kiwifruit
1 (10-ounce) package frozen fruit (strawberries, mixed fruit), thawed
1 teaspoon apple jelly

Arrange the tortillas on a baking sheet. Spray lightly with water and sprinkle with cinnamon-sugar mixture. Bake at 350 degrees until light tan. Combine the apples, kiwifruit and thawed frozen fruit in a food processor container and pulse until desired consistency; do not purée. Spoon into a bowl and stir in the apple jelly. Chill, covered, until serving time. Serve with the sweet tortilla wedges. Yield: 8 to 12 servings.

Dorothy Duerfeldt, Iota Beta
Webster City, Iowa

SPICY FRUIT SALSA

1 (8-ounce) can pineapple tidbits, drained
2 firm mangoes, peeled and chopped
1 red bell pepper, chopped
1 cantaloupe, chopped
1/4 cup chopped fresh cilantro
1/2 honeydew melon, chopped
2/3 cup seasoned rice vinegar
Hot red pepper flakes to taste

Combine the pineapple tidbits, mangoes, bell pepper, cantaloupe, cilantro, and honeydew melon in a large glass or plastic bowl. Drizzle with the vinegar. Add hot red pepper flakes and mix well. Chill, covered, for 8 to 10 hours. Yield: 8 to 10 cups.

Donna Mills, Preceptor Alpha Delta
Kennewick, Washington

STRAWBERRY SALSA

2 cups chopped strawberries
1 tablespoon chopped fresh mint
1/2 teaspoon grated lime zest
1 tablespoon lime juice
1 to 1 1/2 teaspoons honey
4 flour tortillas
2 tablespoons melted butter
2 tablespoons sugar
3/4 teaspoon cinnamon

Combine the strawberries, mint, lime zest, lime juice and honey in a bowl and mix well. Chill, covered, for 1 hour. Brush both sides of tortillas with melted butter; sprinkle both sides with a mixture of the sugar and cinnamon. Place on buttered baking sheets. Bake at 375 degrees for 10 minutes or until crisp and golden. Cut into quarters. Serve with the strawberry salsa. Yield: 4 to 8 servings.

Donna Luus, Alpha Iota Master
Sault Ste. Marie, Ontario, Canada

GEORGIA CAVIAR

2 (15-ounce) cans black-eyed peas, rinsed and drained
1 green bell pepper, chopped
1 small onion, finely chopped
8 jalapeño peppers, chopped
4 scallions, thinly sliced
2 garlic cloves, minced
1 pint cherry tomatoes, diced
2 or 3 dashes Tabasco sauce
8 to 10 ounces Italian salad dressing

Mix all the ingredients in a bowl. Chill, covered, until ready to serve. Serve with tortilla chips.
Yield: 5 to 6 cups.

Joan Pohlman, Mu Master
Weirton, West Virginia

ALMOND BACON DIP

A festive dip for the holidays.

8 ounces cream cheese, softened
1/2 cup mayonnaise-type salad dressing
5 slices bacon, crisp-cooked, finely chopped
1 tablespoon chopped green onions
1/2 teaspoon dill weed
1/2 teaspoon pepper
1/2 cup raw or toasted almonds

Combine the cream cheese, salad dressing, bacon, green onions, dill weed and pepper in a bowl; mix well. Chill, covered, for at least 2 hours. Shape into an almond shape. Decorate with almonds to look like a pinecone. Serve with crackers.
Yield: 12 to 16 servings.

Sandra Moyer, Xi Pi
Brandon, Manitoba, Canada

CHUNKY CHEESE DIP

2 cups (8 ounces) shredded Cheddar cheese
1 bunch green onions, chopped
8 slices bacon, crisp-cooked, crumbled
1/2 cup toasted sliced almonds
Mayonnaise to taste

Combine the cheese, green onions, bacon, almonds and enough mayonnaise to make desired consistency. Serve with assorted crackers. Yield: 8 servings.

Carolyn A. Cunningham, Laureate Beta Gamma
Flint, Texas

BLT DIP

1 cup mayonnaise
1 cup sour cream
1 medium tomato, chopped
1 pound bacon, crisp-cooked, crumbled

Combine the mayonnaise, sour cream, tomato and bacon in a bowl and mix well. Chill, covered, for at least 1 hour. Serve with assorted crackers or small breads. Yield: about 20 servings.

Cindy Bingheim, Chi Psi
Mazon, Illinois

CORNED BEEF DIP

1 (3-ounce) package lemon gelatin
3/4 cup boiling water
1 (12-ounce) can corned beef
1 cup chopped celery
1 large onion, chopped
3 hard-cooked eggs, mashed
1 cup mayonnaise or mayonnaise-type salad dressing

Place the dry gelatin mix in a large bowl and stir in the boiling water. Add the corned beef, celery, onion, eggs and mayonnaise; mix well. Chill, covered, until serving time. Serve with crackers. Yield: 5 cups.

JoAnn Panuska, Laureate Delta
Williamsburg, Virginia

DILLED CORNED BEEF DIP

2 cups sour cream
2 cups Hellmann's mayonnaise
3 tablespoons dried minced onion
2 tablespoons dill weed
3 (3-ounce) packages sliced corned beef, chopped

Combine the sour cream, mayonnaise, minced onion, dill weed and corned beef in a bowl and mix well. Chill, covered, for 8 to 10 hours. Serve with crackers. Yield: 3 1/2 cups.

Ellen Burlin, Xi Gamma Omicron
Chouteau, Oklahoma

SPICY BEEF SAUSAGE DIP

The dip may be cooled and refrigerated for up to 3 days or frozen for up to 1 month. You determine the spiciness with your choice of sausage and salsa.

1 pound ground beef
1 pound Italian sausage (sweet or hot), casings removed
12 ounces Velveeta cheese
1 (16-ounce) jar salsa (mild, medium or hot)

Brown the ground beef and sausage in a skillet, crumbling with a fork; drain. Combine the meat mixture and cheese in the skillet over low heat. Cook for about 5 minutes, stirring frequently. Add about 2/3 of the jar of salsa. Cook until heated through, stirring frequently. Use extra salsa if dip appears too thick. Serve with tortilla chips or crackers.
Yield: 24 servings.

Christine Mazzarella, Psi Kappa
Park Ridge, Illinois

CHICKEN ENCHILADA DIP

16 ounces cream cheese, softened
1 1/2 to 2 cups shredded Cheddar cheese
3 cooked chicken breasts, chopped
1 teaspoon minced garlic
1 (10-ounce) can extra-hot tomatoes with green chiles, drained
Leaves of 1 bunch fresh cilantro, chopped
4 green onions, chopped

Combine the cream cheese and Cheddar cheese in a large bowl and mix well. Add the chicken, garlic, tomatoes with green chiles, cilantro and green onions; mix well. Serve chilled or at room temperature with tortilla chips. Yield: 32 servings.

Ronda Wassenberg, Preceptor Zeta
Marysville, Kansas

SPICY SEAFOOD DIP

Meyer lemons are very good in this dish.

1 pound cooked shrimp, chopped	chopped
1 pound cooked crab meat, chopped	2 or 3 jalapeño peppers, finely chopped
1 (15-ounce) can baby clams, drained and chopped	2 or 3 yellow chile peppers, finely chopped
2 bunches green onions, chopped	Onion powder to taste Garlic salt to taste
1 bunch fresh cilantro, chopped	Salt and pepper to taste Juice of 2 lemons
2 medium tomatoes,	Juice of 2 limes

Combine the shrimp, crab meat, clams, green onions, cilantro, tomatoes, jalapeño peppers and yellow chiles in a large bowl and mix well. Season with onion powder, garlic salt, salt and pepper. Chill, covered, until ready to serve. Stir in the lemon juice and lime juice just before serving. Serve with tortilla chips. Yield: 32 servings.

Betty Erickson, Preceptor Psi
Diamond Bar, California

CLAM DIP

1 (15-ounce) can clams, drained, 1/4 cup liquid reserved	1 1/2 teaspoons Worcestershire sauce
1 garlic clove, minced	2 to 4 drops of Tabasco sauce
8 ounces cream cheese, softened	1/2 teaspoon salt
2 teaspoons lemon juice	Dash of pepper

Chop the clams coarsely. Combine the reserved clam liquid, garlic, cream cheese, lemon juice, Worcestershire sauce, Tabasco sauce, salt and pepper in a mixing bowl and beat at medium speed until smooth. Stir in the clams. Chill, covered, until ready to serve. Serve with celery sticks, cauliflower florets, carrot sticks, potato chips and crackers.
Yield: 10 to 12 servings.

Carol Johannigmeier, Laureate Mu
Fort Collins, Colorado

CRAB DIP

16 ounces cream cheese, softened	2 (6-ounce) cans crab meat, drained and shredded
5 tablespoons Worcestershire sauce	Parsley flakes
1 (8-ounce) bottle cocktail sauce	

Blend together the cream cheese and Worcestershire sauce. Spread the cream cheese mixture on a 12-inch platter. Pour the cocktail sauce evenly over the cream cheese layer. Chill, covered, for at least 1 hour. Layer the crab meat over the cocktail sauce and sprinkle with parsley. Serve with crackers.
Yield: 18 to 24 servings.

Bobbi Herman, Xi
Madison, Mississippi

SPICY CRAB DIP

8 ounces cream cheese, softened	2 tablespoons horseradish sauce
1/4 cup milk	1 (6-ounce) can crab meat
1/2 cup mayonnaise	
1/4 cup chopped green onions	1/2 to 1 teaspoon Worcestershire sauce

Place the cream cheese in a bowl. Whisk the milk into the cream cheese, 1 tablespoon at a time. Stir in the mayonnaise, green onions, horseradish sauce, crab meat and Worcestershire sauce; mix well. Chill, covered, for at least 1 hour. Serve with thin wheat crackers or rye bread chips. Yield: 1 1/2 cups.

Marcia Veltri, Xi Epsilon Delta
Salida, Colorado

SHRIMP DIP

8 ounces cream cheese, softened	1 tablespoon dried minced onion
1 cup mayonnaise	1 tablespoon garlic powder
1 (4-ounce) can shrimp, rinsed, drained	
1 (4-ounce) can chopped olives, drained	

Combine the cream cheese and mayonnaise in a bowl and beat by hand until smooth and creamy. Add the shrimp, olives, minced onion and garlic powder and mix well. Chill, covered, for at least 1 hour before serving. Serve with dip chips. Yield: 3 cups.

Sue Leonard, Alpha Omicron
Pierce, Idaho

COCONUT ALOHA DIP

I scoop out a fresh pineapple and use the hull to hold the dip. Add a fresh flower for decoration.

1 cup sour cream	12 coconut macaroons,
1/4 cup firmly packed	crushed
brown sugar	

Combine the sour cream and brown sugar and stir to blend. Fold in the crushed macaroons. Chill, covered, for 4 to 10 hours. Serve with fresh fruit such as strawberries, sliced apples and pineapple chunks. Yield: 1 1/2 cups.

Trisha Winship, Delta Kappa
Ellisville, Mississippi

AMARETTO CREME

A light, delicious fruit dip. You may substitute 1/4 cup milk plus 1/4 teaspoon almond extract for the amaretto if you like.

8 ounces cream cheese,	1/4 cup amaretto
softened	1/2 cup toasted finely
3 tablespoons brown	chopped almonds
sugar	

Combine the cream cheese, brown sugar and amaretto in a small mixing bowl and beat at medium speed until smooth. Stir in the almonds. Serve with assorted chilled fresh fruits such as melon balls, seedless grapes, strawberries, raspberries and sliced peaches. Yield: 1 1/2 cups.

Mary Prioux, Laureate Zeta Epsilon
Groves, Texas

APPLE DIP

Use Fruit Fresh to keep apples from browning.

8 ounces cream cheese,	1 (12-ounce) jar caramel,
at room temperature	at room temperature
1 (8-ounce) tub apple	1 cup finely chopped
cinnamon cream	pecans
cheese, at room	5 or 6 apples, cut in
temperature	wedges

Combine the cream cheese and apple cinnamon cream cheese in a bowl and mix well. Spread the cream cheese mixture over a large plate. Spread the caramel over the cream cheese mixture and sprinkle with the pecans. Chill, covered with plastic wrap, for 2 to 3 hours. Prepare the apple wedges just before serving and arrange them around the edge of the plate. Yield: 20 to 25 servings.

Margaret Parker, Rho Master
Raton, New Mexico

ENGLISH TOFFEE APPLE DIP

The apples will keep for days in the refrigerator when you store them in pineapple juice, and they will not be tart as they sometimes are if you use lemon juice.

4 red apples, sliced	1/4 cup granulated sugar
4 yellow apples, sliced	1 teaspoon vanilla
1 (6-ounce) can	extract
pineapple juice	1 (10-ounce) package
8 ounces cream cheese,	English toffee bits
softened	
1/3 cup packed brown	
sugar	

Combine the apple slices and pineapple juice in a gallon-size sealable plastic bag. Combine the cream cheese and brown sugar in a bowl and mix well; let stand for 10 minutes. Stir in the granulated sugar and vanilla. Chill, covered, until ready to serve. Stir in the toffee bits just before serving. Arrange the apple slices around a bowl of the dip and serve. Yield: 10 to 12 servings.

Susan Seitzinger, Psi Eta
Paducah, Kentucky

BANANA BREAD DIP

1 cup mashed banana	1 1/2 teaspoons cinnamon
1 teaspoon lemon juice	1 teaspoon vanilla
1/2 cup quick-cooking	extract
oats	1/4 teaspoon salt
1/2 cup sugar	1/4 teaspoon nutmeg

Blend the banana and lemon juice in a small mixing bowl. Stir in the oats, sugar, cinnamon, vanilla, salt and nutmeg and mix well. Serve immediately with fresh fruit. Yield: about 2 cups.

Christi Markin, Zeta Eta
Pancersburg, West Virginia

ORANGE ALMOND FRUIT DIP

8 ounces fat-free cream	1/4 cup confectioners'
cheese, softened	sugar
1 tablespoon honey	1/2 teaspoon grated
1 tablespoon orange	orange zest
juice concentrate	(optional)
3 drops almond extract	

Combine the cream cheese, honey, orange juice concentrate, almond extract, confectioners' sugar and orange zest in a bowl; mix well. Serve as a dip for sliced apples, pears or strawberries, or for salty pretzels. Yield: about 1 cup.

Romita Carol Cohee, Preceptor Delta Theta
Neodesha, Kansas

PUMPKIN DIP

16 ounces cream cheese,
  softened
1 (1-pound) package
  confectioners' sugar
1/2 teaspoon cinnamon

1/4 teaspoon nutmeg
1 (29-ounce) can
  pumpkin
1/4 teaspoon pumpkin
  pie spice

Combine all the ingredients in a bowl and blend well. Spoon into a small cleaned-out pumpkin and serve with apple wedges, pear wedges or gingersnaps. Yield: 1 1/2 quarts.

Barbara Bonner, Xi Zeta Iota
York, Pennsylvania

CARAMEL FRUIT DIP

1 cup (2 sticks) butter
2 1/4 cups packed brown
  sugar
Dash of salt
1 cup light corn syrup

1 (14-ounce) can
  sweetened condensed
  milk
1 teaspoon vanilla
  extract

Melt the butter in a heavy 3-quart saucepan over low heat. Stir in the brown sugar and salt. Stir in the corn syrup. Add the sweetened condensed milk gradually, stirring constantly. Cook over medium heat to the boiling point, stirring constantly. Remove from heat and pour into a bowl. Stir in the vanilla. Cool slightly. Serve warm with assorted fruit. Yield: 3 to 4 cups.

Roberta Eisert, Chi Psi
Marseilles, Illinois

SIMPLE FRUIT DIP

8 ounces cream cheese,
  softened
1/3 cup packed brown
  sugar

1 teaspoon vanilla
  extract

Combine the cream cheese, brown sugar and vanilla in a bowl and mix until smooth. Spoon into a small bowl and place in the center of a serving plate. Surround with fresh fruit. Yield: 20 servings.

Lois Marie Lindsey, Laureate Alpha Sigma
Iola, Kansas

MARSHMALLOW FRUIT DIP

8 ounces cream cheese,
  softened

2 (7-ounce) jars
  marshmallow creme

Place the cream cheese in a mixing bowl and beat until smooth. Add the marshmallow creme; mix until well blended and smooth. Serve with cut-up fruit. Yield: 2 1/2 cups.

Sherry Bingham, Lambda Tau
Meriden, Kansas

QUICK SPINACH MADELINE

4 (10-ounce) packages
  chopped spinach,
  slightly cooked,
  drained
1/4 cup (1/2 stick) butter,
  melted
1 onion, chopped
1 (10-ounce) can cream
  of mushroom soup

1 (6-ounce) roll garlic
  cheese
1 (6-ounce) roll jalapeño
  cheese
Worcestershire sauce to
  taste
Celery salt to taste
Salt and pepper to taste

Mix the spinach, butter, onion, soup, garlic cheese, jalapeño cheese, Worcestershire sauce, celery salt, salt and pepper in a large bowl. Spoon the spinach mixture into a buttered 2-quart baking dish. Sprinkle with cracker crumbs. Bake, uncovered, at 375 degrees for 30 minutes or until bubbly and brown. Serve with crackers. Yield: 10 servings.

Sandra Miletello, Xi Chi
Alexandria, Louisiana

PARMESAN SPINACH SPREAD

1 (10-ounce) package
  frozen chopped
  spinach, thawed and
  drained
3 ounces cream cheese,
  softened
3/4 cup mayonnaise
1 1/4 cups freshly grated
  Parmesan cheese
1/4 cup minced onion

1 teaspoon Italian
  seasoning
1 teaspoon hot red
  pepper sauce
1/2 teaspoon garlic
  powder
1/4 teaspoon freshly
  ground black pepper
1/2 teaspoon paprika

Press the spinach between paper towels to remove excess moisture. Combine the cream cheese and mayonnaise in a bowl; whisk until smooth. Add the spinach, 1 cup of the Parmesan cheese, onion, Italian seasoning, hot red pepper sauce, garlic powder and pepper; mix well. Spoon the spinach mixture into a buttered 1-quart baking dish. Bake, uncovered, at 350 degrees for 10 minutes. Sprinkle with the paprika and the remaining 1/4 cup Parmesan cheese. Bake for 10 minutes longer. Serve with crackers or corn chips. Yield: 2 1/4 cups.

Brenda Westmoreland, Preceptor Mu Kappa
Yoakum, Texas

---

*Elizabeth Flatt, Alpha Master, Kelso, Washington, serves her **Marshmallow Orange Dip** with fresh fruit. She beats 8 ounces cream cheese with a 7-ounce jar of marshmallow creme, 2 tablespoons orange juice, 2 tablespoons confectioners' sugar and 1 teaspoon vanilla extract until smooth and chills before serving.*

BRIE WITH PEAR CRANBERRY CHUTNEY

The chutney is also delicious served as an accompaniment to roast turkey.

3/4 cup packed brown sugar	1 cup chopped red bell pepper
1/2 cup raisins	1/2 cup white vinegar
2 firm ripe pears, peeled and chopped	1 garlic clove, crushed
1/4 cup coarsely chopped onion	1 1/2 teaspoons minced fresh gingerroot
8 ounces cranberries	1 round of Brie cheese

Combine the brown sugar, raisins, pears, onion, cranberries, red bell pepper, vinegar, garlic and gingerroot in a saucepan. Bring to a boil, stirring frequently. Simmer, uncovered, for 1 hour or until thickened, stirring frequently. Store in a covered container in the refrigerator. Place the Brie on a microwave-safe plate. Microwave on High for 1 1/2 minutes. Spoon the chutney over the Brie and serve with favorite crackers. Yield: 2 cups chutney.

Sherry Carlton, Laureate Theta Lambda
Longview, Texas

BAKED BRIE WITH CURRIED WALNUTS

1 tablespoon olive oil	2 tablespoons chopped green onions
1 tablespoon butter	
1/2 to 1 teaspoon curry powder	1 1/2 cups coarsely chopped walnuts
1/3 cup chopped red bell pepper	Salt and pepper to taste
	2 rounds of Brie cheese

Heat the olive oil, butter and curry powder in a large saucepan over medium heat. Add the red bell pepper and green onions and sauté for 2 to 5 minutes or until tender. Add the walnuts and sauté for 1 minute. Remove from heat and season with salt and pepper. Place the Brie in ovenproof serving dishes. Spoon the walnut mixture over the Brie. Bake at 350 degrees for 10 to 15 minutes or until the Brie just starts to melt. Serve with favorite crackers. Yield: 6 to 8 servings.

Paula Brown, Beta Eta Master
Nepean, Ontario, Canada

Gerry Brown, Omicron, Trail, British Columbia, Canada, makes **Simple Brie** *by covering a round of Brie cheese with a mixture of 1/2 cup chopped sun-dried tomatoes, 2 crushed garlic cloves, and 1/4 cup minced parsley and baking at 325 degrees until warm.*

CRESCENT GOUDA SURPRISE

1 (8-count) can crescent rolls	2/3 cup (or to taste) raspberry jelly or raspberry jam
1 (7-ounce) round Gouda cheese	

Separate the dough into 2 rectangles, pressing the perforations to seal. Place one of the rectangles on an ungreased baking sheet. Place the cheese in the center of the rectangle and spread jelly over the cheese. Cover with the other dough rectangle. Press edges together firmly to enclose the cheese. Bake at 350 degrees for 20 minutes or until dough is light brown and cheese is melted. Pierce the center with a knife to test the cheese. Yield: 10 to 12 servings.

Shirley Moorman, Laureate Zeta Alpha
Middleburg, Florida

BAKED BRIE WITH KODIAK SAUCE

1/2 cup sliced almonds	1 sheet frozen puff pastry, thawed
1 (8-ounce) round of Brie cheese	Kodiak Sauce

Layer the almonds over the top of the Brie. Wrap in the puff pastry and brush with melted butter. Bake at 400 degrees for 20 minutes. Prepare Kodiak Sauce and pour into a gravy separator. Pour evenly on the plate, surrounding the warm Brie. Serve with fruit or crackers. Yield: 4 to 6 servings.

KODIAK SAUCE

1/2 cup (1 stick) butter	1 tablespoon fresh lemon juice
1/2 cup packed brown sugar	

Melt the butter in a small saucepan over low heat. Add the brown sugar and lemon juice and cook until sugar is dissolved, stirring constantly.

Jeanette Weiland, Beta Omega
Glenham, South Dakota

TIPSY BRIE

1 wedge of Brie cheese	1/4 cup crushed walnuts
1/4 cup packed brown sugar	1 to 1 1/2 tablespoons bourbon

Place the Brie in a microwave-safe serving dish. Spread a mixture of the brown sugar, walnuts and bourbon evenly over the top and sides of the cheese. Microwave, uncovered, on Medium just until it begins to collapse. Serve warm with crackers. Yield: 4 to 6 servings.

Carlene Moncak, Xi Zeta Psi
E. Stroudsburg, Pennsylvania

KAHLUA BRIE

Serve at holiday dinners or cocktail parties.

³/4 cup pecans, chopped	*1 (14-ounce) round of*
¹/4 cup Kahlúa	*Brie cheese*
3 tablespoons brown	
sugar	

Spread the pecans evenly in a microwave-safe 9-inch pie plate. Microwave on Medium for 4 to 6 minutes. Drizzle the Kahlúa and sprinkle the brown sugar over the pecans; stir until well mixed. Remove and discard the rind of the Brie. Place the Brie in the center of the Kahlúa mixture. Spread the Kahlúa mixture up the side and over the top of the Brie. Microwave on High for 1¹/2 to 2 minutes or until cheese softens. Serve with crackers. Yield: 6 to 8 servings.

Sue Breidenstein, Xi Beta Epsilon
Ocean Pines, Maryland

BAKED BRIE WITH APPLES AND CRANBERRIES

¹/2 cup chopped peeled	*1 tablespoon butter,*
apple	*melted*
¹/4 cup sliced almonds	*1 (8-ounce) round of*
¹/4 cup dried cranberries	*Brie cheese*
1 tablespoon cinnamon	

Combine the apple, almonds, cranberries and cinnamon in a bowl and mix gently. Stir in the butter. Cut the round of cheese in half horizontally. Place one of the halves cut side up on a small baking sheet. Spoon half the apple mixture over the cheese. Top with the remaining cheese, cut side down. Spoon the remaining apple mixture over the top. Bake at 350 degrees for 12 to 15 minutes or until cheese is soft and beginning to melt. Serve with crackers or bread. Yield: 6 to 8 servings.

Diane Fernandez, Preceptor Delta Chi
Hays, Kansas

CRANBERRY BRIE

I like to bake this appetizer in a toaster oven so I can easily remove it before the cheese melts.

1 (8-ounce) round of Brie	*2 tablespoons dried*
cheese	*cranberries*
2 tablespoons brown	*2 tablespoons chopped*
sugar	*walnuts or pecans*

Cut the round of cheese in half horizontally. Sprinkle half the brown sugar, half the cranberries and half the chopped walnuts over one cheese half. Top with the remaining cheese, cut side down. Spoon the remaining brown sugar, cranberries and walnuts over the top. Bake at 350 degrees for 5 to 7 minutes or just until cheese begins to melt. Serve with crackers. Yield: 4 to 6 servings.

Floy M. Grabner, Laureate Iota Lambda
Citrus Heights, California

CARAMEL WALNUT BRIE

2 frozen puff pastry	*Butterscotch caramel*
sheets, thawed	*topping*
1 (12- to 16-ounce)	*¹/2 cup crushed walnuts*
round of Brie cheese	

Place 1 sheet of puff pastry on an ungreased baking sheet. Place the cheese in the center of the pastry. Spread caramel topping over the top and sprinkle walnuts over the caramel. Cover with the second sheet of pastry and seal the edges to enclose the cheese. Chill, covered, for 2 to 10 hours. Bake at 350 degrees for 20 minutes or until lightly browned. Serve warm with crackers, garlic bread and fruits. Yield: 8 to 10 servings.

Bonnie Wiktor, Xi Gamma Rho
Romeo, Michigan

REUBEN SPREAD

1 cup (4 ounces)	*¹/2 pound corned beef,*
shredded Swiss	*chopped*
cheese	*1 cup mayonnaise*
1 cup (4 ounces)	*1 (16-ounce) can*
shredded American	*sauerkraut, drained*
cheese	*and chopped*

Combine the Swiss cheese, American cheese, corned beef, mayonnaise and sauerkraut in a bowl and mix well. Spoon into a glass 8×12-inch baking dish. Bake at 350 degrees for 30 minutes. Serve with party rye, bagels or crackers. Yield: 12 to 15 servings.

Naomi E. Golden, Alpha Nu Master
Van Buren, Ohio

SAVORY SAUSAGE SPREAD

1 pound sausage	*1 teaspoon hot red*
1 pound ground beef	*pepper flakes*
16 ounces Velveeta	*1 teaspoon oregano*
cheese, cubed	*1 teaspoon garlic powder*

Brown the sausage and ground beef in a skillet, stirring until crumbly; drain. Add the remaining ingredients and cook over medium-low heat for about 5 minutes, stirring frequently. Remove from heat. Let stand until the cheese is melted. Spread on party rye bread. Yield: 30 to 40 servings.

Gloria Cobb, Alpha Alpha
Decatur, Alabama

APPETIZER BEEF PIE

8 ounces cream cheese, softened	2 tablespoons finely chopped green bell pepper
2 tablespoons milk	
1 (3-ounce) jar sliced dried beef, finely chopped	1/8 teaspoon black pepper
2 tablespoons minced onion	1/2 cup sour cream
	1/4 cup coarsely chopped walnuts

Combine the cream cheese and milk in a medium bowl and stir until smooth. Add the dried beef, onion, bell pepper and black pepper and mix well. Stir in the sour cream. Spoon evenly into an 8-inch pie plate or shallow baking dish. Sprinkle with walnuts. Bake at 350 degrees for 15 minutes. Serve hot with assorted crackers. Yield: 12 to 15 servings.

Constance Novak, Lambda Laureate
Selinsgrove, Pennsylvania

WARM BACON CHEESE SPREAD

1 round loaf sourdough bread	1 1/2 cups sour cream
8 ounces cream cheese, softened	1 1/2 teaspoons Worcestershire sauce
2 cups (8 ounces) shredded Cheddar cheese	3/4 pound bacon, crisp-cooked, crumbled
	1/2 cup chopped green onions

Slice off the top 1/4 of the bread loaf. Scoop out the center of the loaf to leave a 1-inch-thick shell. Cut the bread top and the scooped-out bread into cubes. Place the cream cheese in a bowl and beat at medium speed for 10 to 20 seconds. Add the cheese, sour cream and Worcestershire sauce and beat until well mixed. Stir in the bacon and green onions. Spoon the cheese mixture into the bread shell. Wrap in a sheet of heavy-duty foil. Bake at 325 degrees for 1 hour. Serve with crackers and bread cubes. Yield: 4 cups.

Susan Holste, Xi Eta Omicron
Great Bend, Kansas

HOT CLAM SPREAD

A can of chicken plus a few tablespoons of chicken broth may be substituted for the clams.

1 (7-ounce) can minced clams	1/2 cup butter or margarine
1 teaspoon fresh lemon juice	Dash of Tabasco sauce
1 onion, chopped	1/2 cup seasoned bread crumbs
1 clove garlic, crushed	
1/2 green bell pepper, minced	8 ounces Velveeta cheese
1 teaspoon chopped parsley	1/2 cup grated Parmesan cheese
1 teaspoon oregano	

Combine the undrained clams and lemon juice in a saucepan over medium heat; bring to a simmer. Simmer for 5 minutes. Stir in the next 8 ingredients. Spoon into a shallow baking dish. Crumble the Velveeta cheese over the top. Sprinkle with Parmesan cheese. Bake, uncovered, at 350 degrees for 20 minutes. Serve with crackers. Yield: 10 to 12 servings.

Marilyn Falusi, Alpha Beta Epsilon
Titusville, Florida

CHEESY CRAB SPREAD

Freeze on baking sheets, then bag for the freezer. When needed, just broil the desired number.

1 (7-ounce) can crab meat, drained	1/2 teaspoon seasoned salt
1 (8-ounce) jar Ingersoll cheese spread	1/2 teaspoon garlic powder
1/4 cup butter, softened	English muffins
1 1/2 teaspoons mayonnaise	

Combine the crab meat, cheese spread, butter, mayonnaise, seasoned salt and garlic powder in a bowl and mix well. Spread the crab mixture over split English muffins, then cut into quarters. Broil until hot and golden. Serve. Yield: 18 to 24 servings.

Terry Socha, Mu Zeta
Tillsonburg, Ontario, Canada

CUCUMBER SPREAD

8 ounces cream cheese, softened	1 tablespoon chopped parsley
1/2 cup drained shredded cucumber	1/4 teaspoon seasoned salt
2 tablespoons finely chopped onion	Dash of pepper

Combine all the ingredients in a bowl and mix well. Serve with assorted crackers. Keeps well in the refrigerator for one week. Yield: 6 to 10 servings.

Janet Cross, Xi Delta Mu
Abilene, Kansas

Debbie Saranchuk, Alpha Gamma, Ft. Saskatchewan, Alberta, Canada, makes an **Easy Mexican Dip** *by mixing 3 cups shredded Monterey Jack cheese with 4 diced tomatoes, 10 diced green onions, a small can each of diced jalapeños and sliced black olives, 3 tablespoons chopped cilantro, and a 10-ounce bottle of Italian salad dressing. Let the flavors blend for 3 to 6 hours in the refrigerator; serve with assorted crackers or chips.*

AVOCADO PISTACHIO PATE WITH HERB TOASTS

1 1/2 cups mashed avocado	1/4 teaspoon chili powder
4 ounces cream cheese, softened	2 tablespoons chopped pistachios
2 shallots, chopped	1 teaspoon chopped fresh parsley
1 small garlic clove, minced	Herb Toasts
1 teaspoon lemon juice or lime juice	

Combine the avocado, cream cheese, shallots, garlic, lemon juice and chili powder in a blender or food processor container; process until smooth. Line 2 (1-cup) molds with plastic wrap. Sprinkle a tablespoon of chopped pistachios into each mold and pour half the avocado mixture into each. Chill, covered, for 3 hours or until set. Unmold onto lettuce-lined serving plates. Remove the plastic wrap and sprinkle the pistachios with parsley. Serve immediately with Herb Toasts. Yield: about 2 cups.

HERB TOASTS

2 pita bread rounds	1/2 teaspoon each basil, rosemary and thyme
1/2 cup (1 stick) butter	

Split the pita rounds horizontally. Brush each half with melted butter and sprinkle with a mixture of the basil, rosemary and thyme. Arrange on baking sheets. Bake at 350 degrees for 5 minutes or until lightly browned. Cool and break into pieces.

Bronwyn Stich, Preceptor Iota Mu
Fort Pierce, Florida

FESTIVE CRANBERRY CHEESE SPREAD

1 (16-ounce) can whole cranberry sauce	1/2 teaspoon chili powder
1 (4-ounce) can chopped green chiles, drained	1/2 teaspoon cayenne pepper or Tabasco sauce
3 tablespoons chopped onion	8 ounces cream cheese, softened
1 tablespoon lime juice	
1/2 teaspoon garlic sauce	

Combine the cranberry sauce, green chiles, onion, lime juice, garlic sauce, chili powder and cayenne pepper in a bowl and mix well. Place the cream cheese on a serving plate and mash with a fork. Spread the cranberry sauce mixture over the cream cheese. Serve with crackers. Yield: 32 servings.

Alice Fitzgibbon, Laureate Sigma
Scottsbluff, Nebraska

CRANBERRY CHEESE SPREAD

1 (16-ounce) can whole cranberry sauce	2 tablespoons prepared horseradish
1 teaspoon salt	8 ounces cream cheese, softened
1/2 cup sugar	
1/3 cup finely chopped onion	

Combine the cranberry sauce, salt, sugar, onion and horseradish in a heavy saucepan over medium-high heat. Bring to a boil. Remove from heat. Let cool. Spread the cream cheese on a flat plate. Spread the cranberry mixture over the cream cheese. Chill, covered, until ready to serve with crackers. Yield: 3 cups.

Elberta McVicker, Preceptor Alpha Chi
Sheldon, Illinois

HERBED CHEVRE

Chèvre is a soft cheese made from goat's milk.

1 (8-ounce) roll chèvre	1/4 cup chopped oil-pack sun-dried tomatoes
1/2 teaspoon crushed dried rosemary	2 teaspoons chopped parsley
1/2 teaspoon dried basil	1/2 to 1 cup extra-virgin olive oil
1/4 teaspoon pepper	
2 garlic cloves, minced	
1/4 cup chopped black olives	

Chill the chèvre and cut into 1/4- to 1/2-inch-thick slices. Arrange on a serving plate. Sprinkle a mixture of the rosemary, basil, pepper and garlic over the cheese. Sprinkle with the olives and sun-dried tomatoes. Drizzle with the olive oil. Chill, covered tightly with plastic wrap, for 1 or 2 days. Bring to room temperature and serve with crackers or sliced baguette. Yield: 8 servings.

Vi Waud, Laureate Epsilon
Brantford, Ontario, Canada

HOLIDAY BLEU CHEESE SPREAD

My mom used to make this every year for snacking while we opened our Christmas presents.

4 ounces soft bleu cheese, crumbled	1 (4-ounce) can chopped black olives, drained
16 ounces cream cheese, softened	1 (2-ounce) jar chopped pimentos, drained

Combine the bleu cheese, cream cheese, olives and pimentos in a bowl and mix well. Chill, covered, until serving time. May be shaped into a ball and rolled in chopped walnuts. Yield: 2 cups.

Bette Brailey, Preceptor Laureate Beta Rho
Kentwood, Michigan

OLIVE NUT SPREAD

1/2 cup green olives, drained, liquid reserved
6 ounces cream cheese, softened
1/2 cup mayonnaise
Dash of pepper
1/2 cup chopped walnuts or pecans

Chop the olives. Combine the cream cheese and mayonnaise in a bowl and blend until smooth. Stir in the pepper and 2 tablespoons of the olive liquid. Fold in the olives and walnuts. Spread over crackers or party rye bread to make open-face appetizers.
Yield: 1 1/4 cups.

Doris Paquette, Epsilon Master
Manchester, New Hampshire

PEACH BRANDIED CHEESE SPREAD

Try peaches, nectarines, pears, or strawberries for the fresh fruit.

8 ounces cream cheese, softened
1/4 cup confectioners' sugar
1 tablespoon peach-flavored brandy
2 pounds fresh fruit, sliced

Combine the cream cheese, confectioners' sugar and brandy in a small bowl and blend until smooth. Mound the cream cheese mixture in the center of a large serving plate and swirl with a knife to make a pretty shape. Chill, covered, until ready to serve. At serving time, arrange the sliced fruit around the cream cheese mixture. Serve with a small knife for spreading the cream cheese mixture on the fruit.
Yield: 15 servings.

Dayle Nelson, Beta Master
Cheyenne, Wyoming

PEPPERONCINI CREAM CHEESE SPREAD

No barbecue takes place in our family without serving this spread. It is served cold and it never lasts long. Use more pepperoncini if you want a hotter flavor.

1 (10-ounce) jar pepperoncini, drained, stemmed
8 ounces cream cheese, softened
1/4 cup grated Parmesan cheese
1/2 cup sour cream

Combine the pepperoncini, cream cheese and Parmesan cheese in a food processor container and process until smooth. Stir in the sour cream. Chill, covered, until serving time. Serve with chips or crackers. Yield: 20 servings.

Pat Raugust, Laureate Gamma Theta
Kalama, Washington

BLEU CHEESE WALNUT SPREAD

8 ounces cream cheese, softened
4 ounces bleu cheese, crumbled
1/2 cup sour cream
1 teaspoon Worcestershire sauce
1/2 cup chopped walnuts
2 tablespoons chopped chives

Combine the cream cheese, bleu cheese, sour cream and Worcestershire sauce in a bowl and mix well. Stir in the walnuts and chives. Chill, covered, for 1 to 10 hours to marry the flavors. Serve with crackers.
Yield: 2 cups.

Doris White, Epsilon Iota
Memphis, Missouri

SHERRY CHEESE PATE

Use your favorite chutney. I prefer peach mango.

6 ounces cream cheese, softened
1 cup (4 ounces) shredded sharp Cheddar cheese
4 teaspoons dry sherry
1/2 teaspoon curry powder
1/4 teaspoon salt
1 (8-ounce) jar chutney
3 or 4 green onions, tops included, finely sliced
Sesame crackers or wheat crackers

Combine the cream cheese, Cheddar cheese, sherry, curry powder and salt in a bowl and mix well. Spread the cheese mixture 1/2 inch thick on a serving platter. Chill for 30 minutes or until firm. Spread the chutney over the cheese layer and sprinkle with green onions. Serve with crackers. Yield: 25 servings.

Joanne Woods, Xi Alpha Nu
Atlanta, Georgia

JEZEBEL SAUCE FOR CREAM CHEESE BLOCKS

Jezebel sauce is a traditional sweet, spicy condiment. It will keep for months in the refrigerator.

1 (1-ounce) can dry mustard
1 (4-ounce) jar horseradish
1 (16-ounce) jar pineapple preserves
1 (16-ounce) jar apple jelly
1 tablespoon black pepper

Place the dry mustard and horseradish in a bowl and mix into a paste. Add the pineapple preserves, apple jelly and pepper, and stir by hand until well mixed. Serve over an 8-ounce block of cream cheese. Surround with assorted crackers and a small knife for spreading. Yield: 1 quart.

Jackie Miller, Laureate Delta
Suffolk, Virginia

MUFFALATA

Muffalata is a celebrated savory sandwich spread that is beloved in New Orleans. You may chop the ingredients by hand or in a food processor.

1/2 cup chopped pepperoncini	5 tablespoons chopped shallots
1/2 cup chopped cherry peppers	5 tablespoons capers, drained and chopped
1/4 cup each chopped black and green olives	1/2 teaspoon minced garlic
1/2 cup chopped roasted red bell pepper	1 to 2 cups extra-virgin olive oil
1/2 cup chopped artichoke hearts	Tabasco sauce to taste

Combine the pepperoncini, cherry peppers, black olives, green olives, roasted red pepper, artichoke hearts, shallots, capers and garlic in a bowl and mix well. Stir in the olive oil. Season with Tabasco sauce. Serve with garlic toast or crackers. Yield: 5 cups.

Babs Donoho, Gamma Psi
Chico, California

ROASTED RED PEPPER AND ARTICHOKE TAPENADE

1 (7-ounce) jar roasted red bell peppers, drained	1/2 cup freshly grated Parmesan cheese
1 (6-ounce) jar marinated artichoke hearts, drained	1 teaspoon fresh lemon juice
1/2 cup minced fresh parsley	Salt and pepper to taste

Place the roasted red peppers and artichoke hearts in a food processor container and pulse until coarsely chopped. Add the parsley, Parmesan cheese and lemon juice and process until finely chopped. Season with salt and pepper. Yield: 2 cups.

Mary Phillips, Xi Omicron Theta
Sugar Land, Texas

HERBED CHEESECAKE

24 ounces cream cheese, softened	2 tablespoons minced fresh basil, or 1 teaspoon dried
1 (10-ounce) can cream of celery soup	1 tablespoon minced fresh thyme, or 1 teaspoon dried
2 cups sour cream	
3 eggs	
1/2 cup grated Romano cheese	1/2 teaspoon Italian seasoning
3 garlic cloves, minced	1/2 teaspoon coarsely ground pepper
1 tablespoon cornstarch	

Combine the cream cheese, soup and 1 cup of the sour cream in a large mixing bowl and beat at high speed until smooth. Add the eggs, Romano cheese, garlic, cornstarch, basil, thyme, Italian seasoning and pepper; beat until smooth. Pour into a buttered 9-inch springform pan. Place the pan on a baking sheet. Bake at 350 degrees for 55 to 60 minutes or until center is almost set. Cool on a wire rack for 10 minutes. Carefully run a knife around the edge of the pan to loosen. Let stand for 1 hour longer. Chill, covered, for 4 to 10 hours. Remove the side of the pan. Spread the remaining 1 cup sour cream over the top of the cheesecake. Serve with assorted crackers. Keep leftovers in the refrigerator. Yield: 24 servings.

Ethel M. Goble, Pi Master
Brighton, Illinois

TACO APPETIZER CHEESECAKE

Serves a large group and makes an excellent presentation.

1 cup crushed tortilla chips	1 (4-ounce) can chopped green chiles
3 tablespoons melted margarine	1 cup sour cream
24 ounces cream cheese, softened	1/4 cup chopped green onions
3 eggs	1/4 cup shredded Cheddar cheese
8 ounces Colby cheese or Monterey Jack cheese, shredded	1/4 cup each chopped red, yellow and green bell peppers
1/2 cup medium salsa	1 tomato skin rose

Combine the tortilla chips and margarine in a small bowl and mix well. Press the chip mixture over the bottom of a 9-inch springform pan. Bake at 325 degrees for 15 minutes. Place the cream cheese in a large mixing bowl and beat for 1 minute at medium speed. Add the eggs 1 at a time, beating well after each addition. Add the Colby cheese, salsa and green chiles and stir until well mixed. Pour over the baked tortilla crust. Bake for 40 minutes. Cool on a wire rack for 10 minutes. Carefully run a knife around the edge of the pan to loosen. Let cool completely. Chill, covered, for 8 to 10 hours. Remove the side of the pan. Remove cheesecake to a serving plate. Spread sour cream over the top. Divide the top into six equal sections with aluminum foil strips and decorate with the chopped vegetables and the Cheddar cheese. Remove the foil strips. Place the tomato skin rose in the center. Serve at room temperature with chips or crackers. Yield: 16 to 20 servings.

Joyce Fred, Alpha Iota Master
Springfield, Illinois

ROAST BEEF SALAD SPREAD

2 cups chopped cooked roast beef	1/3 cup chopped green bell pepper
2 cups chopped celery	1/3 cup chopped pimentos
1 (8-ounce) can green peas, drained	1/2 cup sliced black olives
4 chopped hard-cooked eggs	1 small onion, chopped
1/2 cup diced American cheese	Salt and pepper to taste
	3/4 cup mayonnaise-type salad dressing

Combine the roast beef, celery, peas, eggs, cheese, bell pepper, pimentos, olives and onion in a large bowl and mix gently. Season with salt and pepper. Stir in the salad dressing, adding more if necessary to moisten. Chill, covered, for at least 2 hours. Serve over a bed of lettuce with crackers. Yield: 12 servings.

Joyce Bell, Preceptor Delta Tau
Isabel, Kansas

CHICKEN LIVER PATE

1 1/2 pounds chicken livers	1/2 to 3/4 cup mayonnaise
1/2 teaspoon garlic powder	1/2 onion, chopped
	1/2 teaspoon salt

Place the chicken livers in a saucepan. Sprinkle with the garlic powder and add enough water to cover. Simmer for 15 minutes or until tender. Drain and cool. Combine the cooked chicken livers, mayonnaise, onion and salt in a food processor container and process until smooth. Serve with assorted crackers. Yield: 8 to 10 servings.

Jean Kuhn, Preceptor Beta Gamma
Wyoming, Michigan

SWISS BACON PARTY SPREAD

Do not use a baking sheet when you broil these appetizers or they will become soggy—use a broiler pan.

1 cup (4 ounces) shredded Swiss cheese	1/4 cup chopped black olives
1/4 cup bacon bits	1 tablespoon chopped chives
1/4 cup mayonnaise	

Combine the cheese, bacon bits, mayonnaise, olives and chives in a bowl and mix well. Chill, covered, until ready to serve. Spread over party rye or pumpernickel. Broil 6 inches from the heat source for 3 to 5 minutes or until bubbly. Yield: 8 to 10 servings.

Barbara Potter, Laureate Lambda
Fort Pierce, Florida

HOAGIE SPREAD

4 ounces salami	3 tablespoons mayonnaise
4 ounces cooked ham	Oregano or Italian seasoning to taste
4 ounces each American cheese and provolone cheese	Tomato, chopped
1 tablespoon sour cream	Lettuce, chopped

Chop the salami, ham, American cheese and provolone cheese into 1/4-inch pieces. Place in a bowl and stir in the sour cream and mayonnaise. Sprinkle with oregano. Chill, covered, for at least 1 hour. Stir in tomato and lettuce 1 hour before serving. Spread over slices of Italian bread, toasted if desired, and serve. Yield: 18 to 20 servings.

Kathy Lombardo, Xi Zeta Psi
Stroudsburg, Pennsylvania

HAM AND MUSHROOM PATE

4 ounces mushrooms, coarsely chopped	3 ounces cream cheese, softened
1 tablespoon butter or margarine	1/4 teaspoon thyme
2 (4-ounce) cans deviled ham	

Sauté the mushrooms in butter in a skillet for 10 minutes. Mix the deviled ham, cream cheese and thyme in a bowl. Stir in the mushrooms. Chill, covered, for 8 to 10 hours. Serve with party bread. Yield: 1 3/4 cups.

Shirley Petersen, Laureate Kappa
Beatrice, Nebraska

HAM AND CHEESE SPREAD

8 ounces cream cheese, softened	5 ounces chopped cooked ham
1 cup sour cream	2 or 3 green onions, thinly sliced
1/4 teaspoon garlic powder	

Combine the cream cheese, sour cream and garlic powder in a bowl and blend well. Stir in the ham and onions. Chill, covered, until serving time. Serve on miniature bagels. Yield: 2 1/4 cups.

Carol Fielder, Laureate Kappa
Beatrice, Nebraska

*Joan P. Marr, Beta Eta Master, Ottawa, Ontario, Canada, makes **Swiss Almond Spread** by mixing 8 ounces cream cheese with 1 1/2 cups shredded Swiss cheese, 1/2 cup mayonnaise, 1/3 cup sliced almonds, and 2 tablespoons chopped green onion and baking at 350 degrees for 15 minutes, stirring once.*

SMOKED SALMON MOUSSE

*1 (16-ounce) can salmon,
    red or pink*
1/3 cup mayonnaise
*1 to 2 tablespoons
    prepared horseradish*
*3 to 4 green onions,
    finely chopped*
*16 ounces cream cheese,
    softened*
*1/2 teaspoon liquid
    smoke*
Juice of 1 lemon

Remove skin and dark flesh from the salmon. Crush the bones and mash with the light flesh in a medium bowl. Add the mayonnaise, horseradish, green onions, cream cheese, liquid smoke and lemon juice and mix well. Chill, covered, to marry the flavors. Serve as a spread with crackers or bread.
Yield: 20 to 30 servings.

*Karen Millan, Preceptor Xi
St. Johns, Arizona*

SMOKED SALMON PATE

*8 ounces smoked
    salmon, flaked*
*12 ounces cream cheese,
    softened*
*2 tablespoons prepared
    horseradish*
*1/2 teaspoon ground
    black pepper*
*2 tablespoons chopped
    parsley*
*1 tablespoon minced
    garlic*
*1/4 cup finely chopped
    red onion*
*1/4 cup chopped red bell
    pepper*
Salt to taste

Combine all the ingredients in a bowl and mix well. Line a deep bowl with plastic wrap. Press the salmon mixture firmly in the plastic-lined bowl. Cover with additional plastic wrap. Chill for 2 to 10 hours. Unmold onto a serving plate. Remove any plastic wrap. Serve with assorted crackers.
Yield: 20 to 30 servings.

*Janet Wetzel, Xi Zeta Omega
Offerle, Kansas*

❖ SWEET-AND-SOUR SALMON

3 1/2 pounds fresh salmon
*1 1/2 pounds onions,
    sliced*
3/4 cup sugar
3/4 cup vinegar
3/4 cup ketchup
1 1/2 tablespoons salt
1/2 tablespoon pepper
1 1/2 cups sliced gherkins

Steam the salmon until the fish flakes easily with a fork. Break into chunks and spread in a glass dish. Add enough water to the fish liquid to make 2 cups and pour into a saucepan. Stir in the onions, sugar, vinegar, ketchup, salt, pepper and gherkins and bring to a boil. Pour the hot liquid over the salmon.

Cover with foil and chill for 8 to 10 hours. Drain; serve with crackers or miniature bagels.
Yield: 6 to 8 cups.

*M.B. Herczeg, Lambda Master
Vancouver, British Columbia, Canada*

SMOKED SALMON CHEESECAKE

*1/4 cup toasted bread
    crumbs*
*2 tablespoons grated
    Romano cheese or
    Parmesan cheese*
*28 ounces cream cheese,
    softened*
4 large eggs
*1/2 cup (2 ounces) grated
    Asiago cheese*
1/3 cup heavy cream
*3 tablespoons fresh
    lemon juice*
*1/2 teaspoon white
    pepper*
1 1/2 teaspoons coriander
*1/2 to 3/4 pound smoked
    salmon, diced*
*4 or 5 green onions,
    finely chopped*
*1/4 to 1/3 cup chopped
    fresh dill weed*
Salt to taste

Lightly butter the bottom and side of a springform pan. Coat the buttered surfaces with a mixture of the bread crumbs and Romano cheese. Place the cream cheese in a large mixing bowl and beat until smooth and light. Add the eggs, Asiago cheese, cream, lemon juice, white pepper and coriander; beat until uniformly mixed. Fold in the salmon, green onions, dill weed and salt. Pour the salmon mixture into the prepared springform pan. Bake in the center of the oven at 325 degrees for 35 minutes. Let cool for 10 minutes. Remove from the pan to a serving plate. Chill, covered, until serving time. Serve with assorted crackers.
Yield: 16 to 18 servings.

*Dorothy Feagan, Alpha Nu
Goderich, Ontario, Canada*

TUNA PATE

*8 ounces cream cheese,
    softened*
*2 tablespoons chili
    sauce*
*2 tablespoons chopped
    fresh or dried parsley*
*1 teaspoon instant
    minced onion*
Dash of pepper
*2 (6-ounce) cans tuna,
    well drained*

Combine the cream cheese, chili sauce, parsley, onion, pepper and tuna in a blender container and process until smooth. Serve with assorted crackers and chips. Yield: 20 to 30 servings.

*Lil Blasko, Laureate Rho
Kindersley, Saskatchewan, Canada*

CRAB SPREAD

Every Christmas Eve our family has soup and finger foods, including this crab spread. It is "help-yourself" serving for several delightful hours.

8 ounces cream cheese, softened
2 (6-ounce) cans crab meat, drained and chopped
1½ teaspoons lemon juice
1½ cups ketchup
1½ teaspoons sugar
2 dashes Worcestershire sauce
1½ tablespoons prepared horseradish

Place the cream cheese on a serving plate. Combine the crab meat, lemon juice, ketchup, sugar, Worcestershire sauce and horseradish in a bowl and mix well. Pour the crab meat mixture over the cream cheese. Serve with assorted crackers.
Yield: 20 to 30 servings.

Eleanor Lohr, Iota Master
Quincy, Illinois

SHRIMP AND VEGETABLE SPREAD

8 ounces cream cheese, softened
½ cup sour cream
¼ cup mayonnaise
1 (4-ounce) can shrimp, rinsed, drained
1 cup seafood cocktail sauce
2 cups (8 ounces) shredded mozzarella cheese
1 cup chopped green bell pepper
3 green onions, chopped
1 or 2 tomatoes, diced (optional)

Combine the cream cheese, sour cream and mayonnaise in a bowl and blend until smooth. Spread the cream cheese mixture in a serving dish. Layer the shrimp, cocktail sauce, mozzarella cheese, bell pepper, green onions and tomato over the cream cheese mixture. Chill, covered, until serving time. Serve with tortilla chips or crackers. Yield: 20 to 30 servings.

Marie Holms, Alpha Master
Souris, Manitoba, Canada

SHRIMP PASTE

My mother prepares this appetizer in a fish-shaped mold and serves it on a bed of lettuce, using olive and pimento to make a fish eye and mouth.

2 pounds peeled boiled shrimp
½ small onion
2 hard-cooked eggs
¾ teaspoon Worcestershire sauce
Juice of 1 to 1½ lemons
½ teaspoon celery salt
3 tablespoons (about) mayonnaise
Hot red pepper sauce to taste
Salt and pepper to taste

Put the shrimp, onion and eggs through a medium meat grinder. Place the shrimp mixture in a large bowl. Mix in the Worcestershire sauce, lemon juice, celery salt and enough mayonnaise to make desired consistency. Season with hot red pepper sauce, salt and pepper. Shape into a ball or spoon into a mold. Chill, covered, for 8 to 10 hours. Serve with club crackers. Yield: 15 to 20 servings.

Esther Crandall, Preceptor Alpha Alpha
North Charleston, South Carolina

SHRIMP BUTTER

The ingredients are often on hand and it elicits raves.

½ cup butter or margarine, softened
8 ounces cream cheese, softened
1 tablespoon lemon juice
1 small onion or 3 or 4 scallions, finely chopped
3 tablespoons mayonnaise
1 (4-ounce) can tiny shrimp, drained
Salt and pepper to taste
Minced garlic to taste

Cream the butter and cream cheese together in a mixing bowl until creamy. Beat in the lemon juice, onion and mayonnaise. Add the shrimp, salt, pepper and garlic; beat by hand until well mixed. Spoon into a serving bowl. Chill, covered, for 24 hours. Serve with crackers. Yield: 16 to 20 servings.

Kathleen Frontz, Xi Iota Pi
Trinity, Florida

CUCUMBER SPREAD

A hand mixer or a food processor works best to mix this spread.

1 medium cucumber
8 ounces cream cheese, softened
2 tablespoons mayonnaise
Garlic salt to taste
Sprinkle of dill weed

Shred the unpeeled cucumber, reserving the juice. Combine the cream cheese and mayonnaise in a bowl and beat until smooth. Add the cucumber, garlic salt and dill weed and mix well, adding a little cucumber juice if consistency is too thick. Serve with crackers or chips. May also be used as a spread for open-face party sandwiches with a slice of cucumber or sprig of parsley. Yield: 10 to 12 servings.

Rosalyn Guyton, Psi Master
Ballwin, Missouri

PIMENTO CHEESE SPREAD

Excellent with a variety of crackers. Makes a pretty Christmas appetizer with its red pimento and green parsley.

12 ounces cream cheese, at room temperature	1½ teaspoons garlic powder
¾ cup purchased Cheddar cheese spread, at room temperature	1½ teaspoons finely chopped onion
1½ teaspoons chopped pimento	Chopped parsley Chopped pimento

Combine the cream cheese, Cheddar cheese spread, pimento, garlic powder and onion in a bowl and mix well. Place in a serving bowl and sprinkle with parsley and additional pimento. Serve with crackers. Yield: 20 to 30 servings.

Julia Gatsos, Laureate Beta Omicron
New Albany, Indiana

PECAN PARTY SANDWICH FILLING

¾ cup chopped pecans	3 tablespoons chopped pimentos
¼ cup chopped green bell pepper	½ teaspoon (or less) salt
1 tablespoon ketchup	Dash of pepper
3 hard-cooked eggs, chopped	8 ounces cream cheese, softened
¼ cup chopped onion	

Combine the pecans, bell pepper, ketchup, hard-cooked eggs, onion, pimentos, salt, pepper and cream cheese in a bowl and mix well. Spread sandwich bread lightly with salad dressing, mayonnaise or butter. Fill sandwiches with pecan filling. Cut each sandwich diagonally twice to make 4 triangles. Yield: 32 servings.

Pat Duncan, Laureate Alpha Xi
Durant, Oklahoma

LEMON PEPPER CHICKEN SALAD

May also be used to stuff tomatoes or as a sandwich filling.

2 boneless skinless chicken breast halves	¼ cup chopped green onions
2 teaspoons lemon pepper	¼ cup chopped green bell pepper
¼ cup chopped cucumber	3 to 4 tablespoons fat-free mayonnaise

Rinse the chicken and pat dry. Place the chicken breasts in an 8×8-inch baking dish that has been sprayed with nonstick cooking spray. Sprinkle 1 teaspoon of lemon pepper over each chicken breast.

Cover dish tightly with foil and bake at 350 degrees for 30 minutes. Remove foil and let chicken stand until cool. Chop the chicken and place in a bowl. Add the cucumber, green onions, bell pepper and mayonnaise and mix well. Serve with crackers. Yield: 1 to 2 cups.

Lisa Neisen, Tau Delta
Ewing, Missouri

CHICKEN SALAD

Add a small jar of pimentos to the chicken salad to make a Christmas appetizer.

2 (10-ounce) cans white chicken, drained	1 teaspoon garlic powder
2 ribs celery, finely chopped	1 cup Hellman's light mayonnaise
2 hard-cooked eggs, finely chopped	Salt and pepper to taste

Combine the chicken, celery, eggs, garlic powder, mayonnaise, salt and pepper in a bowl and mix well. Chill, covered, for at least 2 hours. Serve with crackers, celery sticks or carrot sticks, or serve with cocktail bread to make party sandwiches. Yield: 20 servings.

Ellen Edmonds, Eta Xi
Birmingham, Alabama

FRUITED CHICKEN SALAD

2 cups chopped cooked chicken	1 cup pineapple tidbits
1 cup pecan halves	1 cup white seedless grapes
1 cup chopped peeled Granny Smith apples	Mayonnaise to taste

Combine the chicken, pecans, apples, pineapple, grapes and mayonnaise in a bowl and mix well. Chill, covered, until ready to serve. Serve with crackers. Yield: 32 servings.

Lana Puckett, Theta Theta
Clintwood, Virginia

ZESTY CHICKEN SPREAD

1 (4-ounce) can chicken spread	1 teaspoon lemon juice
8 ounces cream cheese, softened	1 teaspoon Worcestershire sauce

Combine the chicken spread, cream cheese, lemon juice and Worcestershire sauce in a bowl and mix well. Chill, covered, until ready to serve. Serve with butter crackers. Yield: 8 to 10 servings.

Lynn Baker, Epsilon Gamma
Canton, Missouri

GARLIC CHEESE ROLL

To soften the cream cheese, I let it stand overnight at room temperature.

¹/₂ cup pecans	*16 ounces cream cheese,*
Desired number of	*softened*
peeled garlic cloves	*16 ounces sharp*
1 teaspoon cayenne	*Cheddar cheese,*
pepper	*shredded*

Combine the pecans, garlic and cayenne pepper in a food processor container and chop by pulsing 4 or 5 times. Add the cream cheese and Cheddar cheese and process until well mixed. Shape into rolls. Wrap the rolls in sheets of waxed paper that have been sprinkled with paprika; tie the ends closed. Chill until ready to serve. Serve with crackers. Yield: 2 or 3 rolls.

Marge Royster, Preceptor Alpha Mu
Chesapeake, Virginia

CREAM CHEESE BALL

This recipe will make 1 large cheese ball or 2 small ones. It is better if prepared a day before serving. Use full-fat cream cheese, not the low-fat kind.

1 (7-ounce) package dry	*1 (2-ounce) jar chopped*
Italian salad dressing	*pimentos, drained*
mix	*1 cup (or more) finely*
3 tablespoons sour	*chopped pecans*
cream	*¹/₃ cup dried parsley*
24 ounces cream cheese,	*flakes*
at room temperature	

Combine the salad dressing mix and sour cream in a large bowl and whisk to blend. Let stand for about 15 minutes to thicken. Add the cream cheese and pimentos and mix well. Roll into a ball. Chill, wrapped in plastic wrap, for at least 2 hours. Remove plastic wrap. Butter hands and roll the cheese ball in a mixture of the chopped pecans and parsley flakes. Serve with crackers. Yield: 32 servings.

Alice McBride, Preceptor Theta Omega
McKinney, Texas

RANCH CHEESE BALL

16 ounces cream cheese,	*1 envelope dry ranch*
softened	*dressing mix*
1 cup (4 ounces) shredded	*¹/₂ cup bacon bits*
Cheddar cheese	*¹/₂ cup chopped pecans*

Combine the cream cheese, Cheddar cheese, ranch dressing mix and bacon bits in a bowl and mix well. Roll into 2 balls. Roll in chopped pecans. Chill,

wrapped in plastic wrap. Remove from refrigerator about ¹/₂ hour before serving to soften. Serve with crackers, pretzels, and raw vegetables such as celery and carrots. Yield: 32 servings.

Cathy Anderson, Xi Alpha Zeta
Duluth, Georgia

LEMON BASIL TREE

This easy, pretty cheese ball is perfect for Christmas parties. It can be prepared in advance and stored in the refrigerator for up to 2 weeks, then rolled in parsley on the day of the party.

16 ounces cream cheese,	*2 teaspoons grated*
softened	*lemon zest*
1 cup (4 ounces)	*¹/₄ teaspoon garlic*
shredded Havarti	*powder*
cheese	*¹/₄ cup chopped fresh*
2 tablespoons chopped	*parsley or basil*
fresh basil, or	
2 teaspoons dried	

Combine the cream cheese, Havarti cheese, basil, lemon zest and garlic powder in a bowl and mix well. Shape into a cone to look like a Christmas tree, or roll into a ball or log. Roll in the parsley. Chill, wrapped in plastic wrap, for at least 2 hours until firm. Top with a star cut from lemon peel or yellow cheese. Variation: Omit the parsley and roll tree in 1 cup shredded Monterey Jack cheese. Decorate with chopped red bell pepper and top with a small star cut from lemon peel. Yield: 24 servings.

Robin Chase, Upsilon
Claremore, Oklahoma

PURPLE CHEESE BALL

8 ounces sharp Cheddar	*¹/₂ cup mayonnaise*
cheese, shredded	*10 butter crackers,*
¹/₂ large purple onion,	*crumbled*
finely chopped	*Chopped jalapeño*
¹/₄ cup chopped green	*peppers to taste*
onion tops	

Combine the cheese, purple onion, green onions, mayonnaise, cracker crumbs and jalapeño peppers in a bowl and mix well. Roll into a ball or a loaf. Sprinkle with paprika. Chill, wrapped in plastic wrap, for 8 to 10 hours. Yield: 18 to 20 servings.

Belinda Stephens, Alpha Beta Chi
Lufkin, Texas

EASY CHUTNEY ALMOND BALL

16 ounces cream cheese, softened
½ teaspoon curry powder
½ teaspoon dry mustard
1 (9-ounce) jar hot mango chutney
⅔ cup sliced blanched almonds

Combine the cream cheese, curry powder and dry mustard in a bowl and blend until smooth. Mix in the chutney a little at a time. Roll into a ball. Roll in the sliced almonds. Wrap in plastic wrap and chill for at least 2 hours. Serve with crackers. Yield: 25 servings.

Virginia Lee, Laureate Eta Nu
Houston, Texas

PINEAPPLE CHEESE BALL

16 ounces cream cheese, softened
1 (8-ounce) can crushed pineapple, drained
1 bunch green onions, finely chopped
1 cup chopped pecans

Combine the cream cheese, pineapple and green onions in a bowl and mix well. Roll into a ball. Roll in pecans to coat and wrap in plastic wrap. Chill for at least 2 hours. Serve with crackers. Yield: 16 servings.

Susan E. Guglielmo, Xi Theta Delta
Riverview, Florida

SAVORY CHEESE BALL

1 envelope dry onion soup mix
2 tablespoons hot water
16 ounces cream cheese, softened
1 cup chopped pecans

Whisk the soup mix and hot water together in a large bowl. Add the cream cheese and mix well. Wrap in plastic wrap and chill until firm. Roll into a ball. Roll in pecans to coat. Serve with crackers. Yield: 18 servings.

Sarah Dunn, Preceptor Beta Omicron
Indianapolis, Indiana

CREAM CHEESE LOG

16 ounces cream cheese, softened
½ cup chopped green bell pepper
½ cup chopped onion
1¼ teaspoons seasoned salt
1 (20-ounce) can crushed pineapple, well drained
1 to 1½ cups chopped pecans

Combine the cream cheese, bell pepper, onion, seasoned salt and pineapple in a bowl; mix well. Wrap in plastic wrap and chill until firm. Roll into a log. Roll in the pecans to coat. Chill, wrapped in plastic wrap, for at least 2 hours before serving. Serve with crackers. Yield: 12 servings.

Karen Dieken, Laureate Rho
Gilbert, Arizona

NUTTY FRUITED CHEESE BALLS

3 ounces cream cheese, softened
3 tablespoons drained crushed pineapple
¼ cup chopped pecans
Pretzel sticks

Beat the cream cheese in a mixing bowl until creamy. Mix in the pineapple. Shape into ½-inch balls. Roll the balls in the pecans. Chill until firm. Pierce each ball with a pretzel stick and serve. Yield: 24 servings.

Louise Long, Alpha Epsilon Master
Bethany, Missouri

SNOWBALL CHEESE BALL

This delicious blend of ingredients makes a great holiday appetizer.

16 ounces cream cheese, softened
1 (8-ounce) can crushed pineapple, drained
½ cup chopped pecans
½ cup chopped green bell pepper
Shredded coconut

Combine the cream cheese, pineapple, pecans and bell pepper in a bowl and mix well. Roll into 2 balls. Roll in coconut. Chill, covered, until serving time. Serve with crackers. Yield: 32 servings.

Marlene M. Jorgenson, Laureate Lambda
Devils Lake, North Dakota

GREEN ONION CHEESE BALL

16 ounces cream cheese, softened
1 teaspoon cayenne pepper
2 tablespoons mayonnaise
3 dashes of Tabasco sauce
2 bunches green onions, chopped
½ teaspoon garlic salt
½ teaspoon garlic powder
½ teaspoon onion powder
Real bacon bits

Mix all the ingredients in a bowl. Roll into 1 or 2 balls. Chill, wrapped in plastic wrap, until serving time. Serve with crackers. Yield: 24 servings.

Karen Johnson, Xi Gamma Omicron
Clarksville, Arkansas

CHOCOLATE CHIP CHEESE BALL

8 ounces cream cheese, softened	2 tablespoons brown sugar
1/2 cup (1 stick) butter, softened	3/4 cup miniature chocolate chips
1/4 teaspoon vanilla extract	3/4 cup finely chopped pecans
3/4 cup confectioners' sugar	

Beat the cream cheese, butter and vanilla in a mixing bowl until creamy. Add the confectioners' sugar and brown sugar a few tablespoons at a time, beating just until combined. Stir in the chocolate chips. Chill, covered, for 2 hours. Place the cream cheese mixture on a large piece of plastic wrap and shape into a ball. Chill for at least 1 hour. Just before serving, roll the cheese ball in pecans. Serve with graham crackers. Yield: 24 servings.

Rexie Eaker, Pi Master
Bethalto, Illinois

BEEFY CHEESE BALL

24 ounces cream cheese, softened	1 tablespoon soy sauce
1 medium onion, chopped	3 or 4 (3-ounce) packages thin smoked sliced beef, chopped

Combine the cream cheese, onion, soy sauce and half the chopped beef in a bowl and mix well. Roll into a ball. Roll in the remaining chopped beef. Chill, wrapped in plastic wrap, until ready to serve with crackers. Yield: 32 servings.

Nancy Tillette, Preceptor Gamma
Lansing, West Virginia

ZESTY BEEFY CHEESE BALL

8 ounces cream cheese, softened	1 tablespoon dried parsley flakes
1/4 pound dried beef	1 tablespoon mayonnaise
1 teaspoon prepared horseradish	1 teaspoon Worcestershire sauce

Combine the cream cheese, dried beef, horseradish, parsley flakes, mayonnaise and Worcestershire sauce in a bowl and mix well. Roll into a ball. Chill, wrapped in plastic wrap, for at least 2 hours. Serve with crackers. Yield: 24 servings.

Mary Elizabeth Arnold, Alpha Epsilon Master
Lebanon, Pennsylvania

CHICKEN CHEESE BALL

8 ounces cream cheese, at room temperature	1/2 teaspoon Worcestershire sauce
1 (10-ounce) can white chicken, drained	Garlic powder to taste
1 onion, finely chopped	1/2 cup (about) chopped parsley
Lemon juice to taste	

Combine the cream cheese, chicken, onion, lemon juice, Worcestershire sauce and garlic powder in a bowl and mix well. Roll into a ball. Roll in the parsley. Chill, wrapped in plastic wrap, for 8 to 10 hours. Serve with crackers. Yield: 20 servings.

Marcy Mouzaffar
Washington, Pennsylvania

HAM CHEESE BALL

2 (6-ounce) cans chunk ham	1 teaspoon minced onion
11 ounces cream cheese, softened	1 teaspoon hot red pepper sauce
2 tablespoons parsley flakes	1/4 cup mayonnaise
	1 cup chopped pecans

Combine the ham, cream cheese, parsley flakes, onion, hot red pepper sauce and mayonnaise in a bowl and mix well. Chill, covered, for 8 to 10 hours. Roll into a ball. Roll in the pecans. Serve with crackers. Yield: 32 servings.

Mary Free-Phelps, Xi Mu
Jeffersonville, Indiana

BLEU CHEESE BALL

8 ounces cream cheese, softened	1/2 teaspoon dill weed
1/2 cup mayonnaise	Salt and pepper to taste
5 slices bacon, crisp-cooked, crumbled	8 ounces bleu cheese, crumbled
3 tablespoons chopped green onions	1/2 cup (about) chopped pecans or walnuts

Beat the cream cheese and mayonnaise together until creamy. Add the bacon, green onions, dill weed, salt and pepper and mix well. Add the bleu cheese and mix lightly. Roll into a ball. Roll in chopped pecans. Chill, wrapped in plastic wrap, until serving time. Serve with crackers. Yield: 24 servings.

Cheryl Kramer, Preceptor Lambda Mu
Ridgecrest, California

BACON ALMOND CHEESE BALL

10 slices bacon, crisp-
  cooked, crumbled
2 cups (8 ounces)
  shredded Cheddar
  cheese
1/3 cup slivered almonds
1/2 cup chopped green
  onions
1 cup real mayonnaise

Combine the bacon, cheese, almonds, green onions
and mayonnaise in a large bowl and mix well. Roll
into a ball. Chill, wrapped in plastic wrap, until serving time. Serve with assorted crackers.
Yield: 15 to 20 servings.

Vanessa Summerlin, Nu Psi
Lexington, Missouri

BACON CREAM CHEESE BALL

1 pound bacon, crisp-
  cooked, crumbled
16 ounces cream cheese,
  softened
1 tablespoon
  Worcestershire sauce
1 teaspoon seasoned salt
1 teaspoon minced
  garlic
1 cup chopped pecans
  (optional)

Combine the bacon and cream cheese in a bowl and
mix well. Add the Worcestershire sauce, seasoned
salt, garlic and pecans and mix well. Roll into a ball.
Chill, wrapped in plastic wrap, for at least 1 hour
before serving. Serve with crackers.
Yield: 20 servings.

Diane F. Smith, Preceptor Gamma Zeta
Ballwin, Missouri

SALMON MOUSSE LOG

1 (8-ounce) can salmon,
  drained
1 teaspoon grated onion
4 ounces cream cheese,
  softened
1/2 teaspoon prepared
  horseradish
1 cup (4 ounces)
  shredded Swiss cheese
1 teaspoon liquid smoke
1 teaspoon lemon juice
Salt and pepper to taste
1/3 cup finely chopped
  green onions

Combine the salmon, onion, cream cheese, horseradish, Swiss cheese, liquid smoke, lemon juice, salt and
pepper in a large bowl and mix well. Chill, covered,
for 1 hour. Roll into a log or a ball. Roll in green
onions. Chill, wrapped in plastic wrap, for 8 to 10
hours. Serve with crackers. Yield: 24 servings.

Lois L. Drobot, Beta Iota
Porcupine Plain, Saskatchewan, Canada

CLAM ASPIC

1 (7-ounce) can minced
  clams
1 1/2 envelopes
  unflavored gelatin
1 (10-ounce) can cream
  of mushroom soup
8 ounces cream cheese,
  softened
1 cup mayonnaise
1 small green onion,
  minced
1 cup chopped celery

Drain the clams, reserving the liquid. Add water to
the reserved clam liquid to measure 1/4 cup. Soften
the gelatin in the liquid. Combine with the soup in a
saucepan over medium-low heat. Heat until the
gelatin dissolves, stirring occasionally. Let stand until
cool. Beat the cream cheese in a mixing bowl until
creamy. Add the mayonnaise, green onion, celery
and soup mixture, beating after each addition. Pour
into a 4-cup mold. Chill, covered, for 8 to 10 hours.
Unmold onto a serving plate. Decorate with thinly
sliced red bell peppers and parsley if desired. Serve
with crackers or sliced baguette. Yield: 30 servings.

Rose C. Gaspari, Beta Chi Master
Santa Rosa, California

OYSTER CHEESE BALL

*The bit of curry powder is an important ingredient in
this tasty appetizer.*

1 (4-ounce) can smoked
  oysters, lightly
  drained
8 ounces cream cheese,
  softened
1 tablespoon
  Worcestershire sauce
Dash of curry powder,
  or to taste
1/2 cup chopped pecans

Combine the oysters, cream cheese, Worcestershire
sauce and curry powder in a bowl and mix well. Roll
into a ball. Roll in the pecans to coat. Chill, wrapped
in plastic wrap, until ready to serve. Serve with
crackers. Yield: 12 to 15 servings.

Krista M. Forrest, Preceptor Beta Tau
Poquoson, Virginia

*A block of cream cheese topped with a fantastic con-
trasting flavor and a selection of crackers makes for
an instant party. Try this topper.*

*Eleanor Clark, Xi Mu, Moores Mills, New Bruns-
wick, Canada, makes **Peach and Pepper Relish** by
boiling 12 large peeled chopped peaches, 12 finely
chopped red bell peppers, 1 cup red wine vinegar, 1
teaspoon salt, and 2 lemons cut into halves for 30
minutes. Discard the lemons and stir in 5 cups
sugar. Simmer for 30 minutes or until thickened and
ladle in hot sterilized jars to seal for storage. The relish is also delicious with cold pork or chicken.*

Canapés & First Courses

PARMESAN BRUSCHETTA

1/4 cup cream-style
  cottage cheese
1/4 cup sour cream
1/4 cup sliced green
  onions

1/4 cup mayonnaise
11/2 cups (6 ounces)
  grated Parmesan
  cheese
French bread

Combine the first 5 ingredients in a medium bowl; mix well. Cut the bread into 1/2-inch slices. Toast the bread slices and spread with the cottage cheese mixture. Broil 6 inches from the heat source for 4 to 5 minutes or until lightly browned and bubbly. Serve warm. Yield: 12 to 15 servings.

Joanne McQuary, Xi Alpha Kappa
Clarkston, Washington

BRUSCHETTA

2 or 3 garlic cloves,
  minced
2 tablespoons capers
2 anchovy fillets
1/4 cup chopped black
  olives
2 medium tomatoes,
  chopped
1/2 cup olive oil

1 cup (4 ounces)
  shredded mozzarella
  cheese
1/4 cup grated Parmesan
  cheese
1 teaspoon oregano
1/2 teaspoon pepper
1/4 teaspoon basil
Baguette

Combine the garlic, capers, anchovies and olives in a food processor container and pulse until finely chopped. Add the tomatoes and pulse several times to combine. Place the vegetable mixture in a bowl. Stir in the next 6 ingredients. Let stand at room temperature, covered, for 2 to 3 hours. Slice the baguette thinly either crosswise or lengthwise. Arrange the slices on a nonstick baking sheet and toast lightly in a 450-degree oven. Spread the tomato mixture over the slices and return to the oven for a few minutes or until bubbly. Yield: about 8 servings.

Norma Robb, Preceptor Alpha Delta
Lively, Ontario, Canada

❖ TWO-TOMATO BRUSCHETTA

2 large plum tomatoes,
  seeded and chopped
12 sun-dried tomatoes
  in oil, drained and
  chopped
1 cup (4 ounces)
  shredded Italian
  6-cheese blend
1/3 cup crumbled bleu
  cheese

1/4 cup minced onion
1 tablespoon minced
  fresh basil
1 teaspoon minced fresh
  rosemary
1/4 teaspoon garlic
  pepper
24 baguette slices

Preheat the oven to 350 degrees. Combine the plum tomatoes, sun-dried tomatoes, Italian cheese, bleu cheese, onion, basil, rosemary and garlic pepper in a bowl and mix well. Arrange the baguette slices on a nonstick baking sheet. Spoon tomato mixture evenly over the slices. Bake for 7 or 8 minutes or until cheese melts. Serve warm or at room temperature. Yield: 2 dozen.

Carla Morley, Laureate Gamma Tau
Jefferson City, Missouri

SAVORY PARTY BREAD

Use any kind of bread you like. I have prepared this recipe many times, but because I change the ingredients my guests think it is a new recipe every time. You can use fresh mushrooms, green or red bell peppers, canned crab meat or shrimp, dill weed, or anything else you can think of.

1 unsliced round loaf of
  bread
16 ounces Monterey Jack
  cheese, sliced
1/2 pound bacon, crisp-
  cooked, crumbled

1/2 cup melted butter
1/2 cup chopped green
  onions

Cut into the bread loaf lengthwise, then crosswise, without cutting through the bottom crust. Fill the cuts with cheese slices and bacon. Drizzle with a mixture of the melted butter and green onions. Wrap in foil and place on a nonstick baking sheet or pie plate. Bake at 350 degrees for 15 minutes. Uncover and bake for 10 minutes longer or until the cheese melts. Serve hot. Yield: 2 dozen.

Shelley Jersak, Alpha Delta
Swan River, Manitoba, Canada

PARMESAN HASTY HOTS

4 green onions, finely
  chopped
1/2 cup (2 ounces) grated
  Parmesan cheese

6 tablespoons
  mayonnaise
1 (12-ounce) package
  English muffins

Combine the green onions, Parmesan cheese and mayonnaise in a small bowl and stir until well blended. Stir in additional mayonnaise if necessary to make a firm spreading consistency. Split the English muffins and arrange cut side up on a nonstick baking sheet. Broil 6 inches from the heat source until light brown. Turn and broil other side for 2 to 3 minutes. Spread the cheese mixture over the cut sides of the muffins and broil until bubbly and lightly browned. Watch carefully, as they brown quickly. Cut in half to serve. Yield: 2 dozen.

Mary Jo Rossini, Xi Rho Chi
Orangevale, California

HOT CHEESE BREAD

Be sure to use butter, not margarine.

1/2 cup (1 stick) butter
1 cup (4 ounces)
  shredded Monterey
  Jack cheese or
  mozzarella cheese
1 cup mayonnaise-type
  salad dressing

1 (4-ounce) can chopped
  green chiles, or 4 to
  6 ounces jalapeño
  peppers, sliced and
  chopped
1 loaf French bread,
  sliced

Melt the butter in a saucepan over medium heat. Add the cheese and cook until melted and smooth, stirring frequently. Stir in the salad dressing and green chiles. Arrange the bread slices on a nonstick baking sheet and spread with the cheese mixture. Bake at 350 degrees for 15 minutes or until the cheese mixture is bubbling. Yield: 2 dozen.

Elizabeth Kaye Hunt, Xi Delta Nu
Winchester, Kentucky

COOL CUCUMBER CANAPES

Mayonnaise to taste
15 slices sandwich
  bread, crusts trimmed
1 cucumber, peeled and
  thinly sliced

Cavender's Greek
  Seasoning to taste

Spread mayonnaise over bread slices. Cut each slice into 4 squares. Place a cucumber slice over each bread square and sprinkle with Cavender's Seasoning. Yield: 15 servings.

Lucy Ude, Alpha Delta Omicron
Bonne Terre, Missouri

PUMPERNICKEL BITES

8 ounces cream cheese,
  softened
1 envelope Italian salad
  dressing mix
1 loaf cocktail
  pumpernickel bread

2 cucumbers, peeled and
  thinly sliced
Dash of paprika

Combine the cream cheese and salad dressing mix in a bowl and blend well. Spread over the bread slices. Top each with a slice of cucumber. Sprinkle with paprika. Yield: 20 servings.

Beverly Mertens, Preceptor Gamma Lambda
Fort Madison, Iowa

PESTO MOZZARELLA SLICES

1 loaf French bread
1/4 cup (1/2 stick) butter
8 teaspoons pesto

8 tomato slices
8 chunks mozzarella
  cheese

Cut the bread into 8 slices and arrange on a nonstick baking sheet. Spread 1 1/2 teaspoons butter over each slice. Layer 1 teaspoon pesto, 1 tomato slice and 1 chunk mozzarella cheese over each slice in the order given. Bake at 350 degrees for 10 to 15 minutes or until cheese melts. Yield: 8 servings.

Jane Hajdukiewicz, Eta Master
Tallahassee, Florida

GOAT CHEESE AND SUN-DRIED TOMATO ROUNDS

1/4 cup sun-dried
  tomatoes in oil,
  drained and minced
8 ounces creamy goat
  cheese
1/4 cup chopped fresh
  parsley

3 tablespoons light
  cream
1/2 teaspoon grated
  lemon zest
Baguette or crackers

Combine the sun-dried tomatoes, goat cheese, parsley, light cream and lemon zest in a bowl and mix well. Chill, covered, for 1 to 24 hours. Spread the cheese mixture over baguette slices. Garnish with black olive slices and serve. Yield: 4 dozen.

Sharon Francis, Laureate Omicron
St. Albert, Alberta, Canada

PIMENTO SPREAD AND HERBED CROSTINI

Crostini is Italian for "croutons."

2 dried tomato halves	*¹/₄ cup drained pimentos*
¹/₄ small jalapeño pepper	*¹/₄ teaspoon red wine*
1 garlic clove	*vinegar*
¹/₈ teaspoon freshly	*¹/₄ teaspoon basil*
ground black pepper	*Crostini*

Place the tomato halves in a small bowl and add enough boiling water to cover. Let stand for 2 minutes; drain well. Combine the jalapeño pepper and garlic in a small food processor container; process until minced. Add the tomato halves, pepper, pimentos, red wine vinegar and basil; process until smooth. Chill, covered, until ready to serve. Spread over the crostini at serving time. Yield: 10 to 20 servings.

CROSTINI

¹/₂ cup olive oil	*2 garlic cloves, minced*
2 tablespoons minced	*1 sourdough baguette,*
fresh parsley	*sliced*

Combine the olive oil, parsley and garlic in a small bowl and mix well. Arrange the baguette slices on a nonstick baking sheet and brush with the olive oil mixture. Broil 6 inches from the heat source for about 2 minutes or until lightly toasted.

Liane Wobito, Xi Epsilon Xi
Stouffville, Ontario, Canada

MINIATURE EGGS BENEDICT

24 thin slices deli	*24 bread rounds, toasted*
ham	*on both sides*
24 slices hard-cooked	*Hollandaise sauce*
egg	*to taste*

Cut the ham slices into rounds with a cookie cutter. Layer a ham round and an egg slice over each bread round. Spread Hollandaise sauce over the top. Broil 6 inches from the heat source until hot and bubbly. Sprinkle with chopped parsley or sliced pimento-stuffed olives and serve at once. Yield: 2 dozen.

Mary Reinhart, Gamma Master
Fox Point, Wisconsin

CHEESE AND BACON SNACKS

2 eggs, beaten	*¹/₄ teaspoon savory*
1 cup (4 ounces)	*¹/₂ teaspoon soy sauce*
shredded Cheddar	*4 bread slices*
cheese	*8 thick tomato slices*
Freshly ground pepper	*2 slices uncooked bacon,*
to taste	*each cut into 4 pieces*

Combine the eggs and cheese in a bowl and mix well. Sprinkle with pepper. Add the savory and soy sauce; mix well. Cut the bread slices in half. Spread the cheese mixture over each half. Add a tomato slice and a piece of bacon. Broil 6 inches from the heat source for about 10 minutes or until bacon is cooked through. Serve hot. Yield: 8 servings.

Janice W. Craig, Preceptor Laureate
Ormond Beach, Florida

TOMATO SALAMI ANTIPASTO

¹/₃ cup olive oil	*1 tablespoon basil*
1 tablespoon chopped	*4 tomatoes, thickly*
fresh parsley	*sliced*
¹/₂ teaspoon grated	*4 ounces salami, thickly*
lemon zest	*sliced*
1 tablespoon lemon	*1 baguette, cut into*
juice	*¹/₄-inch slices*
1 garlic clove, minced	

Place the olive oil, parsley, lemon zest, lemon juice, garlic and basil in a jar with a lid; shake vigorously to combine. Arrange overlapping slices of tomato and salami in a deep serving platter. Drizzle with the olive oil mixture. Let stand for at least 1 hour. Serve a slice of tomato and a slice of salami on each baguette slice. Yield: 2 to 3 dozen.

Gale Smyth, Omicron
Trail, British Columbia, Canada

MOZZARELLA AND TOMATO CANAPES

8 ounces fresh	*2 tablespoons vinegar*
mozzarella cheese	*1 tablespoon olive oil*
2 medium tomatoes	*Salt and pepper to taste*
6 or 7 fresh basil leaves,	*1 loaf Italian bread*
chopped	*1 garlic clove*

Slice the mozzarella cheese and tomatoes ¹/₄ inch thick and sprinkle with basil, vinegar, olive oil, salt and pepper. Set aside for several minutes. Slice the bread ³/₄ inch thick, toast on 1 side and sprinkle with additional olive oil. Rub each slice with the garlic clove and place a slice of cheese and tomato on each bread slice. Yield: 1 to 2 dozen.

Angela Theobald, Laureate Epsilon Omega
Bradenton, Florida

MARINATED SHRIMP CANAPES

1 pound cooked peeled	*30 rounds garlic Melba*
medium shrimp	*toast*
¹/₂ cup Italian salad	*Salt and pepper to taste*
dressing	*¹/₃ cup sour cream*
1 cucumber	

Marinate the shrimp in the salad dressing in the refrigerator for several hours. Score the cucumber lengthwise with a fork and slice thinly. Drain the shrimp. Place a cucumber slice on each toast. Sprinkle with salt and pepper. Add a small amount of sour cream and top with a shrimp. Garnish with parsley. Yield: 2½ dozen.

Carolyn Powell, Laureate Iota
Boone, North Carolina

SOUTHERN SARDINE CANAPES

²⁄₃ cup mustard-pack
sardines, finely
chopped
1 teaspoon lemon juice
1½ tablespoons ketchup
Salt and pepper to taste

1 teaspoon
Worcestershire sauce
1 tablespoon Italian
salad dressing
2 teaspoons minced
onion

Combine the sardines, lemon juice, ketchup, salt, pepper, Worcestershire sauce, salad dressing and onion in a bowl and mix well. Chill, covered, until serving time. Spread over crackers or toast rounds and sprinkle with paprika. Yield: 25 pieces.

Nadine Traynor, Laureate Mu
Clermont, Florida

MELTAWAY CRAB WEDGES

2 tablespoons
mayonnaise
½ cup (1 stick) butter or
margarine, softened
¼ teaspoon garlic salt
1 (7-ounce) can crab
meat, drained

1 (5-ounce) jar sharp
Cheddar cheese
spread
½ teaspoon salt
⅛ teaspoon dry mustard
8 English muffins, split

Combine the mayonnaise, butter, garlic salt, crab meat, cheese spread, salt and dry mustard in a mixing bowl and beat at medium speed until well mixed. Spread the English muffin halves generously with the crab mixture. Cut each muffin half into 8 wedges, as if cutting a pie. Holding the shapes, move with a pancake turner to a nonstick baking sheet and freeze for at least 30 minutes and up to several weeks. Broil the frozen muffins 6 inches from the heat source until puffy and slightly brown and bubbly, being sure to watch closely. Break into wedges. Yield: 15 to 20 servings.

Delores Overacker, Xi Nu
Weiser, Idaho

CUCUMBER SLICES ON PARTY RYE

Hellmann's mayonnaise
to taste
2 loaves party rye bread
Seasoned salt to taste

2 to 3 cucumbers, peeled
and sliced
Seasoned pepper to taste

Spread mayonnaise on each slice of party rye and sprinkle with seasoned salt. Top each with a cucumber slice and sprinkle with seasoned pepper. Layer the appetizers on a tray with sheets of plastic wrap separating the layers. Chill, covered, for 3 to 10 hours before serving. Yield: 3 dozen.

Marilyn A. Williams, Preceptor Epsilon Xi
Athens, Ohio

CALLA LILIES

8 ounces cream cheese,
softened
2 tablespoons orange
marmalade
1 (2-ounce) package
slivered almonds

2 or 3 drops yellow food
coloring
54 slices white
sandwich bread

Combine the cream cheese and marmalade in a small bowl and mix well. Place the almonds and yellow food coloring in a covered jar and shake vigorously until almonds are evenly coated. Roll each bread slice to ⅛ inch thickness with a rolling pin. Cut rounds using a biscuit cutter. Spread about 1 teaspoon marmalade mixture over each bread round. Pinch the edges of one part of the round to make a lily shape. Press a tinted almond sliver into the pinched portion for the flower's stamen. Yield: 4½ dozen.

Billie Cochran, Delta Kappa
Ellisville, Mississippi

ONION PUFFS

½ cup water
¼ cup (½ stick) butter
or margarine
1 envelope onion soup
mix
2 teaspoons caraway
seeds

1 teaspoon dry mustard
½ cup flour
1 cup (4 ounces)
shredded Swiss
cheese
2 large eggs

Combine the water, butter, soup mix, caraway seeds and dry mustard in a medium saucepan and bring to a boil. Reduce heat to low and add the flour all at once; stir vigorously with a wooden spoon for about 30 seconds or until mixture leaves the side of the saucepan and forms a ball. Remove from heat. Beat in the cheese immediately. Beat in the eggs immediately, continuing to beat until mixture is smooth and cheese almost melted. Drop by rounded teaspoons 2 inches apart on a large greased baking sheet. Bake at 375 degrees for 15 minutes or until puffed and golden. Turn off the oven; let puffs stand in the closed oven for 10 minutes. Serve warm. Yield: 2 dozen.

Irene Hitzeman, Alpha Delta Master
Lisle, Illinois

NUTTY CHICKEN PUFFS

1 cup chicken broth	1/8 teaspoon cayenne
1/2 cup vegetable oil	pepper
2 teaspoons	1 cup flour
Worcestershire sauce	4 eggs
1 teaspoon dried parsley	1 1/2 cups finely chopped
flakes	cooked chicken
1 teaspoon seasoned	1/3 cup chopped almonds,
salt	toasted
1/2 to 1 teaspoon celery	
seed	

Combine the chicken broth, vegetable oil, Worcestershire sauce, parsley flakes, seasoned salt, celery seed and cayenne pepper in a large saucepan; bring to a boil. Add the flour all at once; stir until mixture leaves the side of the saucepan and forms a smooth ball. Remove from heat; let stand for 5 minutes. Add the eggs 1 at a time, beating well after each addition. Beat until smooth. Stir in a mixture of the chicken and almonds. Drop by rounded teaspoons onto a greased baking sheet. Bake at 450 degrees for 12 to 14 minutes or until golden brown. Serve warm. Yield: 6 dozen.

Patricia D. Wanta, Laureate Alpha Gamma
Osprey, Florida

✧ HOT SHRIMP BOUCHEES

Bouchées are puff pastry shells that hold fillings or stuffings.

1/2 cup water	1 cup (4 ounces)
1/2 teaspoon salt	shredded sharp
1/4 cup shortening	Cheddar cheese
1/2 cup flour	1 (10-ounce) can cream
2 eggs	of mushroom soup
2 (4-ounce) cans shrimp,	1/4 cup mayonnaise
drained	Salt and pepper
2 tablespoons finely	to taste
chopped onion	1/4 to 1/2 cup Parmesan
2 tablespoons chopped	cheese
green bell pepper	Paprika to taste
2 tablespoons chopped	
pimentos	

Combine the water, the 1/2 teaspoon salt and shortening in a small saucepan over medium-high heat; bring to a boil. Add the flour all at once; stir vigorously until mixture leaves the side of the saucepan and forms a ball. Remove from heat. Cool slightly. Add the eggs 1 at a time, beating well after each addition. Drop by tablespoons onto a greased baking sheet. Bake at 450 degrees for 15 minutes. Reduce heat to 350 degrees and bake for 10 minutes longer. Cool. Combine the shrimp, onion, bell pepper, pimentos, Cheddar cheese, soup and mayonnaise in a bowl and mix well. Add salt and pepper. Cut off and discard the tops of the bouchées. Fill the shells with the shrimp mixture; sprinkle with Parmesan cheese and paprika. Bake at 350 degrees for about 20 minutes or until hot and bubbly. Yield: 2 1/2 dozen.

Sharon Hutchison, Alpha Gamma
Fort Saskatchewan, Alberta, Canada

CHEESE TRIANGLES

4 eggs, well beaten	Dash of Worcestershire
16 ounces Monterey Jack	sauce
cheese or pepperjack	1/2 teaspoon garlic salt
cheese	1/2 teaspoon onion salt
1 cup cottage cheese or	1 cup (2 sticks) butter,
grated Romano	melted
cheese	1 pound phyllo dough,
1 cup grated Romano	thawed
cheese or Parmesan	Jalapeño peppers
cheese	(optional)
Dash of Tabasco sauce	

Combine the eggs, Monterey Jack cheese, cottage cheese, Romano cheese, Tabasco sauce, Worcestershire sauce, garlic salt and onion salt in a bowl and mix well. Phyllo dough dries out very quickly, so do not open the package until the filling has been prepared. Unroll the phyllo and cover it with waxed paper topped with a damp towel. Keep the unused portion covered until needed. Cut each phyllo sheet in half lengthwise. Brush a half-sheet of the phyllo dough with melted butter; fold from the long edge to make a 3-inch-wide strip. Brush lightly with butter and place a rounded teaspoon of the cheese mixture at one end of the strip. Fold diagonally, as if folding a flag, until a triangle is formed. Brush with butter. Arrange on a nonstick baking sheet and freeze. Once frozen, the triangles may be bagged for easier storage. At serving time, place desired number of frozen triangles on a nonstick baking sheet and bake at 375 degrees for 12 to 15 minutes or until golden. Garnish with jalapeños. Serve hot. Yield: about 40 pieces.

Lori Jo McLean, Alpha Chi
Onfino, Idaho

SPINACH-STUFFED PHYLLO TRIANGLES

1/2 cup (1 stick)	1 (10-ounce) package
margarine	frozen chopped
1/4 cup chopped	spinach, thawed and
onion	well drained
1/4 teaspoon minced	1/8 teaspoon pepper
garlic	Dash of nutmeg
8 ounces cream cheese,	6 frozen phyllo sheets,
softened	thawed

Melt 2 tablespoons of the margarine in a skillet over medium heat. Sauté the onion and garlic in the margarine for 5 to 10 minutes or until tender. Combine the onion mixture, cream cheese, spinach, pepper and nutmeg in a bowl and mix well. Melt the remaining margarine. Phyllo dough dries out very quickly, so do not open the package until the filling has been prepared. Unroll the phyllo and cover it with waxed paper topped with a damp towel. Keep the unused portion covered until needed. Lay 1 sheet of phyllo dough on a flat surface. Brush with margarine and cut into 4 strips lengthwise. Spoon about 1 tablespoon spinach mixture 1 inch from the end of a strip. Fold the end over the filling at a 45-degree angle. Continue folding as you would fold a flag to form a triangle that encloses the filling. Repeat with remaining phyllo and filling. Arrange on a nonstick baking sheet. Bake at 375 degrees for 12 to 15 minutes or until golden brown. Serve, or wrap securely and freeze. To bake frozen triangles, heat oven to 375 degrees and bake for 10 to 12 minutes or until heated through. Yield: 2 dozen.

Janice DiBeneditto, Theta Master
Waterbury, Connecticut

MY BIG FAT GREEK APPETIZERS

16 ounces ricotta cheese
16 ounces feta cheese
3 medium eggs
1 pound phyllo dough, thawed
2 cups (4 sticks) butter, melted

Combine the ricotta cheese, feta cheese and eggs in a medium bowl and mix well. Prepare the phyllo dough using the package directions; it dries out very quickly, so do not open the package until the filling has been prepared. Unroll the phyllo and cover it with waxed paper topped with a damp towel. Keep the unused portion covered until needed. Spread each of 3 phyllo sheets with butter and stack one on top of the other. Cut into 6 or 7 equal strips lengthwise. Place 2 rounded teaspoons of the cheese mixture at one end of a strip. Fold the end over the filling at a 45-degree angle. Continue folding as you would fold a flag to form a triangle that encloses the filling. Repeat until all the cheese mixture is used. Arrange on a nonstick baking sheet. Freeze, separating with waxed paper. At serving time, place frozen triangles on an ungreased baking sheet and bake at 400 degrees for about 20 minutes or until light brown. Yield: about 40 pieces.

Betty Carmichael, Phi Master
Sun City West, Arizona

RANCH PARTY PINWHEELS

16 ounces cream cheese, softened
1 envelope ranch salad dressing mix
2 green onions, minced
4 (12-inch) flour tortillas
1/2 cup diced red bell pepper
1/2 cup diced celery
1/2 cup sliced black olives

Combine the cream cheese, salad dressing mix and green onions in a bowl and mix well. Spread evenly over the tortillas. Sprinkle with bell pepper, celery and olives. Roll up tightly. Chill, covered, for 2 hours. Cut off ends of rolls and slice rolls into 1-inch pieces. Yield: 3 dozen.

Carol Finanger, Preceptor Rho
Merrill, Wisconsin

SPICY MEXICAN ROLL-UPS

8 ounces cream cheese, softened
1 (4-ounce) can sliced black olives, drained
1 envelope ranch salad dressing mix
1 (4-ounce) can chopped green chiles, drained
6 flour tortillas

Combine the cream cheese, olives, salad dressing mix and chiles in a bowl and mix well. Spread the cream cheese mixture evenly over the tortillas. Wrap each tortilla tightly into a roll. Chill, wrapped in plastic wrap, for 3 to 4 hours. Slice tortilla rolls into 1-inch pieces. Yield: 2 dozen.

Alison Lewis, Xi Phi
Wrangell, Alaska

BLACK BEAN PINWHEELS

4 ounces cream cheese, softened
1/2 cup (2 ounces) shredded Monterey Jack cheese with jalapeño peppers
1/4 cup sour cream
1/4 teaspoon onion salt
1 cup canned black beans, rinsed and drained
3 flour tortillas

Combine the cream cheese, Monterey Jack cheese, sour cream and onion salt in a mixing bowl and beat at medium speed until well blended. Place the black beans in a food processor container and process until smooth. Spread a thin layer of puréed black beans over each tortilla; spread cheese mixture over the bean layer. Roll tightly as for a jelly roll. Chill, wrapped in plastic wrap, for 30 minutes. Cut into 1/2-inch slices. Serve with salsa. Yield: 10 servings.

Diana Adams, Theta
Vincennes, Indiana

BEAN DIP ROLL-UPS

1 (9-ounce) can bean dip	1/4 cup chopped red bell
4 ounces cream cheese,	pepper
softened	1 (4-ounce) can chopped
6 (8-inch) flour tortillas	green chiles, drained

Combine the bean dip and cream cheese in a medium bowl and mix well. Spread 1/6 of the bean dip mixture over each tortilla. Sprinkle with the bell pepper and chiles. Roll up tightly as for a jelly roll. Chill, wrapped in plastic wrap, for at least 2 hours. Cut each roll into 8 pieces and serve. Yield: 2 dozen.

Elaine R. Cernik, Theta Master
Rogers, Arkansas

VEGETABLE ROLL-UPS

1 large stalk broccoli,	1 (8-ounce) tub whipped
trimmed	cream cheese with
1 medium carrot	chives or garden
1/2 cucumber, seeded	vegetables
1 small tomato, seeded	1 garlic clove, minced
1/4 cup pitted black	3 or 4 (9- or 10-inch)
olives (optional)	flour tortillas

Peel the broccoli and cut into 1-inch pieces. Place in a food processor container and process until finely chopped (will make about 1 cup). Peel the carrot, cut into 1-inch pieces, place in food processor container and process until finely chopped (about 1/3 cup). Repeat procedure with cucumber and tomato, pouring off any liquid. Place the olives in the food processor container and process until finely chopped. Combine the chopped vegetables, cream cheese and garlic in a bowl and mix well. Spread about 1/2 cup of the cream cheese mixture over each tortilla to within 1/2 inch of the edge. Roll tightly as for a jelly roll. Chill, wrapped in plastic wrap, for 1 hour or longer. Cut into 1-inch slices and arrange on a serving plate. If you like, garnish by piping a star or dollop of mayonnaise on each slice and topping with a thin carrot flower or cucumber triangle. Yield: 2 to 3 dozen.

Fran Greiner, Alpha Preceptor
Bedford, New Hampshire

HAM TORTILLA ROLL-UPS

1/2 pound ham, ground	2 tablespoons chopped
3 ounces cream cheese,	green onions
softened	1 teaspoon honey
1/4 cup crushed pineapple,	4 (8-inch) tortillas
well drained	

Combine the ham and cream cheese in a mixing bowl and beat at medium speed until smooth. Stir in the pineapple, green onions and honey. Spread 1/4 cup of the ham mixture over each tortilla to within 1/2 inch of the edge. Roll up each tortilla tightly. Chill, wrapped in plastic wrap, for 3 to 8 hours. Cut each tortilla roll into 1/2-inch slices. Top each slice with an olive and spear with a wooden pick. Arrange on a serving platter. Serve with a dip made of a mixture of 6 tablespoons mayonnaise, 1/4 cup mustard and 2 tablespoons honey. Yield: 40 pieces.

Nancy Poling, Preceptor Alpha Tau
Wheeling, West Virginia

DEVILED CHICKEN ROLLS

1 loaf white sandwich	8 ounces cream cheese,
bread, crusts trimmed	at room temperature
1 cup finely chopped	1/2 cup sour cream
green onions	3/4 to 1 cup sour cream
1 (4-ounce) can deviled	1 (12-ounce) bag potato
chicken	chips, crushed

Flatten each slice of bread with a rolling pin. Combine the green onions, deviled chicken, cream cheese and 1/2 cup sour cream in a mixing bowl and beat at medium speed until well mixed. Spread the deviled chicken mixture over each flattened slice of bread. Roll up tightly as for a jelly roll. Coat the outside of each roll with sour cream and roll in crushed potato chips. Cut each roll in half crosswise. Arrange on a greased baking sheet. Bake at 350 degrees for 20 to 25 minutes or until lightly toasted. Serve warm. Yield: 20 servings.

Christine Crowell, Laureate Alpha Chi
San Leandro, California

CREAMY MUSHROOM BITES

4 ounces cream cheese,	1/4 teaspoon seasoned
softened	salt
1 (4-ounce) can	1 (8-count) can crescent
mushrooms,	rolls
drained and finely	1 egg, beaten
chopped	1 tablespoon poppy seeds

Combine the cream cheese, mushrooms and seasoned salt in a bowl and mix well. Unroll the dough. Separate into 2 rectangles, pressing the perforations to seal. Spread half the mushroom mixture over each rectangle to within 1/2 inch of the edge. Roll as for a jelly roll, sealing the edge and ends. Cut into 1-inch slices with a floured knife. Arrange on an ungreased baking sheet. Brush with the beaten egg and sprinkle with poppy seeds. Bake at 375 degrees for 20 minutes or until golden brown. Yield: 30 servings.

Barbara H. Dick, Preceptor Gamma Nu
Miami, Florida

SPINACH AND FETA STRUDEL

12 ounces fresh spinach	2 garlic cloves, crushed
1 cup crumbled feta cheese	Salt and pepper to taste
¼ cup freshly grated Parmesan cheese	5 sheets phyllo dough, thawed
2 eggs, beaten	¼ cup melted butter
1 tablespoon chopped fresh dill weed	1 tablespoon sesame seeds

Bring ½ inch of water to a boil in a large kettle. Reduce heat to medium. Add the spinach and cook for a few minutes or just until wilted. Cool spinach in cold water, then drain, pressing out as much moisture as possible. Chop coarsely. Combine the spinach, feta cheese, Parmesan cheese, eggs, dill weed, garlic, salt and pepper in a bowl and mix well. Phyllo dough dries out very quickly, so do not open the package until the filling has been prepared. Unroll the phyllo and cover it with waxed paper topped with a damp towel. Layer the phyllo sheets in a buttered baking dish, brushing each sheet with melted butter. Spread the spinach mixture down the center in a long narrow strip. Roll as for a jelly roll. Make small cuts about 1 inch long in top of pastry. Brush the top with melted butter and sprinkle with sesame seeds. Bake at 350 degrees for 25 to 30 minutes or until golden brown. Serve warm. Yield: 18 slices.

Vicky Williams, Xi Alpha Phi
Campbell River, British Columbia, Canada

LUMPIA SHANGHAI

This special dish may also be called Philippine Fried Egg Rolls, Shanghai Style.

½ pound ground pork or beef	1 tablespoon soy sauce
½ pound shrimp, finely chopped	1 teaspoon salt
½ cup chopped water chestnuts	1 teaspoon freshly ground pepper
½ cup green onions, finely chopped	1 (16-ounce) package egg roll wrappers
1 egg	Vegetable oil for deep-frying

Combine the ground pork, shrimp, water chestnuts, green onions, egg, soy sauce, salt and pepper in a bowl; mix well. Place 2 tablespoons of the pork mixture in the center of each egg roll wrapper and seal with a few drops of water. Deep-fry in hot oil and drain on paper towels. Serve with sweet-and-sour sauce. Yield: about 2 dozen.

Josephine Campbell, Alpha
Everett, Washington

SAUSAGE CUPS

1 pound bulk pork sausage	1 cup prepared ranch dressing
1¼ cups (5 ounces) shredded Cheddar cheese	1 (4-ounce) can sliced black olives, drained
1¼ cups (5 ounces) shredded Monterey Jack cheese	¼ teaspoon cayenne pepper
	1 (10-ounce) package won ton wrappers

Brown the sausage in a skillet, stirring until crumbly; drain well. Combine the sausage, Cheddar cheese, Monterey Jack cheese, ranch dressing, olives and cayenne pepper in a large bowl and mix well. Press 1 won ton wrapper into each of 2 dozen lightly buttered muffin cups. Bake at 350 degrees for 5 minutes. Remove from muffin cups and arrange on a nonstick baking sheet. Fill each won ton shell with sausage mixture. Bake an additional 10 minutes or until cheese is bubbly. Yield: 2 dozen.

Deanne Nowlan, Xi Eta Kappa
Sterling, Kansas

PEPPER JELLY TARTS

2 cups (8 ounces) shredded Cheddar cheese	1 teaspoon paprika
	⅛ teaspoon cayenne pepper
½ cup (1 stick) butter, softened	1 cup flour
	⅔ cup hot pepper jelly

Combine the cheese, butter, paprika and cayenne pepper in a mixing bowl and beat at medium speed until blended. Add the flour, mixing with a fork until the mixture forms a ball of dough. Roll into 30 small balls and press each into a miniature muffin cup to make a tart shell. Spoon 1 teaspoon hot pepper jelly into the center of each shell. Bake at 400 degrees for 10 minutes or until golden brown. Cool in the pans for 5 minutes. Remove tarts from pans to a wire rack to cool completely. Serve warm or at room temperature. Yield: 8 to 10 servings.

Pat Robusky, Xi Zeta
Crossfield, Alberta, Canada

Bernice D'Agostino, Zeta Upsilon, Portales, New Mexico, prepares her **Cocktail Chicken Croissants** *by finely chopping the meat of 2 cooked chickens, adding a 6-ounce can each of finely chopped black and green olives and a finely chopped onion with 4 finely chopped celery stalks. After adding enough of a mixture of 1 cup mayonnaise, 2 tablespoons fresh lemon juice, salt and pepper to bind the mixture, she has enough to fill about 30 cocktail croissants.*

SAUSAGE ROLLS

Whenever I make these appetizers, guests line up at the oven to take them before I can put them on a serving plate! Use your favorite kind of sausage.

1 (16-ounce) package frozen puff pastry, thawed	1 pound bulk pork sausage

Roll the pastry on a floured surface into a 9×15-inch rectangle. Cut into three smaller rectangles, each 3 inches wide. Divide the sausage meat into thirds; roll each third into a 15-inch log. Wrap the pastry around each log and seal the edge. Cut each roll into 1/2-inch pieces and arrange on an ungreased baking sheet. Bake at 400 degrees for 10 minutes or until pastry is puffed and golden brown.
Yield: about 30 servings.

Gina Aleo, Laureate Epsilon Zeta
Wilkes-Barre, Pennsylvania

SWEET SAUSAGE ROLLS

1 (8-count) can crescent rolls	3 tablespoons honey
24 miniature smoked sausages	3 tablespoons brown sugar
1/2 cup melted butter	1/2 cup chopped pecans

Unroll the dough and separate into triangles. Cut each triangle into 3 smaller triangles. Place a sausage on each triangle and roll up tightly. Place the rolls seam side down in an ungreased 9×13-inch baking dish. Drizzle a mixture of the butter, honey and brown sugar over the sausage rolls. Sprinkle with the pecans. Bake at 400 degrees for 15 minutes. Yield: 2 dozen.

Karen A. Long, Preceptor Alpha Gamma
Cumming, Georgia

SAUSAGE SQUARES

2 (8-count) cans crescent rolls	1/4 teaspoon pepper
1 pound bulk pork sausage	1/2 teaspoon dried parsley
2 eggs, well beaten	1 cup (4 ounces) shredded Swiss cheese
1/4 teaspoon garlic powder	2 tablespoons grated Parmesan cheese
1/4 teaspoon salt	

Unroll the dough. Separate into 2 rectangles, pressing the perforations to seal. Line the bottom of a 9×13-inch baking dish with half the flattened dough, patting and stretching to fit. Brown the sausage in a skillet, stirring until crumbly; drain. Remove 2 tablespoons of the beaten eggs and set aside. Mix the remaining eggs with the sausage, garlic powder, salt, pepper and parsley. Spread the sausage mixture in the dough-lined baking dish. Sprinkle with the Swiss cheese and Parmesan cheese. Roll the remaining dough into a 9×13-inch rectangle and fit over the top. Brush with the 2 tablespoons beaten egg. Bake at 350 degrees for 30 minutes or until hot and browned. Let cool for about 15 minutes. Cut into squares or diamonds and serve. Yield: 32 servings.

Victoria Mozgai, Laureate Alpha Epsilon
Longmont, Colorado

WRAPPED SAUSAGE BITES

1 (8-count) can crescent rolls	1 teaspoon prepared horseradish (optional)
3 ounces cream cheese, softened	5 ounces precooked sausage links
2 teaspoons Dijon mustard	

Unroll the dough. Separate into 8 triangles; cut each triangle in half. Cut each half in half, making 32 small triangles. Beat the cream cheese in a mixing bowl until fluffy. Beat in the mustard and horseradish. Spread a spoonful of the cream cheese mixture along one edge of each triangle. Cut each sausage link in half lengthwise, then cut each length in half. Place a sausage piece over the cream cheese mixture on each rectangle. Bring the tip of the triangle over the sausage piece to the base of the triangle and press to form a wrap. Arrange on an ungreased baking sheet. Bake at 400 degrees for 10 minutes or until golden. Serve warm. Yield: 32 servings.

Patricia Kelley Lahey, Xi Alpha Iota
Rochester, Minnesota

HOT MUSHROOM TURNOVERS

These appetizers can be made up to a week ahead of time and frozen.

8 ounces cream cheese, softened	1 large onion, minced
1 1/2 cups flour	3 tablespoons margarine
1/2 cup (1 stick) margarine, softened	1/4 cup sour cream
1 pound mushrooms, minced	1/4 teaspoon thyme
	1/2 teaspoon salt
	1 egg, beaten

Combine the cream cheese, flour and 1/2 cup margarine in a mixing bowl and blend. Roll into a ball and chill, wrapped in plastic wrap, for 1 hour. Sauté the mushrooms and onion in 3 tablespoons margarine until tender. Combine the mushroom mixture, sour cream, thyme and salt in a bowl and mix well.

Roll the chilled dough into ¹/₄-inch thickness and cut in 3-inch circles. Place a slightly drained teaspoon of the mushroom mixture on each circle, near the center. Brush the edges of the dough circles with egg. Fold each circle over to enclose the filling and seal by pressing the edge with a fork. Arrange on an ungreased baking sheet. Pierce the top of each with the point of a sharp knife in 2 or 3 places. Brush the top with egg. Bake at 400 degrees for 10 to 20 minutes or until light brown. Yield: 24 pieces.

Susan Grove Talpalar, Xi Zeta Alpha
St. Augustine Beach, Florida

CHEESE PUFFS

The puffs may be prepared in advance, arranged on a baking sheet before baking, and frozen. Bake frozen puffs at 375 degrees for 15 to 20 minutes.

1 egg	³/₄ cup (1¹/₂ sticks) butter
¹/₄ cup milk	or margarine, melted
¹/₈ teaspoon salt	1¹/₂ cups (6 ounces)
12 thin slices white	grated Parmesan
bread, crusts trimmed	cheese

Combine the egg, milk and salt in a bowl and mix well. Dip 1 slice of bread in the egg mixture and sandwich it between 2 undipped bread slices. Cut into 4 squares. Dip each small square in butter and roll in Parmesan cheese to coat heavily. Repeat with remaining bread slices. Arrange in a buttered shallow baking dish or 10×15-inch cake pan. Bake at 375 degrees for 10 minutes. Serve hot. Yield: 16 servings.

Vivian Leiting, Alpha Beta
Forrest City, Arkansas

RANCH CHEESE PUFFS

1 cup (2 sticks) butter,	1 envelope ranch salad
softened	dressing mix
2 (5-ounce) jars Old	1 loaf sandwich bread,
English cheese spread	sliced, crusts trimmed

Combine the butter, cheese spread and salad dressing mix in a bowl; beat until fluffy. Spread a spoonful of the cheese mixture over each of 2 slices of bread. Stack the slices cheese side up. Place a third slice without cheese mixture on top. Cut the bread stack into quarters. Spread cheese mixture over the top and sides of each small puff and arrange on a nonstick baking sheet. Repeat with remaining bread and cheese spread. Bake at 350 degrees for 12 to 15 minutes or until piping hot. Yield: 25 servings.

Pam Schwarz, Preceptor Eta
Lincoln, Illinois

DANISH BLEU CHEESE PIZZA

1 (10-ounce) package	¹/₂ cup crumbled bleu
frozen pie pastry,	cheese
thawed	¹/₂ cup mayonnaise

Preheat the oven to 400 degrees. Unroll the dough and press to fit a buttered 10×15-inch cake pan. Bake for 7 minutes; remove from oven. Spread a mixture of the bleu cheese and mayonnaise over the crust. Bake for 11 minutes longer. Cool. Cut into 12 pieces. Yield: 12 servings.

Jeanette Powell, Xi Phi Rho
Houston, Texas

PARTY PIZZA SNACKS

¹/₄ cup chopped black	¹/₄ cup bacon bits
olives	1 teaspoon chopped
¹/₄ cup mayonnaise	chives
1 cup (4 ounces) shredded	18 slices party rye bread
Swiss cheese	

Combine the black olives, mayonnaise, cheese, bacon bits and chives in a bowl and mix well. Spread over party rye and serve. Yield: 18 servings.

Barbara J. Sherwood, Preceptor Delta Theta
Berea, Ohio

PARTY RYE PIZZA

1 pound ground beef	4 cups (16 ounces)
1 pound Italian sausage,	shredded Cheddar
casings removed	cheese
1 medium onion, chopped	1 teaspoon oregano
1 tablespoon	1 loaf party rye
Worcestershire sauce	

Brown the ground beef and sausage with the onion in a skillet, stirring until crumbly; drain. Remove from heat. Add the Worcestershire sauce, cheese and oregano to the hot meat mixture and stir until well mixed; heat from the meat will melt the cheese. Spread over slices of party rye and arrange on a nonstick baking sheet. Bake at 400 degrees for 10 minutes or until sizzling. Serve hot. Yield: about 40 servings.

Judy Miller, Xi Iota Pi
Palm Harbor, Florida

---

*Jean K. Dunn, Laureate Gamma, Halifax, Nova Scotia, Canada, prepares **Salmon Tea Sandwiches** by mixing a 7-ounce can of salmon with 2 ounces cream cheese, 2 tablespoons each chili sauce and minced celery and salt and pepper. She spreads on thin-sliced bread cut into shapes and garnishes with cucumber, paprika, olive slices or sieved hard-cooked egg.*

CHICKEN CAESAR SALAD PIZZA

1 prebaked pizza crust	**2 cups (8 ounces)**
1 (12-ounce) bottle	**shredded mozzarella**
Caesar salad dressing	**cheese**
1/2 cup chopped onion	**1 cup shredded lettuce**
2 cups chopped cooked	**1/2 cup bacon bits**
chicken	

Place the crust on a pizza stone. Drizzle with desired amount of salad dressing and top with onion, chicken and mozzarella cheese. Bake at 350 degrees for 15 minutes. Top with lettuce, bacon bits and additional salad dressing. Yield: 6 to 8 servings.

Dianna DeMint, Preceptor Delta Nu
University Heights, Ohio

BUBBLE PIZZA APPETIZER

It looks terrible in the bowl, but brace yourself and pour the mess into the pan—the finished dish is a million-dollar winner!

4 (5-count) cans biscuits	**1/2 cup chopped black**
1 (16-ounce) jar pizza	**olives**
sauce	**8 to 16 ounces pepperoni**
1/2 cup chopped green	**or Canadian bacon**
bell pepper	**8 to 12 ounces**
1/2 cup sliced mushrooms	**mozzarella cheese,**
1/2 cup chopped onion	**shredded**

Cut biscuits in half. Place the half-biscuits, pizza sauce, bell pepper, mushrooms, onion, black olives and pepperoni in a large bowl and stir to combine. Pour the biscuit mixture into a buttered 9×13-inch baking dish. Bake at 400 degrees for 10 minutes. Sprinkle with the cheese and return to the oven; bake until the cheese is melted and beginning to brown. Yield: 4 to 6 servings.

Connie Weber, Alpha Iota
Rapid City, South Dakota

CHEESY QUESADILLAS

3/4 cup (3 ounces)	**1/2 cup chopped cooked**
shredded Cheddar	**turkey, ham or**
cheese	**chicken (optional)**
3/4 cup (3 ounces)	**1/2 cup chopped black**
shredded Monterey	**olives (optional)**
Jack cheese	**3 tablespoons butter or**
6 flour tortillas	**margarine**
1/3 cup chopped green	**Taco sauce for dipping**
onions (optional)	

Sprinkle 1/4 cup Cheddar cheese and 1/4 cup Monterey Jack cheese evenly over each of 3 tortillas to within 1/2 inch of the edge. Sprinkle green onions, turkey and black olives over the cheese. Cover each with another tortilla. Heat 1 to 2 teaspoons of butter in a skillet over medium heat. Place a tortilla stack in the skillet and cook until lightly browned; turn and cook until lightly browned on other side. Remove from pan and let cool slightly. Repeat to make 3 tortilla stacks. Cut into wedges. Serve warm with taco sauce. Yield: about 12 servings.

Michelle Keely, Xi Gamma Zeta
Quincy, California

TURKEY QUESADILLAS

1/2 pound ground turkey	**2 cups (8 ounces)**
1/2 envelope	**shredded Cheddar**
(3 tablespoons) taco	**cheese**
seasoning mix	**1/2 cup chunky salsa**
2/3 cup water	**1 tomato, diced**
8 flour tortillas	**Sour cream (optional)**

Brown the ground turkey in a skillet, stirring until crumbly; drain. Combine the turkey, taco seasoning mix and water in the skillet and simmer for 5 minutes. Place 4 tortillas in the bottom of a lightly buttered 9-inch pie plate; tortillas will overlap. Layer the turkey and half the cheese over the tortillas; cover with the remaining 4 tortillas. Spread the salsa over the top and sprinkle with tomatoes. Cover with the remaining 1 cup cheese. Bake, uncovered, at 350 degrees for 20 minutes. Serve with sour cream. Yield: 6 to 8 servings.

Lori Ponn, Xi Delta Gamma
Marshall, Virginia

SOUTHWESTERN EGG ROLLS

1 boneless skinless	**2 tablespoons chopped**
chicken breast	**canned jalapeño**
Cajun or Southwestern	**peppers**
seasoning	**1 1/2 teaspoons minced**
2 tablespoons vegetable	**cilantro**
oil	**1/2 teaspoon cumin**
2 tablespoons minced	**1/2 teaspoon chili**
red bell pepper	**powder**
2 tablespoons minced	**1/4 teaspoon salt**
green onions	**Dash of cayenne pepper**
1/3 cup frozen corn,	**3/4 cup (3 ounces)**
thawed	**shredded Monterey**
1/4 cup canned black	**Jack cheese**
beans, rinsed and	**5 (7-inch) flour tortillas**
drained	**Avocado Ranch Dipping**
2 tablespoons frozen	**Sauce**
chopped spinach,	**4 to 6 cups peanut oil**
thawed and drained	

Cut up chicken into small bite-size pieces and season with Cajun seasoning. Heat 1 tablespoon of oil in a skillet over medium-high heat. Sauté the chicken in the hot oil for 5 minutes or until it begins to brown on the edges. Remove from heat. Heat the remaining 1 tablespoon of oil in a separate skillet over medium-high heat. Sauté the bell pepper and green onions in the hot oil for 4 or 5 minutes or until tender. Stir in the chicken, corn, black beans, spinach, jalapeño peppers, cilantro, cumin, chili powder, salt and cayenne pepper; cook for 4 minutes longer, stirring constantly so that spinach separates and is incorporated into the mixture. Remove from heat. Add the cheese and stir until it is melted by the heat of the spinach mixture. Wrap the tortillas in a moist cloth and microwave on High for 1½ minutes or until hot. Spoon ⅕ of the spinach mixture in the center of each tortilla. Fold in the ends and roll the tortilla over the mixture. Roll very tight and pierce with a wooden pick to hold together. Arrange the 5 rolls on a plate and freeze, covered with plastic wrap, for 4 to 10 hours. About 1 hour before serving time, prepare the Avocado Ranch Dipping Sauce. Deep-fry the egg rolls in peanut oil at 375 degrees for 12 to 15 minutes or until golden brown; remove to paper towels to drain. Slice each egg roll diagonally and arrange on a plate around a small bowl of Avocado Ranch Dipping Sauce. Yield: 10 servings.

AVOCADO RANCH DIPPING SAUCE

¼ cup mashed fresh avocado	⅛ teaspoon dried parsley
¼ cup mayonnaise	⅛ teaspoon onion powder
1 tablespoon buttermilk	Dash of dried dill weed
1½ teaspoons white vinegar	Dash of garlic powder
⅛ teaspoon salt	Dash of pepper

Combine all the ingredients in a small bowl and whisk to blend.

Denise Trouard, Xi Rho
Sulphur, Louisiana

GREEN ONION FINGER SANDWICHES

3 ounces cream cheese, softened	½ green bell pepper, finely chopped
2 tablespoons lemon juice	20 slices white sandwich bread, buttered
¼ cup mayonnaise	
4 green onions, finely chopped	

Combine the cream cheese, lemon juice and mayonnaise in a blender container and process until smooth. Combine the green onions, bell pepper and cream cheese mixture in a bowl and mix well. Chill, covered, for 8 to 10 hours. Spread the cream cheese mixture over 10 slices of buttered bread. Top each

with another slice of buttered bread, buttered side facing center. Cut off the crusts. Cut each sandwich into 3 finger slices. Yield: 30 fingers.

Margaret N. Camp, Xi Beta Lambda
Leesville, South Carolina

ORANGE CHEESE FINGERS

4 ounces Neufchâtel cheese, softened	1 tablespoon honey
1 teaspoon grated orange zest	½ cup Grape Nuts
½ teaspoon vanilla extract	½ (1-pound) loaf sliced whole wheat bread, crusts trimmed

Combine the cheese, orange zest, vanilla and honey in a small bowl and blend well. Stir in the Grape Nuts. Spread 2 tablespoons of the cheese mixture on ½ of the bread slices. Top with the remaining bread slices. Cut each sandwich into thirds.
Yield: 18 fingers.

Carolyn M. Cline, Laureate Omicron
Jamestown, New York

RAISIN FINGER SANDWICHES

8 ounces cream cheese, softened	½ cup chopped pecans
¼ cup mayonnaise	10 slices raisin bread

Combine the cream cheese and mayonnaise in a mixing bowl and beat until smooth. Stir in the pecans. Spread over 5 slices of raisin bread; top with remaining bread. Cut into strips or triangles. Serve immediately. Yield: 10 servings.

Marjorie A. Green, Laureate Epsilon
Abilene, Kansas

MINIATURE GRILLED CHEDDAR HAM SANDWICHES

1 (16-ounce) package cocktail rye or cocktail pumpernickel	8 ounces Cheddar cheese, thinly sliced
1 (1-pound) package sliced ham	Dijon mustard to taste
	5 tablespoons butter, melted

Preheat the oven to 450 degrees. Top half the bread slices with ham folded to fit and cheese trimmed to fit. Spread with Dijon mustard. Top with the remaining bread slices. Brush a baking sheet with melted butter. Arrange the sandwiches on the baking sheet; brush tops with melted butter. Bake for 5 minutes or until lightly browned. Turn sandwiches, brush with butter and bake for 3 to 4 minutes longer.
Yield: about 22 servings.

Lynn Sewell, Xi Beta Delta
Chesterfield, Virginia

CHEESY ARTICHOKE SQUARES

4 eggs, beaten
½ cup dry bread crumbs
1 garlic clove, minced
1 teaspoon Greek
   seasoning
Pinch of chile flakes
½ teaspoon salt
1 (14-ounce) can
   artichoke hearts,
   drained and chopped

1 onion, finely chopped
1 cup (4 ounces)
   shredded Cheddar
   cheese
2 tablespoons grated
   Parmesan cheese
1 tablespoon fines
   herbes (mixed minced
   fresh herbs)

Combine the eggs, bread crumbs, garlic, Greek seasoning, chile flakes and salt in a medium bowl and mix well. Stir in the artichokes, onion and Cheddar cheese. Pour into an 8×8-inch baking dish that has been sprayed with nonstick cooking spray. Sprinkle with Parmesan cheese and fines herbes. Bake at 325 degrees in center of oven for 30 minutes or until firm. Serve hot or at room temperature. May be frozen and reheated. Yield: 16 squares.

Sylvia Labelle, Xi Mu
Edmonton, Alberta, Canada

CHEESE PEPPER SQUARES

2 (4-ounce) cans chopped
   hot green chiles
4 cups (16 ounces)
   shredded sharp
   Cheddar cheese

1 dozen eggs, well
   beaten

Spread the chile peppers in a buttered 9×13-inch baking dish. Layer the cheese over the peppers. Pour the eggs evenly over the cheese layer. Bake at 325 degrees for 30 minutes or until edges are lightly browned. Serve warm or cold. Yield: 18 servings.

Vee Falk, Laureate Zeta
Mesa, Arizona

MEXICAN QUICHE APPETIZER

½ cup (1 stick) butter
10 eggs
½ cup flour
1 teaspoon baking
   powder
Dash of salt
2 cups cottage cheese

1 (8- to 12-ounce) can
   chopped mild green
   chiles
4 cups (16 ounces)
   shredded Monterey
   Jack cheese

Melt the butter in a 9×13-inch baking dish. Combine the eggs, flour, baking powder and salt in a large mixing bowl and beat until smooth. Add the melted butter, leaving a buttered baking dish. Add the cottage cheese, chiles and Monterey Jack cheese; mix well. Spoon into the buttered baking dish. Bake,

uncovered, at 350 degrees for 45 to 60 minutes or until a knife inserted in the center comes out clean. Cut into bite-size squares while hot; allow to cool slightly before removing to a serving plate.
Yield: 24 to 30 servings.

Barbara J. Gates, Alpha Epsilon Master
Bethany, Missouri

JALAPENO PIE

1 (11-ounce) can
   jalapeño peppers,
   drained and
   chopped

4 cups (16 ounces)
   shredded Cheddar
   cheese
4 eggs, beaten

Spread the jalapeño peppers in a buttered 9-inch pie plate. Layer the cheese over the peppers. Pour the eggs evenly over the cheese layer. Bake at 375 degrees for 30 minutes or until edges are slightly browned. Yield: 10 to 12 servings.

Carolyn Sigler, Epsilon Alpha
Lake Charles, Louisiana

SPINACH BROWNIES

2 (10-ounce) packages
   frozen chopped
   spinach, thawed
1 cup flour
1 cup milk
2 eggs, beaten
2 teaspoons salt

1 tablespoon baking
   powder
½ cup (1 stick) butter or
   margarine, melted
4 cups (16 ounces)
   shredded sharp
   Cheddar cheese

Drain the spinach and press out excess moisture. Combine the spinach and remaining ingredients in a large bowl and mix well. Spread in a lightly greased 8×11-inch baking dish. Bake at 350 degrees for 30 to 35 minutes or until edges are lightly browned. Cut into squares. Yield: 9 to 12 servings.

Frances Knutson, Laureate Epsilon Psi
Leesburg, Florida

FLORENTINE SQUARES

4 eggs, beaten
1 (10-ounce) can cream
   of mushroom soup
2 (10-ounce) packages
   frozen chopped
   spinach, thawed and
   minced
½ cup toasted walnuts,
   chopped

¼ cup minced green
   onions
1 cup (4 ounces)
   shredded Swiss
   cheese
¼ cup grated Parmesan
   cheese
1 (8-count) package
   crescent rolls

Combine the eggs, soup, spinach, walnuts, green onions, Swiss cheese and Parmesan cheese in a large bowl; mix well. Unroll the dough and separate into

2 rectangles. Press into a 9×13-inch baking dish, pressing the perforations and edges to seal. Spread the spinach mixture evenly over the dough. Bake at 350 degrees for 40 minutes or until a knife inserted in the center comes out clean. Cool slightly and cut into 1-inch squares. Yield: 50 pieces.

Elaine Haworth, Xi Chi
Alexandria, Louisiana

SPINACH TOMATO APPETIZER PIE

1 (9-inch) unbaked pie shell	**¼ cup thinly sliced green onions**
1½ cups (8 ounces) shredded Swiss cheese	**¾ teaspoon (or more) minced fresh basil, or**
⅓ cup mayonnaise	**¼ teaspoon (or more) dried**
1 (10-ounce) package frozen chopped spinach, thawed	**½ teaspoon oregano**
	¼ teaspoon salt
4 (or more) medium tomatoes	**¼ teaspoon pepper**
	Garlic powder to taste

Preheat the oven to 425 degrees. Bake the pie shell for 5 minutes and remove from oven. Reduce oven heat to 400 degrees. Combine the Swiss cheese and mayonnaise and mix well. Drain the spinach and squeeze until dry. Spread the spinach over the bottom of the partially baked pie shell. Slice the tomatoes and halve the slices. Arrange tomatoes in circles over the spinach until spinach is completely covered. Sprinkle with green onions, basil, oregano, salt, pepper and garlic powder. Spread the mayonnaise mixture over the top, sealing to the edge. Bake for 40 minutes or until lightly browned. Yield: 8 servings.

Paula Bourcy, Preceptor Lambda
Devils Lake, North Dakota

GRILLED PORTOBELLO MUSHROOMS WITH SMOKED SALMON

1 red onion, thinly sliced	**Salt and pepper to taste**
2 tablespoons butter, melted	**12 ounces smoked salmon**
4 (3- to 4-inch) portobello mushrooms	**10 ounces provolone cheese, sliced**

Sauté the onion in a small amount of the butter in a skillet over medium heat until caramelized; cool slightly. Remove the stems from the mushrooms and brush the mushrooms with the remaining butter. Cook the mushrooms in a skillet over medium heat for 2 to 3 minutes per side or until tender. Arrange the mushrooms smooth side down on a nonstick baking sheet and sprinkle with salt and pepper. Layer

the salmon and sautéed onion over the mushrooms. Top with slices of cheese. Bake at 400 degrees for 5 minutes or until cheese melts. Cut into bite-size pieces and serve. Yield: about 1 dozen.

Erin Oliver, Alpha Epsilon
Stuttgart, Arkansas

ITALIAN WEDGES

1 (9-inch) frozen pie pastry, thawed	**1 cup part skim ricotta cheese**
½ cup Italian bread crumbs	**Dash of nutmeg**
	3 tablespoons olive oil
⅓ cup chopped fresh basil	**3 fresh Italian plum tomatoes, or**
¼ cup grated Romano cheese	**1 (14-ounce) can whole tomatoes, sliced**
¼ teaspoon salt	
¼ teaspoon pepper	

Unfold the pie pastry and use a rolling pin to roll to a 12-inch round. Place on an ungreased pizza pan or baking sheet. Combine the next 8 ingredients in a medium bowl and mix well. Spread the cheese mixture over the pastry to within 3 inches of the edge. Spread sliced tomatoes over the cheese layer. Fold edge of pastry up over the filling and crimp the edge slightly. Bake at 400 degrees for 25 to 35 minutes or until golden. Cool for 15 minutes. Garnish with additional chopped basil. Cut into wedges and serve. Yield: 10 servings.

Barbara Butler, Eta Master
Commack, New York

TOMATO BASIL SQUARES

1 loaf frozen pizza dough, thawed	**⅔ cup mayonnaise**
2 cups (8 ounces) shredded mozzarella cheese	**2 tablespoons snipped fresh basil, or**
	2 teaspoons dried
	1 garlic clove, minced
¼ cup (1 ounce) grated Parmesan cheese	**4 plum tomatoes, thinly sliced**

Roll the dough into a 12×15-inch rectangle on a nonstick baking sheet. Bake at 375 degrees for 5 to 10 minutes. Sprinkle with half the mozzarella cheese. Combine the Parmesan cheese, mayonnaise, basil, garlic and the remaining 1 cup mozzarella cheese in a bowl; mix well. Arrange tomato slices over the mozzarella cheese layer; spread the mayonnaise mixture over the top. Bake for 10 to 15 minutes longer or until crust is golden brown. Serve warm. Yield: 24 pieces.

Norma Smith, Alpha Delta Upsilon
Shell Knob, Missouri

GOAT CHEESE TORTA WITH PESTO AND SUN-DRIED TOMATOES

Great with blackberry wine and fresh fruit.

12 ounces Montrachet cheese (goat cheese)	8 ounces pesto
8 ounces cream cheese, softened	1 jar sun-dried tomatoes, well drained and chopped
1/2 cup (1 stick) unsalted butter, softened	

Combine the Montrachet cheese, cream cheese and butter in a mixing bowl and beat until fluffy. Line an 8-inch cake pan with a piece of damp cheesecloth that is large enough so it can eventually be folded back over the top. Layer 1/3 of the cheese mixture in the cake pan and layer 1/2 of the pesto over the cheese mixture. Repeat the layers. Spread the remaining cheese mixture over the top and cover with sun-dried tomatoes. Place plastic wrap over the top; fold back the cheesecloth extensions to cover the plastic wrap. Chill for at least 1 hour. Remove from pan and place on a cake plate. Serve with assorted crackers and bread. Yield: 15 to 20 servings.

Teresa Blanton, Xi Beta Pi
Trussville, Alabama

QUICK ZUCCHINI FRITTATA

3 cups thinly sliced zucchini	1/2 teaspoon salt
1 cup baking mix	1/2 teaspoon pepper
1/2 cup chopped onion	1/2 teaspoon Italian seasoning
1/2 cup (2 ounces) grated Parmesan cheese	1/2 cup vegetable oil
1 garlic clove, minced	4 eggs, beaten

Combine the zucchini, baking mix, onion, Parmesan cheese, garlic, salt, pepper, Italian seasoning, vegetable oil and eggs in a bowl and mix well. Pour into a buttered 9×13-inch baking dish. Bake at 350 degrees for 25 minutes or until edges begin to brown. Cut into 1-inch squares. Yield: 32 servings.

Wendy Bennett, Xi Pi Rho
Napa, California

❖ NAPA VALLEY QUICHE

1 sheet puff pastry, thawed	1 teaspoon salt
16 ounces cream cheese, softened	1/4 teaspoon pepper
8 ounces goat cheese	2 garlic cloves, minced
9 eggs	2 cups (8 ounces) shredded Monterey Jack cheese
1 teaspoon basil	1 cup heavy cream
1 teaspoon thyme	3 cups shredded zucchini

Roll the pastry into a 10×15-inch rectangle on a heavily floured surface. Fit into a 10×15-inch cake pan. Combine the cream cheese and goat cheese in a mixing bowl and beat until fluffy. Add the eggs 1 at a time, beating well after each addition. Beat in the basil, thyme, salt, pepper, garlic, Monterey Jack cheese, cream and zucchini. Pour evenly into the pastry-lined cake pan. Bake at 350 degrees for 30 minutes or until custard is set and surface is puffy and light brown. Serve at room temperature. Cut into squares. Yield: about 40 pieces.

Christine Hoffman, Epsilon Iota
Blair, Nebraska

MINI VEGGIE QUICHES

2 frozen (9-inch) pie shells, thawed	1 green onion, chopped
1/2 cup milk	1/2 cup (2 ounces) shredded Cheddar cheese
2 eggs, beaten	1 garlic clove, minced
4 slices bacon, crisp-cooked, crumbled	Dash of pepper
1/2 cup shredded zucchini	
1/2 cup chopped mushrooms	

Roll the pie shells flat on a lightly floured surface. Cut into scalloped circles with a scalloped cookie cutter. Press pastry circles into muffin cups sprayed with nonstick cooking spray. Whisk the milk and eggs together in a bowl. Add the bacon, zucchini, mushrooms, green onion, Cheddar cheese, garlic and pepper; mix well. Fill each pastry-lined muffin cup with the zucchini mixture. Bake at 375 degrees for 17 to 20 minutes or until beginning to brown. Cool in the pans for 2 minutes. Serve warm. Yield: 2 dozen.

Michelle Jaramillo, Kappa Iota
Northglenn, Colorado

HAMBURGER CUPCAKES

12 slices white bread, crusts trimmed	1/2 cup (2 ounces) shredded Cheddar cheese
1 pound lean ground beef	1/2 teaspoon oregano
1 egg, beaten	1 (10-ounce) can cream of mushroom soup
1 teaspoon salt	
1/2 cup bread crumbs	
1/2 cup chopped onions or chives	

Butter the bread and fit buttered side down into muffin cups. Combine the ground beef, egg, salt, bread crumbs, onions, cheese, oregano and soup in a large bowl and mix well. Fill each bread-lined muffin cup with 1/12 of the beef mixture. Top with additional shredded cheese. Bake at 350 degrees for 40 to 45 minutes or until cooked through. Serve hot. Yield: 12 servings.

Raquel Schumacher, Theta Nu
Prince George, British Columbia, Canada

MINIATURE HAM QUICHES

1 cup chopped cooked ham	Chopped onion to taste
2 cups (8 ounces) shredded Cheddar cheese	Prepared mustard to taste
2 eggs, beaten	3 (8-count) cans crescent rolls

Combine the ham, cheese, eggs, onion and mustard in a bowl and mix well. Unroll the dough and flatten into a rectangle, pressing the perforations to seal. Sprinkle lightly with flour and cut into 3-inch squares. Fit a square of dough into each of 36 miniature muffin cups; fill with the ham mixture. Bake at 325 degrees for 20 to 30 minutes or until set. Yield: 3 dozen.

Leslie H. Chatman, Kappa Epsilon
Cartersville, Georgia

SAUSAGE CHEESE BARS

1 (8-count) can crescent rolls	4 eggs, beaten
1 pound bulk pork sausage, cooked and drained	3/4 cup milk
	Salt and pepper to taste
2 cups (8 ounces) shredded mozzarella cheese	

Unroll the dough and flatten into a rectangle. Fit into a 9×13-inch baking dish that has been sprayed with nonstick cooking spray, pressing the perforations to seal. Layer the sausage and cheese over the dough. Combine the eggs and milk and mix well; pour evenly over the cheese layer. Season with salt and pepper. Bake at 400 degrees for 25 to 35 minutes or until set. Remove from oven and let stand for 15 minutes. Cut into bars and serve hot. Yield: 2 dozen.

Brenda Price, Alpha Phi
Lavonia, Georgia

CLAM PIE

2 (6-ounce) cans minced clams	1 to 2 tablespoons minced parsley
1 cup bread crumbs	1 tablespoon oregano
Minced garlic to taste	1/2 cup (1 stick) butter, melted
2 cups (8 ounces) shredded mozzarella cheese	

Combine the undrained clams, bread crumbs, garlic, cheese, parsley, oregano and butter in a bowl and mix well. Spoon into a buttered quiche dish. Bake at 350 degrees for 15 minutes or until cheese is melted. If top begins to brown too quickly, place a piece of foil across the top and continue baking until cheese melts. Remove from oven. Serve warm with crackers. Yield: 18 to 20 servings.

Margaret Lawrence, Laureate Phi
Montgomery, New York

BITE-SIZE CRAB QUICHES

1 (5-count) can large buttermilk biscuits	1 egg
1 (6-ounce) can crab meat, drained	1/2 cup milk
	1/2 teaspoon dill weed
1/2 cup (2 ounces) shredded Swiss cheese	1/4 teaspoon salt

Separate each biscuit horizontally into 5 equal pieces. Press each piece over the bottom and up the side of each of 24 ungreased miniature muffin cups. Fill each cup with 5 teaspoons crab meat and 1 teaspoon Swiss cheese. Combine the egg, milk, dill weed and salt in a small bowl and whisk to blend. Spoon about 1 1/2 teaspoons of the egg mixture into each cup. Bake at 375 degrees for 15 to 20 minutes or until edges are golden brown. Let stand for 5 minutes. Serve warm. Yield: 2 dozen.

Marilyn Lee Johnson, Beta Psi
Holbrook, Arizona

SWISS CRAB QUICHE

To make a fuller pie, use 10 ounces of cheese and a pound of crab meat.

2 eggs, beaten	2 cups (8 ounces) shredded Swiss cheese
1 cup milk	
6 tablespoons mayonnaise	1/2 cup chopped green onion tops
2 tablespoons flour	1 recipe (2-crust) pie pastry
Dash of salt	
3/4 pound cooked crab meat, flaked	

Combine the eggs, milk, mayonnaise and flour in a large bowl and blend well. Stir in the salt, crab meat, cheese and green onions. Pour the crab mixture into a pastry-lined 9×13-inch baking dish. Bake at 350 degrees for 45 minutes to 1 hour or until a knife inserted in the center comes out clean. Cut into squares. Yield: 50 squares.

Barbara Latta, Sigma Master
Spokane Valley, Washington

Fingerfood

ANTIPASTO

4 ounces provolone
    cheese, cubed
1/2 cup olive oil
1 teaspoon oregano
Dash of crushed red
    pepper
4 ounces Italian sharp
    cheese
4 ounces prosciutto
1 (10-ounce) jar
    pepperoncini, drained

1 (6-ounce) jar marinated
    mushrooms, chilled
    and drained
1 (7-ounce) jar roasted
    red bell peppers,
    drained
1 (6-ounce) jar
    marinated artichoke
    hearts, drained
4 ounces salami, cubed

Combine the provolone cheese, olive oil, oregano and crushed red pepper in a small bowl and mix well. Chill, covered, for 2 hours. Cut half the Italian sharp cheese into 3-inch sticks and wrap each with a slice of prosciutto. Cut the remaining Italian sharp cheese into bite-size wedges. Line a serving platter with green leaf lettuce. Drain the provolone mixture, reserving the marinade. Arrange the provolone mixture, cheese sticks, cheese wedges, pepperoncini, mushrooms, roasted red bell peppers, artichokes and salami over the lettuce. Drizzle with the reserved marinade and serve. Yield: 40 servings.

Virginia King, Xi Lambda
Salem, Oregon

---

*Keran Cueva, Preceptor Iota Eta, Oregon House, California, wows her guests with a platter of **Waffle Fry Nachos**. She bakes a package of frozen waffle fries using package directions, arranges the fries in batches in a large ovenproof skillet, tops with cooked crumbled bacon, sliced green onions, chopped tomatoes, sliced black olives, salsa, and generous amounts of mixed shredded Cheddar and Monterey Jack cheese. Bake for 5 minutes or until the cheese melts and serve with sour cream.*

HOT ANTIPASTO

2 (14-ounce) cans
    artichoke hearts,
    drained
1 (14-ounce) can sliced
    black olives, drained
2 (14-ounce) cans sliced
    potatoes, drained
2 (14-ounce) jars roasted
    red bell peppers,
    thinly sliced

3 garlic cloves, minced
2 cups Italian-flavored
    bread crumbs
1 1/2 cups olive oil
1/2 cup grated Romano
    cheese
Dash of parsley
Dash of basil

Cut the artichoke hearts into quarters. Combine the black olives, potatoes, roasted red bell peppers, garlic, bread crumbs, olive oil, Romano cheese, parsley and basil in a large bowl and mix well. Stir in the artichokes. Spoon into a 9×9-inch glass baking dish. Bake at 450 degrees for 20 minutes. Yield: 12 to 16 servings.

Johanna Kudlo, Delta Delta
Myrtle Beach, South Carolina

JARDINIERE

Jardinière makes a wonderful gift to give to someone special.

4 cups vinegar
2 cups water
2 cups sugar
1 tablespoon pickling
    and canning salt
3 bay leaves
6 peppercorns
3 garlic cloves, thinly
    sliced
1 zucchini, thinly sliced
2 cups cauliflower
    florets

1 1/2 cups miniature
    white onions
3 ribs celery, diagonally
    sliced
2 carrots, cut into thin
    1 1/2-inch strips
2 red bell peppers, cut
    into strips
1 yellow bell pepper, cut
    into strips
1 green bell pepper, cut
    into strips

Combine the vinegar, water, sugar and salt in a large kettle and bring to a boil. Tie the bay leaves, peppercorns and garlic in cheesecloth to make a bouquet garni and add to the vinegar mixture. Boil for 5 minutes. Add the zucchini, cauliflower, onions, celery and carrots; bring to a boil. Remove from heat. Stir in the bell peppers. Remove and discard the bouquet garni. Ladle into hot sterilized jars, leaving 1/2 inch headspace; seal with 2-piece lids. Process in a boiling water bath for 10 minutes. Let stand until cooled to room temperature. Store in a cool dry place or in the refrigerator. Yield: 5 to 7 pints.

Pierrette Paquet, Xi Eta Kappa
Northbrook, Ontario, Canada

BLOODY MARY SWIZZLERS

1 pint cherry tomatoes	3 or 4 ribs celery, leafy
1 cup lemon-flavored	tops removed,
vodka	diagonally sliced into
1 (10-ounce) jar almond-	1-inch pieces
stuffed green olives or	Celery salt to taste
vermouth green	(optional)
olives	

Pierce the skin of each tomato in several places with a wooden pick. Place the tomatoes and vodka in a sealable plastic bag. Seal the bag and turn several times to coat the tomatoes. Marinate in the refrigerator for 8 to 10 hours, stirring occasionally; drain. Skewer an olive, a piece of celery and a tomato on each cocktail pick or skewer. Arrange over a bed of greens and sprinkle lightly with celery salt.
Yield: 10 to 20 servings.

Thelma Kenney, Preceptor Gamma Kappa
Virginia Beach, Virginia

GOURMET MUSHROOMS AND OLIVES

2 (4-ounce) jars whole	1 tablespoon parsley
mushrooms, drained	flakes
1 (15-ounce) can black	1/4 teaspoon salt
olives, drained	1/4 teaspoon lemon
1 small onion, sliced	pepper
into thin rings	1/8 teaspoon black
1/2 cup red wine vinegar	pepper
1/2 cup vegetable oil	

Combine the mushrooms, black olives and onion rings in a glass dish. Place the vinegar, oil, parsley flakes, salt, lemon pepper and black pepper in a covered jar and shake vigorously to combine. Pour over the mushroom mixture. Chill, covered, for at least 8 hours, stirring occasionally. Yield: 10 to 15 servings.

Mary Nita Wing, Xi Master
Lake Jackson, Texas

MARINATED MUSHROOMS

Two 6-ounce cans of mushrooms, drained, may be substituted for the fresh mushrooms. If you use canned mushrooms, simmer for only 5 or 6 minutes.

1/3 cup red wine vinegar	1 teaspoon dry mustard
1/3 cup vegetable oil	or Grey Poupon
1 small onion, thinly	1 tablespoon brown
sliced	sugar
1 teaspoon salt	1 pound fresh
2 teaspoons chopped	mushrooms, cleaned
fresh parsley	

Combine the red wine vinegar, oil, onion, salt, parsley, dry mustard and brown sugar in a saucepan and bring to a boil. Stir in the mushrooms. Reduce heat and simmer for 15 to 20 minutes. Chill, covered, for at least 3 hours. Drain before serving or serve with a slotted spoon. Yield: 15 servings.

Jennifer Whittemore, Alpha Nu
Littleton, Colorado

RED HOT GREEN OLIVES

1 (7-ounce) jar large	2 garlic cloves, sliced
green olives, well	1 teaspoon crushed red
drained	pepper
1/2 cup tomato juice	1/2 teaspoon oregano
1 tablespoon olive oil	1/2 teaspoon basil

Place the olives in a bowl. Combine the tomato juice, olive oil, garlic, crushed red pepper, oregano and basil and mix well. Pour the tomato juice mixture over the olives and stir. Place all in a jar. Marinate, covered, in the refrigerator for 3 days, turning the jar daily. At serving time, drain and sprinkle with additional crushed red pepper. Yield: 6 to 8 servings.

Mildred E. Mitchke, Preceptor Epsilon
Bigfork, Montana

REFRIGERATOR PICKLES

7 cups sliced cucumbers	2 cups sugar
2 tablespoons salt	1 cup white vinegar
1 cup sliced onion	1 teaspoon celery seed

Combine the cucumbers, salt and onion in a large bowl. Combine the sugar, vinegar and celery seed in a separate bowl and stir well. Pour the vinegar mixture over the cucumber mixture. Chill, covered, in the refrigerator for 24 hours before serving.
Yield: 1 1/2 to 2 quarts.

Kimberly Hertzog, Preceptor Epsilon Beta
Princeton, Missouri

SWEET KOSHER DILLS

To make a gallon of pickles, use 1 gallon whole kosher dill pickles, 2½ cups apple cider vinegar, 1 package pickling spice and 10 cups of sugar.

½ gallon whole kosher dill pickles	*½ (2-ounce) package pickling spice*
1½ cups apple cider vinegar	*6 cups sugar*

Slice the kosher pickles into a bowl; drain. Combine the apple cider vinegar, pickling spice and sugar in a small bowl and stir to dissolve the sugar. Pour over the kosher pickles and stir. Let stand, covered, at room temperature for 8 to 10 hours, stirring occasionally. Spoon into jars, cover and refrigerate. Yield: ½ gallon.

Maysel Wiesenhofer, Zeta Eta
Roosevelt, Arizona

CHEESE-STUFFED CELERY

½ cup (2 ounces) shredded Cheddar cheese	*⅓ cup sour cream*
	¼ teaspoon Italian seasoning
¼ cup drained pickle relish	*12 ribs celery*

Combine the cheese, pickle relish, sour cream and Italian seasoning in a 1-quart bowl and mix well. Chill, covered, for 1 to 2 hours. Stuff each celery rib with 2 tablespoons of the cheese mixture. Cut celery into pieces if desired. Yield: 12 to 24 servings.

Arlene Pankow, Laureate Gamma Theta
Vancouver, Washington

CRAB MOUSSE IN CUCUMBERS

Flake-style imitation or cooked smoked salmon or whitefish may be substituted for the crab meat.

½ pound flaked cooked crab meat	*2 teaspoons prepared horseradish*
3 ounces cream cheese, softened, cut up	*½ teaspoon cayenne pepper*
2 tablespoons mayonnaise	*¼ teaspoon salt*
1 tablespoon Dijon mustard	*4 medium (7 to 8 inches long) cucumbers*
1 tablespoon minced shallots	

Combine the crab meat, cream cheese, mayonnaise, Dijon mustard, shallots, horseradish, cayenne pepper and salt in a food processor container and process until smooth, scraping the side of the container once or twice. Spoon the crab mixture into a pastry bag

fitted with a large star tip. Peel the cucumbers, leaving some strips of the cucumber skin on the vegetable. Cut into ³/₄-inch-thick slices. Use a melon baller to scoop out the center of the slices to form cups. Pipe crab mousse into each cucumber cup. Garnish with additional crab meat or fish. Chill, covered, for 2 hours before serving. Yield: 20 servings.

Beatrice Rice, Laureate Xi
Billings, Montana

CUCUMBER SHRIMP APPETIZERS

1 (8-ounce) can unsweetened crushed pineapple, drained	*2 teaspoons Dijon mustard*
	1½ teaspoons minced fresh dill weed
1 (4-ounce) can tiny shrimp, rinsed and drained	*1 medium cucumber, cut into ¼-inch slices*
¼ cup mayonnaise	
1 green onion, finely chopped	

Combine the pineapple, shrimp, mayonnaise, green onion, Dijon mustard and dill weed in a bowl and mix well. Spoon onto cucumber slices. Garnish with dill sprigs if desired. Yield: 32 servings.

Frances Reynolds, Delta Kappa
Ellisville, Mississippi

DEVILED EGGS PICANTE

12 large eggs	*1 teaspoon minced garlic*
¼ cup finely chopped celery	*1 teaspoon lemon pepper*
2 tablespoons finely chopped onion	*1 teaspoon minced rosemary*
1 (4-ounce) jar pimentos, finely chopped	*1 tablespoon deli-style mustard*
2 tablespoons finely chopped bread-and-butter pickles or sweet pickle relish	*1 tablespoon chunky salsa or picante sauce*
	½ cup mayonnaise-type salad dressing
2 tablespoons pickle juice	

Place eggs in a kettle over medium-high heat with enough water to cover the eggs. Bring to a boil; boil for 5 minutes. Drain the hot water and replace with cold water and 2 trays of ice cubes; let stand for 15 minutes. Drain. Roll each egg to gently crack the shell before peeling. Cut the eggs into halves lengthwise. Scoop the yolks into a medium mixing bowl and mash well. Fold in the celery, onion, pimentos, pickles, pickle juice, garlic, lemon pepper, rosemary, mustard, salsa and salad dressing. Beat with an electric or hand mixer at medium speed for about 3 minutes or until well mixed. Chill, covered, for 8 to 10 hours. Fill the egg whites with the yolk mixture. Sprinkle with paprika and garnish each with a sliced green olive ring. Yield: 24 servings.

Eve Oppedisano, Epsilon Xi
Page, Arizona

BROILED GRAPES AND CREAM

Select green grapes, red grapes, or any color you like.

2 cups seedless grapes
1/2 cup whipped cream
1 1/2 cups sour cream
1/4 cup firmly packed brown sugar

Clean and dry the grapes; place in a 9×9-inch baking dish. Spread a mixture of the whipped cream, sour cream and brown sugar over the grapes. Broil 6 inches from the heat source for 5 to 10 minutes or until top is bubbly and golden brown. Chill, tightly covered, for at least 3 hours before serving.
Yield: 10 to 12 servings.

Ann Doucet, Laureate Zeta Gamma
Deer Park, Texas

CHEESY PECAN GRAPES

8 ounces reduced-fat cream cheese, softened
4 ounces bleu cheese, crumbled
36 seedless green grapes, washed and patted dry
1 1/2 cups chopped pecans

Combine the cream cheese and bleu cheese in a small bowl and mix well. Add the grapes and stir gently to coat. Spread the pecans in a shallow bowl. Roll the cheese-coated grapes in the pecans until coated. Arrange on a serving platter. Chill, covered, for at least 2 hours before serving. Yield: 12 servings.

Selma Ulbrich, Preceptor Beta Psi
La Quinta, California

STUFFED GRAPE LEAVES

1 (1-pint) jar grape leaves
1 pound ground lamb or ground beef or both
1 onion, minced
1/4 cup chopped green bell pepper
3 tablespoons olive oil
2 cups cooked rice
1/2 cup chopped peeled tomato
1/4 cup chopped raw almonds
2 tablespoons minced fresh parsley
1 tablespoon chopped fresh mint
1 tablespoon fresh lemon juice
Salt and pepper to taste
1 cup water or chicken broth

Rinse the grape leaves to remove the brine; drain. Brown the ground lamb with the onion and bell pepper in the olive oil in a skillet, cooking until vegetables are tender and stirring until crumbly; drain. Add the rice, tomato, almonds, parsley, mint, lemon juice, salt and pepper; cook over medium-low heat for 10 minutes or until liquid from tomato is absorbed, stirring occasionally. Spread the grape leaves shiny side down on a flat surface. Place a tablespoon of rice mixture on each leaf. Tuck in sides of leaf and roll. Stack rolled leaves in a 2-quart baking dish. Pour in the water. Bake, covered, at 325 degrees for 40 to 45 minutes or until sizzling hot. Sprinkle with additional lemon juice. Chill, covered, until serving time. Yield: 10 to 12 servings.

Karen Casson, Xi Beta Delta
Encampment, Wyoming

BACON-STUFFED MUSHROOMS

1 pound fresh mushrooms
2 tablespoons chopped onion
2 tablespoons butter
1 slice bread, torn into small pieces
1 cup (4 ounces) shredded Cheddar cheese
1 (3-ounce) jar bacon bits

Clean the mushrooms and remove the stems. Arrange mushroom caps hollow side up on a buttered baking sheet. Chop mushroom stems and place in a skillet over medium-low heat with the onion and butter. Cook for 5 to 10 minutes or until vegetables are tender. Remove from heat. Stir in the bread, cheese and bacon bits. Fill the mushroom caps with the cheese filling. Bake at 400 degrees for 15 minutes. Yield: 6 to 10 servings.

Phyllis Mesker, Preceptor Delta Upsilon
Dayton, Ohio

PINEAPPLE-STUFFED MUSHROOMS

12 large fresh mushroom caps
1 (8-ounce) can crushed pineapple, drained
1 (6-ounce) can chicken
1 tablespoon mayonnaise
1/2 teaspoon lemon juice
12 walnut halves

Arrange the mushroom caps in a microwave-safe baking dish. Combine the pineapple, chicken, mayonnaise and lemon juice in a bowl and mix well. Fill the mushroom caps with the pineapple mixture and garnish with walnut halves. Microwave on High for 2 minutes and serve. Yield: 12 servings.

Lettie Loveleen Turner, Laureate Zeta Alpha
Orange Park, Florida

SAUSAGE-STUFFED MUSHROOMS

*1/4 pound Italian
   sausage, casings
   removed, or bulk
   pork sausage
1 cup chopped onion
1 pound large
   mushrooms
   (about 12)
1/2 cup water*

*1 tablespoon chopped
   fresh parsley
1/2 teaspoon salt
1/8 teaspoon pepper
1/2 cup quick-cooking
   rice
2/3 cup mayonnaise
1/3 cup grated Parmesan
   cheese*

Brown the sausage with the onion in a skillet, stirring until crumbly; drain. Clean the mushrooms and remove the stems. Mince the stems and add to the sausage mixture; cook over medium heat for 10 minutes or until mushrooms begin to brown. Add the water, parsley, salt and pepper; bring to a rolling boil. Stir in the rice. Cover and remove from heat. Let stand for 5 minutes. Combine the mayonnaise and Parmesan cheese in a small bowl and mix well. Stir 1/2 cup of the mayonnaise mixture into the sausage mixture. Fill the mushroom caps with sausage mixture; top each with mayonnaise mixture. Arrange the filled mushroom caps in a shallow baking dish with a little water in the bottom. Bake at 400 degrees for 15 minutes or until brown and puffy. Yield: 12 servings.

*Kathryn Stoterau, Zeta Master
Mesa, Arizona*

CREAM CHEESE-STUFFED MUSHROOMS

*8 ounces cream cheese,
   softened
1/4 cup (1/2 stick)
   margarine
2 tablespoons minced
   fresh parsley*

*1/2 teaspoon garlic salt
1/2 cup (2 ounces) grated
   Parmesan cheese
1 pound fresh
   mushrooms*

Combine the cream cheese, margarine, parsley and garlic salt in a microwave-safe bowl. Microwave on High for 2 minutes or until softened. Stir in the Parmesan cheese. Remove the mushroom stems and hollow out the caps slightly. Fill with the cream cheese mixture and arrange on a microwave-safe baking dish. Microwave on High for 4 minutes. Serve hot. Yield: 12 servings.

*Carol A. Carnell, Xi Delta Omega
Jackson, Tennessee*

BAKED OLIVES

*1 (16-ounce) jar jumbo
   Spanish olives
2 (8-count) cans crescent
   rolls*

*2 tablespoons melted
   butter*

Drain the olives well and pat dry. Unroll the dough and separate into triangles. Cut each triangle into 3 pieces. Wrap a dough piece around each olive and pinch to enclose the olive. Arrange on an ungreased baking sheet. Bake at 350 degrees for 20 minutes or until light brown. Brush with melted butter.
Yield: 30 servings.

*Susan Speer, Alpha Delta Master
Arkansas City, Kansas*

OLIVE CHEESE PUFFS

Freeze unbaked puffs on a baking sheet and store in a plastic bag in the freezer. Bake as needed.

*1/2 cup (1 stick) butter or
   margarine, softened
2 cups (8 ounces)
   shredded Cheddar
   cheese*

*1/2 teaspoon black
   pepper
Dash of cayenne pepper
1 cup sifted flour
50 stuffed green olives*

Combine the butter, cheese, black pepper and cayenne pepper in a bowl and mix well. Add the flour and blend well. Shape about 1 tablespoon of the flour mixture around each stuffed green olive to enclose. Arrange on a nonstick baking sheet and chill, covered, until firm. Bake at 400 degrees for 12 to 15 minutes or until lightly browned. Yield: 50 pieces.

*Vivian M. DeKar, Laureate Gamma Upsilon
Fruitland Park, Florida*

MARINATED STUFFED PASTA

*1 cup chopped fresh
   basil leaves
1/4 cup olive oil
1 tablespoon balsamic
   vinegar*

*Salt and freshly ground
   pepper to taste
8 ounces tortellini,
   cooked, cooled*

Combine the basil, olive oil, balsamic vinegar, salt and pepper in a large bowl and mix well. Add the tortellini and toss to combine. To serve, skewer two pasta pieces onto each of 25 bamboo picks and arrange picks on a serving platter. Yield: 25 servings.

*Karen Ives, Xi Theta Alpha
Grimsby, Ontario, Canada*

---

*Jean Barnett, Zeta Alpha, Sheridan, Arkansas, serves **Confetti Rounds** by scrubbing new potatoes and cooking in boiling water just until cooked through but firm. Rinse with cool water and let stand to cool completely. Slice the potatoes into disks about 1/4 inch thick. Top each with about 1 tablespoon sour cream and sprinkle with thinly sliced green onions, crisp-fried crumbled bacon or bacon bits, and shredded Cheddar cheese.*

SAVORY STUFFED PEPPERS

12 (4- to 6-inch) Italian frying peppers, cleaned, halved	1 cup mayonnaise
2 tablespoons olive oil	1/4 cup chopped onion
1/2 pound sliced bacon, crisp-cooked, crumbled	3 garlic cloves, minced
	1/4 teaspoon thyme
	1/4 teaspoon black pepper
8 ounces cream cheese, softened	1/4 teaspoon celery seed
1 cup (4 ounces) grated Parmesan cheese	1/8 teaspoon cayenne pepper
	8 ounces Cheddar cheese, shredded

Sauté the Italian frying peppers in olive oil in a skillet over medium-low heat for 5 minutes or until softened. Combine the bacon, cream cheese, Parmesan cheese, mayonnaise, onion, garlic, thyme, black pepper, celery seed and cayenne pepper in a bowl and mix well. Fill the frying pepper halves with the cream cheese mixture and arrange in a buttered 11×17-inch baking dish. Sprinkle with Cheddar cheese. Sprinkle with chopped red bell pepper if desired. Bake at 350 degrees for 25 to 30 minutes. Serve warm. Yield: 24 servings.

Esther Westfall, Laureate Psi
Grand Island, New York

LIGHT PEPPER POPPERS

1/2 cup (2 ounces) grated Parmesan cheese	8 large jalapeño peppers
1/2 cup seasoned bread crumbs	8 ounces light garden vegetable cream cheese, softened
1 teaspoon garlic salt	1/2 cup egg substitute

Combine the Parmesan cheese, bread crumbs and garlic salt in a shallow bowl; mix well. Cut the jalapeño peppers into halves lengthwise; if possible, leave half the stem on each piece. Scoop out the seeds, being sure to wear gloves for protection. Fill each jalapeño half with cream cheese. Dip the stuffed pepper in egg substitute and roll in the bread crumb mixture. Arrange on a nonstick baking sheet and freeze. They may be placed in a plastic bag and returned to the freezer. At serving time, remove stuffed jalapeños from freezer, arrange on a nonstick baking sheet and bake at 400 degrees for 20 to 25 minutes. Yield: 16 servings.

Sammie E. Williams, Preceptor Mu
Newton, Kansas

BACON-WRAPPED JALAPENOS

12 jalapeño peppers	12 thin slices of bacon
8 ounces cream cheese, softened	

Cut jalapeño peppers into halves lengthwise. Scoop out the seeds and membranes, being sure to wear gloves for protection. Spread on paper towels and pat dry. Fill each jalapeño half with cream cheese. Cut bacon slices into halves crosswise. Wrap a strip of bacon around each filled jalapeño half and secure with a wooden pick. Arrange on a nonstick baking sheet. Bake at 350 degrees for 35 minutes or until bacon is crisp. Remove to paper towels to absorb some of the drippings. Serve hot. Yield: 24 servings.

Nancy Parr, Xi Sigma Omicron
San Antonio, Texas

JALAPENO TREATS

24 fresh jalapeño peppers	1 teaspoon finely grated onion (optional)
8 ounces cream cheese, softened	Seasoned salt to taste
2 tablespoons shredded Cheddar cheese	

Cut off the top of each jalapeño pepper. Scoop out the seeds and membranes, being sure to wear gloves for protection. Spread on paper towels and pat dry. Combine the cream cheese, Cheddar cheese and onion in a bowl and mix well. Fill the jalapeños with the cream cheese mixture and arrange in a 9×12-inch baking dish. Sprinkle with seasoned salt. Broil 6 inches from the heat source for 10 minutes or until golden brown and crispy. Serve hot or cold.
Yield: about 12 servings.

Phyllis Esquivel, Preceptor Alpha Epsilon
Upton, Wyoming

SPICY POTATO SKINS

15 potatoes	2 (4-ounce) cans chopped green chiles
Salt and pepper to taste	
1 pound bacon, crisp-cooked, crumbled	2 cups (8 ounces) shredded Colby cheese
1 cup chopped green onions	1 1/2 cups sour cream
1 large tomato, diced	

Pierce the potatoes deeply with a fork. Bake at 350 degrees for 45 minutes or until tender. Remove from oven. Raise the oven temperature to 375 degrees. Cut the potatoes into halves lengthwise and scoop out most of the pulp, saving it for another use. Salt and pepper the potato skins. Sprinkle the bacon, green onions, tomato, green chiles and cheese into the potato skins. Arrange on a nonstick baking sheet and bake at 350 degrees for 10 to 15 minutes or until cheese melts. Cut into halves crosswise and serve with sour cream. Yield: 30 servings.

Cindy Esveld, Alpha Lambda
Peoria, Arizona

TOMATO CLAM MINIATURES

50 cherry tomatoes (about 2 pints)	**1 garlic clove, minced**
1 (8-ounce) can minced clams, well drained	**1/2 cup mayonnaise**
1 (5-ounce) can bamboo shoots, well drained	**1 tablespoon apple cider vinegar**
1 (5-ounce) can water chestnuts, drained	**1/2 teaspoon sugar**
1 cup finely chopped celery	**1/2 teaspoon salt**
	1/2 teaspoon dill weed
	1/2 teaspoon soy sauce

Cut a thin slice from the rounded end of each tomato and scoop out the seeds. Place tomatoes cut side down on a paper towel-lined tray to drain. Chill, covered, until ready to fill. Mince the clams, bamboo shoots and water chestnuts together and place in a bowl. Stir in the celery and garlic. Combine the mayonnaise, apple cider vinegar, sugar, salt, dill weed and soy sauce in a cup and blend well. Stir the mayonnaise mixture into the clam mixture. Fill each tomato with 1/2 teaspoon clam mixture.
Yield: 50 servings.

Joanne McCann, Theta Tau
Spokane, Washington

ASPARAGUS IN PHYLLO DOUGH

12 asparagus spears	**3/4 cup grated Parmesan cheese**
3 sheets phyllo dough, thawed	**1 egg and 1 tablespoon milk to make egg wash (optional)**
4 tablespoons butter, melted	
12 thin slices prosciutto	

Steam asparagus until tender-crisp. Phyllo dough dries out very quickly, so do not open the package until the asparagus is cooked. Unroll the phyllo and cover it with waxed paper topped with a damp towel. Keep the unused portion covered until needed. Cut each phyllo sheet into quarters; keep them covered with a damp cloth so they will not dry out as you work with 1 quarter-sheet at a time. Brush the edges and the center of a quarter-sheet with melted butter. Lay 1 slice of prosciutto flat at one end of the dough. Place 1 asparagus spear over the prosciutto with 1/2 inch of the tip extending beyond the dough. Sprinkle the cheese over the asparagus and roll as for a jelly roll. Brush melted butter along the edge and press to seal. Arrange the finished rolls on a nonstick baking sheet. Blend the egg and milk and brush thinly over the rolls. Bake at 450 degrees for 8 to 10 minutes or until lightly browned. Serve warm. Yield: 12 servings.

Maria Farago, Preceptor Nu Xi
Redding, California

ASPARAGUS ROLL-UPS

14 thin slices white bread, crusts trimmed	**1/4 cup melted butter**
1/2 cup (1 stick) butter, softened	**1/4 cup grated Parmesan cheese**
1 (15-ounce) can asparagus spears	

Roll each bread slice flat with a rolling pin and spread with butter. Drain asparagus and pat dry with paper towels. Place 1 asparagus spear at one end of each bread slice and roll as for a jelly roll. Place rolls seam down, side by side on a nonstick baking sheet. Drizzle with melted butter and sprinkle generously with Parmesan cheese. Bake at 350 degrees for 15 to 20 minutes or until browned and crisp. Cut into thirds and serve hot. Yield: 42 servings.

Jan Newton Hicky, Alpha Psi
Knoxville, Arkansas

CHILE FROGS

You may substitute whole fresh green chiles, cut into strips, for the canned chiles if you like.

2 cups baking mix	**1 (7-ounce) can whole green chiles, cut into strips**
2 eggs	
1 cup milk	
24 ounces (about) Cheddar cheese or other firm cheese	**Canola oil for deep-frying**

Combine the baking mix, eggs and milk in a bowl and blend well to make a batter. Cut the cheese into 3/4-inch cubes. Wrap each cube with a chile strip and secure with a wooden pick. Place wrapped cheese cubes in a bowl. When guests arrive, heat 2 to 3 inches of canola oil in a fondue pot until hot enough that a small cube of bread browns easily. Instruct guests to use a fondue or table fork to spear a wrapped cheese cube, dip it in the batter and cook in hot oil until browned. Remove and enjoy.
Yield: 12 to 14 servings.

Marlene Grace, Beta Psi
Holbrook, Arizona

❖ MEATLESS PATTIES

2 cups cooked white rice	**1 cup bread crumbs**
2 cups uncooked instant oats	**2 eggs**
1 cup chopped pecans	**Seasoned salt to taste**
1 medium onion, chopped	**Pepper to taste**

Combine the rice, oats, pecans, onion, bread crumbs and eggs in a large bowl and mix well. Mix in an additional egg if mixture seems too loose to shape into patties. Add seasoned salt and pepper and shape into small patties. Pour enough olive oil into a skillet over medium-high heat to cover the bottom. Fry the patties in the hot olive oil for about 5 minutes on each side or until crispy. Yield: 12 or more servings.

Brenda J. Culbertson, Alpha Phi
Paris, Missouri

FRIED CACTUS PAD TIDBITS

4 to 6 large cactus pads	1¹/2 tablespoons cayenne
6 eggs, well beaten	pepper
1 cup milk	2 tablespoons salt
Bread crumbs from 6	¹/2 cup chopped fresh
stale rolls or 10 slices	cilantro
of bread	2 cups flour
¹/4 (1-pound) package	2 teaspoons salt
saltines, crushed	1 teaspoon black pepper
3 tablespoons chili	Peanut oil for deep-
powder	frying

Remove spiny needles from the cactus pads with a paring knife. Slice pads into ¹/2-inch-wide strips. Wash and drain. Blend the eggs and milk in a bowl. Combine the bread crumbs, saltines, chili powder, cayenne pepper, 2 tablespoons salt and cilantro in a bowl and mix well. Coat the cactus strips with a mixture of the flour, 2 teaspoons salt and black pepper. Dip in the egg mixture and coat with the seasoned crumbs. Deep-fry at 350 degrees for 1 to 2 minutes or until browned. Serve immediately. Yield: 20 servings.

Pat McKelvy, Preceptor Theta Sigma
Brackettville, Texas

BLOOMIN' ONIONS

4 large sweet onions	2¹/2 teaspoons black
¹/3 cup cornstarch	pepper
3¹/2 cups flour	24 ounces beer
2 teaspoons minced	2 teaspoons garlic
garlic	powder
2 tablespoons plus 4	¹/2 teaspoon cayenne
teaspoons paprika	pepper
1 teaspoon salt	

Cut the onions in strips from the top to the core, leaving them connected at the base. Combine the cornstarch, 1¹/2 cups of the flour, minced garlic, 2 tablespoons of the paprika, salt, 2 teaspoons of the black pepper and beer in a bowl and mix well; let stand for about 5 minutes. Coat each onion with a mixture of the remaining 2 cups flour, 4 teaspoons

paprika, the remaining ¹/2 teaspoon black pepper, garlic powder and cayenne pepper. Coat with the cornstarch mixture and coat again with the flour mixture. Deep-fry 1 at a time at 375 degrees for 1¹/2 minutes; turn and fry for 1¹/2 minutes longer. Drain on paper towels. Serve with a dipping sauce made of 2 cups mayonnaise, ¹/2 cup chili sauce and ¹/2 teaspoon cayenne pepper. Yield: 8 to 12 servings.

Norma Gilkey, Laureate Pi
Glendora, California

TOMATOES COUNTRY STYLE

You know it's summer when you can grow your own fresh tomatoes large enough to make this delicious country-style dish.

1 garlic clove, minced	4 to 6 large tomatoes
¹/4 cup minced fresh	¹/2 cup flour
parsley	1 egg, beaten well with
¹/8 teaspoon salt	1 tablespoon milk
8 ounces cream cheese,	²/3 cup dry bread crumbs
softened	3 tablespoons butter
1 teaspoon chopped	3 tablespoons olive oil
fresh basil (optional)	

Combine the garlic, parsley, salt, cream cheese and basil in a food processor container or mixing bowl; mix well. Cut the tomatoes into a total of 12 even slices about ¹/2 inch thick. Spread each of 6 slices with 2 tablespoons of the cream cheese mixture; cover with remaining tomato slices to make 6 sandwiches. Coat each tomato sandwich with flour. Dip in the egg mixture and coat with the bread crumbs. Fry in a mixture of butter and olive oil in a skillet over medium heat until both sides are brown. Garnish with additional fresh basil or parsley if desired. Yield: 6 servings.

Dodie Ashlock, Gamma Zeta
Sand Springs, Oklahoma

ZUCCHINI ROUNDS

¹/2 cup shredded onions	¹/4 cup grated Parmesan
¹/2 cup (2 ounces)	cheese
shredded sharp	¹/8 teaspoon pepper
Cheddar cheese	2 tablespoons butter,
²/3 cup baking mix	melted
4 cups shredded	
zucchini, drained	

Combine the onions, Cheddar cheese, baking mix, zucchini, Parmesan cheese and pepper in a bowl and mix well. Drop by spoonfuls in hot butter in a skillet and bake as for pancakes. Yield: 12 to 15 servings.

Diana Rae Krebs, Alpha Zeta Alpha
Lowry City, Missouri

TATER-DIPPED VEGGIES

Zucchini, mushrooms, broccoli, bell peppers, and cauliflower are good vegetable selections for this dish.

1 cup instant potato flakes	1/4 cup reduced-calorie or regular margarine, melted
1/3 cup grated Parmesan cheese	3 egg whites
1/4 teaspoon celery salt	4 cups assorted raw vegetables, cut into bite-size pieces
1/8 to 1/4 teaspoon garlic salt	

Preheat the oven to 400 degrees. Combine the potato flakes, Parmesan cheese, celery salt, garlic salt and margarine in a small bowl and mix well. Beat the egg whites with a fork in a separate bowl until foamy. Dip the vegetables in the egg whites; coat with the potato flake mixture. Bake for 15 to 20 minutes or until lightly browned. Serve at once.
Yield: 4 cups batter.

Martha Haley, Preceptor Beta Eta
Jackson, Tennessee

DILL PICKLE WRAPS

1 (6- to 8-ounce) tub spreadable cream cheese	12 thin slices cooked ham
	12 dill pickle spears

Spread the cream cheese evenly over the ham slices. Place a pickle spear at the end of each slice and roll as for a jelly roll. Secure with wooden picks. Cut into bite-size pieces. Yield: 48 servings.

Darla Gaus, Epsilon Gamma
Canton, Missouri

BACON-WRAPPED WATER CHESTNUTS

2 (8-ounce) cans whole water chestnuts, drained	1/2 cup packed brown sugar
2 pounds sliced bacon	1 (14-ounce) bottle ketchup
1 cup granulated sugar	

Cut the water chestnuts in half. Cut the bacon into thirds. Wrap each water chestnut half with a piece of bacon and secure with a wooden pick. Arrange in a 9×13-inch baking dish. Bake at 350 degrees for 30 minutes; drain. Combine the granulated sugar, brown sugar and ketchup in a small bowl and mix well. Drizzle the ketchup mixture over the wrapped water chestnuts. Bake for 30 minutes longer.
Yield: 75 servings.

Heather Hill, Preceptor Gamma Psi
Terre Haute, Indiana

BACON-WRAPPED BREADSTICKS

Substitute garlic powder for the garlic salt, or use any other kind of salt or powder you prefer.

24 (4 1/2-inch) sesame breadsticks	1 cup (4 ounces) grated Parmesan cheese
12 slices bacon, cut in half	2 tablespoons garlic salt

Wrap each breadstick in bacon in a spiral, beginning at one end and ending at the other. Arrange on a parchment-lined baking sheet. Bake at 350 degrees for 15 minutes or until bacon is browned. Roll at once in a mixture of the cheese and garlic salt. Let cool. Serve at room temperature. Yield: 24 servings.

Mary A. McCaffrey, Preceptor Iota Mu
Port St. Lucie, Florida

RUMAKI

1 (8-ounce) can whole water chestnuts, drained	1/2 cup soy sauce
	1/4 teaspoon ginger
1/2 pound chicken livers	1/4 teaspoon curry powder
8 bacon slices, cut in half	

Embed a water chestnut in a chicken liver, then wrap in a half-slice of bacon. Secure with a wooden pick. Repeat with the remaining water chestnuts, chicken livers and bacon. Combine the soy sauce, ginger and curry powder in a large glass dish and mix well. Add the wrapped water chestnuts. Marinate, covered, in the refrigerator for 1 hour; drain. Arrange on a rack in a shallow pan. Bake at 400 degrees for 15 to 18 minutes or until bacon is cooked through and crisp. Yield: 16 servings.

Bobbie Quick, Lambda Master
Mentor, Ohio

BACON FRANKFURTER ROLL-UPS

1 pound frankfurters	1 cup (or more) packed brown sugar
1 pound sliced bacon	

Cut the frankfurters and bacon slices into thirds. Wrap each bacon piece around a frankfurter piece and secure with a wooden pick. Arrange in a baking dish that has been sprayed with nonstick cooking spray. Sprinkle brown sugar over the top. Cover tightly with plastic wrap and chill for 8 to 10 hours. Bake, uncovered, at 300 degrees for 2 hours.
Yield: 2 dozen (or more).

Minda Walters, Delta Psi
Highlands Ranch, Colorado

CRAB MEAT BACON ROLLS

1 egg, well beaten
1/4 cup tomato juice
1 (6-ounce) can crab
    meat, drained and
    flaked
1/2 cup fine dry bread
    crumbs
1 tablespoon chopped
    fresh parsley

1 tablespoon lemon
    juice
1/4 teaspoon salt
1/4 teaspoon
    Worcestershire sauce
Dash of pepper
9 slices bacon, cut in
    half

Place the egg and tomato juice in a bowl and whisk to combine. Add the crab meat, bread crumbs, parsley, lemon juice, salt, Worcestershire sauce and pepper; mix well. Roll crab mixture into 18 fingers. Wrap in bacon slices; secure with wooden picks. Arrange on a large flat baking pan. Broil 5 inches from the heat source for 10 minutes, turning frequently to brown evenly. Yield: 18 servings.

Al Briggs, Xi Kappa Upsilon
Cameron, Missouri

CRAB MEAT AND PROSCIUTTO

1/4 cup butter
2 tablespoons finely
    chopped shallots
2 cups cooked crab meat
2 tablespoons chopped
    fresh parsley

2 teaspoons finely
    crushed dried
    tarragon
6 large thin slices
    prosciutto

Melt the butter in a skillet over medium heat. When butter begins to sizzle, add the shallots and sauté for 3 minutes. Add the crab meat and cook just long enough to warm, tossing with the shallots and butter. Remove from heat. Add the parsley and tarragon and toss. Spoon the crab mixture carefully over half of each prosciutto slice; fold the other half back over the crab mixture. Arrange on a nonstick baking sheet. Broil 6 inches from the heat source just long enough to heat the ham. Serve with melba toast or crisp rolls. Yield: 6 servings.

Janice Nelson, Eta Xi
Birmingham, Alabama

❖ SALMON BELLIES

2 cups small cooked
    peeled shrimp
1 cup bottled Alfredo
    sauce
2 tablespoons prepared
    horseradish

Salt and pepper
    to taste
8 thin slices smoked
    salmon

Combine the shrimp, Alfredo sauce, horseradish, salt and pepper in a bowl and mix well. Place 1/8 of the shrimp mixture in the center of each salmon slice and roll into a cornet shape. Serve over a bed of chopped lettuce with lemon wedges. Yield: 4 to 8 servings.

Ethel Armitage, Laureate Beta Delta
Delta, British Columbia, Canada

KOREAN BARBECUED RIBS

3 pounds short ribs
1 cup soy sauce
1/2 cup sugar
4 green onions, finely
    chopped

1/3 cup sesame oil
3 tablespoons toasted
    sesame seeds
4 garlic cloves, minced
Salt and pepper to taste

Place the ribs in a bowl. Combine the soy sauce, sugar, green onions, sesame oil, sesame seeds, garlic, salt and pepper in a bowl and mix well. Pour the soy sauce mixture over the ribs. Marinate, covered, in the refrigerator for at least 6 hours. Grill over medium coals for 15 minutes on each side or until cooked through. Serve hot or cold. Yield: 12 servings.

Cecil Rose and Gail Utter, Beta Epsilon
Austin, Nevada

BEEF TONGUE VINAIGRETTE

1 beef tongue
Salt and pepper to taste
1 tablespoon pickling
    spice
3 tablespoons chopped
    fresh parsley

1/2 cup pimento-stuffed
    olives, sliced
Mustard Vinaigrette
1 teaspoon paprika

Bring enough water to cover the tongue to a boil in a saucepan. Add the tongue, salt, pepper and pickling spice. Simmer for 2 to 3 hours or until tender. Let stand in the broth to cool. Remove skin and cut into thin slices. Layer the tongue slices, parsley and olives alternately in a deep serving dish until all the tongue is used, ending with the olives. Pour the Mustard Vinaigrette over the top. Sprinkle with paprika and garnish with olives and parsley. Chill, covered, for 8 to 10 hours. Serve cold. Yield: 8 to 10 servings.

MUSTARD VINAIGRETTE

1 cup olive oil
1/2 cup red wine vinegar
1 bunch green onions,
    chopped
2 tablespoons prepared
    mustard

3 hard-cooked eggs,
    chopped
Salt and pepper
    to taste

Combine the olive oil, vinegar, green onions, mustard, eggs, salt and pepper in a bowl and mix well.

Dolores T. Fritz, Laureate Zeta Lambda
Houston, Texas

CHICKEN DIJON TIDBITS

2 whole chicken breasts	1 teaspoon lemon juice
1/2 cup (1 stick) margarine	1/8 teaspoon salt
2 teaspoons Dijon mustard	1/4 cup fine dry bread crumbs
1 garlic clove, minced	1/4 cup grated Parmesan cheese
1 tablespoon chopped parsley	

Rinse the chicken and pat dry. Remove and discard the skin and bones. Cut into bite-size pieces. Melt the margarine in a skillet over medium heat. Add the chicken, Dijon mustard, garlic, parsley, lemon juice and salt. Sauté for 5 to 10 minutes or until chicken is lightly browned on all sides. Remove from heat. Sprinkle with bread crumbs and Parmesan cheese and toss to coat the chicken. Yield: 24 servings.

Harriett Goodin, Laureate Delta Beta
Princeton, Missouri

CHICKEN NUGGETS

These may be frozen before baking, then removed from the freezer and baked when needed. Increase the baking time by a few minutes.

4 whole boneless skinless chicken breasts	1/4 cup grated Parmesan cheese
1/2 cup fine dry unseasoned bread crumbs	1/2 teaspoon salt
	1 teaspoon thyme
	1 teaspoon basil
	1/2 cup melted butter

Cut the chicken into 1 1/4- to 1 1/2-inch-square nuggets. Combine the next 5 ingredients in a shallow bowl; mix well. Dip the chicken in melted butter; roll in the crumb mixture to coat. Arrange in a single layer on a foil-lined baking sheet. Bake at 400 degrees for 10 to 12 minutes or until golden. Serve with wooden picks. Yield: 56 to 60 pieces.

Bona L. Beckley, Omega Master
Alma, Michigan

BARBECUED CHICKEN PIECES

You can buy duck sauce in the oriental food section of the grocery store.

3 or 4 boneless skinless chicken breasts	Barbecue-flavor potato chips, crushed
1/2 cup (1 stick) butter, melted	Duck sauce

Cut the chicken into small bite-size pieces. Dip in melted butter and roll in potato chips. Arrange on a baking sheet that has been sprayed with nonstick cooking spray. Bake at 350 degrees for 15 to 20 minutes or until cooked through. Serve with duck sauce. Serve with wooden picks to handle the chicken pieces. Yield: 12 to 15 servings.

Ardith Eleanore Ashworth, Laureate Theta Beta
Windsor, California

CHICKEN FINGERS WITH HONEY MUSTARD

1/2 cup honey	1/2 teaspoon salt
1/4 cup Dijon mustard	1/4 teaspoon pepper
4 (4-ounce) boneless skinless chicken breasts	3/4 cup milk
	Vegetable oil for deep-frying
1 cup flour	

Combine the honey and Dijon mustard in a small bowl and blend well. Chill, covered, for 1 or 2 days before cooking the chicken. Rinse the chicken and pat dry. Cut into finger-size pieces. Combine the flour, salt and pepper in a shallow bowl. Dip the chicken in the milk. Roll it in the flour mixture to coat well. Place coated chicken on waxed paper. Pour 1/4 inch vegetable oil into a large heavy skillet. Heat to 350 degrees or until a cube of white bread dropped in the oil browns evenly in 1 minute. Place chicken in the hot oil 2 pieces at a time. Fry, turning once, for about 3 minutes on each side; drain on paper towels. Serve with honey mustard sauce. Yield: 16 servings.

Shirley Boston-Otis, Preceptor Iota
Lee's Summit, Missouri

PEKING CHICKEN WINGS

6 pounds chicken wings	1/2 cup honey
1/2 cup soy sauce	1/4 cup orange marmalade
1/4 cup dry sherry	1 teaspoon grated orange zest
1/3 cup hoisin sauce	
6 scallions, finely chopped	1 teaspoon grated lemon zest
2 garlic cloves, minced	
1/4 cup apple cider vinegar	1/8 teaspoon Tabasco sauce

Disjoint the wings and discard the tips. Combine the remaining ingredients in a large glass bowl and mix well. Add the chicken. Marinate, covered, in the refrigerator for 4 to 10 hours, stirring occasionally. Drain the chicken, reserving the marinade. Arrange the chicken on the rack of a foil-lined broiler pan. Bake at 375 degrees for 40 minutes, turning once and basting occasionally with reserved marinade. Yield: 24 servings.

Diana Martin, Kappa Alpha
Apex, North Carolina

SLOW-COOKER TERIYAKI WINGS

3 pounds chicken wings
1 onion, chopped
1 cup soy sauce
1 cup packed brown
   sugar
2 teaspoons ginger
2 garlic cloves, minced
1/4 cup dry sherry

Rinse the chicken and pat dry. Disjoint the wings and discard the tips. Place wings in a slow cooker. Combine the onion, soy sauce, brown sugar, ginger, garlic and sherry in a bowl and mix well. Pour the soy sauce mixture over the wings. Cook on High for 2 to 3 hours or on Low for 5 to 6 hours, stirring occasionally. Yield: 12 to 15 servings.

Debbie Beckwith, Alpha Delta Eta
Jefferson City, Missouri

CEBICHE

In Peru's colonial past, fishermen would use cut-up fish as bait ("cebos" means bait or lure), and they would marinate the leftover pieces of fish in lemon juice for their own consumption. The wealthy classes adopted this workingman's dish, adding other seafood and chiles.

4 cups fish stock
2 bay leaves
3 to 5 garlic cloves,
   minced
1 onion, chopped
1 1/2 pounds mixed
   seafood (peeled
   shrimp, squid rings,
   scallops)
3/4 cup ketchup
1/4 cup Mexican chile
   sauce
1/4 cup vinegar
Salt and pepper to taste
1/2 cup chopped fresh
   cilantro
4 tablespoons lime juice
1 avocado

Combine the fish stock, bay leaves, garlic and half the onion in a kettle over medium-high heat. Boil gently for 10 minutes or until onion is tender. Add the seafood and simmer for 5 minutes. Remove from heat. Let stand until cool. Remove the seafood, reserving the stock. Combine the ketchup, chile sauce, vinegar, salt and pepper in a large bowl and mix well. Stir in the seafood, the remaining onion, cilantro, lime juice and 1/2 cup or more of the remaining fish stock. Stir carefully. Peel and pit the avocado and cut into cubes; toss with additional lime juice to prevent discoloration. Serve Cebiche in individual bowls and garnish with avocado.
Yield: 12 to 15 servings.

Maria Guadalupe Amaya, Preceptor Epsilon Phi
Windsor, Ontario, Canada

PARTY SHRIMP

There is no need to serve cocktail sauce with this delicious shrimp appetizer. For the holidays, cover a styrofoam cone with lettuce or any other pretty edible green; spear shrimp with wooden picks and arrange on the green "tree." For color, arrange cherry tomatoes in between the shrimp. Place the "tree" on a serving platter and arrange any unused shrimp around the bottom.

2 pounds fresh or frozen
   large shrimp, peeled
   and deveined
4 envelopes Italian
   salad dressing mix
1 cup (about) lemon
   juice
Garlic powder to taste
Dill weed to taste
Pinch of salt (optional)

Prepare the Italian salad dressing using the package directions with 1 cup white vinegar and 2 cups vegetable oil. Place shrimp in a saucepan. Pour half the prepared salad dressing over the shrimp. Add enough water and lemon juice to cover the shrimp. Add garlic powder and dill weed and bring to a boil. Reduce heat and simmer for a few minutes or until shrimp turns pink; do not overcook. Drain and cool in a colander. Place cooled shrimp in a bowl. Pour the remaining salad dressing over the shrimp. Sprinkle with additional garlic powder, dill weed and salt. Marinate in the refrigerator, covered, for 4 to 10 hours, stirring several times. At serving time, fill a large platter with crushed ice and place a smaller platter over the ice. Arrange the shrimp on the smaller platter. Yield: 20 or more servings.

Marilyn Mason, Preceptor Iota Mu
Ft. Pierce, Florida

COCONUT SHRIMP

1 pound medium shrimp,
   peeled and deveined
1 egg
3/4 cup milk
1/4 cup packed brown
   sugar
1 1/4 cups flour
Vegetable oil for deep-
   frying
2 (4-ounce) packages
   shredded
   unsweetened coconut

Cut shrimp into halves lengthwise. Combine the egg, milk and brown sugar in a mixing bowl and beat until well blended. Add the flour gradually, beating until smooth. Pour vegetable oil in an electric skillet to a depth of 1 inch. Place coconut in a shallow bowl. Dip shrimp in egg mixture, then coat with coconut. Deep-fry at 375 degrees for about 5 minutes or until brown. Serve hot. Yield: about 40 pieces.

Kathy Engel, Laureate Epsilon Psi
Leesburg, Florida

SHRIMP WITH CURRY APRICOT SAUCE

24 jumbo shrimp, peeled
  and deveined
1½ cups shredded
  unsweetened coconut,
  toasted
¼ cup cornstarch
½ teaspoon salt
3 egg whites
2 tablespoons (or more)
  vegetable oil
1 cup mayonnaise
3 tablespoons apricot
  preserves
1 teaspoon curry powder

Rinse the shrimp and pat dry. Combine the coconut, cornstarch and salt in a shallow bowl. Beat the egg whites in a separate bowl until foamy. Dip shrimp 1 at a time in the egg whites, then roll in the coconut mixture. Heat the oil in a skillet over medium-high heat. Cook the shrimp in hot oil until brown, stirring frequently. Drain on paper towels. Serve with a sauce made of a mixture of the mayonnaise, apricot preserves and curry powder. Yield: 24 pieces.

Lorraine Fenton, Xi Omicron
Whitinsville, Massachusetts

SWEET-AND-SOUR KIELBASA

½ cup sugar
½ cup chicken broth or
  water
⅓ cup white vinegar
1 teaspoon vegetable oil
1 teaspoon soy sauce
¼ teaspoon salt
1 garlic clove, crushed
2 tablespoons
  cornstarch
2 tablespoons cold water
1 tomato, cut into
  16 pieces
1 small green bell
  pepper, cut into
  1-inch pieces
1 (8-ounce) can
  pineapple chunks in
  heavy syrup, drained
1 (14- to 16-ounce)
  package kielbasa, cut
  into bite-size pieces

Combine the sugar, chicken broth, vinegar, vegetable oil, soy sauce, salt and garlic in a 2-quart saucepan over medium-high heat and bring to a boil, stirring occasionally. Stir a mixture of the cornstarch and cold water into the sugar mixture. Cook for 10 seconds or until thickened, stirring constantly. Stir in the tomato, bell pepper and pineapple. Bring to a boil. Remove from heat and stir in kielbasa. Keep mixture warm in a slow cooker or large fondue pot. Serve with wooden picks. Yield: 20 to 24 servings.

Jennifer Canada, Beta Nu
Connellsville, Pennsylvania

RED CURRANT KIELBASA

2 (12-ounce) packages
  kielbasa, cut into
  bite-size pieces
1 (12-ounce) bottle chili
  sauce
¾ cup red currant jelly
2 teaspoons prepared
  mustard
1 teaspoon lemon juice
1 (12-ounce) can
  pineapple chunks in
  juice, drained

Place the kielbasa in a saucepan over low heat. Combine the chili sauce, red currant jelly, mustard and lemon juice in a bowl and blend well. Add the chili sauce mixture to the kielbasa. Stir in the pineapple. Bring to a simmer. Simmer for 15 minutes, stirring occasionally. Serve in a chafing dish.
Yield: more than 24 servings.

Mary Miller, Preceptor Upsilon
Omaha, Nebraska

SWEET SAUSAGE BITES

1 (8-count) can crescent
  rolls
1 (16-ounce) package
  small cocktail
  sausages
½ cup melted butter
3 tablespoons honey
3 tablespoons brown
  sugar
¾ cup chopped pecans

Unroll the dough. Separate into 4 rectangles, pressing the perforations to seal. Cut each rectangle into 12 thin strips. Wrap 1 dough strip around each cocktail sausage. Combine the butter, honey and brown sugar in a bowl and blend well. Spread the honey mixture in a 9×13-inch baking dish that has been sprayed with nonstick cooking spray. Sprinkle evenly with the pecans. Arrange the wrapped sausages over the honey mixture. Bake at 350 degrees for 15 to 20 minutes or until dough is golden brown. Yield: 48 servings.

Lynn McMaster, Preceptor Alpha Delta
Spring Lake, Michigan

TENNESSEE BOURBON HOT DOGS

1 pound beef hot dogs,
  cut into bite-size
  pieces
½ cup packed brown
  sugar
1 cup ketchup
¾ cup bourbon
¼ teaspoon grated
  onion

Combine the hot dogs, brown sugar, ketchup, bourbon and onion in a large saucepan over medium-high heat and bring to a boil. Reduce heat and simmer, partially covered, for 1 hour. Serve in a fondue pot. Yield: 32 to 40 servings.

Linda Ling, Laureate Lambda
Memphis, Tennessee

SMOKY FRANKFURTER BITES

1 pound skinless
  frankfurters
2 tablespoons butter or
  margarine
¼ teaspoon onion salt
¼ teaspoon garlic salt
¼ teaspoon celery salt
1½ teaspoons angostura
  bitters

Cut the frankfurters into 1-inch pieces. Melt the butter in a skillet over medium heat. Stir in the onion salt, garlic salt, celery salt and angostura bitters. Add the frankfurter pieces and stir to coat. Cook over medium heat until pieces are dark brown and crusty, stirring occasionally. Spear with wooden picks and serve hot. Yield: 32 to 40 servings.

Lavada Harrison, Laureate Delta Sigma
Poplar Bluff, Missouri

SWEET HOT LITTLE SMOKIES

1 (16-ounce) jar grape jelly	*2 (16-ounce) packages little smoked sausages*
1 (12-ounce) jar chili sauce	

Combine the jelly, chili sauce and sausages in a large saucepan over medium heat. Cook until jelly is dissolved, stirring frequently. Place in a slow cooker to serve. Yield: 48 servings.

Carla Schmitz, Omega Phi
Parnell, Missouri

SAUCY TURKEY MEATBALLS

1 cup old-fashioned rolled oats	*1 teaspoon chili powder*
3/4 cup fat-free evaporated milk	*1/4 teaspoon garlic salt*
1 medium onion, chopped	*1/4 teaspoon pepper*
1 teaspoon salt	*1 1/2 pounds lean ground turkey*
	Sweet Sauce

Combine the oats, evaporated milk, onion, salt, chili powder, garlic salt and pepper in a large bowl. Crumble the turkey over the oats mixture and mix well. Shape into 1-inch balls. Arrange in a 9×13-inch baking dish that has been sprayed with nonstick cooking spray. Bake, uncovered, at 350 degrees for 10 to 15 minutes. Pour the Sweet Sauce evenly over the meatballs. Bake, uncovered, for 35 to 45 minutes longer. Yield: 15 servings.

SWEET SAUCE

2 cups ketchup	*2 tablespoons liquid smoke*
1 1/2 cups packed brown sugar	*1/2 teaspoon garlic salt*
1/4 cup chopped onion	

Combine the ketchup, brown sugar, onion, liquid smoke and garlic salt in a bowl and mix well.

Sharron Wooldridge, Alpha Zeta Alpha
Clinton, Missouri

ROSY MEATBALLS

1 (16-ounce) can whole cranberry sauce	*1/2 cup bread crumbs*
1 (8-ounce) can tomato sauce	*1 egg, beaten*
1 pound ground beef	*1 teaspoon minced onion*
	1/4 teaspoon dry mustard
	Salt and pepper to taste

Combine the cranberry sauce and tomato sauce in a small bowl and mix well. Combine the remaining ingredients in a bowl and mix well. Shape into 1-inch balls. Brown on all sides in a large skillet over medium heat; drain. Pour the cranberry mixture over the meatballs and simmer, covered, for 30 minutes. Yield: 8 to 12 servings.

Mary Lou Markley, Laureate Pi
Glendora, California

COCKTAIL MEATBALLS

2 pounds ground beef	*1 cup crushed cornflakes*
1/3 cup dried parsley	*1 (16-ounce) can jellied cranberry sauce*
2 eggs	*2 tablespoons brown sugar*
2 tablespoons soy sauce	
1/3 cup ketchup	*1 (12-ounce) bottle chili sauce*
2 tablespoons instant chopped onions	*1 tablespoon lemon juice*
1/4 teaspoon garlic powder	

Combine the first 8 ingredients in a large bowl and mix well. Shape into walnut-size balls. Arrange in a 10 1/2×15 1/2 glass baking dish. Combine the cranberry sauce, brown sugar, chili sauce and lemon juice in a medium bowl and mix well. Pour over the meatballs. Bake, uncovered, at 350 degrees for 45 minutes or until cooked through. Serve with wooden picks. Yield: 2 dozen.

Sheila Merrill, Epsilon Beta
Princeton, Missouri

EASY BEER AND KETCHUP MEATBALLS

1 (28-ounce) bottle ketchup	*2 teaspoons garlic powder*
24 ounces beer	*1 onion, chopped*
1 1/2 pounds ground beef	

Pour the ketchup and beer into a slow cooker on High. Combine the ground beef, garlic powder and onion in a large bowl and mix well. Shape into 3/4-inch balls. Arrange meatballs in a 9×13-inch baking dish. Bake at 400 degrees for 20 minutes. Add the meatballs to the ketchup mixture in the slow cooker and cook on High for 3 hours. Yield: 2 1/2 to 3 dozen.

Betty West, Laureate Omicron
Pahrump, Nevada

GLAZED MEATBALLS

1 pound ground beef	1/2 teaspoon
1/2 cup fine bread crumbs	Worcestershire sauce
1/2 cup minced onion	2 tablespoons vegetable
1/4 cup milk	oil
1 egg, beaten	1/2 cup bottled chili
1 tablespoon chopped	sauce
parsley	1 cup (12-ounce jar)
1 teaspoon salt	grape jelly
1/8 teaspoon pepper	

Combine the ground beef, bread crumbs, onion, milk, egg, parsley, salt, pepper and Worcestershire sauce in a large bowl; mix well. Shape into 1-inch balls. Cook in hot oil in a skillet over medium heat for 10 to 15 minutes or until browned. Drain on paper towels. Combine the chili sauce and grape jelly in a medium saucepan over medium heat; stir well. Add the meatballs and simmer, uncovered, for 30 minutes, stirring occasionally. Serve in a chafing dish. Yield: 2 dozen.

Carol Sizemore, Preceptor Alpha Upsilon
Northfork, West Virginia

❖ BRANDY MEATBALLS

1 egg, beaten	1 tablespoon brandy
2 tablespoons milk	1 tablespoon
1 pound ground beef	Worcestershire sauce
1 pound ground pork	2 tablespoons chopped
1 teaspoon garlic	green onions
powder	2 tablespoons chopped
1 teaspoon prepared	green bell pepper
horseradish	Brandy Sauce

Whisk the egg and milk together in a large bowl. Add the ground beef, ground pork, garlic powder, horseradish, brandy, Worcestershire sauce, green onions and bell pepper and mix well. Shape into 1-inch balls and arrange in a 9×13-inch baking dish. Bake at 350 degrees for 15 minutes or until cooked through; drain well. Pour hot Brandy Sauce over the meatballs in a serving dish. Serve with wooden picks. Yield: about 2 dozen.

BRANDY SAUCE

1 tablespoon cornstarch	3 tablespoons honey
1/4 cup red wine vinegar	2 tablespoons brandy
1/4 cup soy sauce	1/2 teaspoon ginger
3 tablespoons brown	1/2 teaspoon garlic
sugar	powder

Whisk the cornstarch and 1/4 cup cold water together in a saucepan. Whisk in the red wine vinegar, soy sauce, brown sugar, honey, brandy, ginger and garlic powder. Cook over medium heat until thickened, stirring constantly.

Wendy Lauer, Xi Gamma Theta
Waterloo, Ontario, Canada

FANCY COVERED MEATBALLS

1 pound lean ground	1 (8-count) can crescent
beef	rolls
1 envelope onion soup	Miscellaneous
mix	seasonings and seeds

Combine the ground beef and onion soup mix in a bowl and mix well. Shape into sixteen 1-inch balls. Unroll the crescent roll dough and separate into triangles. Cut each triangle in half to make 16 pieces. Press each piece of dough with the palm of the hand to flatten. Place a meatball on the wide end and roll up, bringing sides together and pinching to enclose. Arrange the meatballs on a baking sheet. Spray the top of the dough-wrapped meatballs with nonstick cooking spray and sprinkle with various toppings such as Italian seasoning, sesame seeds and poppy seeds. Bake at 375 degrees for 13 to 15 minutes or until lightly browned. Serve with a mustard dipping sauce. Yield: 16 servings.

Faye A. Magers, Laureate Beta Upsilon
Chester, Illinois

SAUERKRAUT BITES

1/2 pound bulk pork	1 teaspoon prepared
sausage	mustard
1 (14-ounce) can	1 teaspoon minced
sauerkraut, drained	garlic
and chopped	1/4 cup flour
2 tablespoons dry bread	1/2 teaspoon pepper
crumbs	2 eggs, well beaten
4 ounces cream cheese,	1/4 cup milk
softened	3/4 cup dry bread crumbs
2 tablespoons chopped	Vegetable oil for
fresh parsley	deep-frying

Brown the sausage in a skillet, stirring until finely crumbled; drain. Stir in the sauerkraut and 2 tablespoons bread crumbs. Combine the cream cheese, parsley, mustard and garlic and mix well. Stir the cream cheese mixture into the sausage mixture. Chill, covered, for at least 2 hours. Shape into 3/4-inch balls. Coat with a mixture of the flour and pepper. Whisk the eggs and milk together. Dip the floured sausage balls in the egg mixture; roll in the 3/4 cup bread crumbs. Deep-fry 3 or 4 at a time in 375-degree oil for 30 to 60 seconds or until golden brown. Yield: 2 1/2 dozen.

Vicky Williams, Xi Alpha Phi
Campbell River, British Columbia, Canada

SAUERKRAUT BALLS

1/4 cup (1/2 stick) butter	3 cups sauerkraut,
1 medium onion,	drained and chopped,
finely chopped	1/2 cup liquid reserved
(about 1/2 cup)	1 tablespoon chopped
1 1/3 cups chopped cooked	fresh parsley
ham	1 egg
1/2 garlic clove	1 cup milk
1/4 cup flour	Dry bread crumbs

Melt the butter in a skillet and lightly brown the onion. Stir in the ham and garlic and brown slightly. Add the flour and cook over medium heat for a few minutes or until light brown, stirring vigorously. Add the sauerkraut, reserved liquid and parsley. Cook and stir a few minutes longer. Chill, covered, for at least 1 hour. Shape into 1-inch balls. Combine the egg and milk in a shallow bowl and whisk until smooth. Dip the sauerkraut balls in the egg mixture; roll in additional flour, then in dry bread crumbs. Deep-fry in 375-degree oil until golden brown. Yield: 4 dozen.

Kathy Traster, Laureate Delta Psi
Barberton, Ohio

SPINACH BALLS

2 (10-ounce) packages	1 tablespoon garlic
frozen spinach,	powder
thawed	1 tablespoon minced
1 (8-ounce) package	onion
stove-top stuffing	1/3 cup butter, melted
mix	2/3 cup grated Parmesan
3 large eggs	cheese

Drain the spinach, pressing out the excess moisture. Prepare the stuffing using the package directions. Combine the spinach, stuffing, eggs, garlic powder, onion, butter and Parmesan cheese in a bowl and mix well. Shape into 2-inch balls. Arrange on a greased baking sheet. Bake at 350 degrees for 20 minutes or until lightly browned. Yield: 2 dozen.

Donna Straub, Xi Zeta Psi
Stroudsburg, Pennsylvania

HAWAIIAN HAM BALLS

1 egg	2 tablespoons
2 tablespoons milk	cornstarch
1/2 cup fine bread crumbs	1 cup pineapple juice
1/8 teaspoon pepper	1/4 cup vinegar
1 pound ground cooked	2 tablespoons sugar
ham	2 tablespoons soy sauce
2 tablespoons vegetable	1 tablespoon butter
oil	1 beef bouillon cube

Combine the egg, milk, bread crumbs and pepper in a large bowl and mix well. Add the ham and mix well. Shape into 1-inch balls. Brown the ham balls in the oil in a heavy skillet, 3 or 4 at a time. Remove the ham balls from skillet. Stir the cornstarch into the drippings. Add the pineapple juice, vinegar, sugar, soy sauce, butter and bouillon cube. Cook over medium heat until thick and bubbly, stirring constantly. Stir in the ham balls. Simmer for 5 to 7 minutes or until piping hot. Serve in a chafing dish with wooden picks. Yield: 5 dozen.

Mary Sheron, Preceptor Zeta
Fallon, Nevada

ARMADILLO EGGS

8 ounces Monterey Jack	15 to 18 fresh jalapeño
cheese, shredded	peppers
8 ounces Cheddar	1 egg, beaten
cheese, shredded	1 (12-ounce) package
1/2 pound bulk pork	Shake 'n Bake pork
sausage, hot	coating mix
1 1/2 cups baking mix	

Combine half the Monterey Jack cheese, half the Cheddar cheese, sausage and baking mix in a bowl and mix well. Slit the jalapeño peppers carefully and remove seeds and membranes; do not rinse. Stuff the peppers with the remaining cheeses. Pinch off a piece of sausage dough and pat into a 1/4-inch-thick square. Place a cheese-stuffed pepper in the center of the dough and roll to enclose, pressing seams and forming an egg shape. Roll in beaten egg and coat with the pork coating mix. Arrange coated armadillo eggs on a nonstick baking sheet. Bake at 350 degrees for 20 minutes or until lightly browned. Yield: 15 to 18 servings.

Sandy Stretcher, Xi Rho Psi
Port Neches, Texas

SAUSAGE BALLS

1 pound mild bulk pork	1 1/2 to 2 cups baking mix
sausage	
10 ounces sharp Cheddar	
cheese, shredded	

Combine the sausage and cheese in a large bowl and mix well. Mix in the baking mix a little at a time, using the hands. Roll into 1-inch balls. Arrange on an ungreased baking sheet. Bake at 350 degrees for 30 minutes or until brown and cooked through. Yield: 13 servings.

Kathey Sherrard, Preceptor Nu Omicron
Corsicana, Texas

HALFTIME CORNED BEEF SANDWICHES

1 (12-ounce) can corned beef	1/2 envelope onion soup mix
1 cup sour cream	12 hamburger buns

Put the corned beef through a food mill. Combine the corned beef, sour cream and onion soup mix in a bowl and mix well. Fill each hamburger bun with 1/12 of the corned beef mixture; wrap each sandwich in foil and arrange in a single layer on a nonstick baking sheet. Bake at 350 degrees for 15 minutes. Yield: 12 servings.

Katherine Radford, Xi Gamma Alpha
Waterford, Michigan

CORNED BEEF SANDWICHES

1 (16-ounce) can corned beef	1/2 cup chopped celery
4 hard-cooked eggs, chopped	1/2 cup mayonnaise
1 bunch green onions	1 teaspoon Worcestershire sauce
1/4 teaspoon pepper	1 loaf rye bread

Heat the corned beef in a skillet over medium heat, stirring until crumbly. Remove from heat. Combine the eggs, green onions, pepper and celery in a bowl and mix well. Add the mayonnaise and mix well. Stir in the Worcestershire sauce and corned beef mixture. Spread additional mayonnaise over slices of rye bread. Top each slice with corned beef mixture and a leaf of lettuce. Yield: 12 servings.

Madeline Parker, Xi Alpha Beta Omega
Jasper, Texas

HEARTY SHRIMP SALAD SANDWICHES

1 small head lettuce	4 hard-cooked eggs, thickly sliced
1 cup cooked green beans, cut into 1-inch pieces	2/3 cup olive oil
1 cup radishes, sliced	1 teaspoon salt
1 cucumber, peeled and thinly sliced	1/8 teaspoon pepper
3 tomatoes, peeled and sliced	1/3 cup white vinegar or lemon juice
1 (4-ounce) can shrimp, rinsed, drained	1 loaf bread, sliced

Wash, drain and separate the lettuce leaves. Place the lettuce, green beans, radishes, cucumber, tomatoes, shrimp and hard-cooked eggs in a bowl and toss to combine. Chill, covered, for at least 1 hour. Place the olive oil, salt and pepper in a covered jar and shake vigorously to combine. Add the olive oil mixture to the lettuce mixture and toss until well coated. Just at serving time, add the vinegar to the salad and toss again. Spread salad immediately between slices of buttered bread. Yield: 6 or more servings.

Anna Mae Staradumsky, Xi Beta Mu
Myrtle Beach, South Carolina

TUNA BUNSTEADS

1 cup (4 ounces) cubed American cheese	2 tablespoons each chopped green bell pepper, onion, black olives and sweet pickle
3 hard-cooked eggs, chopped	
1 (7-ounce) can tuna, drained	6 hot dog buns
1/2 cup Italian salad dressing	

Combine the cheese, eggs, tuna, salad dressing, bell pepper, onion, black olives and pickle; mix lightly. Split the hot dog buns and fill with the tuna mixture. Wrap in foil and arrange on a nonstick baking sheet. Bake at 250 degrees for 30 minutes or until filling is heated through and cheese is melted. Yield: 6 servings.

Jeannie Duffy, Mu Master
Weirton, West Virginia

STILTON WALNUT BISCUITS

These snacks can be made ahead and stored between sheets of waxed paper in an airtight container for up to 2 days, or they can be frozen for up to 1 month. Reheat at 375 degrees for 5 minutes.

1/2 cup (1 stick) butter, softened	1/2 cup finely chopped walnuts
2 cups (8 ounces) crumbled Stilton cheese	1/4 teaspoon salt
	1/4 teaspoon black pepper
	Pinch of nutmeg
4 egg yolks	Pinch of cayenne pepper
1 2/3 cups flour	

Combine the butter and cheese in a mixing bowl and beat until smooth. Beat in the egg yolks. Combine the flour, walnuts, salt, black pepper, nutmeg and cayenne pepper in a separate bowl and blend well. Add the flour mixture 1/3 cup at a time to the egg mixture, mixing to form a ragged dough. Roll into a ball. Chill, wrapped in plastic wrap, for 30 minutes. Roll into 1/8-inch thickness on a lightly floured surface. Cut out circles with a 1 1/2-inch cookie cutter. Arrange on a parchment paper-lined or buttered baking sheet and chill for 15 minutes. Bake at 400 degrees for 15 minutes or until light brown. Use top and bottom oven racks, switching baking sheets halfway through the baking time. Yield: about 2 dozen.

Margaret Smalyga, Xi Theta
Fonthill, Ontario, Canada

HERB BISCUITS

Another way to prepare these biscuits is to chill the ball of dough for 1 hour, roll to ¼-inch thickness on a lightly floured surface, and cut into shapes. Bake for 8 to 10 minutes, depending on the size of the shapes.

½ cup (1 stick) butter, softened	⅛ teaspoon salt
1 cup (4 ounces) shredded sharp Cheddar cheese	1 cup flour
	½ teaspoon dried dill weed or thyme or chives
⅛ teaspoon hot red pepper sauce	1 egg

Combine the butter, cheese, hot red pepper sauce, salt, flour, dill weed and egg in a bowl and mix until smooth. Roll into 4 thin logs and chill, wrapped in plastic wrap, for 1 hour. Slice into coins and arrange on a lightly buttered baking sheet. Bake in a preheated 400-degree oven for 8 to 10 minutes or until beginning to brown. Yield: 4 dozen.

Shirley S. Boon, Laureate Alpha Delta
Roanoke, Virginia

SAVORY BREAD

10 sun-dried tomato halves	1 tablespoon chopped fresh oregano, or 1 teaspoon dried
2 cups baking mix	
8 ounces feta cheese, coarsely crumbled	1 tablespoon chopped fresh basil, or 1 teaspoon dried
¾ cup milk	
1 (7-ounce) jar roasted red bell peppers, drained and finely chopped	1 garlic clove, minced
	2 tablespoons olive oil

Place the sun-dried tomatoes in a bowl and cover with boiling water. Let stand for 10 minutes; drain. Chop the tomatoes. Combine the tomatoes, baking mix, half the feta cheese and milk in a medium bowl, stirring until dough forms. Combine the remaining cheese, roasted red bell peppers, oregano, basil, garlic and olive oil in a small bowl and mix well. Drop half the dough mixture by tablespoons close together in an irregular pattern in a 9×9-inch baking dish that has been sprayed with nonstick cooking spray. Spread half the cheese mixture over the dough. Drop the remaining dough mixture over the cheese layer. Top with the remaining cheese mixture. Bake at 425 degrees for 20 minutes or until golden.
Yield: 6 to 8 servings.

Dianne Walsh, Kappa Beta
Clifton Park, New York

ANTIPASTO BREAD

1 (7-ounce) jar marinated artichoke hearts, drained and chopped	2 garlic cloves, minced
	2 (8-count) cans dinner rolls
⅓ cup sliced hard salami, chopped	½ cup (1 stick) butter, melted
⅓ cup chopped green or red bell pepper	4 ounces fresh Parmesan cheese, grated
½ cup sliced pitted black olives	

Place the artichokes, salami, bell pepper, black olives and garlic in a bowl; toss to combine. Cut each dinner roll into quarters. Dip 16 quarters in melted butter and roll in grated cheese. Fill a buttered bundt pan with the coated dough. Sprinkle ⅓ of the artichoke mixture over the dough quarters. Repeat the layers twice and top with a layer of dough quarters. Bake at 375 degrees for 27 to 30 minutes. Cover top loosely with foil if necessary to keep from overbrowning. Cool for 10 minutes. Invert onto a serving plate. Yield: 10 to 12 servings.

Patricia Shaffer, Xi Beta Upsilon
Decatur, Alabama

CHEESE PARTY BREAD

1 round sourdough bread loaf	½ cup chopped green onions
1 pound Monterey Jack cheese	2 to 3 teaspoons poppy seeds
½ cup butter or margarine, melted	

Cut the bread loaf carefully lengthwise and crosswise to but not through the bottom to form fingerlike pieces. Slice the cheese and insert the cheese slices into the bread cuts. Combine the butter, green onions and poppy seeds in a bowl and mix well. Drizzle the mixture over the bread, allowing the mixture to flow into the cuts. Wrap the loaf in foil and place on a baking sheet. Bake at 350 degrees for 15 minutes. Open the foil and bake for 10 minutes longer or until the cheese is melted. Yield: 6 to 8 servings.

Dorothy Thompson, Alpha Sigma Master
St. Charles, Missouri

---

*Crystal Livingstone, Theta Nu, Prince George, British Columbia, Canada, prepares **Salsa Tuna Melt** by combining 1 drained 6-ounce can tuna and ½ cup salsa in a bowl, spreading the mixture on 2 or 3 hamburger buns, sprinkling with ½ cup shredded Cheddar cheese, and broiling on Low until the cheese melts.*

Snacks & Beverages

CARAMEL CRACKERS

4 (5-ounce) packages
   mini butter crackers
1 cup dry-roasted
   peanuts
1/2 cup (1 stick) butter or
   margarine

1 cup sugar
1/2 cup light corn syrup
1 teaspoon vanilla
   extract
1 teaspoon baking soda

Combine the butter crackers and peanuts in a greased 9×13-inch baking pan. Combine the butter, sugar and corn syrup in a saucepan over medium-high heat. Bring to a boil and cook for 5 minutes. Remove from heat. Stir in vanilla and baking soda. Pour the sugar mixture over the cracker mixture; mix well. Bake in a preheated 250-degree oven for 1 hour, stirring every 15 minutes. Pour onto sheets of waxed paper. Let cool and break into pieces. Store in airtight containers. Yield: 9 cups.

Jacque-Faye Truitt, Laureate Beta Rho
Richmond, Indiana

NUTTY CRACKER DELIGHTS

42 original club
   crackers
1/2 cup (1 stick) butter
1/2 cup sugar

1 teaspoon vanilla
   extract
1 1/2 to 2 cups walnuts or
   pecans

Spread crackers in a single layer in a nonstick 10×15-inch cake pan. Melt the butter in a saucepan over medium heat. Add the sugar and bring to a boil, stirring constantly. Boil for 2 minutes without stirring. Remove from heat and stir in the vanilla. Pour evenly over the cracker layer. Sprinkle with the walnuts. Bake at 350 degrees for 10 to 12 minutes or until lightly browned. Break into pieces. Yield: 42 pieces.

Patricia Grant, Preceptor Kappa Epsilon
Arlington, Texas

WHITE CHOCOLATE NIBBLE

2 cups white chocolate
   wafers
1 cup cashews, chopped

4 cups Golden Grahams
1/4 cup dried cranberries
   (optional)

Place the white chocolate wafers in a large glass bowl and microwave on High for about 1 1/2 minutes or until melted, stirring once after 1 minute. Stir in the cashews, Golden Grahams and dried cranberries. Mix until well coated. Pour over a foil-lined baking sheet and spread evenly. Chill for at least 1 hour. Break into bite-size pieces. Yield: variable.

Marina Cram, Xi Zeta
Brandon, Manitoba, Canada

CHOCOLATE CEREAL SNACK

3 cups Cheerios
2 cups rice Chex
2 cups wheat Chex
1 pound "M & M's"
   Chocolate Candies

Peanuts and pretzels to
   taste
2 pounds white
   chocolate

Combine the Cheerios, rice Chex, wheat Chex, "M & M's," peanuts and pretzels in a large container and mix well. Melt the white chocolate; pour over the cereal mixture and mix well. Pour onto sheets of waxed paper. Let stand until set. Break into pieces and store in sealable plastic bags. Yield: about 3 quarts.

Myrna Zielinski, Xi Gamma Eta
Grand Rapids, Michigan

PRALINE PECAN CRUNCHIES

1 (16-ounce) package oat
   squares cereal
2 cups pecans, whole or
   coarsely chopped
1/2 cup light corn syrup
1/2 cup packed brown
   sugar

1/4 cup (1/2 stick) butter
   or margarine
1 teaspoon vanilla
   extract
1/2 teaspoon baking soda

Combine the cereal and pecans in a 9×13-inch baking dish. Combine the corn syrup, brown sugar and butter in a 2-cup microwave-safe bowl. Microwave butter mixture on High for 1½ minutes and stir. Microwave for ½ to 1½ minutes longer or until boiling. Stir in the vanilla and baking soda. Pour the butter mixture over the cereal and pecans; stir to coat. Bake in a preheated 250-degree oven for 1 hour, stirring every 20 minutes. Pour onto a baking sheet and let cool. Break apart. Yield: 10 cups.

Carole Cox, Xi Zeta Iota
Polk City, Florida

CLEVELAND CANDY

3 cups rice Chex
3 cups corn Chex
2 cups Cheerios
2 cups dry-roasted
   peanuts
2 to 3 cups pretzel sticks

1 (12-ounce) package "M
   & M's" Chocolate
   Candies
2 pounds white
   chocolate

Combine the rice Chex, corn Chex, Cheerios, peanuts, pretzel sticks and "M & M's" in a large roasting pan. Melt the white chocolate and pour over the cereal mixture. Stir gently to coat. Pour the coated ingredients onto sheets of waxed paper to harden. Break into pieces. Yield: 3 quarts.

Mariam G. Hasan, Delta Master
Glendale, California

EASY RANCH SNACK MIX

10 cups Crispix
2½ cups cheese crackers
2½ cups small pretzels
1 cup peanuts or pecans

¼ cup vegetable oil
1 envelope ranch salad
   dressing mix

Combine the Crispix, crackers, pretzels and peanuts in a 2-gallon plastic bag; close tightly and toss to combine. Add the vegetable oil to the cereal mixture and toss to coat. Sprinkle with dry ranch salad dressing mix and toss to distribute evenly. Store in airtight containers. Yield: 4 quarts.

Grace M. Baylor, Laureate Theta
Waynesboro, Pennsylvania

ALMOND COCONUT MIX

½ (16-ounce) package
   corn Chex
½ (18-ounce) package
   Golden Grahams
½ (16-ounce) package
   rice Chex
2 cups mixed nuts

2 cups slivered almonds
2 cups unsweetened
   flaked coconut
1½ cups (3 sticks) butter
2 cups sugar
2 cups light corn syrup

Combine the corn Chex, Golden Grahams, rice Chex, mixed nuts, almonds and coconut in a large bowl and mix well. Combine the butter, sugar and corn syrup in a saucepan over medium heat and bring to a boil. Boil for 5 minutes. Remove from heat. Pour over the dry ingredients and mix well. Pour onto sheets of waxed paper. Cool for 3 to 4 hours and break into pieces. Yield: 2 quarts.

Sue Simon
Meeteetse, Wyoming

NUTS AND BOLTS PARTY MIX

The party mix keeps for at least two months in coffee tins with tight lids, or you may store the mix in sealable plastic bags inside a container with a tight lid.

1 (15-ounce) package
   Cheerios
1 (12-ounce) package
   rice Chex or corn
   Chex
1 (17-ounce) package
   Crispix
2 (15-ounce) packages
   stick pretzels
4 pounds pecan halves
5 (9-ounce) cans cashew
   halves and pieces
2 cups vegetable oil
1 cup (2 sticks)
   margarine

2 cups bacon drippings,
   strained
2 tablespoons
   Worcestershire sauce
2 tablespoons Tabasco
   sauce
2 tablespoons garlic salt
2 teaspoons garlic
   powder
2 teaspoons celery salt
1 teaspoon onion
   powder

Divide a combination of the Cheerios, rice Chex, Crispix, pretzels, pecans and cashews between 2 large aluminum roasting pans. Combine the vegetable oil, margarine, bacon drippings, Worcestershire sauce, Tabasco sauce, garlic salt, garlic powder, celery salt and onion powder in a medium saucepan over medium-high heat. Bring to a boil, stirring often. Remove from heat and pour over the cereal mixture in both pans. Toss to coat evenly. Preheat the oven to 200 degrees. Bake for 1 hour. Every 15 minutes, remove pan from oven and toss cereal mixture several times to recoat and to prevent mixture from burning. This tossing time should not be counted as part of the hour of baking time. After baking, spread the mixture over layered newspaper or brown paper. Let cool for 30 to 40 minutes. Yield: 30 or more servings.

Mary Duncan, Eta Nu
Mobile, Alabama

❖ CRANBERRY ORANGE CHEX MIX

3 cups corn Chex
3 cups rice Chex
3 cups wheat Chex
1 cup sliced almonds
1/4 cup (1/2 stick) butter
   or margarine
1/4 cup packed brown
   sugar
1/4 cup frozen orange
   juice concentrate
1/2 to 3/4 cup dried
   cranberries

Combine the corn Chex, rice Chex, wheat Chex and almonds in a large bowl and mix well. Melt the butter in a saucepan over medium heat. Add the brown sugar and orange juice concentrate and stir well. Pour the butter mixture over the cereal mixture, stirring until evenly coated. Pour into a large ungreased roasting pan. Bake at 300 degrees for 30 to 45 minutes, stirring after every 15 minutes of baking. Stir in the cranberries. Let stand until cool. Store in airtight containers or plastic bags. Yield: 10 cups.

Margaret J. McDaniel, Laureate Gamma
Anchorage, Alaska

CAYENNE PRETZELS

1 cup vegetable oil
1 envelope ranch salad
   dressing mix
1 teaspoon garlic salt
1 teaspoon cayenne
   pepper
2 (10-ounce) packages
   pretzel sticks

Combine the vegetable oil, salad dressing mix, garlic salt and cayenne pepper in a small bowl and mix well. Spread the pretzels in 2 ungreased 10×15-inch cake pans. Drizzle the oil mixture over the pretzels and stir to coat. Bake at 300 degrees for 1 1/4 to 1 1/2 hours or until golden brown, stirring occasionally. Cool and store in airtight containers. Yield: 3 1/2 quarts.

Gwyn Bacot, Xi Alpha Upsilon
Natchez, Mississippi

PRETZELS WITH AN ATTITUDE

Adjust the spiciness to your taste.

1 (15-ounce) package
   pretzel sticks
1 (15-ounce) package
   pretzel twists
1 cup Cheez-It party
   mix
1 cup peanuts
3/4 cup vegetable oil
1 teaspoon cayenne
   pepper
1/2 teaspoon lemon
   pepper
1/2 teaspoon garlic
   powder
1 envelope ranch salad
   dressing mix

Combine the pretzel sticks, pretzel twists, Cheez-It party mix and peanuts in a large container. Place the vegetable oil, cayenne pepper, lemon pepper, garlic powder and dry salad dressing mix in a covered jar and shake vigorously to combine. Pour over the pretzel mixture, stirring to coat. The mixture may seem greasy but after standing awhile it will be a good consistency. Yield: 1 1/2 quarts.

Carol McLennan, Preceptor Alpha Tau
Lawton, Oklahoma

CORNY SNACK MIX

The vanilla chips may be melted in the microwave oven.

3 quarts popped popcorn
1 (15-ounce) package
   Corn Pops
1 (15-ounce) package
   small corn chips
2 (10- to 12-ounce)
   packages vanilla
   chips

Divide the popcorn, Corn Pops and corn chips between 2 large bowls. Melt half the vanilla chips and toss with the popcorn mixture in one of the bowls. Melt the remaining vanilla chips and toss with the popcorn mixture in the other bowl. Spread in two 10×15-inch cake pans and let cool. Store in airtight containers. Yield: 7 1/2 quarts.

Veronica Filipek, Laureate Epsilon
Minot, North Dakota

CANDY CORN SNACK MIX

You can find "wheat nuts" in the nuts section in the grocery store, but they are not real nuts, so they are safe for those who have nut allergies.

1 (8-ounce) package
   candy corn
1 (12-ounce) can honey-
   roasted peanuts
1 jar "wheat nuts"
   (optional)
1 package "M & M's"
   Chocolate Candies
   (optional)
1 (10-ounce) can mixed
   nuts (optional)
1 (2-ounce) package
   Reese's Pieces
   (optional)
1 (7-ounce) jar
   macadamia nuts
   (optional)
1 (10-ounce) package
   candy-coated pretzels
   (optional)

Combine the candy corn, peanuts and optional ingredients of your choice in a large bowl; mix well. Be sure to add 1 salty item for each sweet item you use and shake excess salt from nuts before adding to the mix. Store in airtight containers. Yield: 2 quarts.

Carol Bellairs, Iota Upsilon
Clarinda, Iowa

JACK-O'-LANTERN TUMBLE

8 cups Crispix
1 cup salted peanuts
1/4 cup (1/2 stick) butter
1/4 cup peanut butter
2 1/4 teaspoons
    Worcestershire sauce
1/2 teaspoon salt
1/4 teaspoon garlic
    powder
1 cup candy corn

Combine the Crispix and peanuts in a large bowl. Combine the butter, peanut butter, Worcestershire sauce, salt and garlic powder in a saucepan over low heat. Cook until all is melted, stirring frequently. Pour over the peanut mixture and stir to coat. Spread in a 10×15-inch cake pan. Bake at 250 degrees for 1 hour. Let stand until cool. Stir in the candy corn. Yield: 2 1/2 quarts.

Holly Crowell, Zeta Kappa
Red Oak, Iowa

FALL HARVEST POPCORN

2 quarts cooked popcorn
2 (9-ounce) cans
    shoestring potato
    snacks
1 cup salted peanuts or
    pecans
1/4 cup melted butter
1 teaspoon dill weed
1 teaspoon
    Worcestershire sauce
1/2 teaspoon lemon
    pepper
1/2 teaspoon garlic
    powder
1/2 teaspoon onion
    powder

Combine the popcorn, shoestring potatoes and peanuts in a large roasting pan. Combine the remaining ingredients in a small bowl and mix well. Pour the butter mixture evenly over the popcorn mixture; stir until coated. Bake at 325 degrees for 8 to 10 minutes or until hot and fragrant. Store in airtight containers. Yield: 2 1/2 quarts.

Barbara Kennedy, Laureate Lambda
Fort Pierce, Florida

PIZZA POPCORN

1 to 2 quarts popped
    popcorn
1/3 cup butter, melted
1/4 cup grated Parmesan
    cheese
1/2 teaspoon garlic salt
1/2 teaspoon crushed
    oregano
1/2 teaspoon basil
1/2 teaspoon salt
1/4 teaspoon onion
    powder

Spread the popcorn in a shallow baking pan. Combine the remaining ingredients in a small bowl and whisk to blend. Pour over the popcorn and mix well. Heat in a 300-degree oven for 15 minutes, stirring occasionally. Yield: 1 to 2 quarts.

Heidi McAllister, Beta Eta
Wichita, Kansas

BAKED CARAMEL CORN

1 cup (2 sticks) butter or
    margarine
2 cups packed light
    brown sugar
1/2 cup light corn syrup
1/2 teaspoon baking soda
1 teaspoon vanilla
    extract
1 cup chopped walnuts
    or pecans (optional)
3 bags popped
    microwave popcorn

Melt the butter in a saucepan over medium heat. Stir in the brown sugar and corn syrup. Bring to a boil, stirring just enough to blend well. Boil for 5 minutes without stirring. Remove from heat. Stir in the baking soda and vanilla; mix well. Place the walnuts and popcorn in a large bowl. Pour the brown sugar mixture over the popcorn mixture; mix well. Spread the popcorn mixture in 3 ungreased 9×13-inch baking pans. Bake at 350 degrees for 1 hour, stirring every 15 minutes. Yield: 9 to 18 servings.

Jane Van Doren, Preceptor Gamma Theta
Manchester, Michigan

HOLIDAY PECANS

1 egg white
4 cups pecan halves
1/2 cup sugar
1/4 teaspoon salt
1 1/2 tablespoons
    cinnamon

Beat the egg white in a large bowl until foamy. Add the pecans and stir until coated. Sprinkle with a mixture of the sugar, salt and cinnamon; stir gently until coated. Spread the pecan mixture in a lightly greased 10×15-inch cake pan. Bake at 300 degrees for 30 minutes, stirring every 10 minutes. Cool completely and store in an airtight container. Yield: 4 cups.

Sandra Mayo, Xi Mu Upsilon
Grayslake, Illinois

JACK'S PARTY PECANS

1/4 cup (1/2 stick) butter
1/4 cup Jack Daniel's
    whiskey
1 to 2 tablespoons
    Tabasco sauce
3 tablespoons sugar
1/2 teaspoon salt
1/2 teaspoon garlic
    powder
4 cups pecan halves

Combine the first 6 ingredients in a large saucepan over medium heat; bring to a boil. Reduce heat and simmer, uncovered, for 3 minutes, stirring occasionally. Remove from heat. Stir in the pecans; toss well to coat. Spread the pecan mixture in a single layer in a shallow baking pan. Bake at 300 degrees for 25 to 30 minutes or until crisp, stirring occasionally. Pour onto a foil-lined flat surface and cool. Store in airtight containers. Yield: 4 cups.

Marianne Funk, Laureate Beta Theta
Aurora, Colorado

SPICED PECAN HALVES

1 cup sugar	2 cups pecan halves
1/2 teaspoon cinnamon	1 teaspoon vanilla
1/3 cup evaporated milk	extract

Combine the sugar, cinnamon and evaporated milk in a heavy saucepan. Cook over medium heat to 234 to 240 degrees on a candy thermometer, soft-ball stage. Remove from heat. Stir in the pecan halves and vanilla. Pour onto waxed paper. Let stand until cool and dry. Yield: 2 cups.

Jessie R. Neighbors, Xi Beta Chi
Alexander City, Alabama

HOT SPICED PECANS

1 to 1 1/2 teaspoons chili powder	3 tablespoons olive oil
1 teaspoon curry powder	1 teaspoon Worcestershire sauce
1 teaspoon garlic salt	1/4 to 1/2 teaspoon hot red pepper sauce
1/4 teaspoon cumin	3 cups pecan halves
1/4 teaspoon ginger	
1/4 teaspoon cinnamon	

Combine the chili powder, curry powder, garlic salt, cumin, ginger and cinnamon in a skillet over low heat. Stir in the olive oil, Worcestershire sauce and hot red pepper sauce. Cook for 5 minutes to mellow and blend the flavors, stirring constantly. Place the pecans in a large bowl. Add the spice mixture and toss well to coat. Spread in a single layer in a 10×15-inch pan. Bake at 325 degrees for 15 minutes, shaking the pan occasionally. Cool completely. Store in a covered container. Yield: 3 cups.

Ann Miles, Xi Zeta Phi
Meriden, Kansas

CAJUN ROASTED PECANS

1 pound mammoth pecans	Garlic powder and white pepper to taste
1 tablespoon olive oil	Dried lemon peel to taste
2 tablespoons garlic-infused olive oil	Tony Chachere's Old Bay Seasoning to taste
Tarragon, rosemary, thyme and marjoram to taste	3 tablespoons butter, softened

Combine the pecans, olive oil and garlic-infused olive oil in a very large bowl; stir until mixed. Spread the pecans in a single layer on a large baking sheet. Bake at 350 degrees for 10 minutes. Remove from oven and return to the bowl. Add the remaining ingredients; stir until coated. Return to the oven and bake for 5 minutes. Cool and serve. Yield: 1 pound.

Mary D. Stockwell, Xi Lambda
Baton Rouge, Louisiana

TOASTED NUTS WITH ROSEMARY

1 egg white	4 teaspoons minced fresh rosemary, or
3 cups pecans, walnuts, hazelnuts or almonds	2 teaspoons crushed dried rosemary
1/2 teaspoon pepper	
1/2 teaspoon salt	

Beat the egg white in a large bowl until frothy. Add the walnuts and toss to coat. Toss in a mixture of the pepper, salt and rosemary. Spread in a 9×13-inch baking dish that has been lightly sprayed with nonstick cooking spray and lined with foil. Bake at 350 degrees for 15 to 20 minutes. Yield: 3 cups.

Eileen Sonnenberg, Iota Master
Sterling, Colorado

ORANGE-GLAZED PECANS

4 cups pecan halves	1 1/2 cups sugar
1/2 cup frozen orange juice concentrate	1/4 teaspoon cinnamon

Bake the pecans at 350 degrees in a shallow baking pan for 10 to 15 minutes or until toasted, stirring occasionally. Combine the orange juice concentrate, sugar and cinnamon in a heavy saucepan and bring to a boil. Boil for about 1 minute, stirring constantly. Remove from heat and stir in the toasted pecans. Drop the pecans 1/2 inch apart onto a foil-lined baking sheet. Let stand until cool and firm. Yield: 4 cups.

Dal'rene Hinson, Laureate Alpha Alpha
North Little Rock, Arkansas

CHEDDAR HA'PENNIES

1/2 cup (1 stick) butter, softened	1 cup sifted flour
8 ounces sharp Cheddar cheese, shredded	1/4 teaspoon salt
	3 tablespoons dry onion soup mix, crushed

Combine all the ingredients in a bowl and mix well. Shape into 1-inch-diameter logs. Wrap in foil and chill or freeze. When ready to bake, slice into 1/8-inch-thick coins. Arrange on an ungreased baking sheet. Bake at 375 degrees for 10 minutes or until golden brown. Serve hot. Yield: about 6 1/2 dozen.

Terry Skidgmore, Xi Kappa
Kingston, Nova Scotia, Canada

Ellie O'Donnell, Alpha Beta Master, Nazareth, Pennsylvania, makes a **Low-Cal Chickpea Snack** *by rinsing and draining a can of chickpeas, tossing with 1 teaspoon olive oil and baking at 350 degrees for 1 hour or until brown, shaking the pan several times. Season with butter flavoring or favorite seasoning.*

CHEDDAR CRISPS

Be sure to use real butter. You may freeze the dough instead of chilling it, but let it thaw for about 30 minutes before slicing.

2 cups (8 ounces) shredded sharp Cheddar cheese
1/2 cup (1 stick) butter
1 1/4 cups flour
3/4 cup chopped pecans

1/4 teaspoon garlic powder
1/8 teaspoon cayenne pepper
1/2 teaspoon salt

Combine the cheese, butter, flour, pecans, garlic powder, cayenne pepper and salt in a bowl and mix well. Shape into a log with one flat side. Chill, wrapped well in plastic wrap, for at least 2 hours. Slice into desired widths and arrange on an ungreased baking sheet. Bake at 350 degrees for about 10 minutes or until done to taste. Sprinkle lightly with paprika if desired. Yield: about 2 dozen.

Mary Ann Simmons, Preceptor Alpha Rho
Santa Maria, California

CHEESE COOKIES

1 cup (2 sticks) margarine, at room temperature
2 cups (8 ounces) shredded medium or sharp Cheddar cheese, at room temperature

2 cups flour
1/4 teaspoon (or more) hot red pepper flakes
2 cups crisp rice cereal

Cream the margarine and cheese in a mixing bowl until light and smooth. Mix in the flour and red pepper flakes. Mix in the crisp rice cereal with your hands, dipping fingers in flour if dough is too sticky. Drop by teaspoonfuls 2 inches apart onto a greased cookie sheet. Roll into balls and flatten with a fork in a crisscross pattern. Bake at 350 degrees for 15 to 20 minutes or until beginning to brown. Yield: 7 dozen.

Cheri L. Brown, Laureate Kappa
Fort Washington, Maryland

CHEESE STRAWS

I use a fancy serrated rolling cutter to cut the strips, but a knife may be used as well.

2 cups (8 ounces) shredded sharp Cheddar cheese
2 cups flour
1/2 teaspoon salt

1/4 cup (1/2 stick) butter, softened
Dash of pepper
5 1/2 tablespoons water

Combine the cheese, flour, salt, butter, pepper and water in a bowl and mix well. Roll very thin on a floured surface. Cut into strips of desired length. Arrange on an ungreased baking sheet. Bake at 350 degrees for 10 to 12 minutes or until beginning to brown. Yield: about 2 dozen.

Kathleen Radcliffe, Laureate Beta
Lancaster, Pennsylvania

SAVORY BUTTER CRACKER BITS

1/2 cup vegetable oil
1 envelope ranch salad dressing mix
1 tablespoon dill weed
1 teaspoon celery salt

1 teaspoon garlic powder
2 (10-ounce) packages miniature butter crackers with cheese

Combine the vegetable oil, salad dressing mix, dill weed, celery salt and garlic powder in a bowl and mix well. Place the miniature butter crackers in a large plastic container with a tight lid. Pour the well-stirred seasoned oil over the crackers. Shake gently to distribute the seasoned oil evenly. Chill for at least 24 hours, turning the container upside down several times to mix thoroughly. Yield: 20 servings.

Patricia Goodger, Xi Alpha Zeta
Laurel, Maryland

OYSTER CRACKER SNACK

1 (16-ounce) package oyster crackers
1/2 cup canola oil

1 teaspoon dill weed
1 tablespoon (or more) garlic powder

Combine the oyster crackers, canola oil, dill weed and garlic powder in a large bowl and mix well. Let stand for at least 8 to 10 hours, stirring occasionally to distribute the oil evenly. Yield: 6 to 8 servings.

Delores Schmidt, Beta Mu Master
Susanville, California

PARMESAN CRISPS

If you want curvy hors d'eouvres, place the hot circles over a rolling pin or bottle to cool.

1 cup (4 ounces) grated fresh Parmesan cheese or asiago cheese

Drop the Parmesan cheese by scant tablespoonfuls 2 inches apart onto a baking sheet lined with parchment paper. Bake at 375 degrees for 8 to 10 minutes or until golden. Yield: 10 servings.

Kris Weishaupt, Omicron
Fruitvale, British Columbia, Canada

CARAWAY TWIST STICKS

1 egg, beaten
1 tablespoon water
1 teaspoon country-
  style Dijon mustard
  or prepared mustard
3/4 cup (3 ounces)
  shredded Swiss
  cheese
1/4 cup finely chopped
  onion

2 teaspoons snipped
  parsley
1 1/2 teaspoons caraway
  seed
1/4 teaspoon garlic salt
1/2 (17-ounce) package
  frozen puff pastry,
  thawed

Whisk the egg, water and Dijon mustard together in a small bowl. Combine the cheese, onion, parsley, caraway seed and garlic salt in a medium bowl and mix well. Unfold the sheet of puff pastry onto a flat surface and brush generously with some of the egg mixture. Sprinkle the cheese mixture lengthwise over half the rectangle. Fold the plain pastry over the cheese layer, lining up the edges and pressing to seal. Brush the remaining egg mixture over the top. Slice horizontally into 1/2-inch-wide strips with a sharp knife. Twist each strip several times and place 1 inch apart on a greased baking sheet, pressing down the ends of each twisted strip. Bake at 350 degrees for 18 to 20 minutes or until light brown. Serve warm. Yield: 18 pieces.

Ruth Drummond, Xi Master
Pueblo, Colorado

POPPY STRIPS

Sesame seeds or caraway seeds may be substituted for the poppy seeds.

2 cups baking mix
1/4 teaspoon basil
1/2 cup milk
2 tablespoons melted
  butter

1 cup (4 ounces)
  shredded Cheddar
  cheese
1 teaspoon poppy seeds

Mix the baking mix and basil together in a bowl. Stir in the milk to form a soft dough. Roll into a soft ball and knead several times. Roll into a 10×16-inch rectangle on a floured surface. Brush with 1 tablespoon of the melted butter and sprinkle with the cheese. Fold into thirds lengthwise. Brush with the remaining butter and sprinkle with the poppy seeds. Bake at 425 degrees for 10 minutes or until golden brown. Yield: 15 to 16 servings.

Barbara Winquist, Alpha Pi Master
Seattle, Washington

TORTILLA CRISPS

I use kitchen scissors to cut each tortilla into wedges, cutting across the circle in both directions and then slicing the resulting quarters into halves. Use up all the cheese mixture; it may seem like too much, but once cooked, it will be just right.

3/4 cup (1 1/2 sticks)
  butter, softened
1/2 cup (2 ounces) grated
  Parmesan cheese
2 teaspoons parsley
  flakes
1/4 cup sesame seeds

1/2 teaspoon oregano
1/4 teaspoon onion
  powder
1/4 teaspoon garlic
  powder
12 (6-inch) flour
  tortillas

Combine the butter, Parmesan cheese, parsley flakes, sesame seeds, oregano, onion powder and garlic powder in a bowl and mix well. Spread each tortilla with a thick layer of the cheese mixture. Cut each tortilla into 8 wedges. Arrange on an ungreased baking sheet. Bake at 350 degrees for 12 to 15 minutes or until crisp and browned. Serve with salsa or a sour cream-based dip, or enjoy "as is." Yield: 96 pieces.

Linda McMullan, Alpha Rho
Hope, British Columbia, Canada

CHEESY SOFT PRETZELS

I enjoy these pretzels most when my younger sister and cousin, both age nine, come over after school. The recipe is simple enough for them to do most of the work, and we all love the results.

1 1/2 cups flour
1/2 cup (2 ounces)
  shredded Cheddar
  cheese
2 teaspoons baking
  powder
1 teaspoon sugar
3/4 teaspoon salt

2 tablespoons cold
  butter or margarine
2/3 cup milk
1 egg, beaten
Coarse salt
Ranch dressing
  (optional)

Combine the flour, cheese, baking powder, sugar and salt in a bowl. Cut in the butter until mixture resembles coarse crumbs. Stir in the milk until moistened. Knead on a floured surface for 1 minute. Divide dough in half. Roll each half into an 8×12-inch rectangle. Cut into 8-inch strips. Shape into pretzels and arrange on a greased baking sheet. Brush with egg and sprinkle with coarse salt. Bake at 400 degrees for 12 to 15 minutes or until golden brown. Serve with ranch dressing. Yield: about 25 pretzels.

Amanda Long, Alpha Epsilon Sigma
Memphis, Missouri

SORORITY PUNCH

3 cups sugar
3 (3-ounce) packages
   orange pineapple
   gelatin
2 (20-ounce) cans
   pineapple juice
1 (12-ounce) can frozen
   lemonade concentrate

2 (12-ounce) cans frozen
   orange juice
   concentrate
1 (2-liter) bottle ginger
   ale

Combine the sugar and 3 cups of water in a kettle and bring to a boil. Place 6 cups of water in a separate saucepan and bring to a boil; stir the gelatin into the boiling water. Stir the sugar water into the gelatin mixture. Let cool. Stir in the pineapple juice, lemonade and orange juice. Chill until serving time. Add the ginger ale just before serving. Yield: 50 servings.

Betty Foshee, Chi Master
Mount Carmel, Illinois

LEMON ORANGE REFRESHER

1 (6-ounce) can frozen
   lemonade concentrate
1 (6-ounce) can frozen
   orange juice
   concentrate

1 teaspoon vanilla
   extract
2 teaspoons almond
   extract
1/2 cup sugar

Prepare the lemonade and orange juice using the package directions. Add the vanilla, almond extract and sugar and mix well. Pour into ice-filled glasses. Yield: 6 to 8 servings.

Barbara Ross, Preceptor Iota Sigma
Carrollton, Texas

GOLD RUSH PUNCH

2 cups orange juice
2 cups lemon juice
2 cups cold water

1 cup sugar
1 gallon ginger ale

Combine the orange juice, lemon juice, water and sugar in a large punch bowl; stir to dissolve the sugar. Chill until serving time. When ready to serve, pour the ginger ale down the inside side of the bowl to reduce foaming. Garnish with floating orange and lemon slices. Yield: 20 cups.

Cathy Beaver, Preceptor Gamma Eta
Tulsa, Oklahoma

RHUBARB PUNCH

8 cups rhubarb cut into
   1-inch pieces
8 cups water
2 cups sugar

1/2 cup lemon juice
3/4 cup orange juice
Pinch of salt

Combine the rhubarb and water in a saucepan over medium-high heat and bring to a boil. Reduce heat and simmer for 15 minutes. Strain through cheesecloth or a sieve. Combine the rhubarb liquid, sugar, lemon juice, orange juice and salt in a punch bowl and mix well. Chill until serving time. Pour desired amount of rhubarb syrup into glasses and add ice and ginger ale to taste. Yield: 8 cups syrup.

Carolynne Campbell, Xi Zeta Phi
Tweed, Ontario, Canada

GRADUATION PINEAPPLE PUNCH

Select a drink mix flavor that will correspond with your school colors. Cherry plus raspberry makes a great red.

2 envelopes drink mix,
   any flavor
2 cups sugar
2 quarts water

1 (46-ounce) can
   pineapple juice
1 quart ginger ale

Combine the drink mix, sugar and water in a punch bowl and mix well. Stir in the pineapple juice. Chill until serving time. Add the ginger ale just before serving. Yield: 50 (1/2-cup) servings.

Carol Anderson, Xi Zeta Rho
LeMars, Iowa

❖ ORANGE LEMONADE

This recipe is from the late 1950s and early 1960s. My mother and our next-door neighbor took turns making it so we could have it almost every night as we sat outside enjoying the evening while the children played.

2 cups sugar
2 1/2 cups water
Juice of 3 oranges (about
   1 1/2 cups)
Juice of 6 lemons (about
   1 1/2 cups)

2 tablespoons finely
   shredded orange zest
1/4 cup lightly packed
   fresh mint leaves
   (optional)

Combine the sugar and water in a saucepan over medium heat. Heat until sugar dissolves, stirring occasionally. Remove from heat and let cool. Add the juices and the orange zest to the syrup and stir well. Place the mint leaves in a bowl. Pour the juice mixture over the mint leaves. Let stand at room temperature, covered, for 1 hour. Strain into glass jars. Chill, covered, until serving time. At serving time, fill glasses with ice; pour equal parts water and fruit syrup over the ice. Stir to combine.
Yield: 12 (8-ounce) servings.

Susan Mercer, Xi Beta Gamma
Prairie Village, Kansas

ICED TEA PUNCH

5 tablespoons instant tea	1 (6-ounce) can frozen lemonade concentrate
1 envelope unsweetened drink mix	2¹/₂ cups sugar
	1 gallon water

Combine the instant tea, unsweetened drink mix, lemonade, sugar and water in a punch bowl and mix well. Ladle into ice-filled glasses.
Yield: more than 30 servings.

Alice L. Mitchell, Xi Alpha Alpha Eta
Benbrook, Texas

VIRGIN SANGRIA

3 cups unsweetened purple or white grape juice	1 unpeeled small lemon, sliced and seeded
³/₄ cup frozen apple juice concentrate, thawed	1 unpeeled small orange, sliced and seeded
1 tablespoon fresh lime juice	1 unpeeled small apple, cored, cut into eighths
1 tablespoon fresh lemon juice	³/₄ cup sparkling water

Combine the grape juice, apple juice concentrate, lime juice, lemon juice, lemon, orange and apple in a large pitcher. Mix well. Chill until serving time. Add the sparkling water just before serving. Serve in ice-filled wineglasses. Yield: 5 to 6 servings.

Amy Phillips, Alpha Epsilon
Claymont, Delaware

BANANA PUNCH

3 cups sugar	1 (12-ounce) can frozen pineapple juice concentrate
4 cups water	
2 (12-ounce) cans frozen orange juice concentrate	4 large ripe bananas, mashed
1 (12-ounce) can frozen lemonade concentrate	

Combine the sugar and water in a saucepan over medium heat; heat until sugar is dissolved, stirring constantly. Cool. Combine the orange juice, lemonade and pineapple juice in a large bowl and mix well. Stir in the bananas and sugar water or, better, process the punch in a blender in small amounts. Pour into 2- or 3-gallon sealable plastic bags and freeze. Thaw for 30 minutes before adding 2 large bottles of ginger ale or lemon-lime soda. Yield: 20 servings.

Gaye Noble, Gamma Chi
Cynthiana, Kentucky

PEACH PUNCH

1 (3-ounce) package peach gelatin	1 (12-ounce) can frozen lemonade concentrate
2 cups sugar	1 (46-ounce) can pineapple juice
4 cups boiling water	2 quarts ginger ale

Dissolve the gelatin and sugar in the boiling water. Stir in the lemonade and pineapple juice. Freeze in a large covered container or sealable plastic bags. Let stand at room temperature for 2 hours. Stir in the ginger ale. Yield: 36 cups.

Rachel Compere
Springfield, Missouri

PINEAPPLE VANILLA PUNCH

2 (46-ounce) cans unsweetened pineapple juice	14 (12-ounce) cans lemon-lime soda
¹/₂ gallon pineapple sherbet, softened	1 quart vanilla ice cream, softened

Combine all the ingredients in a punch bowl 1 at a time in the order listed. Be sure to add the lemon-lime soda 1 can at a time, stirring carefully to avoid too much fizzing. Yield: 50 servings.

Sandra L. Salyers, Xi Alpha Phi
Paintsville, Kentucky

RASPBERRY PUNCH

1 (10-ounce) package frozen raspberries	1 cup sugar
1 pint raspberry sherbet	1 cup lemon juice
2 cups apple juice	1 (28-ounce) bottle carbonated grapefruit beverage, chilled
2 cups water	

Partially thaw the raspberries. Spoon the sherbet into a punch bowl. Combine the apple juice, water, sugar and lemon juice in separate bowl; stir until sugar dissolves. Add the raspberries to the apple juice mixture and stir until raspberries separate. Add to the sherbet and stir. Stir in the carbonated beverage.
Yield: 25 (¹/₂-cup) servings.

Kim Beyer, Epsilon Omega
Sidney, Nebraska

Anna Handsaker, Omicron Omega, Bettendorf, Iowa, prepares **Red Hot Cinnamon Wassail** *by combining two thawed 12-ounces cans frozen lemonade concentrate, 1 thawed 12-ounce can orange juice concentrate, 1 gallon apple cider and ¹/₄ cup red hot cinnamon candies and about 1 gallon of water in a large kettle over medium heat. She heats until the candies melt and serves the wassail either hot or cold.*

TROPICAL COOLER

Add a little rum if you like.

8 ounces frozen strawberries, partially thawed	1 cup pineapple juice
	1/4 cup grenadine
	1 cup ice
1 banana	2 fresh strawberries
2 tablespoons coconut cream	

Place the frozen strawberries, banana, coconut cream, pineapple juice, grenadine and ice in a blender container in the order listed. Blend on high speed for about 30 seconds until ice is crushed and drink is slushy. Garnish with fresh strawberries. Yield: 2 servings.

Diane Heyman, Preceptor Delta Alpha
Paxton, Illinois

RHUBARB SLUSH

8 cups chopped red rhubarb	2 cups vodka
	1 (6-ounce) can frozen lemonade concentrate, thawed
8 cups water	
2 1/2 cups sugar	
2 (3-ounce) packages strawberry gelatin	Lemon-lime soda

Combine the rhubarb, water and sugar in a kettle and bring to a boil. Reduce heat and simmer for 10 to 20 minutes or until rhubarb is tender. Strain through a fine-mesh strainer and discard the pulp. Dissolve the gelatin in the hot strained liquid. Stir in the vodka and lemonade. Keep in the freezer in an ice cream bucket for several hours or until slushy. Fill glasses 3/4 full and add some lemon-lime soda. Yield: 20 servings.

Julie Pomerico, Beta Xi
Huron, South Dakota

MARGARITAS

For convenience, use the empty frozen juice cans to measure the tequila, triple sec, and water.

6 (12-ounce) cans frozen lemonade concentrate	3 lemonade cans tequila
	1 1/2 lemonade cans triple sec
3 (12-ounce) cans frozen limeade concentrate	9 lemonade cans water

Divide the lemonade, limeade, tequila, triple sec, and water evenly among 3 clean 5-quart ice cream buckets. Cover and freeze until serving time. Serve in salt-rimmed glasses garnished with lime wedges. Yield: 8 1/2 quarts.

Jennifer Elarton, Xi Gamma Theta
Red Oak, Iowa

PINK COLADA

2 (12-ounce) cans frozen limeade concentrate	1/2 cup grenadine
	2 (28-ounce) bottles sparkling water, chilled
1 (16-ounce) can coconut cream	

Combine the limeade, coconut cream and grenadine in a blender or bowl; blend well. Stir in the sparkling water. Serve in ice-filled glasses. Garnish with lime slices and maraschino cherries. Yield: 24 servings.

Jennifer Kirchhoff, Chi Nu
Kingsville, Missouri

ORANGE SMOOTHIE

1 cup orange juice	3/4 teaspoon vanilla extract
1 cup water	
2 egg whites	1 generous cup ice
1/4 cup sugar	

Combine the orange juice, water, egg whites, sugar, vanilla and ice in a blender container. Process on high speed for 15 to 30 seconds or until fairly smooth. Yield: 2 servings.

Storm Harding, Delta Omega
Albuquerque, New Mexico

FRESH FRUIT COOLER

1 large ripe mango or 2 1/2 cups fresh raspberries	3 tablespoons pure maple syrup
	1/4 teaspoon ginger or nutmeg (optional)
2 cups plain yogurt	

Peel the mango and slice the fruit from the stone. Chop the fruit coarsely, then place in a food processor fitted with a steel blade. Pulse until fruit is puréed. Add the yogurt, maple syrup and ginger; purée until smooth. Taste and add additional maple syrup for desired sweetness. Pour into 4 chilled glasses. You may garnish each with a small skewer of fresh summer berries. Yield: 4 servings.

Nancy Mercer, Omicron
Trail, British Columbia, Canada

STRAWBERRY CHAMPAGNE PUNCH

5 cups cool water	1 pint strawberries, sliced
3 (6-ounce) cans frozen lemonade concentrate, thawed	4 cups champagne
	1 (1-liter) bottle ginger ale

Combine all the ingredients in the order listed in a large punch bowl, stirring after each addition. Yield: 4 1/2 quarts.

Kaye Clay, Laureate Alpha Master
Guthrie, Oklahoma

SANGRIA

½ cup lemon juice
½ cup orange juice
½ cup sugar
1 liter dry red wine
¼ cup brandy
1 (7-ounce) bottle club
   soda, chilled

1 cup sliced fruit such as
   oranges, lemons,
   apples, peaches,
   bananas

Combine the lemon juice, orange juice, sugar, red wine and brandy in a large punch bowl. Chill until serving time. Stir in the club soda, fruit and a tray of ice cubes just before serving. Yield: 12 servings.

Nancy Jerose, Preceptor Beta Eta
Hendersonville, North Carolina

WINE PUNCH

1 cup water
1 cup sugar
6 cups orange juice
3 cups grape juice

1½ cups pineapple juice
¾ cup lemon juice
3 liters sangria

Combine the water and sugar in a saucepan and bring to a boil. Boil until sugar is dissolved, stirring frequently. Pour into a large punch bowl. Stir in the remaining ingredients. Chill until serving time. Yield: 5 quarts.

Laura Barham, Preceptor Iota
Jackson, Mississippi

AMARETTO PUNCH

1 (12-ounce) can frozen
   orange juice
   concentrate
1 (12-ounce) can frozen
   lemonade concentrate
2 cups amaretto

4 teaspoons instant tea
   granules
Splash of lemon juice
10 cups water
1 (2-liter) bottle lemon-
   lime soda

Combine the orange juice, lemonade, amaretto, tea granules, lemon juice and water and freeze for several hours or until slushy. Add the lemon-lime soda just before serving. Garnish with lemon slices. Yield: 6 quarts.

Barbara B. Eakin, Alpha
Cheyenne, Wyoming

BRANDY SLUSH

1 (12-ounce) can
   lemonade concentrate
6 or 8 ounces frozen
   orange juice
   concentrate

2 tea bags
2 cups sugar
2 cups brandy
Lemon-lime soda

Combine the lemonade, orange juice and 7 cups water in a large container; mix well. Combine the tea bags, sugar and 2 cups water in a saucepan over medium-high heat. Bring to a boil, stirring occasionally. Remove and discard the tea bags and add the sweetened tea to the lemonade mixture. Stir in the brandy and freeze for several hours or until slushy. Spoon into glasses at serving time, and fill with lemon-lime soda. Yield: 1 gallon.

Sarah Kapla, Chi Omicron
Romeoville, Illinois

CHOCOLATE IRISH CREAM

3 eggs
1½ tablespoons
   chocolate syrup
1 (14-ounce) can
   sweetened condensed
   milk

1 tablespoon instant
   coffee granules
1 pint Irish coffee cream
12 ounces Irish whiskey

Combine the eggs, chocolate syrup, condensed milk and coffee granules in a blender container and process until smooth. Add the coffee cream and whiskey and process for 1 minute. Chill, covered, until serving time. Shake before serving. May be refrigerated for 30 days. Yield: 1½ quarts.

Idell Henderson, Preceptor Theta
Virginia, Minnesota

❖ COFFEE PUNCH

2 cups water
2 cups sugar
1 (2-ounce) jar instant
   coffee granules

1 gallon milk, very cold
½ gallon chocolate
   ripple ice cream

Bring the water and sugar to a boil in a medium saucepan. Remove from heat and dissolve the coffee granules in the sugar water. Keep in an airtight container in the refrigerator until serving time; may prepare up to this point several days in advance. At serving time, combine the coffee mixture and milk in a 2-gallon glass punch bowl. Float large scoops of the ice cream in the punch. Yield: 20 servings.

Diann C. Walters, Delta Kappa
Ellisville, Mississippi

BUTTER BRICKLE DREAM

1 pint butter brickle ice
   cream

1⅓ cups milk
¼ cup hazelnut liqueur

Combine the ice cream, milk and hazelnut liqueur in a blender and process until smooth. Serve at once in 4 glasses. Yield: 4 (6-ounce) servings.

Shelly Allison, Nu Kappa
Guthrie, Oklahoma

CITRUS GIN PUNCH

1 (12-ounce) can frozen
  orange juice
  concentrate
1 (12-ounce) can frozen
  limeade concentrate
1 juice can milk
1 juice can gin or vodka
2 eggs

Combine the orange juice, lime juice, milk, gin and eggs in a blender and process until smooth. Serve over ice. Yield: 6 to 8 servings.

Laura Wilson, Xi Omega
Murphysboro, Illinois

WHISKEY FLIP

3 eggs, separated
1 cup sugar
1/2 cup rye whiskey
Juice and grated zest of
  1 lime
1/8 teaspoon cream of
  tartar
1 cup whipping cream

Combine the egg yolks and half the sugar in a large bowl; beat until creamy. Add the whiskey, the lime juice and most of the lime zest, reserving some of the zest for garnish. Place the egg whites in a small bowl and beat at high speed until stiff peaks form. Fold the egg whites into the yolk mixture. Place the cream and the remaining 1/2 cup sugar in a separate bowl and beat at high speed until stiff peaks form. Fold into the egg mixture and spoon into individual glasses. Freeze, covered, for 4 to 10 hours. Remove glasses to the refrigerator 1 hour before serving. Garnish each with a mint leaf and a sprinkle of grated lime zest. Yield: 4 to 6 servings.

Jeanne Gordon, Preceptor Epsilon Pi
Trenton, Ontario, Canada

DRINKABLE CUSTARD

4 eggs
1/2 cup sugar
1 quart homogenized
  milk
1 teaspoon vanilla, or
  to taste

Combine the eggs and sugar in a small bowl and beat until smooth. Scald the milk in a heavy saucepan over medium heat. Whisk in the egg mixture gradually. Cook over low heat until the mixture coats a metal spoon with a thin film, stirring constantly. Remove from heat and stir in the vanilla. Serve chilled or at room temperature. Top with whipped topping if desired. Yield: about 1 quart.

Erika F. Wells, Eta Rho
Joplin, Missouri

MOCK EGGNOG

2 quarts cold milk
1 (3-ounce) package
  vanilla instant
  pudding mix
1/4 cup sugar
1 teaspoon nutmeg
1 teaspoon vanilla
  extract
1/8 teaspoon salt
  (optional)
1 cup whipping cream

Combine the milk and pudding mix in a mixing bowl and beat at low speed for 2 minutes. Beat in the sugar, nutmeg, vanilla and salt. Place the cream in a separate mixing bowl and beat at high speed for about 3 minutes or until soft peaks form. Stir the whipped cream into the pudding mixture. Chill, covered, until ready to serve. Sprinkle with additional nutmeg if desired. Yield: about 2 1/2 quarts.

Eileen Sanders, Preceptor Iota
Eugene, Oregon

THE WORLD'S GREATEST EGGNOG

10 eggs, separated
2 cups sugar
2 quarts half-and-half,
  scalded
2 cups whiskey
1 cup apricot brandy
1 cup sugar
2 cups whipping cream,
  whipped

Beat the egg yolks at high speed until thick and pale yellow; place in the top of a double boiler over boiling water. Whisk in the half-and-half; cook over boiling water until the mixture coats a metal spoon with a thin film, stirring constantly. Stir in the whiskey and apricot brandy. Chill, covered, for 8 to 10 hours. At serving time, beat the egg whites at medium speed until soft peaks form. Combine the whiskey mixture, egg whites, sugar and whipped cream in a punch bowl and blend well. Dust with grated nutmeg and serve. Yield: 20 servings.

Janet Hamilton, Preceptor Alpha Beta
Kalamazoo, Michigan

TOMATO TODDY

1 (10-ounce) can tomato
  soup
1 (10-ounce) can beef
  consommé
1 soup can water
1/4 teaspoon marjoram
1/4 teaspoon thyme

Combine the soup, consommé, water, marjoram and thyme in a saucepan and bring to a boil. Reduce heat and simmer for 2 minutes. Serve hot in punch cups. Dot each serving with butter and garnish with 2 or 3 oyster crackers. Yield: 6 servings.

Lorraine Connors, Xi Zeta Chi
Southampton, Ontario, Canada

BLOODY MARY MIX

3 (46-ounce) cans tomato juice	2 tablespoons celery salt
2 tablespoons old-fashioned horseradish	2 tablespoons Worcestershire sauce
3 tablespoons lemon juice	2 or 3 squirts Tabasco sauce
	1 tablespoon garlic powder

Combine all the ingredients in a large container, or divide ingredients among 3 (2-quart) containers; mix well. Chill, covered, in the refrigerator. Shake before serving. Yield: 24 (8-ounce) servings.

Sandra Thrasher, Preceptor Beta Mu
Prineville, Oregon

MEXICAN CINNAMON CAFE

3/4 to 1 cup freshly ground dark coffee	1 teaspoon pure vanilla extract
1/2 teaspoon ground cinnamon	Raw natural sugar crystals (optional)
1 cup whipping cream	12 cinnamon sticks
1/4 cup sugar	

Brew the coffee with the ground cinnamon in a 12-cup drip coffeemaker. Beat the cream with the sugar and vanilla at high speed until stiff peaks form. Moisten the rims of heavy coffee mugs and roll the rims in raw sugar crystals. Pour the coffee into the mugs and top with dollops of the whipped cream. Serve with cinnamon sticks for stirring.
Yield: 3 quarts.

Kathleen Landreth, Xi Alpha
Albuquerque, New Mexico

VANILLA ALMOND COFFEE

1 (13-ounce) can auto drip coffee	1 ounce pure almond extract
1 ounce pure vanilla extract	

Place the coffee in a large sealable plastic bag or large bowl. Add the vanilla extract and almond extract; blend well. Store in the plastic bag or an airtight container in the refrigerator until ready to brew. Brew as usual in a coffeemaker. Yield: 80 to 90 cups.

Claudia M. Long, Kappa Kappa
Meriden, Kansas

HOT SPICED PUNCH

2 quarts cranberry juice	2 teaspoons whole cloves
2 quarts apple juice	
1 cup water	1/2 cup packed brown sugar
3 cinnamon sticks	

Combine the cranberry juice, apple juice and water in a percolator. Place the cinnamon, cloves and brown sugar in the percolator basket. Perk using the manufacturer's instructions. Serve hot. Yield: about 4 quarts.

Jean Saunders, Laureate Beta Delta
Shawnee, Kansas

SPICED TEA MIX

1 1/2 cups orange drink mix	2 1/2 cups sugar
1 1/2 cups unsweetened instant tea with lemon	3 teaspoons cinnamon
	3 teaspoons ground cloves

Combine the orange drink mix, instant tea, sugar, cinnamon and cloves in a jar; mix well. Store in the closed jar in a cool area. At serving time, mix with cold water and add ice. Yield: 8 servings.

Judy Silver, Xi Rho Chi
Roseville, California

HOT CRANBERRY CITRUS DRINK

12 ounces fresh or frozen cranberries	1 1/2 cups pineapple juice
2 1/2 quarts water	3 (3-inch) cinnamon sticks
2 cups orange juice	1 cup sugar
2 tablespoons lemon juice	

Combine the cranberries and water in a large saucepan and bring to a boil. Reduce heat and simmer for 5 to 7 minutes or until cranberries split. Stir in the orange juice, lemon juice, pineapple juice, cinnamon sticks and sugar; return to a boil. Reduce heat and simmer, uncovered, for 25 to 30 minutes. Strain through cheesecloth; discard pulp and cinnamon sticks. Serve warm. Yield: about 3 quarts.

Cindy Kruckenberg, Xi Theta Zeta
Gilbert, Iowa

HOT CRANAPPLE PUNCH

3 quarts apple juice	Dash of salt
2 quarts cranberry juice	4 cinnamon sticks
1/2 cup packed brown sugar	1 whole clove

Combine the apple juice, cranberry juice, brown sugar and salt in a percolator. Place the cinnamon sticks and clove in the percolator basket. Perk using the manufacturer's instructions. Serve hot with a small dot of butter in each cup. Yield: 20 cups.

Kay Stukenholtz, Alpha Rho
Perry, Iowa

Endings

Cakes

APPLE CAKE

2¼ cups flour	5 cups coarsely chopped
1 teaspoon baking soda	peeled apples
1 teaspoon salt	2 tablespoons lemon
1 teaspoon nutmeg	juice
2 teaspoons cinnamon	1 cup chopped walnuts
2 cups sugar	or pecans
1 cup vegetable oil	1 cup raisins
2 eggs	

Mix the flour, baking soda, salt, nutmeg and cinnamon together. Combine the sugar, vegetable oil, eggs, flour mixture, apples, lemon juice, nuts and raisins in the order listed in a large bowl, mixing by hand after each addition. Mixture will be thick. Spread in a buttered 9×13-inch cake pan. Bake for 1 hour or until cake tests done. Frost warm cake with a mixture of 3 ounces softened cream cheese, 1 cup confectioners' sugar, 2 teaspoons softened butter and 1 teaspoon vanilla extract. Yield: 15 servings.

Nadine Clevenger, Preceptor Gamma Theta
Richmond, Maryland

APPLESAUCE CAKE

½ cup shortening	½ teaspoon nutmeg
1½ cups packed brown	1 teaspoon baking soda
sugar	1 teaspoon cinnamon
½ cup granulated sugar	½ teaspoon ground
2 eggs	cloves
2½ cups flour	1 (16-ounce) can
1½ teaspoons baking	applesauce
powder	1 cup chopped pecans
1 teaspoon salt	1 cup raisins

Cream the shortening and sugars in a mixing bowl until light and fluffy. Add the eggs 1 at a time, beating well after each addition. Add a mixture of the flour, baking powder, salt, nutmeg, baking soda, cinnamon and cloves; mix well. Add the applesauce and mix well. Stir in the pecans and raisins. Pour into a tube pan that has been sprayed with nonstick cooking spray. Bake at 325 to 350 degrees for 45 minutes or until a wooden pick inserted in the center comes out clean. Do not overbake. Cool in the pan for 5 minutes. Remove to a wire rack to cool completely. Place in a sealable plastic bag to keep moist. Let stand at room temperature for 3 days before slicing.
Yield: 16 servings.

Wanda Blake, Laureate Alpha Epsilon
Lewisburg, West Virginia

LIGHT APPLE SPICE CAKE

5 Granny Smith apples,	1 teaspoon allspice
peeled, cored, cut into	1 tablespoon sugar
½-inch slices	1 (18-ounce) package
7 tablespoons apple	spice cake mix
juice	1 cup chopped pecans
1 (21-ounce) can apple	3 tablespoons butter
pie filling	¼ cup light pancake
1 teaspoon cinnamon	syrup
1 teaspoon nutmeg	

Place the apple slices in a glass bowl. Drizzle with 2 tablespoons of the apple juice. Cover with plastic wrap and microwave on High for 5 minutes; stir. Microwave on High for 5 minutes longer or until apples are tender. Stir in the pie filling. Pour into a buttered 9×13-inch cake pan. Sprinkle a mixture of the cinnamon, nutmeg, allspice and sugar over the apples. Layer the dry cake mix evenly over the top. Scatter the pecans over the cake mix layer. Combine the butter, syrup and remaining 5 tablespoons apple juice in a glass measuring cup. Microwave until butter melts; stir. Drizzle evenly over the top of the unbaked cake. Bake at 350 degrees for 45 to 55 minutes or until browned. Serve warm with ice cream.
Yield: 15 servings.

Nedral Brown-Gockel, Xi Epsilon Pi
Centerville, Ohio

APPLE TORTE

1/4 cup (1/2 stick) butter, at room temperature	1/4 teaspoon nutmeg
1 cup sugar	2 cups finely chopped apples
1 egg	1/2 cup chopped walnuts
1 cup flour	1 teaspoon almond extract or vanilla extract
1 teaspoon baking soda	
1 teaspoon cinnamon	

Cream the butter and sugar in a mixing bowl until light and fluffy. Beat in the egg. Sift the flour, baking soda, cinnamon and nutmeg together. Add the sifted dry ingredients to the butter mixture; mix well. Stir in the apples, walnuts and almond extract. Spoon into a large buttered pie plate. Bake at 350 degrees for 35 to 40 minutes or until cake tests done. Serve with ice cream or whipped cream. Yield: 6 to 8 servings.

Jane DePew, Laureate Phi
Montgomery, New York

GLAZED APPLE RING

1 cup (2 sticks) butter	2 eggs
4 apples, peeled and sliced	1 1/2 cups sifted flour
1 cup packed brown sugar	1 1/2 teaspoons baking powder
1 cup granulated sugar	1/2 teaspoon salt
1 teaspoon vanilla extract	1/2 cup milk

Melt half the butter in a skillet over medium heat. Add the apple slices and brown sugar; cook for 10 to 15 minutes or until apples are tender, stirring frequently to prevent burning. Cream the remaining butter and granulated sugar in a mixing bowl until light and fluffy. Stir in the vanilla. Beat in the eggs 1 at a time. Sift the flour, baking powder and salt together. Add to the egg mixture alternately with the milk, mixing well after each addition. Spoon the cooked apples with syrup into a bundt or tube pan. Pour in the cake batter. Bake at 375 degrees for about 40 minutes or until cake tests done. Invert immediately onto a serving plate. Serve warm.
Yield: 8 servings.

Rose Daniels, Laureate Beta Gamma
Comanche, Iowa

---

*Elaine McCulloch, Xi Beta Rho, Lamar, Missouri, makes her fresh apple cake especially moist and delicious by adding her **Brown Sugar Icing**. Boil 1 cup brown sugar, 1/4 cup milk and 1 stick margarine for 3 minutes. Stir in 1/2 cup pecans and 1 teaspoon vanilla extract and pour over the hot cake that has been pierced all over with a fork.*

APPLE PAN WALNUT CAKE

1 (21-ounce) can apple pie filling	2 eggs, beaten
2 cups flour	1 teaspoon vanilla extract
1 cup sugar	2/3 cup vegetable oil
1 1/2 teaspoons baking soda	3/4 cup chopped walnuts
1 teaspoon salt	Sour Cream Topping

Spread the apple pie filling in a buttered 9×13-inch baking pan. Sprinkle a mixture of the flour, sugar, baking soda and salt evenly over the pie filling. Combine the eggs, vanilla, vegetable oil and half the walnuts in a bowl and mix well. Pour over the ingredients in the baking pan. Stir in the pan just until blended; smooth the top with a spatula or spoon. Bake at 350 degrees for 40 to 50 minutes or until cake tests done. Prick the warm cake with a fork. Pour Sour Cream Topping over the warm cake. Sprinkle with the remaining walnuts. Serve warm or cold. Serve plain or with whipped cream or ice cream. Yield: 10 to 15 servings.

SOUR CREAM TOPPING

1 cup sugar	1/2 teaspoon baking soda
1 cup sour cream	

Combine the sugar, sour cream and baking soda in a small saucepan over medium heat. Bring to the boiling point, stirring constantly.

Helen A. Heath, Laureate Alpha Kappa
Muncie, Indiana

APRICOT NECTAR CAKE

1 (2-layer) package lemon cake mix	4 eggs
1 cup apricot nectar	1/2 cup vegetable oil
	1/2 cup sugar

Combine the dry cake mix, apricot nectar, eggs, vegetable oil and sugar in a mixing bowl and beat at high speed for 3 minutes. Pour into a buttered bundt pan. Bake at 325 degrees for 1 hour. Pour Rich Apricot Nectar evenly over the warm cake. Cool in the pan for 20 minutes. Remove to a wire rack to cool completely. Yield: 16 servings.

RICH APRICOT NECTAR

1 cup confectioners' sugar	3 ounces apricot nectar
	1/4 cup melted margarine

Combine the confectioners' sugar, apricot nectar and margarine in a small bowl and blend well.

Jennifer Jeffries, Alpha Rho
Madison, Indiana

BANANA CAKE

2 cups self-rising flour	3 eggs, beaten
2 cups sugar	3 bananas, mashed
1 cup vegetable oil	1 cup chopped walnuts
1 tablespoon vanilla	or pecans
extract	

Combine the flour, sugar, vegetable oil, vanilla and eggs in a large bowl; mix well by hand. Stir in the bananas. Fold in the walnuts. Pour into a buttered and floured bundt pan. Bake at 350 degrees for 55 minutes. Cool in the pan on a wire rack. Invert onto a serving plate. Yield: 16 servings.

Janice Lavoie, Beta Omega
Virginia Beach, Virginia

PINEAPPLE BANANA CAKE

3 eggs, beaten	1 1/3 cups vegetable oil
3 cups flour	2 cups cut-up bananas
3 cups sugar	1 (8-ounce) can crushed
1 teaspoon salt	pineapple
1 teaspoon cinnamon	1/2 cup walnuts or
1 1/2 teaspoons vanilla	pecans
extract	Powdered Sugar Glaze

Combine the eggs, flour, sugar, salt, cinnamon, vanilla, vegetable oil, bananas, undrained pineapple and walnuts in a large bowl. Stir just until mixed; do not beat. Pour into a buttered and floured bundt pan. Bake at 350 degrees for 1 hour. Cool in the pan on a wire rack. Invert onto a serving plate. Spread Powdered Sugar Glaze over the cake. Yield: 16 servings.

CONFECTIONERS' SUGAR GLAZE

1 cup (2 sticks) butter or	2 cups confectioners'
margarine, softened	sugar
1 teaspoon vanilla	Milk
extract	

Combine the butter, vanilla and confectioners' sugar in a small bowl and blend well. Blend in enough milk to make a thin glaze.

Dorothy Jones, Alpha Phi
Paris, Missouri

BANANA CAKE WITH PENUCHE FROSTING

2 eggs, well beaten	1 teaspoon baking
1 1/2 cups sugar	powder
1 cup mashed bananas	Pinch of salt
2 cups flour	1 cup heavy cream
1 teaspoon baking soda	Penuche Frosting

Combine the eggs and sugar in a large mixing bowl and mix well. Stir in the bananas. Sift the flour, baking soda, baking powder and salt together. Add to the egg mixture alternately with the cream, mixing well after each addition. Spread in a buttered 9×13-inch cake pan. Bake at 375 degrees for 25 to 30 minutes or until cake tests done. Cool in the pan on a wire rack. Frost with Penuche Frosting.
Yield: 12 servings.

PENUCHE FROSTING

1/2 cup (1 stick) butter	1/4 cup milk
1 cup packed brown	2 cups (or more) sifted
sugar	confectioners' sugar

Melt the butter in a heavy saucepan over medium-low heat. Stir in the brown sugar and milk. Boil gently for 2 minutes, stirring constantly. Cool to lukewarm. Add the confectioners' sugar gradually, beating until spreading consistency. Add a little hot water if frosting becomes too thick.

Kathy Dabestani, Xi Alpha Tau
Twin Falls, Idaho

❖ BLACKBERRY WINE CAKE

1 (2-layer) package	4 eggs
white cake mix	1/2 cup vegetable oil
1 (3-ounce) package	1 cup blackberry wine
blackberry or black	1/2 cup pecans
cherry gelatin	Blackberry Glaze

Combine the cake mix and gelatin mix in a bowl. Add the eggs, vegetable oil and blackberry wine. Beat at low speed until moistened; beat at medium speed for 5 minutes. Sprinkle the pecans in a buttered and floured bundt pan. Pour the batter into the pan. Bake at 325 degrees for 45 to 50 minutes or until cake tests done. Remove from oven. Drizzle 2/3 of the warm Blackberry Glaze over the hot cake in the pan. Cool in the pan on a wire rack for 30 minutes. Invert onto a serving plate. Add additional confectioners' sugar to the remaining Blackberry Glaze to thicken. Spread or pour over the cake. Yield: 12 to 24 servings.

BLACKBERRY GLAZE

1 cup confectioners'	1/2 cup (1 stick) butter
sugar	1/2 cup blackberry wine

Combine the confectioners' sugar, butter and blackberry wine in a heavy saucepan and bring to a hard boil, stirring frequently.

Ann Biddy, Tau Master
Sanford, Florida

BLUEBERRY CAKE

1 cup (2 sticks) butter
2 cups sugar
4 eggs, separated
2 teaspoons vanilla
  extract
3 cups flour
2 teaspoons baking
  powder
1/2 teaspoon salt
2/3 cup milk
3 cups fresh blueberries

Cream the butter and 1½ cups of the sugar in a mixing bowl. Add the egg yolks and vanilla and beat until light and fluffy. Sift the flour, baking powder and salt together. Add to the egg yolk mixture alternately with the milk, mixing well after each addition. Beat the egg whites in a mixing bowl until soft peaks form. Add the remaining ½ cup sugar gradually, beating until stiff peaks form. Fold gently into the batter. Toss the blueberries in a tablespoon of flour and fold into the batter. Pour into a buttered 9×13-inch cake pan. Bake at 350 degrees for 50 minutes or until cake tests done. Cool completely. Sprinkle top with confectioners' sugar. Yield: 15 servings.

Anna Maye Sigel, Preceptor Gamma Pi
Warfordsburg, Pennsylvania

KENTUCKY BUTTER CAKE

1 cup (2 sticks) butter,
  softened
1 cup sugar
4 eggs
1 cup buttermilk
3 cups flour
1/2 teaspoon baking soda
1 teaspoon baking
  powder
1 teaspoon salt
2 teaspoons vanilla
  extract
Butter Sauce

Cream the butter and sugar in a mixing bowl until light and fluffy. Beat in the eggs 1 at a time. Beat in the buttermilk. Add a mixture of the flour, baking soda, baking powder and salt gradually, beating after each addition. Beat in the vanilla. Pour into a lightly buttered 9×13-inch cake pan. Bake at 325 degrees for 55 to 65 minutes or until a wooden pick inserted in the center comes out clean. Remove from oven and poke holes all over the top of the hot cake with a fork. Drizzle with hot Butter Sauce, covering the top of the cake completely. Cool and serve. Yield: 15 servings.

BUTTER SAUCE

1/2 cup butter
1 cup sugar
1/4 cup water
1 teaspoon vanilla
  extract

Bring a mixture of the butter, sugar and water to a boil in a heavy saucepan. Remove from heat and stir in the vanilla.

Denise Johnson-Williams, Xi Zeta
Boulder City, Nevada

HOT CINNAMON BUTTERMILK CAKE

1/2 cup (1 stick) butter
2 cups sugar
2 cups buttermilk
3 cups flour
1½ teaspoons baking
  soda
1 teaspoon baking
  powder
1 teaspoon salt
1 teaspoon cinnamon
1/4 teaspoon nutmeg
1/8 teaspoon ground
  cloves
1 cup raisins
1 cup chopped walnuts
  or pecans (optional)
Vanilla Sauce

Cream the butter and sugar in a mixing bowl until light and fluffy. Add the buttermilk and a mixture of the flour, baking soda, baking powder, salt, cinnamon, nutmeg and cloves; mix well. Stir in the raisins and chopped nuts. Pour into a buttered 9×13-inch cake pan. Bake at 350 degrees for 35 minutes or until a wooden pick inserted in the center comes out clean. Serve hot with Vanilla Sauce. Yield: 16 servings.

VANILLA SAUCE

3/4 cup sugar
2 tablespoons
  cornstarch
1 cup boiling water
2 teaspoons vanilla
  extract
2 tablespoons butter

Blend the sugar and cornstarch together in a bowl. Add the water, vanilla and butter and blend well. Serve warm.

Jeanne Felix, Xi Alpha Eta
Truchee, California

BUTTERSCOTCH SPICE PUDDING CAKE

1 (2-layer) package spice
  cake mix
1 (4-ounce) package
  butterscotch cook-
  and-serve pudding
2 cups butterscotch
  chips
1/2 cup chopped walnuts
  and pecans

Place the dry cake mix in a large bowl. Prepare the pudding using the package directions and stir into the cake mix. Pour into a buttered 9×13-inch cake pan. Sprinkle evenly with butterscotch chips and walnuts. Bake at 350 degrees for 25 to 30 minutes or until cake tests done. Yield: 12 to 16 servings.

Betty Holtzen, Laureate Epsilon
Abilene, Kansas

*Christy Shvalmire, Eta Beta, Mansfield, Louisiana, likes to serve her fresh apple cake with **Buttermilk Sauce**. She brings ½ cup sugar, ¼ cup buttermilk, 2 tablespoons margarine and ⅛ teaspoon baking soda to a boil and spoons it over a warm cake pierced with holes about an hour before serving.*

❖ CARAMEL CAKE WITH RUM CARAMEL SAUCE

1 (2-layer) package caramel cake mix	1 teaspoon cinnamon
3/4 cup prepared caramel topping	1/2 cup crushed milk chocolate English
1 tablespoon rum	toffee bars

Prepare and bake the cake mix using the package directions for a 9×13-inch cake pan. Let cool in the pan for 10 minutes. Spread a mixture of the caramel topping, rum, and cinnamon over the warm cake. Sprinkle with the crushed candy. Serve warm with whipped cream. Yield: 12 to 16 servings.

Tammy Dighero, Xi Zeta Rho
Lamar, Missouri

CARROT CAKE

2 cups sugar	2 teaspoons baking soda
1 1/2 cups vegetable oil	1/2 cup chopped walnuts
4 eggs	or pecans
2 teaspoon cinnamon	2 (3-ounce) jars junior
2 cups flour	baby food, carrots
2 teaspoons salt	Cream Cheese Frosting

Combine the sugar, vegetable oil, eggs and cinnamon in a mixing bowl; mix well. Add a mixture of the flour, salt and baking soda; mix well. Mix in the chopped walnuts and baby food. Pour into a 9×13-inch cake pan that has been sprayed with nonstick cooking spray. Bake at 300 degrees for 1 hour. Let cool completely. Frost with Cream Cheese Frosting. Yield: 15 servings.

CREAM CHEESE FROSTING

8 ounces cream cheese, softened	1/4 cup (1/2 stick) margarine, softened
1 (1-pound) package confectioners' sugar	2 teaspoons vanilla extract

Combine the cream cheese, confectioners' sugar, margarine and vanilla in a mixing bowl. Beat at high speed for at least 3 minutes.

Phyllis M. Carver, Alpha Theta Master
Lakeland, Florida

---

*Joanne Haines, Preceptor Delta Gamma, Lawrenceville, Illinois, makes her **Super Coconut Pecan Cake** by preparing the batter from a package of yellow cake mix directions then beating in a can of coconut pecan frosting. Bake in a prepared bundt pan at 350 degrees for 55 to 60 minutes. Cool for 10 minutes and invert onto a serving plate.*

CHERRY LOAF

3/4 cup sugar	1/2 cup chopped walnuts
1 egg	or pecans
1 tablespoon butter, softened	1 (9-ounce) jar red maraschino cherries
2 cups flour	1 (9-ounce) jar green
2 teaspoons baking powder	maraschino cherries

Combine the sugar, egg and butter in a mixing bowl and mix well. Add a mixture of the flour and baking powder; mix well. Fold in the walnuts. Drain the cherries, reserving the juice. Combine enough milk and enough juice from both jars of cherries to make 1 cup liquid. Halve the cherries and toss in a little flour to coat. Mix into the batter. Pour into a buttered and floured loaf pan. Bake at 300 degrees for 1 hour. Yield: 12 slices.

June Kendall, Precepter
Gananoque, Ontario, Canada

CHERRY POUND CAKE

1 cup shortening	1/2 teaspoon almond
1/2 cup (1 stick) margarine, softened	extract
	3 3/4 cups flour
3 cups sugar	3/4 cup milk
6 eggs	1/2 cup maraschino
1/2 teaspoon vanilla extract	cherries, drained and chopped

Cream the shortening, margarine and sugar in a mixing bowl until light and fluffy. Beat in the eggs, vanilla and almond extract. Add the flour alternately with the milk, mixing well after each addition. Stir in the cherries. Pour into a buttered and floured tube pan. Place in an unheated oven. Turn the oven temperature to 275 degrees immediately and bake for 2 hours. Cool and invert onto a serving plate. Frost with Cherry Frosting. Yield: 16 servings.

CHERRY FROSTING

3 ounces cream cheese, at room temperature	1/2 (9-ounce) jar maraschino cherries,
2 cups confectioners' sugar	drained and chopped
	1/2 cup chopped walnuts
1/4 cup (1/2 stick) margarine, softened	or pecans
1 teaspoon vanilla extract	1/2 cup shredded coconut

Beat the first 4 ingredients in a mixing bowl until creamy. Stir in the cherries and enough milk to make of spreading consistency. Stir in the walnuts and coconut.

Judy Ramer, Xi Beta Xi
North Little Rock, Arkansas

CHOCOLATE CHERRY CAKE

1 (2-layer) package
    deluxe chocolate
    cake mix
1 (21-ounce) can cherry
    pie filling
1 teaspoon vanilla
    extract or almond
    extract

2 eggs, beaten
1 cup sugar
5 tablespoons butter
1/2 cup half-and-half
1 cup chocolate chips

Combine the cake mix, cherry pie filling, vanilla and eggs in a large bowl and mix well by hand. Pour into a buttered and floured 9×13-inch cake pan. Bake at 350 degrees for 25 to 30 minutes or until cake tests done. Combine the sugar, butter and half-and-half in a small saucepan and bring to a rolling boil. Boil for about 1 minute. Remove from heat and whisk in the chocolate chips. Pour over the warm cake. Cool and serve. Yield: 12 to 16 servings.

Pat Galloway, Laureate Alpha Alpha
Maumelle, Arkansas

QUICK MOIST CHOCOLATE CAKE

1 1/2 cups flour
1 cup sugar
1/4 cup baking cocoa
1 scant teaspoon baking
    soda
1/2 teaspoon salt
1/2 cup vegetable oil
1 cup water

1/4 teaspoon red food
    coloring
1 teaspoon white
    vinegar
1 teaspoon vanilla
    extract
Chocolate Frosting

Combine the flour, sugar, baking cocoa, baking soda, salt, vegetable oil, water, food coloring, vinegar and vanilla in a large mixing bowl and beat at medium speed until well blended. Pour into a buttered 7×11-inch cake pan. Bake at 350 degrees for 20 minutes. Spread with Chocolate Frosting. Yield: 12 servings.

CHOCOLATE FROSTING

3 tablespoons margarine
3 tablespoons milk

3/4 cup sugar
1/4 cup chocolate chips

Combine the margarine, milk and sugar in a saucepan; bring to a boil. Boil for 1 minute. Remove from heat and add the chocolate chips, stirring until chips are melted by the heat.

Ellarea Davison, Preceptor Alpha Sigma
Corydon, Iowa

❖ CHOCOLATE UPSIDE-DOWN CAKE

1 cup chopped pecans
1 cup shredded coconut
1 (2-layer) package
    German chocolate
    cake mix
1 (1-pound) package
    confectioners' sugar

8 ounces cream cheese,
    softened
1/2 cup (1 stick) butter
1/4 cup (1/2 stick) butter,
    melted

Spread the pecans and coconut in the bottom of an ungreased metal 9×13-inch cake pan. Prepare the cake mix using the package directions, adding the confectioners' sugar. Blend the cream cheese and butter together and stir into the batter. Spread evenly over the nuts and coconut. Bake at 350 degrees for 45 minutes to 1 hour; do not bake longer than 1 hour. Invert immediately onto a serving plate.
Yield: 12 to 15 servings.

Lois Lawler, Gamma Master
Chattanooga, Tennessee

SOUR CREAM CHOCOLATE CAKE

2 cups sugar
1/2 cup baking cocoa
1/2 cup (1 stick) butter or
    margarine, at room
    temperature
1/2 cup sour cream
1 1/4 teaspoons baking
    soda

1/4 teaspoon salt
1 cup boiling water
2 cups flour
2 eggs, well beaten
1/2 teaspoon vanilla
    extract
Rich Chocolate Frosting

Combine the sugar, baking cocoa, butter, sour cream, baking soda, salt and boiling water in a large bowl and beat with a rotary beater until blended. Add the flour and eggs; beat until smooth. Pour into 2 buttered and floured 9-inch cake pans. Bake at 350 degrees for 30 to 35 minutes or until cake tests done. Frost the cooled cake with Rich Chocolate Frosting. Yield: 8 to 10 servings.

RICH CHOCOLATE FROSTING

1/2 cup (1 stick) butter,
    softened
2 1/2 cups confectioners'
    sugar
1 egg

3 ounces unsweetened
    chocolate, melted
1 teaspoon vanilla
    extract

Combine the butter, confectioners' sugar, egg, chocolate and vanilla in a mixing bowl and beat until smooth. Add milk if necessary to make of spreading consistency.

Sondra Drake, Preceptor Delta Tau
Ridgecrest, California

TRIPLE-CHOCOLATE FANTASY CAKE

For a special touch, melt dark or white chocolate pieces and drizzle over the top of the frosted cake.

3/4 cup (1 1/2 sticks) butter	1 teaspoon salt
2 ounces unsweetened chocolate	1 3/4 cups buttermilk
2 1/4 cups flour	2 eggs, at room temperature
2 cups sugar	2 1/2 cups semisweet chocolate chips
1/4 cup baking cocoa	
2 teaspoons baking soda	3/4 cup heavy cream

Melt the butter and unsweetened chocolate in a saucepan over low heat. Combine the flour, sugar, baking cocoa, baking soda and salt in a large mixing bowl; mix well. Stir in the butter mixture, buttermilk and eggs. Beat at low speed for 1 minute. Beat at high speed for 2 minutes or until light and fluffy. Stir in 1/2 cup of the semisweet chocolate chips. Pour into 2 buttered and floured 9-inch cake pans. Bake at 350 degrees for 25 to 30 minutes or until top of cake springs back when lightly pressed. Pour the cream into a heavy saucepan and bring to the boiling point. Remove from heat and add the remaining 1 1/2 cups semisweet chocolate chips, stirring until smooth. Frost the cooled cake with the chocolate mixture. Yield: 10 servings.

Sharon Brunn, Laureate Gamma Delta
Yakima, Washington

CHOCOLATE SHEET CAKE

1/2 cup (1 stick) margarine	1/2 cup milk
1/4 cup vegetable oil	1 teaspoon baking soda
1/4 cup baking cocoa	1 teaspoon salt
1 cup water	1 teaspoon cinnamon
2 cups flour	1 teaspoon vanilla extract
2 cups sugar	
2 eggs	1/2 cup chopped walnuts or pecans (optional)

Combine the margarine, vegetable oil, baking cocoa and water in a saucepan over medium-low heat. Heat until margarine is melted, stirring to blend. Pour the margarine mixture into a large mixing bowl. Beat in the flour, sugar, eggs, milk, baking soda, salt, cinnamon and vanilla; beat until smooth. Stir in the walnuts. Pour into a buttered and floured 10×15-inch cake pan. Bake at 350 degrees for 15 minutes or until top springs back when touched lightly. Frost with chocolate frosting or serve unfrosted and topped with vanilla ice cream. Yield: 12 to 24 servings.

Rogene M. Schneider, Preceptor Beta Alpha
Bellevue, Nebraska

QUICK COCOA CAKE

It's great when served warm with vanilla ice cream.

2 cups sugar	1 teaspoon vanilla extract
1/2 cup shortening	
3 tablespoons baking cocoa	1 cup boiling coffee or boiling water
2 eggs	6 tablespoons melted butter
1/2 cup buttermilk	
2 cups flour	1/2 cup evaporated milk
1 teaspoon baking soda	1 cup chopped walnuts or pecans
1/2 teaspoon salt	

Combine the sugar, shortening, baking cocoa, eggs, buttermilk, flour, baking soda, salt, vanilla and coffee in a large bowl and mix well. Pour into a buttered 9×13-inch cake pan. Bake at 375 degrees for 26 to 30 minutes or until cake tests done. Spread a mixture of the melted butter, evaporated milk and chopped nuts over the hot cake. Broil 6 inches from the heat source for 3 minutes or until brown and bubbly and a little crusty; watch closely to avoid burning. Serve hot or cold. Yield: 16 to 20 servings.

DeeDee Pomper, Alpha Rho Lambda
Farwell, Texas

SLOW-COOKER CHOCOLATE CAKE

1 (4-ounce) package chocolate instant pudding mix	2 cups sour cream
	4 eggs
	1 cup water
1 (2-layer) chocolate cake mix	3/4 cup vegetable oil
	1 cup chocolate chips

Combine the dry pudding mix, dry cake mix, sour cream, eggs, water and vegetable oil in a mixing bowl. Beat for 2 minutes or until smooth. Stir in the chocolate chips. Pour into a slow cooker. Cook on Low for 6 to 7 hours. Serve with whipped topping or ice cream. Yield: 16 servings.

Ginger Clawson, Xi Zeta Sigma
Ackley, Iowa

CHOCOLATE CHIP ZUCCHINI CAKE

1/2 cup (1 stick) margarine, softened	1/2 cup buttermilk
	1 teaspoon baking soda
1 2/3 cups sugar	1 teaspoon salt
1/2 cup olive oil or grape oil	2 cups shredded zucchini
	3/4 cup finely chopped walnuts or pecans
2 eggs	
2 1/2 cups flour	1/2 to 3/4 cup chocolate chips
1/4 cup baking cocoa	

Combine the margarine, sugar, olive oil and eggs in a large mixing bowl and beat until smooth. Add a mixture of the flour, baking cocoa, buttermilk, baking soda and salt. Beat for 2 minutes longer or until smooth. Stir in the zucchini. Pour into an ungreased 9×13-inch cake pan. Sprinkle with the chopped nuts and chocolate chips. Bake at 325 degrees for 45 to 50 minutes or until cake tests done. Yield: 15 servings.

Paula Schwenk, Xi Eta Tau
Pennsdale, Pennsylvania

CHOCOLATE POUND CAKE

In addition to this being my husband's favorite cake, it has been entered in seven county fairs, winning six blue ribbons and one red.

1 cup (2 sticks) butter or margarine, softened	1 cup sour cream
2 cups granulated sugar	1/4 teaspoon baking soda
1 cup firmly packed light brown sugar	2 1/2 cups flour
6 eggs, separated	1/2 cup baking cocoa
	1 teaspoon vanilla extract

Cream the butter and sugars in a mixing bowl until light and fluffy. Add the egg yolks 1 at a time, beating well after each addition. Stir the sour cream and baking soda together. Sift the flour and baking cocoa together. Add to the egg yolk mixture alternately with the sour cream mixture, beginning with flour mixture and ending with flour mixture, mixing well after each addition. Stir in the vanilla. Beat the egg whites in a mixing bowl until stiff peaks form. Fold gently into the batter. Pour into a buttered and floured 10-inch tube pan. Cut through the batter with a knife to eliminate air pockets. Bake at 325 degrees for 1 hour and 15 minutes. Cool in the pan for 15 minutes. Invert onto a serving plate. Yield: 16 servings.

Delona Shockey, Laureate Eta
Palmyra, Tennessee

MISSISSIPPI MUD CAKE

1 cup melted margarine	4 eggs
1/3 cup baking cocoa	2 cups sugar
1 1/2 cups chopped walnuts or pecans	1 (8-ounce) jar marshmallow creme
1 cup sweetened flaked coconut	Cocoa Frosting

Combine the margarine, baking cocoa, chopped nuts, coconut, eggs and sugar in a large bowl and mix well. Pour into an ungreased 9×13-inch cake pan. Bake at 350 degrees for 30 minutes. Spread the marshmallow creme over the hot cake. Frost the cooled cake with Cocoa Frosting. Yield: 12 to 15 servings.

COCOA FROSTING

1 pound confectioners' sugar	1/3 cup baking cocoa
1/2 cup (1 stick) margarine, softened	1/2 cup evaporated milk
	1 teaspoon vanilla extract

Combine the confectioners' sugar, margarine, baking cocoa, evaporated milk and vanilla in a mixing bowl and beat until smooth.

Jan Angotti, Laureate Lambda
Walla Walla, Washington

MOIST DEVIL'S FOOD CAKE

Be sure not to bake the cake longer than 40 minutes. The secret to baking a good cake is not to overbake!

2/3 cup (1 1/3 sticks) butter	1/2 cup baking cocoa
2 cups sugar	2 teaspoons baking soda
2 eggs	1 teaspoon salt
1 teaspoon vanilla extract	1 cup buttermilk
2 1/2 cups flour	1 cup boiling water
	Fudge Frosting

Cream the butter and sugar in a mixing bowl until light and fluffy. Add the eggs and beat well. Add the vanilla. Sift the flour before measuring; then sift three more times with the baking cocoa, baking soda and salt. Add the dry ingredients to the egg mixture alternately with the buttermilk, mixing well after each addition. Stir in the boiling water. Pour into two buttered and floured 9-inch cake pans, three 8-inch cake pans or a 9×13-inch cake pan. Bake at 350 degrees for 35 to 40 minutes. Let stand until cool. Frost the cooled cake with Fudge Frosting. Yield: 12 to 16 servings.

FUDGE FROSTING

3 cups sugar	1 teaspoon vanilla extract
3/4 cup (1 1/2 sticks) butter	
3/4 cup evaporated milk	1 cup chopped pecans (optional)
3/4 cup baking cocoa	

Combine the sugar, butter, evaporated milk, baking cocoa and vanilla in a 2-quart saucepan over medium heat. Bring to a full boil. Cook, stirring constantly, for 2 minutes or until a soft ball is formed when a small spoonful is dropped into ice-cold water. Remove from heat and beat until the mixture begins to thicken. Add the pecans and beat by hand until the frosting is of spreading consistency.

Shiela Shallcross, Xi Eta Pi
Arlington, Texas

FOUR-DAY CHOCOLATE CAKE

Use a chocolate cake mix without pudding in the mix.

1 (2-layer) chocolate
  cake mix
2¹/2 cups whipped
  topping
2 cups sour cream
2 cups shredded coconut

Prepare and bake the cake mix using the package directions for 8- or 9-inch cake pans. Slice the cooled cake into 4 layers. Spread a mixture of the whipped topping, sour cream and 1¹/2 cups of the coconut between the layers and over the top and side of the stacked 4 layers. Sprinkle the remaining coconut over the top. Chill in the refrigerator, covered, for at least 4 days. Yield: 16 servings.

Shirley Wolfe, Preceptor Alpha Lambda
Springfield, Missouri

CHOCOLATE CHIP PUDDING CAKE

1 (2-layer) chocolate
  cake mix
2 large eggs
6 snack pudding cups
1 to 2 cups chocolate
  chips
1 cup chopped walnuts
  or pecans

Combine the dry cake mix, eggs and pudding cups in a mixing bowl and beat at medium speed for 2 minutes. Batter will be thick. Pour into a lightly buttered or sprayed 9×13-inch cake pan. Top with chocolate chips and chopped nuts. Bake at 325 degrees for 45 minutes. Yield: 16 servings.

Donna Perrelle, Preceptor Gamma Psi
Terre Haute, Indiana

MOCHA CAKE

1 cup chocolate chips
¹/2 cup (1 stick) butter
3 eggs
3 egg yolks
1 (18-ounce) package
  brownie mix
2 tablespoons Kahlúa
1 quart coffee ice cream
Chocolate syrup for
  drizzling

Place the chocolate chips and butter in a microwave-safe bowl and microwave on High for 1 minute, stirring every 15 seconds. Let stand for 5 minutes. Combine the eggs and egg yolks in a mixing bowl and beat at medium speed for 5 minutes. Add the dry brownie mix; mix well. Fold in the melted chocolate mixture and Kahlúa. Fill 12 buttered muffin cups ²/3 full. Bake at 400 degrees for 12 minutes. Centers will be soft. Serve hot topped with ice cream and drizzled with chocolate syrup. Yield: 12 servings.

Lorraine Keatley, Laureate Lambda
Omaha, Nebraska

SWISS CHOCOLATE CAKE

1 (2-layer) package Swiss
  chocolate cake mix
3 eggs
¹/2 cup vegetable oil
Strawberry jam
2 to 3 tablespoons
  baking cocoa
12 ounces whipped
  topping

Prepare and bake the cake mix using the package directions, using 3 eggs and ¹/2 cup vegetable oil, in three or four 9-inch cake pans. Spread strawberry jam over the hot cake layers. Let stand until cool. Whisk the baking cocoa into the whipped topping in a bowl and spread between the layers and over the top of the cake to make a 3- or 4-layer cake. Serve with strawberries and cheese straws.
Yield: 12 to 16 servings.

Linda Smiley, Xi Beta Gamma
North Augusta, South Carolina

CHOCOLATE PRALINE TORTE

1 cup packed brown
  sugar
¹/2 cup (1 stick) butter
  (no substitute)
¹/4 cup heavy cream or
  evaporated milk
³/4 cup chopped pecans
1 (2-layer) package
  devil's food cake mix
1³/4 cups whipping cream
¹/4 cup confectioners'
  sugar
¹/4 teaspoon vanilla
  extract

Combine the brown sugar, butter and heavy cream in a saucepan. Cook over low heat until butter is melted, stirring constantly. Pour into two buttered 9-inch cake pans. Sprinkle the pecans over the top. Prepare the cake mix using the package directions. Pour the batter over the pecans. Bake at 325 degrees for 35 to 45 minutes or until cake tests done. Cool in the pans for 10 minutes; invert onto wire racks to cool completely. Beat the whipping cream until soft peaks form. Add the confectioners' sugar and vanilla; beat until stiff peaks form. Place a cake layer pecan side up on a serving plate. Spread with half the whipped cream mixture. Top with the second cake layer, pecan side up. Spread with the remaining whipped cream mixture. Garnish with chocolate curls.
Yield: 8 to 10 servings.

Lynda McDaniel, Iota Rho
Cornelius, North Carolina

---

*Lois Kotas, Laureate Kappa, Milligan, Nebraska, produces her **Incredible Chocolate Cake** by baking chocolate cake in a 9×13-inch pan, punching holes in the hot cake with a wooden spoon handle and pouring a can of sweetened condensed milk and a jar of caramel ice cream topping on top. Serve the cooled cake with whipped topping and crushed Heath bars.*

KATHRYN'S PROPOSAL CAKE

1 (2-layer) package
  Swiss chocolate cake
  mix
8 ounces cream cheese,
  softened
1 cup confectioners'
  sugar

½ cup granulated sugar
10 (2-ounce) milk
  chocolate candy bars
  with almonds
12 ounces whipped
  topping

Prepare the cake mix using the package directions. Pour into three buttered and floured 8-inch cake pans. Bake at 325 degrees for 20 to 25 minutes or until a wooden pick inserted in the center comes out clean. Remove from pans to a wire rack to cool completely. Combine the cream cheese, confectioners' sugar and granulated sugar in a mixing bowl and beat at medium speed until creamy. Finely chop 8 of the candy bars and fold into the cream cheese mixture. Spread between the layers and over the top and side of the cooled cake. Coarsely chop the remaining 2 candy bars and press on the top and side of the cake to decorate. Serve with whipped topping. Yield: 12 servings.

Kim DeCorte, Zeta Alpha
Sheridan, Arkansas

ENGLISH TOFFEE BAR CAKE

1 (2-layer) German
  chocolate cake mix
1 (14-ounce) can
  sweetened condensed
  milk
1 (12-ounce) jar caramel
  topping

1 cup whipped topping
3 (2-ounce) milk
  chocolate English
  toffee bars, crushed

Prepare and bake the cake mix using the package directions for a 9x13-inch cake pan. Remove from oven and immediately poke holes in the cake with a straw. Drizzle the condensed milk evenly over the top. Drizzle the caramel topping evenly over the condensed milk. Cool completely. Spread whipped topping over the top and sprinkle with the crushed candy bars. Chill until serving time. Yield: 12 servings.

Gerry Tetrault, Rho Master
Coralville, Iowa

SELF-FILLED CHOCOLATE CUPCAKES

1 (2-layer) package
  chocolate cake mix
8 ounces cream cheese,
  softened

⅓ cup sugar
1 egg
1 cup semisweet
  chocolate chips

Prepare the cake mix using the package directions. Fill paper-lined muffin cups ⅔ full. Cream the cream cheese and sugar in a mixing bowl until light and fluffy. Beat in the egg. Stir in the chocolate chips. Drop 1 rounded teaspoon of cream cheese mixture into each cupcake. Bake using the package directions for muffins. Yield: 30 cupcakes.

Stellene Matzdorff, Preceptor Beta Alpha
Lake Havasu City, Arizona

BLACKBOTTOM CUPCAKES

1½ cups flour
1⅓ cups sugar
¼ cup baking cocoa
1 teaspoon baking soda
½ teaspoon salt
1 cup water
½ cup vegetable oil
1 teaspoon vanilla
  extract

1 tablespoon white
  vinegar
8 ounces cream cheese,
  softened
1 egg, unbeaten
1 cup semisweet
  chocolate chips

Combine the flour, 1 cup of the sugar, baking cocoa, baking soda and salt in a mixing bowl and blend. Add the water, vegetable oil, vanilla and vinegar; beat at medium speed until smooth. Fill buttered muffin cups ⅓ full. Combine the cream cheese, egg and remaining ⅓ cup sugar in a separate bowl and beat until smooth. Stir in the chocolate chips. Drop cream cheese mixture by tablespoons, 1 over each cupcake. Sprinkle with nuts and additional sugar if desired. Bake at 350 degrees for 20 to 25 minutes or until cupcakes test done. Yield: about 18 cupcakes.

Joanne K. Mohr, Laureate Alpha Alpha
Brunswick, Georgia

FUDGY CUPCAKES

4 ounces semisweet
  chocolate
1 cup (2 sticks) butter
¼ teaspoon butter
  flavoring
1½ cups chopped pecans

1¾ cups sugar
4 large eggs
1 cup unsifted flour
2 teaspoons vanilla
  extract

Melt the chocolate and butter in a saucepan over medium-low heat, stirring frequently. Add the butter flavoring and pecans, stirring until nuts are well coated. Combine the sugar, eggs, flour and vanilla in a bowl and mix gently just until blended. Mix in the chocolate mixture; do not beat. Fill muffin cups ⅔ full. Bake at 325 degrees for 35 minutes or until cupcakes test done. Yield: 1 dozen.

Carolyn Waters, Xi Psi
Crestview, Florida

BROWNIE CUPCAKES

4 ounces unsweetened chocolate	1 cup flour
1 cup (2 sticks) butter	1³/4 cups sugar
1¹/2 cups chopped walnuts or pecans	4 eggs
	1 teaspoon vanilla extract

Place the chocolate in a microwave-safe bowl and microwave on High for 1 minute. Add the butter and microwave for 1 to 1¹/2 minutes longer or until melted. Stir in the chopped nuts. Combine the flour, sugar, eggs and vanilla in a bowl and mix well. Add to the chocolate mixture; blend well. Fill paper-lined muffin cups almost full. Bake at 325 degrees for 30 minutes. Yield: 18 cupcakes.

Anna L. Maiselson, Alpha Lambda Master
Thornton, Colorado

COCONUT CAKE WITH LEMON FILLING AND MARSHMALLOW FROSTING

Lemon Filling	¹/4 teaspoon salt
6 tablespoons butter, at room temperature	³/4 cup milk
1¹/2 cups sugar	1 teaspoon vanilla extract
3 eggs, separated	Marshmallow Frosting
2¹/4 cups flour, sifted	1 to 2 cups sweetened
1 tablespoon baking powder	shredded coconut

Prepare the Lemon Filling and chill, covered, in the refrigerator. Cream the butter and sugar in a mixing bowl for 4 minutes or until light and fluffy. Add the egg yolks 1 at a time, beating after each addition until thick and pale yellow. Place the egg whites in a separate mixing bowl and beat until stiff peaks form. Mix the flour, baking powder and salt together. Add to the sugar mixture alternately with the milk, mixing well after each addition. Stir in the vanilla. Fold in the beaten egg whites. Pour batter into three buttered and floured 8-inch cake pans. Bake at 350 degrees for 20 minutes. Cool completely and remove from pans. Spread the chilled filling between the cooled layers. Spread the Marshmallow Frosting over the top and the side of the cake. Sprinkle coconut over the entire cake and press gently into the side. Yield: 16 servings.

LEMON FILLING

Juice and grated zest of 2 lemons	2 eggs, beaten
1 cup sugar	2 tablespoons butter, melted

Combine the ingredients in the top of a double boiler. Cook over simmering water for 15 to 20 minutes or until thickened. Chill until ready to fill the cake.

MARSHMALLOW FROSTING

¹/3 cup water	Pinch of salt
1 cup sugar	2 egg whites
¹/8 teaspoon cream of tartar	1 teaspoon vanilla extract

Combine the water, sugar, cream of tartar and salt in a small heavy saucepan. Hook a candy thermometer to the side of the pan and cook to 240 degrees without stirring. Beat the egg whites until stiff peaks form. Pour the hot syrup over the beaten egg whites in a thin stream, beating constantly until thick and glossy. Stir in the vanilla.

Lynn Gustin, Alpha Zeta
Missoula, Montana

GRAHAM STREUSEL COFFEE CAKE

2 cups graham cracker crumbs (about 28 squares)	1 (2-layer) yellow cake mix
³/4 cup chopped pecans	1 cup water
³/4 cup packed brown sugar	¹/3 cup vegetable oil
¹/4 teaspoon cinnamon	3 eggs
³/4 cup (1¹/2 sticks) margarine, softened	1 cup confectioners' sugar

Combine the graham cracker crumbs, pecans, brown sugar and cinnamon in a bowl; mix well. Cut in the margarine until crumbly. Combine the cake mix, water, vegetable oil and eggs in a mixing bowl; beat at medium speed for 2 minutes or until moistened. Pour into a buttered and floured 9×13-inch cake pan. Sprinkle the crumb mixture evenly over the top. Bake at 350 degrees for 45 to 50 minutes or until cake tests done. Cool in the pan. Drizzle a mixture of the confectioners' sugar and 2 tablespoons water over the crumb layer. Yield: 15 servings.

Nancy A. Tosetti, Omicron Delta
Witt, Illinois

JEWISH COFFEE CAKE

1 cup (2 sticks) margarine, at room temperature	2 cups sour cream
	2 teaspoons baking soda
3 cups sugar	3 cups flour
4 eggs	¹/2 teaspoon salt
2 teaspoons vanilla extract	4 teaspoons cinnamon
	1 cup chopped walnuts or pecans (optional)

Cream the margarine and 2 cups of the sugar in a mixing bowl until light and fluffy. Add the eggs 1 at a time, beating well after each addition. Mix in the vanilla. Place the sour cream in a separate bowl and stir in the baking soda. Let stand for at least

5 minutes. Add the sour cream mixture to the sugar mixture and mix well. Fold in a mixture of the flour and salt. Combine the remaining 1 cup sugar, cinnamon and walnuts in a small bowl; mix well. Pour half the cake batter in a buttered and floured 9×13-inch cake pan. Spread half the cinnamon mixture over the batter. Cut through the batter with a knife. Pour the remaining batter over the top and sprinkle with the remaining cinnamon mixture. Bake at 350 degrees for 1 hour or until cake tests done. Yield: 15 servings.

Nicole Wieters, Xi Eta Pi
Fort Worth, Texas

ITALIAN COFFEE CAKE

1 cup sugar	1 teaspoon lemon extract
2 eggs	1/4 teaspoon cream of
1/2 cup milk	tartar
1/2 cup vegetable oil	1/2 cup chopped walnuts
2 cups flour	1/2 cup chopped
1/2 teaspoon baking	maraschino cherries
powder	1/2 cup semisweet
1/4 teaspoon baking soda	chocolate chips

Combine the sugar and eggs in a mixing bowl and beat at high speed until light. Whisk the milk and vegetable oil together and beat into the sugar mixture. Add a mixture of the flour, baking powder and baking soda. Add the lemon extract and cream of tartar; mix just enough to make a uniform batter. Mix in the walnuts, maraschino cherries and chocolate chips by hand. Pour into an unbuttered 10-inch tube pan. Bake at 325 degrees for 45 minutes; raise oven temperature to 350 degrees and bake for 10 or 15 minutes longer or until the cake tests done. Invert on a funnel to cool. Loosen the cake from the side of the pan. Invert onto a cake plate. Yield: about 12 servings.

Dianne "Dee" Ames, Xi Alpha Tau
Sanford, Maine

AMAZING CORN CAKE

1 (17-ounce) can cream-	1 tablespoon baking
style corn	powder
1/2 cup packed brown	1 teaspoon baking soda
sugar	1 teaspoon salt
3/4 cup granulated sugar	1 teaspoon cinnamon
3 eggs	1/2 cup raisins
1 cup vegetable oil	1/2 cup chopped walnuts
21/4 cups flour	or pecans

Combine the corn, brown sugar and granulated sugar in a mixing bowl and mix well. Beat in the eggs and oil. Add a mixture of the flour, baking powder, baking soda, salt and cinnamon; mix well. Stir in the raisins and nuts. Pour into a buttered 9×13-inch cake

pan. Bake at 350 degrees for 30 to 35 minutes or until cake tests done. Let stand until cool. Frost with caramel frosting. Yield: 18 servings.

Mildred Farr Cox, Alpha Master
Lexington, Kentucky

CRANBERRY PECAN POUND CAKE

11/2 cups (4 sticks)	2 cups flour
butter, softened (no	1 teaspoon baking
substitute)	powder
23/4 cups sugar	1/2 teaspoon salt
6 eggs	1 cup sour cream
21/2 teaspoons grated	1 cup chopped pecans
orange zest	1/2 cup shredded coconut
1 teaspoon vanilla	11/2 cups chopped fresh
extract	or frozen cranberries

Cream the butter and sugar in a mixing bowl for 5 to 7 minutes or until light. Beat in the eggs 1 at a time. Stir in the orange zest and vanilla. Sift the flour, baking powder and salt together; add to the creamed mixture alternately with the sour cream, beating at low speed just until moistened after each addition. Fold in the pecans, coconut and cranberries. Pour into a buttered and floured bundt pan or tube pan. Bake at 350 degrees for 65 to 70 minutes or until cake tests done. Cool in the pan for 10 minutes. Remove to a wire rack to cool completely. Yield: 12 servings.

Hollis McCright, Preceptor Delta
Big Spring, Texas

CRACKER CAKE

11/2 cups crushed saltine	2 teaspoons baking
crackers	powder
2 cups finely chopped	6 egg whites
pecans	12 ounces whipped
2 cups sugar	topping

Combine the cracker crumbs, pecans, sugar and baking powder in a bowl. Beat the egg whites in a separate bowl until stiff peaks form. Add the dry ingredients gradually to the egg whites; mix well. Spread in 3 heavily buttered and floured 8-inch cake pans. Bake at 325 degrees for 40 minutes. Cool in the pans for 10 minutes. Remove to a wire rack to cool completely. Spread a layer of whipped topping evenly over a serving plate. Place a cake layer over the whipped topping. Alternate layers of whipped topping and cake, ending with a cake layer. Spread whipped topping over the top and side of the 3-layer cake. Let stand, covered, in the refrigerator for 12 hours before serving. Yield: 12 to 14 servings.

Pamela S. Jones, Epsilon Alpha
Garland, Texas

COCOLA CAKE

2 cups sifted flour
2 cups sugar
3 rounded tablespoons
   baking cocoa
1/2 teaspoon salt
1/2 cup (1 stick)
   margarine
1/2 cup vegetable oil
1 cup cola beverage

1/2 cup buttermilk or
   sour milk
1 teaspoon baking soda
2 eggs, unbeaten
1 teaspoon vanilla
   extract
11/2 cups miniature
   marshmallows
Hot Cola Frosting

Sift the flour, sugar, baking cocoa and salt into a large bowl. Combine the margarine, vegetable oil and cola beverage in a saucepan and bring to a boil. Pour the hot cola mixture over the dry ingredients. Add the buttermilk, baking soda, eggs and vanilla; beat until smooth. Fold in the marshmallows. Pour into a buttered 9×13-inch cake pan. Smooth the top with a rubber spatula. Bake at 350 degrees for 45 to 50 minutes or until cake tests done. Spread Hot Cola Frosting over the warm cake. Cool in the pan.
Yield: 15 to 18 servings.

HOT COLA FROSTING

1/4 cup (1/2 stick)
   margarine
3 tablespoons cola
   beverage
2 tablespoons baking
   cocoa

11/2 cups confectioners'
1/2 teaspoon vanilla
   extract
1 cup chopped pecans or
   coconut

Combine the margarine, cola and baking cocoa in a saucepan and bring to a boil. Stir in the confectioners' sugar, vanilla and chopped pecans.

Jan Charbonneau, Preceptor Zeta
Yakima, Washington

CREAM CHEESE COCONUT POUND CAKE

1/2 cup (1 stick) butter,
   softened
1/2 cup shortening
8 ounces cream chese,
   softened
3 cups sugar
6 eggs
3 cups flour
1/4 teaspoon salt

1/4 teaspoon baking
   powder
1 (6-ounce) package
   frozen coconut,
   thawed
1 teaspoon coconut
   extract
1 teaspoon vanilla
   extract

Beat the butter, shortening and cream cheese in a mixing bowl until well blended. Add the sugar gradually, beating at medium speed until light and fluffy. Beat in the eggs 1 at a time. Add a mixture of the flour, salt and baking soda and beat until blended.

Stir in the coconut and flavorings. Spoon the batter into a greased and floured tube pan. Bake at 350 degrees for 11/4 hours or until the cake tests done. Cool in the pan for 10 to 15 minutes and invert onto a wire rack or serving plate to cool completely.
Yield: 12 to 16 servings.

Marilyn Borras, Preceptor Alpha Zeta
Stafford, Virginia

DATE CAKE

11/2 cups chopped dates
1 teaspoon baking soda
1/4 cup (1/2 stick) butter
11/2 cups boiling water
1 egg, beaten
1 teaspoon salt
1 teaspoon vanilla
   extract

1 cup sugar
11/2 cups flour
1 teaspoon baking
   powder
Date Topping

Combine the dates, baking soda, butter and boiling water in a bowl; let stand for at least 10 minutes. Combine the egg, salt, vanilla and sugar in a separate bowl and mix well. Stir into the dates mixture. Add a mixture of the flour and baking powder gradually, stirring well. Bake at 350 degrees for 30 minutes. Remove from oven. Spread warm Date Topping over the hot cake. Let stand until cool. Serve with whipped cream if desired. Yield: 12 to 15 servings.

DATE TOPPING

1 cup chopped dates
3/4 cup water
1/8 teaspoon salt
1 cup sugar

1 tablespoon butter
1 cup halved walnuts or
   pecans

Combine the dates, water, salt, sugar and butter in a saucepan over medium heat. Cook until thickened. Stir in the walnuts.

Juanita Shaffer, Preceptor Mu Chi
Atascadero, California

MEXICAN FRUIT CAKE

1 (15-ounce) can crushed
   pineapple
2 cups flour
1 cup pecan or walnut
   pieces
2 teaspoons baking soda
2 cups sugar
2 eggs

8 ounces cream cheese,
   softened
2 cups confectioners'
   sugar
1/2 cup (1 stick)
   margarine, softened
1 teaspoon vanilla
   extract

Combine the undrained pineapple, flour, nuts, baking soda, sugar and eggs in a large bowl and mix well. Spread in a buttered 9×13-inch cake pan. Bake at

350 degrees for 45 minutes. Combine the remaining ingredients in a mixing bowl and beat until smooth. Spread over the cooled cake. Yield: 12 to 15 servings.

Lecieta Taylor, Theta Theta
Independence, Kansas

MINIATURE FRUITCAKES

3/4 cup sugar
1/4 cup flour
1/2 teaspoon baking
  powder
1/8 teaspoon salt
1 1/2 cups chopped
  walnuts
1 cup chopped dates

3/4 cup (4 ounces)
  chopped mixed
  candied fruits
2 eggs, separated
1/2 teaspoon vanilla
  extract
Candied cherries, halved

Combine the sugar, flour, baking powder, salt, walnuts, dates and mixed candied fruits in a bowl; mix well. Blend the egg yolks and vanilla in a small bowl; stir into the date mixture. Beat the egg whites in a small mixing bowl until stiff peaks form. Fold the egg whites into the date mixture. Fill buttered and floured muffin cups 2/3 full. Cover tightly with heavy-duty foil. Bake at 275 degrees for about 1 hour. Uncover when almost done. Top with cherry halves for the last 5 minutes of baking. Yield: 1 dozen.

Connie Tillison, Laureate Omicron
Elberton, Georgia

PECAN FRUITCAKE

1 pound candied cherries
1 pound candied
  pineapple
1 pound pitted dates
7 cups pecans
2 cups flour
2 teaspoons baking
  powder

2 (8-ounce) packages
  frozen coconut,
  thawed
2 (14-ounce) cans
  sweetened condensed
  milk

Chop the cherries, pineapple, dates and pecans finely and combine in a large bowl. Sift the flour and baking powder together. Sprinkle enough of the flour mixture over the fruit mixture to coat and separate the pieces, tossing until well mixed. Add the coconut and toss to mix. Add the remaining flour mixture and toss. Stir in the condensed milk and mix well. Pack the mixture into 2 greased 5×9-inch loaf pans, leaving no air pockets. Bake at 350 degrees for 45 minutes to 1 hour or until the cakes begin to pull from the sides of the pans and are golden brown. Cool for several minutes and turn onto wire racks to cool completely. Cut into thin slices. Yield: variable.

Dorothy Stembridge, Lambda Master
Tampa, Florida

THIRTY-DAY FRIENDSHIP CAKE

The 1 1/2 cups of fruit is prepared as you make the starter.

1 1/2 cups drained
  Friendship fruit
2/3 cup vegetable oil
1 cup shredded coconut
1 (2-layer) package
  butter recipe cake mix

1 (4-ounce) package
  vanilla instant
  pudding mix
4 eggs, beaten
1 cup chopped pecans or
  walnuts

Combine all the ingredients in a large bowl and mix well. Pour into a buttered and floured tube pan or bundt pan. Bake at 300 degrees for 1 to 1 1/2 hours or until a straw inserted in the center comes out clean. If top of cake browns too quickly, place a sheet of foil across the top of the pan for the last part of the baking time. For best results, make each cake 1 at a time. Yield: 3 (16-serving) cakes.

FRIENDSHIP STARTER

1 1/2 cups Starter juice or
  peach brandy
5 cups sugar
1 (16-ounce) can sliced
  peaches in juice, cut
  into small pieces

1 (20-ounce) can
  pineapple tidbits
  in juice
2 (9-ounce) jars
  maraschino cherries,
  drained and halved

Day One: Combine the starter juice or peach brandy, 2 1/2 cups of the sugar and undrained peaches in a large nonmetallic bowl. Let stand at room temperature, loosely covered, for 10 days; stir daily with a nonmetallic spoon. Sugar may not dissolve completely for several days. Day Ten: Add the remaining 2 1/2 cups sugar and undrained pineapple. Stir daily for 10 more days. Fruit may begin to foam when stirred. Day Twenty: Add the cherries. Stir daily for 10 more days. Day Thirty: Drain the fruit, reserving the juice to make Starter. Note: Never refrigerate the Starter; Day One must start within a week after the fruit has drained. Yield: 3 starters.

Tamera Erskine, Eta Xi
Alabaster, Alabama

*Sharon Fitzgerald, Xi Omega, Washington, Indiana, makes a favorite **Peaches and Cream Cake** by preparing a yellow cake mix with a large package of vanilla pudding mix, 1 cup water, 1 cup vegetable oil and 4 eggs and pouring the batter into a prepared 9×13-inch pan. She arranges a large can of drained peach slices on the batter and pours a mixture of 8 ounces cream cheese, 1 cup sugar and 6 tablespoons of the peach syrup over the top. Bake at 350 degrees for about 50 minutes.*

FRUIT COCKTAIL CAKE

1½ cups plus ¾ cup sugar	½ (12-ounce) can evaporated milk
2 cups flour	½ cup (1 stick) butter
2 teaspoons baking soda	½ teaspoon vanilla extract
2 eggs	
1 cup fruit cocktail	

Combine the 1½ cups sugar, flour, baking soda, eggs and undrained fruit cocktail in the order listed in a bowl, mixing after each addition. Pour into a buttered and floured 9×13-inch cake pan. Bake at 350 degrees for 45 minutes or until cake tests done. Combine the ¾ cup sugar, evaporated milk and butter in a saucepan; bring to a boil. Boil for 1 minute without stirring. Remove from heat. Stir in the vanilla. Drizzle evenly over the warm cake. Yield: 15 servings.

Cheryl Baxley, Zeta Theta
Hobbs, New Mexico

GINGERBREAD

1⅓ cups flour	¾ teaspoon cinnamon
½ cup packed brown sugar	½ teaspoon ginger
½ teaspoon baking powder	½ cup shortening
½ teaspoon baking soda	½ cup boiling water
¼ teaspoon salt	½ cup molasses
	1 egg, slightly beaten

Butter the bottom of a 9×9-inch cake pan; do not butter the sides. Combine the flour, brown sugar, baking powder, baking soda, salt, cinnamon and ginger in a large bowl and mix well. Add the remaining ingredients; blend well. Pour into the prepared pan. Bake at 350 degrees for 25 to 35 minutes or until cake tests done. Serve with a lemon sauce or brown sugar sauce. Yield: 9 to 16 servings.

Erma Henderson, Laureate Delta
Truro, Nova Scotia, Canada

GELATIN CAKE

1 (2-layer) package white cake mix	8 ounces whipped topping
1 (3-ounce) package gelatin, any flavor	

Prepare and bake the cake mix using the package directions for a 9×13-inch cake pan. Pierce cake with a fork several times. Prepare the gelatin using the package directions; pour the hot gelatin mixture over the warm cake. Cool. Spread with whipped topping. Yield: 15 servings.

Tamara Jahnke, Alpha
Vinita, Oklahoma

FOURTH OF JULY JELLY ROLL

4 eggs, separated	¾ teaspoon baking soda
¾ cup sugar	¼ teaspoon salt
1 teaspoon vanilla extract	Cherry, strawberry or grape jam
¾ cup sifted flour	Confectioners' sugar

Place the egg yolks in a mixing bowl and beat until light and pale yellow. Add the sugar and vanilla gradually, mixing well. Sift the flour and baking soda together and add to the sugar mixture gradually, beating until smooth. Beat the egg whites and salt in a bowl until stiff peaks form. Fold into the flour mixture. Line a 10×15-inch cake pan with buttered parchment paper. Spread the batter evenly in the pan. Bake at 375 degrees for 13 minutes. Dust a clean kitchen towel generously with confectioners' sugar. Invert the cake onto the towel. Remove the parchment paper and trim the edges. Roll the warm cake in the towel as for a jelly roll from the short side and place on a wire rack to cool. Unroll the cooled cake carefully and remove the towel. Spread the jam to within 1 inch of the edge and reroll. Wrap in waxed paper and chill until serving time. Sprinkle with confectioners' sugar; insert a candle in one end and light the candle. Yield: 8 servings.

Nancy Aufderheide, Pi Iota
Shawnee, Kansas

MELTED ICE CREAM CAKE

1 (2-layer) package white cake mix	⅓ (16-ounce) can fudge frosting
2 cups melted cherry ice cream (or flavor of choice)	⅓ (16-ounce) can white frosting
3 large eggs	⅓ (16-ounce) can cherry frosting

Spray a bundt pan lightly with nonstick cooking spray and dust with flour. Combine the cake mix, melted ice cream and eggs in a large mixing bowl. Beat at low speed for 1 minute, scraping the side of the bowl. Beat at medium speed for 2 minutes. Pour into the prepared bundt pan, smoothing the surface with a rubber spatula. Bake at 350 degrees for 38 to 42 minutes or until cake begins to pull away from the side of the pan and top springs back when touched lightly. Cool in the pan for 20 minutes. Invert on a wire rack to cool completely. Place on waxed paper. Microwave the fudge frosting on High for 15 to 20 seconds; drizzle over the cooled cake. Repeat with white frosting and cherry frosting. Yield: 16 servings.

Jean Saveraid, Xi Theta Zeta
Huxley, Iowa

ICE CREAM POUND CAKE

1 cup (2 sticks) butter
1 cup (2 sticks)
  margarine
2 cups sugar
8 eggs
1 teaspoon vanilla
  extract
4 cups cake flour
1 teaspoon baking
  powder
1 cup vanilla ice cream,
  softened

Combine the butter, margarine, sugar, eggs, vanilla, flour, baking powder and ice cream in the order listed in a mixing bowl, mixing at medium speed after each addition. Pour into a buttered and floured large tube pan. Bake at 300 degrees for 1½ hours. Cool in the pan. Invert cooled cake onto a serving plate. Sprinkle with confectioners' sugar and serve. Yield: 12 or more servings.

Edna Buesing, Laureate Alpha Zeta
Wallkill, New York

AMARETTO SOUR CREAM CAKE

2 eggs, separated
½ cup firmly packed
  brown sugar
1 cup shredded coconut
½ cup ground pecans
1 cup sour cream
1 (2-layer) package
  butter recipe cake mix
½ cup amaretto
½ cup water
2 whole eggs
Amaretto Glaze

Generously butter a 10-inch tube pan. Beat the egg whites in a mixing bowl until foamy. Add the brown sugar gradually, beating until stiff peaks form (about 3 minutes). Fold in the coconut and pecans. Spread the meringue over the bottom and up the side of the prepared tube pan. Combine the sour cream, cake mix, amaretto, water, whole eggs and egg yolks in a mixing bowl and mix at low speed until moistened. Beat at high speed for 2 minutes. Pour the batter into the meringue-lined tube pan. Bake at 350 degrees for 55 to 65 minutes or until cake tests done. Cool in the pan for 15 minutes. Loosen the cake from the side of the pan. Invert onto a cake plate. Drizzle with Amaretto Glaze. Yield: 16 servings.

AMARETTO GLAZE

2 tablespoons amaretto
1 tablespoon margarine,
  softened
1 tablespoon light corn
  syrup
2 to 4 teaspoons water
2 teaspoons ground
  pecans

Combine the amaretto, margarine, corn syrup, water and pecans in a small bowl and blend well.

Cheryl Powell, Preceptor Nu Nu
Calipatria, California

SIMPLE LEMON CAKE

1 cup (2 sticks) butter,
  softened
2½ cups sugar
4 large eggs
2 teaspoons baking
  powder
1 teaspoon salt
3 cups unbleached flour
1 cup whole milk
Grated zest of 2 large
  lemons
⅓ cup fresh lemon juice

Cream the butter and 2 cups of the sugar in a mixing bowl until light and fluffy. Add the eggs 1 at a time, beating well after each addition. Add a mixture of the baking powder, salt and flour alternately with the milk, mixing well after each addition. Stir in the lemon zest. Pour into a bundt pan or tube pan that has been oiled and floured. Bake at 350 degrees for 60 to 70 minutes or until cake tests done. Cool in the pan for 5 minutes. Loosen the cake from the side of the pan. Invert onto a cake plate. Brush the hot cake with a mixture of the lemon juice and the remaining ½ cup sugar. Yield: 10 to 12 servings.

Louise Doll-Borr, Delta Alpha Master
Yuba City, California

LEMON POUND CAKE

1 cup shortening
3 cups sugar
6 eggs
3 cups flour
½ teaspoon salt
¼ teaspoon baking soda
1 cup buttermilk
1 teaspoon lemon
  extract
1 teaspoon vanilla
  extract

Cream the shortening and sugar in a mixing bowl until light and fluffy. Add the eggs 1 at a time, beating well after each addition. Sift the flour, salt and baking soda together. Add to the creamed mixture alternately with the buttermilk, mixing well after each addition. Add the lemon extract and vanilla. Pour into a buttered 9-inch tube pan. Bake at 350 degrees for 1 hour and 15 minutes. Cool in the pan for 15 minutes. Invert onto a cake plate.
Yield: 16 servings.

Gloria Wells, Xi Beta Epsilon
Ocean Pines, Maryland

Debbie Morgan, Alpha Gamma, Marshalltown, Iowa, makes a hit with **Summertime Lemon Poke Cake.** *She prepares and bakes a lemon cake mix in a 9×13-inch pan, cools for 15 minutes, pokes holes every ½ inch with a fork, and pours a mixture of a 6-ounce can of frozen lemonade concentrate and ¾ cup confectioners' sugar over the warm cake. Chill and serve topped with whipped topping or white or lemon canned frosting.*

SWEET-AND-SOUR CAKE

1 (2-layer) package	4 eggs
white cake mix	2 cups confectioners'
1½ cups water	sugar
⅓ cup vegetable oil	⅓ cup lemon juice
3 tablespoons flour	

Beat the cake mix, water, vegetable oil, flour and eggs in a mixing bowl until smooth. Pour into a buttered and floured 9×13-inch cake pan. Bake at 375 degrees for 30 minutes or until cake tests done. Poke holes in the warm cake with a fork and drizzle with a mixture of the confectioners' sugar and lemon juice. Serve with whipped topping if desired. Yield: 15 servings.

Kathy Ryder, Xi Alpha Gamma
Rock Springs, Wyoming

HOT MILK CAKE

2 eggs	1 teaspoon plus
1 cup granulated sugar	2 tablespoons butter,
1 teaspoon vanilla	softened
extract	5 tablespoons brown
1 cup flour	sugar
1 teaspoon baking	3 tablespoons cream or
powder	milk
Pinch of salt	½ cup shredded coconut
½ cup milk	or chopped nuts

Place the eggs in a mixing bowl and beat until pale yellow. Add the granulated sugar and vanilla gradually, beating until light and fluffy. Sift the flour, baking powder and salt together. Fold the flour mixture into the batter. Warm the milk in a saucepan over low heat and stir in the 1 teaspoon butter. Add to the batter and beat well. Pour into a buttered and floured 9×9-inch cake pan. Bake at 350 degrees for 25 to 30 minutes or until cake tests done. Combine the brown sugar, the 2 tablespoons butter, cream and coconut; mix well. Spread the brown sugar mixture over the cooled cake. Broil 6 inches from a heat source until browned. Yield: 9 servings.

Sherry Hayes, Xi Beta Pi
Coeur d'Alene, Idaho

MINCEMEAT CAKE

1 (9-ounce) package	1 teaspoon each ground
mincemeat	cloves, allspice,
3 cups sugar	cinnamon, ginger and
1 cup shortening	nutmeg
3 eggs	1 cup chopped walnuts
2 teaspoons baking soda	1 (9-ounce) jar
1 cup buttermilk	maraschino cherries,
4 cups flour	drained and halved

Place 2 cups of water in a saucepan over medium-high heat and bring to a boil. Add the mincemeat and stir well. Stir in 1 cup of the sugar. Reduce heat to low and cook for a few minutes, stirring occasionally. Remove from heat. Cream the shortening and remaining 2 cups sugar in a mixing bowl until light and fluffy. Add the eggs 1 at a time, beating well after each addition. Dissolve the baking soda in the buttermilk. Combine the flour, cloves, allspice, cinnamon, ginger and nutmeg in a bowl and mix well. Add the buttermilk mixture to the creamed mixture alternately with the dry ingredients. Stir in the mincemeat mixture, walnuts and cherries. Pour into a greased and floured 10-inch tube pan. Bake at 325 degrees for 1 hour. Yield: 16 servings.

Luella Finton, Beta Omicron
Poteau, Oklahoma

OATMEAL CAKE

1 cup quick-cooking	1 teaspoon nutmeg
oats	1 teaspoon vanilla
½ cup (1 stick)	extract
margarine	1½ teaspoons cinnamon
1 cup packed brown	1⅓ cups flour
sugar	1 teaspoon baking soda
1 cup granulated sugar	1 teaspoon salt
2 eggs	Coconut Pecan Topping

Place the oats in a bowl. Pour 1¼ cups boiling water over the oats. Let stand for 20 minutes. Cream the margarine and sugars in a mixing bowl until light and fluffy. Beat in the eggs, nutmeg, vanilla and cinnamon. Stir in the oat mixture. Stir in a mixture of the flour, baking soda and salt. Pour into a buttered 9×11-inch cake pan. Bake at 350 degrees for 30 minutes. Pour the Coconut Pecan Topping over the warm cake and return to the oven for 10 minutes longer. Serve warm or cold. Yield: 12 servings.

COCONUT PECAN TOPPING

⅔ cup packed brown	3 tablespoons melted
sugar	margarine
1 cup shredded coconut	1 cup chopped pecans
3 to 4 tablespoons	1 egg
heavy cream or	
half-and-half	

Combine the brown sugar, coconut, cream, margarine, pecans and egg in a bowl and mix well.

Cora J. Slaughter, Xi Alpha Eta
Vero Beach, Florida

AMBROSIA CAKE

1 (2-layer) package
    orange supreme cake
    mix
2 eggs
1/2 cup vegetable oil
1 (11-ounce) can
    mandarin oranges

1 (20-ounce) can crushed
    pineapple
1 (4-ounce) package
    vanilla instant
    pudding mix
8 ounces whipped
    topping

Combine the cake mix, eggs, vegetable oil and undrained mandarin oranges in a bowl and mix well. Pour into a buttered 9×13-inch cake pan. Bake at 350 degrees for 40 minutes or until top of cake springs back when lightly pressed. Cool in the pan. Place the undrained pineapple and dry pudding mix in a bowl; mix well. Let stand for 5 minutes. Spread over the cooled cake. Spread whipped topping over the pineapple layer. Cut in squares to serve. Top each square with a spoonful of whipped topping topped with an orange slice and pineapple chunk and sprinkled with shredded coconut. Yield: 18 to 20 servings.

Sheila Schlarb, Gamma Iota
Trenton, Missouri

FUZZY NAVEL CAKE

1 (2-layer) package
    orange cake mix
1 (21-ounce) can peach
    pie filling
2 eggs
1 cup sour cream
8 ounces cream cheese,
    softened

1 (20-ounce) can crushed
    pineapple
1 (4-ounce) package
    vanilla instant
    pudding mix
8 ounces whipped
    topping

Combine the cake mix, peach pie filling, eggs and sour cream in a large bowl and mix well by hand. Pour into a buttered and floured 9×13-inch cake pan. Bake at 350 degrees for 25 to 30 minutes or until cake tests done. Cool in the pan. Beat the cream cheese, pineapple, pudding mix and whipped topping in a mixing bowl at medium speed until well blended. Pour evenly over the cooled cake. Chill, covered, until ready to serve. Yield: 15 servings.

Deborah R. Childress, Theta Theta
Clintwood, Virginia

Amberlee O'Connor, Zeta, Ottawa, Ontario, Canada, shares her **Pineapple Cake** *recipe. Combine 2 cups flour, 2 cups undrained crushed pineapple, 2 cups sugar, 2 teaspoons baking soda, 2 eggs and 1 cup walnuts and mix well. Bake in a prepared 9×12-inch pan at 350 degrees for 30 to 35 minutes. Frost with a cream cheese frosting.*

CARAMEL-GLAZED PINEAPPLE CAKE

2 cups granulated sugar
2 cups flour
1 teaspoon baking soda
1/2 teaspoon salt
2 eggs, slightly beaten
1 (20-ounce) can crushed
    pineapple
1/2 cup packed brown
    sugar

1/2 cup chopped walnuts
    or pecans
1/2 cup (1 stick)
    margarine
1 cup sweetened
    condensed milk
1 teaspoon vanilla
    extract

Combine 1 1/2 cups of the granulated sugar, flour, baking soda and salt in a large bowl and mix well. Add the eggs and undrained pineapple; mix well. Pour into a buttered 9×13-inch cake pan. Sprinkle a mixture of the brown sugar and walnuts over the top. Bake at 350 degrees for 40 minutes or until cake tests done. Combine the margarine, condensed milk, vanilla and remaining 1/2 cup sugar in a saucepan; bring to a boil. Pour evenly over the hot cake. Cool in the pan. Serve with whipped topping.
Yield: 12 servings.

Roberta Renville, Laureate Beta Omega
Kankakee, Illinois

PINEAPPLE CAKE WITH CREAM CHEESE FROSTING

1/2 cup egg substitute
2 cups sugar
2 cups flour
2 teaspoons baking soda
1 (20-ounce) can crushed
    pineapple, drained

1 teaspoon vanilla
    extract
1/4 cup chopped walnuts
    or pecans (optional)
Cream Cheese Frosting

Beat the egg substitute and sugar in a mixing bowl at medium speed until smooth. Mix the flour and baking soda together; beat into the egg mixture. Add the pineapple; beat until well blended. Stir in the vanilla and walnuts. Pour into a 9×13-inch cake pan that has been sprayed with nonstick cooking spray. Bake at 350 degrees for 35 to 40 minutes or until cake tests done. Frost with Cream Cheese Frosting. Yield: 15 servings.

CREAM CHEESE FROSTING

8 ounces fat-free cream
    cheese, softened
1 1/2 cups confectioners'
    sugar

1/4 teaspoon vanilla
    extract

Stir the cream cheese until creamy. Stir in the confectioners' sugar a little at a time. Stir in the vanilla. If frosting becomes too runny, add a bit of dry vanilla instant pudding mix.

Ann Joy Hardy, Xi Zeta Iota
Winter Haven, Florida

ICED PINEAPPLE PECAN CAKE

2 cups sugar
2 cups flour
2 eggs
2 teaspoons baking soda
1 (20-ounce) can crushed
    pineapple, slightly
    drained
1 1/2 cups finely chopped
    pecans

8 ounces cream cheese,
    softened
1/2 cup (1 stick) butter,
    softened
1 cup confectioners'
    sugar
1 teaspoon vanilla
    extract

Combine the sugar, flour, eggs, baking soda, pineapple and 1 cup of the pecans in a large bowl and mix well. Pour into a buttered 9×13-inch cake pan. Bake at 350 degrees for 45 minutes. Cool in the pan. Combine the cream cheese and butter in a bowl; stir until well blended. Stir in the confectioners' sugar and vanilla. Spread over the top of the cooled cake. Sprinkle with the remaining 1/2 cup pecans. Yield: 12 to 15 servings.

Helen Schoenrock, Lambda Master
Fairbury, Nebraska

PINEAPPLE COCONUT CAKE

2 cups sifted flour
1 1/2 cups granulated
    sugar
1 1/2 teaspoons baking
    soda
1 teaspoon salt
2 eggs, well beaten

1 (20-ounce) can crushed
    pineapple in syrup
1/3 cup packed brown
    sugar
1/3 cup chopped pecans
Coconut Topping

Combine the flour, granulated sugar, baking soda and salt in a large bowl; mix well. Add the eggs and undrained pineapple a little at a time; stir until moistened. Pour into a buttered 9×13-inch cake pan. Sprinkle with a mixture of the brown sugar and pecans. Bake at 350 degrees for about 40 minutes or until golden brown. Pour warm Coconut Topping over the warm cake, or the topping may be poured over individual pieces of cake at serving time. Yield: 12 to 14 servings.

COCONUT TOPPING

1/4 cup (1/2 stick) butter
6 ounces evaporated
    milk
1 cup granulated sugar

3 tablespoons brown
    sugar
1/3 cup flaked coconut
1/3 cup chopped pecans

Melt the butter in a saucepan over low heat. Add the next 3 ingredients gradually, stirring constantly. Stir in the coconut and pecans.

E. Irene Piper, Alpha Beta
Bedford, Indiana

PEANUT BUTTER CAKE

1 (2-layer) yellow cake
    mix
1 cup creamy peanut
    butter
3/8 cup margarine,
    softened
2 cups confectioners'
    sugar

1 teaspoon vanilla
    extract
3 tablespoons creamy
    peanut butter
2 to 4 tablespoons milk

Prepare and bake the cake mix using the package directions for a 9×13-inch cake pan, reducing the amount of vegetable oil by 1 tablespoon, increasing the amount of water by 1 tablespoon and mixing in 1 cup of the peanut butter. Bake a little longer than directed if necessary. Cool in the pan. Combine the margarine, confectioners' sugar, vanilla and remaining 3 tablespoons peanut butter in a mixing bowl; beat until smooth. Beat in enough milk to make the mixture of spreading consistency. Frost the cooled cake. Yield: 15 servings.

Christine Page, Preceptor Beta Sigma
Niagara Falls, New York

PISTACHIO CAKE

1 (2-layer) package
    white cake mix
1 (4-ounce) package
    pistachio instant
    pudding mix
3 eggs

3/4 cup vegetable oil
1 cup lemon-lime soda
1/2 cup chopped walnuts
    or pecans
1/2 cup shredded coconut
Pistachio Frosting

Combine the cake mix, pudding mix, eggs, vegetable oil and lemon-lime soda in a mixing bowl. Beat using the directions on the cake mix package. Stir in the walnuts and coconut. Pour into a buttered 9×13-inch cake pan or 2 greased and floured round cake pans. Bake using the package directions. Frost cooled cake with Pistachio Frosting. Store the cake in the refrigerator. Yield: 12 to 15 servings.

PISTACHIO FROSTING

1 (4-ounce) package
    pistachio instant
    pudding mix
1 1/2 cups milk

2 envelopes whipped
    topping mix
3 ounces cream cheese,
    softened

Combine the pudding mix, milk, whipped topping mix and cream cheese in a mixing bowl. Beat until the mixture is of spreading consistency.

Cheryl High, Xi Sigma Zeta
Chatsworth, California

PUMPKIN CAKE

2 cups sugar
1½ cups vegetable oil
1 (15-ounce) can pumpkin
4 eggs
2 cups sifted cake flour
1 teaspoon salt
2 teaspoons cinnamon
2 teaspoons baking powder
2 teaspoons baking soda
1 cup chopped pecans
1 cup shredded coconut

Combine the sugar, vegetable oil, pumpkin and eggs in a mixing bowl; beat until smooth. Place the flour, salt, cinnamon, baking powder and baking soda in a separate bowl; stir to combine. Add the flour mixture to the pumpkin mixture. Stir in the pecans and coconut. Pour into a buttered and floured 9×13-inch cake pan or bundt pan. Bake at 350 degrees for 45 to 60 minutes or until a wooden pick inserted in the center comes out clean. Top with a glaze or with a cream cheese frosting that contains nuts and coconut. Yield: about 15 servings.

Sandra Chamblee, Xi Zeta Mu
Belle Glade, Florida

PUMPKIN CAKE ROLL

¾ cup flour
½ teaspoon baking powder
½ teaspoon baking soda
½ teaspoon cinnamon
½ teaspoon ground cloves
¼ teaspoon salt
3 large eggs
1 cup sugar
⅔ cup canned pumpkin
1 cup chopped pecans
8 ounces cream cheese, softened
1 cup confectioners' sugar
6 tablespoons butter, softened
1 teaspoon vanilla extract

Mix the first 6 ingredients in a small bowl. Beat the eggs and sugar in a large bowl until thick. Beat in the pumpkin. Stir in the flour mixture. Spread in a waxed paper-lined 10×15-inch cake pan. Sprinkle with pecans. Bake at 375 degrees for 13 to 15 minutes or until cake tests done. Dust a clean kitchen towel with confectioners' sugar. Invert the cake onto the towel. Remove the waxed paper and trim the edges. Roll the warm cake in the towel as for a jelly roll from the short side and place on a wire rack to cool. Combine the cream cheese, confectioners' sugar, butter and vanilla in a mixing bowl and beat until smooth. Unroll the cooled cake carefully and remove the towel. Spread the cream cheese mixture to within 1 inch of the edge and reroll. Wrap in plastic wrap and chill until serving time. Unwrap cake and sprinkle with confectioners' sugar before serving. Yield: 10 servings.

Thelma McDonald, Beta Gamma Master
El Paso, Texas

PUMPKIN PIE CAKE

1 (29-ounce) can pumpkin
1 (12-ounce) can evaporated milk
3 eggs
½ teaspoon salt
1 cup sugar
1 teaspoon cinnamon
½ teaspoon nutmeg
½ teaspoon ginger
1 (2-layer) package spice cake mix
1 cup chopped pecans
¾ cup (1½ sticks) margarine, melted

Combine the pumpkin, evaporated milk, eggs, salt, sugar, cinnamon, nutmeg and ginger in a bowl; mix well. Pour into a buttered 9×13-inch cake pan. Sprinkle dry spice cake mix evenly over the pumpkin mixture. Layer pecans over the cake mix. Drizzle with melted margarine. Bake at 350 degrees for 1 hour or until a wooden pick inserted in the center comes out clean. Serve with cinnamon-flavored whipped topping. Yield: 12 servings.

Dorothy Miles, Laureate Alpha Rho
Cape Girardeau, Missouri

POPPY SEED CAKE

3 cups flour
1½ teaspoons baking powder
1½ cups milk
1½ tablespoons poppy seeds
1½ teaspoons vanilla extract
¼ teaspoon baking soda
2½ cups sugar
1 cup plus 1 tablespoon vegetable oil
3 eggs
1½ teaspoons almond extract
1½ teaspoons salt
Orange Glaze

Combine the flour, baking powder, milk, poppy seeds, vanilla, baking soda, sugar, vegetable oil, eggs, almond extract and salt in a mixing bowl; beat at medium speed for 2 minutes. Pour into 2 buttered and floured loaf pans. Bake at 350 degrees for 1 hour and 10 minutes. Poke holes in the warm cake and drizzle with Orange Glaze. Yield: 20 servings.

ORANGE GLAZE

¾ cup sugar
¼ cup orange juice
2 tablespoons melted margarine
½ teaspoon vanilla extract
½ teaspoon almond extract

Combine the sugar, orange juice, margarine, vanilla and almond extract in a bowl; whisk until smooth.

Wendy Golec, Iota Omega
Acworth, Georgia

POPPY SEED RUM CAKE

Be sure to use a cake mix that does not have "pudding in the mix."

Butter	1/4 cup flour
Sugar	1/2 cup water
1 (2-layer) package	1/2 cup dark rum
yellow cake mix	1/2 cup vegetable oil
1 (4-ounce) package	4 eggs, beaten
vanilla instant	1 cup (2 sticks) butter
pudding mix	1 cup sugar
3 tablespoons poppy	1/4 cup dark rum
seeds	

Butter a bundt pan with a generous amount of softened butter and sprinkle generously with sugar. Set aside. Combine the cake mix, pudding mix, poppy seeds and flour in a bowl and mix well by hand. Combine the water, 1/2 cup of the dark rum, vegetable oil and eggs in a separate bowl and mix until smooth. Add to the mixture of dry ingredients and mix well by hand. Pour into the prepared bundt pan. Bake at 350 degrees for 38 minutes. Combine the butter, sugar and remaining 1/4 cup dark rum in a saucepan and bring to a boil. Pour the boiling rum mixture over the hot cake; let stand for 5 minutes. Invert onto a serving plate. Serve warm or cold. Yield: 12 or more servings.

Sue Allen, Eta Delta
Ponca City, Oklahoma

PECAN RUM CAKE

1 cup chopped pecans	1/2 cup dark or amber
1 (2-layer) package	rum
yellow cake mix	1/2 cup (1 stick) butter
1 (4-ounce) package	1 cup sugar
vanilla instant	1/4 cup water
pudding mix	1/2 cup dark or amber
4 eggs	rum
1/2 cup vegetable oil	

Sprinkle the pecans in a buttered and floured bundt pan. Combine the cake mix, pudding mix, eggs, 1/2 cup cold water, vegetable oil and 1/2 cup rum in a mixing bowl and mix well. Pour over the pecans in the bundt pan. Bake at 325 degrees for 1 hour. Cool. Invert onto a serving plate. Melt the butter in a saucepan. Stir in the sugar and 1/4 cup water and bring to a boil. Boil for 5 minutes, stirring constantly. Remove from heat and stir in the 1/2 cup rum. Poke holes in the cake all over with a fork. Drizzle the glaze evenly over the top and side of the cake. Let stand until glaze is absorbed. Yield: 12 to 16 servings.

Peggy Houghton, Gamma Iota
Sault Ste. Marie, Ontario, Canada

POUND CAKE

1 cup (2 sticks) butter or	3 cups flour
margarine	1 cup milk
1/2 cup shortening	1 teaspoon vanilla
3 cups sugar	extract
5 eggs	1 teaspoon almond
1/2 teaspoon baking	extract
powder	

Cream the butter, shortening and sugar in a mixing bowl until light and fluffy. Add the eggs 1 at a time, beating well after each addition. Sift together the baking powder and flour; add to the sugar mixture alternately with the milk, mixing well after each addition. Mix in the vanilla and almond extract. Pour into a buttered bundt pan or 2 loaf pans. Place in an unheated oven. Turn oven temperature to 325 degrees. Bake for 90 minutes. Cool. Invert onto a serving plate. Dust with confectioners' sugar. Yield: 15 to 18 servings.

Barbara Smith, Zeta Sigma
Fairfield Bay, Arkansas

CONFECTIONERS' SUGAR POUND CAKE

Simply use the empty sugar box to measure the flour.

1 1/2 cups margarine	1 teaspoon vanilla
1 (1-pound) package	extract
confectioners' sugar	1 teaspoon lemon
6 eggs	extract
1 package flour	

Cream the margarine and sugar in a mixing bowl until light and fluffy. Add the eggs, beating well. Add the flour, vanilla and lemon extract; beat well. Pour into a heavily greased and floured tube pan. Bake at 300 degrees for 1 hour and 15 minutes. Yield: 16 servings.

Glenda Cardwell, Xi Beta Chi
Rockford, Alabama

ONE-STEP POUND CAKE

This cake is very good served with fresh fruit.

2 1/4 cups flour	1 cup (2 sticks) butter,
2 cups sugar	softened
1/2 teaspoon salt	1 (8-ounce) container
1/2 teaspoon baking soda	yogurt, any flavor
1 teaspoon grated lemon	3 eggs
zest (optional)	

Combine the flour, sugar, salt, baking soda, lemon zest, butter, yogurt and eggs in a large bowl. Beat at low speed to blend. Beat at medium speed for 3 minutes, scraping the side of the bowl occasionally. Pour into a buttered 10-inch tube or bundt pan. Bake at 325 degrees for 60 to 70 minutes or until cake tests done. Cool in the pan for 15 minutes. Remove to a serving plate to cool completely. Yield: 8 to 10 servings.

Kandee Graham, Alpha Lambda Master
Hershey, Pennsylvania

POOR MAN'S RAISIN CAKE

2 cups raisins	2 cups applesauce or
1 cup packed brown	drained crushed
sugar	pineapple
1 cup granulated sugar	3¹/₂ cups plus
2 cups water	2 tablespoons flour
1 cup (2 sticks) butter or	2 teaspoons baking soda
margarine	¹/₂ teaspoon salt
2 teaspoons vanilla	1 cup chopped walnuts
extract	

Combine the raisins, brown sugar, granulated sugar, water and butter in a saucepan; bring to a boil. Reduce heat and simmer for 20 minutes, stirring occasionally. Remove from heat; cool slightly. Stir in the vanilla and applesauce. Add a mixture of the 3¹/₂ cups flour, baking soda and salt; mix by hand. Toss the walnuts in the 2 tablespoons flour to coat; fold into the batter. Pour into a buttered and floured 9×13-inch cake pan. Bake at 325 degrees for 1 hour or until cake tests done. Yield: 12 servings.

Gerry Wiehe, Preceptor Alpha Zeta
Leavenworth, Kansas

RED VELVET CAKE

1 (2-ounce) bottle red	2¹/₄ cups sifted cake
food coloring	flour
3 tablespoons chocolate	1 teaspoon salt
drink mix	1 cup buttermilk
¹/₂ cup shortening	1 tablespoon white
1¹/₂ cups sugar	vinegar
2 eggs	1 teaspoon baking soda
1 teaspoon vanilla	
extract	

Whisk together the red food coloring and chocolate drink mix in a bowl. Cream the shortening and sugar in a mixing bowl until light and fluffy. Beat in the eggs. Add the chocolate drink mixture and vanilla. Add a mixture of the flour and salt to the batter alternately with the buttermilk, beating well after each addition. Stir in the vinegar and baking soda. Pour into 3 buttered and floured cake pans or a 9×13-inch cake pan. Bake at 325 degrees for 40 minutes or until a wooden pick inserted in the center comes out clean. Frost cooled cake with Red Velvet Frosting.
Yield: 15 to 18 servings.

RED VELVET FROSTING

¹/₂ cup (1 stick) butter,	3 tablespoons flour
softened	²/₃ cup milk
¹/₂ cup shortening	1 teaspoon vanilla
1 cup sugar	extract

Place the butter in a mixing bowl and beat until fluffy. Add the shortening; beat until light and fluffy. Add the sugar, flour, milk and vanilla gradually, beating constantly. Beat at high speed for 5 to 10 minutes or until fluffy and stiff.

Teresa Quiñones, Alpha Rho
Havana, Illinois

UPSIDE-DOWN RHUBARB CAKE

4 cups chopped rhubarb	1 cup sugar
1 (2-layer) package	1 cup heavy cream
yellow cake mix	

Spread the rhubarb in a buttered 9×13-inch cake pan. Prepare the cake mix using the package directions; pour evenly over the rhubarb layer. Whisk the sugar and cream together; drizzle evenly over the cake batter. Bake at 350 degrees for about 35 minutes. or until cake tests done. Invert immediately onto a serving plate. Yield: 15 servings.

LaVern Hayworth, Laureate Alpha Sigma
Hermiston, Oregon

BLACK RUSSIAN CAKE

1 (2-layer) package	4 eggs
yellow cake mix	¹/₄ cup vodka
¹/₂ cup granulated sugar	¹/₂ cup Kahlúa
1 (6-ounce) package	³/₄ cup water
chocolate instant	¹/₂ cup confectioners'
pudding mix	sugar
1 cup vegetable oil	

Place the cake mix, granulated sugar and pudding mix in a large mixing bowl; stir to combine. Combine the vegetable oil, eggs, vodka, ¹/₄ cup of the Kahlúa and water in a separate mixing bowl and blend well. Add the liquid mixture to the dry ingredients; beat at medium speed for 4 minutes. Pour into a buttered bundt pan. Bake in a preheated 350-degree oven for 45 to 50 minutes or until cake tests done. Cool in the pan for 10 minutes. Invert onto a serving plate. Poke the cake all over with a wooden pick. Blend the confectioners' sugar and the remaining ¹/₄ cup Kahlúa and drizzle evenly over the cake. Dust with confectioners' sugar. Yield: 12 to 15 slices.

Michelle Steinbeck, Zeta Sigma
Hines, Oregon

KAHLUA WHITE RUSSIAN CAKE

*3 tablespoons Kahlúa or
   other coffee liqueur
2 tablespoons vodka
1 (3-ounce) white baking
   bar with cocoa butter
2 cups sifted cake flour,
   or 1³/4 cups sifted
   all-purpose flour
¹/2 teaspoon baking
   powder*

*³/4 teaspoon baking soda
¹/2 cup (1 stick) butter
2 tablespoons
   shortening
1¹/4 cups sugar
3 eggs
³/4 cup buttermilk
¹/3 cup apricot jam
Kahlúa White Russian
   Cream*

Combine the Kahlúa, vodka and white baking bar in a heavy medium saucepan over low heat. Cook until melted, stirring constantly; cool slightly. Place the flour, baking powder and baking soda in a small bowl; stir to combine. Cream the butter, shortening and sugar in a mixing bowl until light and fluffy. Add the eggs 1 at a time, beating well after each addition. Beat in the cooled Kahlúa mixture. Add the flour mixture alternately with the buttermilk, beating at low to medium speed after each addition just until combined. Pour into 3 buttered and lightly floured 8-inch cake pans. Bake at 350 degrees for 20 to 25 minutes. Cool in the pan for 10 minutes. Remove to a wire rack to cool completely. Place one layer bottom up on a serving plate. Spread with 3 tablespoons apricot jam and ¹/3 cup Kahlúa White Russian Cream. Place a second layer bottom side up over the first. Spread with the remaining apricot jam and another ¹/3 cup cream. Place the third layer bottom side up over the second. Swirl the remaining Russian Cream over the top and side. You may decorate with baking bar curls. Chill for 24 hours. Yield: 12 to 15 servings.

KAHLUA WHITE RUSSIAN CREAM

*2 cups whipping cream
¹/2 cup confectioners'
   sugar*

*¹/4 cup Kahlúa
2 teaspoons vodka*

Combine the whipping cream, confectioners' sugar and vodka in a mixing bowl; beat at low speed until soft peaks form. Do not overbeat.

*Sundy Fuemmeler, Kappa Mu
Mexico, Missouri*

---

*Donna Bailey, Preceptor Alpha Lambda, Emporia, Kansas, makes her son's favorite **Chocolate Pudding Cake** by baking a chocolate cake mix in a 9×13-inch pan, cooling completely and spreading prepared chocolate instant pudding on top and adding a layer of whipped topping when the pudding is set. Chill.*

KAHLUA CAKE

*1 (2-layer) package
   devil's food cake mix
1 (6-ounce) package
   vanilla instant
   pudding mix
1 cup sour cream
4 eggs*

*³/4 cup vegetable oil
³/4 cup plus 2 to
   3 tablespoons Kahlúa
1 cup semisweet
   chocolate chips
1 (8-ounce) package
   chocolate frosting*

Combine the cake mix, pudding mix, sour cream, eggs, vegetable oil and the ³/4 cup Kahlúa in a large mixing bowl; mix well. Fold in the chocolate chips. Pour into an oiled and floured 12-cup bundt pan. Bake at 350 degrees for 45 minutes. Cool in the pan for 15 minutes. Invert onto a cake plate. Combine the chocolate frosting and the 2 to 3 tablespoons Kahlúa in a mixing bowl or blender and blend well. Spread over the top only of the cooled cake.
Yield: 12 servings.

*Erika Schultz, Iota Rho
Huntersville, North Carolina*

HARVEY WALLBANGER CAKE

*1 (2-layer) package
   yellow cake mix
1 (4-ounce) package
   vanilla instant
   pudding mix*

*1 cup vegetable oil
4 eggs
¹/4 cup vodka
¹/4 cup galliano
³/4 cup orange juice*

Combine the cake mix, pudding mix, vegetable oil, eggs, vodka, galliano and orange juice in a large mixing bowl; beat at high speed for 4 minutes. Pour into a buttered 10-cup bundt pan. Bake at 350 degrees for 45 to 50 minutes or until cake tests done. Cool in the pan for 10 minutes. Invert onto a serving plate.
Yield: 10 to 12 servings.

*Anita Karl, Laureate Zeta
Cheyenne, Wyoming*

CREAM SHERRY CAKE

*1 (2-layer) package
   yellow cake mix
1¹/2 (3-ounce) packages
   butterscotch instant
   pudding mix*

*3 tablespoons poppy
   seeds
4 eggs
1 cup vegetable oil
1 cup cream sherry*

Combine the cake mix, pudding mix and poppy seeds in a large mixing bowl. Stir in the eggs, half the vegetable oil and half the cream sherry; beat at low speed. Continue to beat at low speed while adding the remaining ¹/2 cup vegetable oil and remaining ¹/2 cup sherry. Beat at medium speed for 2 minutes. Pour into a bundt pan that has been sprayed with nonstick baking spray. Bake at 350 degrees for 50 to

60 minutes or until cake tests done. Cool in the pan for 10 minutes. Invert onto a serving plate.
Yield: 12 servings.

Olga Sisnetsky, Laureate Gamma Psi
Miami, Florida

SPICE CAKE

3/4 cup shortening	*1/2 teaspoon cinnamon*
1 1/2 cups sugar	*3/4 cup buttermilk*
3 eggs	*1 teaspoon vanilla*
1 3/4 cups flour	*extract*
1/2 teaspoon baking soda	*1 teaspoon lemon*
1/2 teaspoon baking	*extract*
powder	*Cocoa Frosting*
3/4 teaspoon nutmeg	*1/2 cup chopped walnuts*
1/2 teaspoon salt	*or pecans (optional)*

Cream the shortening and sugar in a mixing bowl until light and fluffy. Add the eggs 1 at a time, beating well after each addition. Add a mixture of the flour, baking soda, baking powder, nutmeg, salt and cinnamon alternately with the buttermilk, mixing well after each addition. Add the vanilla and lemon extract. Pour into two 8- or 9-inch cake pans that have been sprayed with nonstick cooking spray. Bake at 350 degrees for 35 minutes or until cake tests done. Remove to a wire rack to cool. Frost cooled cake with Cocoa Frosting. Sprinkle with walnuts.
Yield: 12 to 15 servings.

COCOA FROSTING

6 tablespoons butter,	*1 1/2 tablespoons baking*
softened	*cocoa*
3 cups confectioners'	*1 teaspoon cinnamon*
sugar	*1 1/2 tablespoons hot*
1 egg yolk	*coffee*

Combine the butter, confectioners' sugar, egg yolk, baking cocoa, cinnamon and hot coffee in a mixing bowl. Beat until mixture is of spreading consistency.

Anna Jean Dicks, Preceptor Gamma Psi
Terre Haute, Indiana

STRAWBERRY CAKE

1/2 cup boiling water	*3 large eggs*
1 (3-ounce) package	*1 cup thawed frozen*
strawberry gelatin	*strawberries*
1 (2-layer) package	*1/2 cup (1 stick)*
white cake mix	*margarine, softened*
1 tablespoon flour	*1 (1-pound) package*
3/4 cup vegetable oil	*confectioners' sugar*

Combine the boiling water and dry strawberry gelatin mix in a large bowl and stir to dissolve. Add the cake mix, flour, vegetable oil, eggs and 1/2 cup of the strawberries and mix well. Pour into a bundt pan that has been sprayed with nonstick cooking spray, or 2 prepared 8-inch cake pans. Bake at 350 degrees for 25 to 30 minutes or until cake tests done. Cool in the pan for 10 minutes. Invert onto a serving plate. Combine the margarine, confectioners' sugar and remaining 1/2 cup strawberries in a bowl; beat until well mixed. Frost the cooled cake. Serve with strawberry ice cream and fresh strawberries.
Yield: 12 to 16 servings.

Velma P. Simpson, Preceptor Alpha Nu
Cordova, Tennessee

STRAWBERRY SHORTCAKE

Fresh strawberries	*1/2 teaspoon salt*
Sugar	*1/2 cup (1 stick)*
2 cups flour	*margarine*
2 tablespoons sugar	*2/3 cup cold milk*
1 tablespoon baking	*1 egg*
powder	*Whipped topping*

Hull and slice the desired amount of strawberries. Add sugar to taste and mix. Set aside. Combine the flour, 2 tablespoons sugar, baking powder and salt in a bowl. Cut in the margarine until the mixture resembles coarse crumbs. Stir in the cold milk. Mix in the egg. Spread the batter evenly in an 8-inch cake pan that has been sprayed with nonstick cooking spray. Bake at 450 degrees for 20 minutes. Serve hot with sugared sliced strawberries. Top with whipped topping. Yield: 6 to 8 servings.

Joan Grabber, Xi Lambda Psi
Englewood, Florida

EASY STRAWBERRY SHORTCAKE

1 (2-layer) package	*12 ounces whipped*
white cake mix	*topping*
1 (12-ounce) can	
evaporated milk	
2 (10-ounce) packages	
frozen strawberries,	
thawed and drained	

Prepare and bake the cake using the package directions for a 9×13-inch cake pan. Cool slightly. Poke holes in the cake with a fork. Drizzle the evaporated milk over the cake and top with the strawberries. Cover with whipped topping and chill.
Yield: 12 servings.

Wanda Rapp, Alpha Pi Master
El Campo, Texas

TOMATO SOUP CAKE

2 cups sifted cake flour	1 cup seedless raisins,
2¹/₂ teaspoons baking	chopped
powder	¹/₂ cup shortening
¹/₂ teaspoon baking soda	1 cup sugar
¹/₂ teaspoon ground	2 eggs, well beaten
cloves	1 (10-ounce) can tomato
¹/₂ teaspoon cinnamon	soup
¹/₂ teaspoon grated	
nutmeg	

Sift the flour, baking powder, baking soda, cloves, cinnamon and nutmeg together. Roll the raisins in a small amount of the flour mixture. Cream the shortening and sugar in a mixing bowl until light and fluffy. Add the eggs 1 at a time, beating well after each addition. Add the flour mixture alternately with the tomato soup concentrate, mixing well after each addition. Fold in the floured raisins. Pour into 2 buttered 8-inch cake pans. Bake at 375 degrees for 35 minutes or until cake tests done. Frost the cooled cake with your choice of frosting. Yield: 8 servings.

Rita Cane, Preceptor Epsilon Lambda
Whitby, Ontario, Canada

TENNESSEE BLACK WALNUT CAKE

³/₄ cup butter, softened	1 cup chopped black
¹/₂ cup shortening	walnuts
2 cups sugar	1 cup shredded coconut
5 eggs, separated	8 ounces cream cheese,
2 cups flour	softened
1 teaspoon baking soda	1 (1-pound) package
1 cup buttermilk	confectioners' sugar
2¹/₂ teaspoons vanilla	
extract	

Cream ¹/₂ cup of the butter, shortening and sugar in a mixing bowl until light and fluffy. Beat in the egg yolks. Add the flour alternately with a mixture of the baking soda and buttermilk, mixing well after each addition. Beat in 1¹/₂ teaspoons of the vanilla. Beat the egg whites until stiff peaks form; fold gently into the flour mixture. Fold in the black walnuts and coconut. Pour into 3 buttered and floured 8-inch cake pans. Bake at 350 degrees for 30 minutes or until cake tests done. Remove to a wire rack to cool. Combine the cream cheese and remaining ¹/₄ cup butter in a mixing bowl; beat until smooth. Add the confectioners' sugar and remaining 1 teaspoon vanilla gradually, beating until mixture is of spreading consistency. Spread between the layers and over the top and side of the cooled cake. Yield: 16 servings.

Barbara H. Norton, Laureate Epsilon
Seaford, Delaware

WINE CAKE

1 (2-layer) package	³/₄ cup vegetable oil
yellow cake mix	¹/₄ cup sherry
1 (4-ounce) package	¹/₄ cup brandy
vanilla instant	¹/₄ cup water
pudding mix	1 teaspoon nutmeg
4 eggs	

Combine the cake mix, pudding mix, eggs, vegetable oil, sherry, brandy, water and nutmeg in a large mixing bowl and beat at medium speed for 5 minutes. Pour into a buttered tube pan or bundt pan. Bake at 350 degrees for 50 minutes. Cool in the pan for 15 minutes. Remove to a wire rack to cool completely. Yield: 12 servings.

Julie Van Etten, Laureate Theta Chi
Pleasanton, California

HONEY BUN CAKE

1 (2-layer) package	1 cup packed brown
yellow cake mix	sugar
4 eggs	1 cup confectioners'
³/₄ cup vegetable oil	sugar
1 cup sour cream	5 tablespoons milk
¹/₂ cup granulated sugar	¹/₂ teaspoon vanilla
1 teaspoon cinnamon	extract

Combine the first 5 ingredients in a large bowl; mix well. Pour into a buttered 9×13-inch cake pan. Sprinkle evenly with a mixture of the cinnamon and brown sugar. Cut in a swirling pattern with a knife. Bake at 350 degrees for 1 hour. Combine the confectioners' sugar, milk and vanilla in a small mixing bowl and beat until smooth. Pour evenly over the hot cake. Cool and serve. Yield: 15 servings.

Helen A. Ord, Xi Tau
Kingwood, West Virginia

CHRISTMAS NUT CAKE

2¹/₂ cups self-rising flour	1¹/₂ cups sugar
1 cup buttermilk	1 teaspoon baking cocoa
1¹/₂ cups vegetable oil	1 teaspoon white
1 teaspoon baking soda	vinegar
1 teaspoon vanilla	2 large eggs
extract	Pecan Frosting
2 (1-ounce) bottles red	¹/₂ cup chopped pecans
food coloring	

Combine the flour, buttermilk, vegetable oil, baking soda, vanilla, red food coloring, sugar, baking cocoa, vinegar and eggs in a large mixing bowl and beat until well mixed. Pour into three 8- or 9-inch buttered and floured cake pans. Bake at 350 degrees for 20 minutes or until a wooden pick inserted in the center comes out clean. Cool in pans for 10 minutes. Remove to a wire rack to cool completely. Frost the cooled cake with Pecan Frosting. Sprinkle top with pecans. Yield: 12 to 15 servings.

PECAN FROSTING

1/3 pound (11/3 sticks) butter, softened	1 (1-pound) package confectioners' sugar
10 ounces cream cheese, softened	11/2 cups chopped pecans

Cream the butter, cream cheese and confectioners' sugar in a mixing bowl until light and fluffy. Fold in the pecans.

Ellen S. Caspers, Beta Xi
Huron, South Dakota

MAYONNAISE CAKE

2 cups mayonnaise	4 teaspoons baking soda
2 cups sugar	1/2 cup baking cocoa
2 teaspoons vanilla extract	2 teaspoons cinnamon
4 cups flour	1 teaspoon salt
	2 cups lukewarm water

Combine the mayonnaise and sugar in a large mixing bowl and blend well. Blend in the vanilla. Sift the flour, baking soda, baking cocoa, cinnamon and salt together. Add the mayonnaise mixture alternately with the water, mixing well after each addition. Pour into a buttered 9×13-inch cake pan. Bake at 350 degrees for 25 minutes or until cake tests done. Frost the cooled cake with your favorite frosting. Yield: 9 to 12 servings.

Roberta Slocum, Preceptor Zeta Pi
Madison, Ohio

GLAZED SOUR CREAM CAKE

1 (2-layer) package butter recipe golden cake mix	1/4 cup granulated sugar
4 eggs	1 tablespoon butter or margarine
1 cup sour cream	2 tablespoons milk
1/3 cup vegetable oil	11/2 cups confectioners' sugar

Combine the cake mix, eggs, sour cream, vegetable oil and granulated sugar in a large mixing bowl and beat at medium speed for 2 minutes. Pour into a buttered bundt pan. Bake at 375 degrees for 50 minutes. Melt the butter in a small saucepan over medium-low heat; whisk in the milk and confectioners' sugar. Drizzle over the warm cake. Cool in the pan for 20 minutes. Invert onto a serving plate. Yield: 16 servings.

Tina Barsanti, Preceptor Omicron Rho
Bedford, Texas

WACKY CAKE

This cake was created by Women's Army Corps nurses during WWII. The WACs mixed this cake in their helmets and baked it in a surgical instrument tray. Eggs were impossible to get abroad, so this recipe provided the only way to enjoy cake during that time.

3 cups flour	3/4 cup vegetable oil
2 cups sugar	2 tablespoons white vinegar
6 tablespoons baking cocoa	2 teaspoons vanilla extract
2 teaspoons baking soda	2 cups cold water
1 teaspoon salt	

Combine the flour, sugar, baking cocoa, baking soda and salt in a large bowl. Make 2 small holes and 1 large hole in the mixture. Pour the vegetable oil in the large hole, the vinegar in one of the small holes and the vanilla in the other small hole. Add the cold water and mix by hand until moistened; do not use an electric mixer. Pour into an ungreased 9×12-inch cake pan. Bake at 350 degrees for 30 to 40 minutes or until cake tests done. Cool in the pan. Frost the cooled cake with Gourmet Frosting. Yield: 15 servings.

GOURMET FROSTING

This frosting does not do well in extreme heat. When serving outside in the summer, chill the iced cake for 1 hour before taking it outside.

4 tablespoons flour	1/2 cup (1 stick) margarine, at room temperature
1 cup whole milk	
1/2 cup (1 stick) butter, at room temperature	1 cup sugar

Combine the flour and milk in a medium saucepan over medium-low heat. Cook until very thick, stirring constantly. The spoon should stand in the mixture. Chill for 1 hour. Combine the flour mixture, butter, margarine and sugar in a mixing bowl and beat at high speed until smooth. Beat in more sugar if necessary to make of spreading consistency.

Judy Dorsey, Laureate Delta
Wilmington, Delaware

*Kim E. Davis, Theta Delta, Burlington, Colorado, makes her **Special Strawberry Cake** using a strawberry cake mix, 11/4 cups water, 1/3 cup vegetable oil, 3 eggs and two 6-ounce cartons of strawberry yogurt. Bake in a prepared 9×13-inch pan and bake at 350 degrees for 30 to 35 minutes or until the cake tests done. Cool completely before spreading a blend of 2 cartons of strawberry yogurt and 8 to 12 ounces of whipped topping over the top. Store the cake in the refrigerator.*

HORNET'S NEST CAKE

This cake actually resembles a hornet's nest. It can be further enhanced with a dollop of whipped topping. Don't worry about stings . . . maybe just a few extra pounds.

1 (6-ounce) package
   vanilla cook-and-
   serve pudding
1 (2-layer) package
   yellow cake mix

1 (11-ounce) package
   butterscotch morsels
1 cup chopped pecans

Prepare and cook the pudding mix using the package directions. Cool. Combine the dry cake mix and cooked pudding in a large bowl and stir to combine; do not beat. Mixture may be a little lumpy. Pour into a buttered 9×13-inch cake pan. Sprinkle the butterscotch morsels evenly over the top. Sprinkle with the pecans. Do not mix. Bake at 350 degrees for 30 minutes or until cake tests done. Yield: 10 to 12 servings.

Betty B. DePaola, Beta Master
Daytona Beach, Florida

HUMMINGBIRD CAKE

5 eggs, lightly beaten
1¹/₂ cup vegetable oil
2 cups sugar
1 teaspoon salt
1 teaspoon baking soda
1 teaspoon cinnamon
2¹/₂ teaspoons vanilla
   extract
1 (8-ounce) can crushed
   pineapple

2 cups mashed ripe
   bananas
1¹/₂ cups chopped pecans
3 cups flour
8 ounces cream cheese,
   softened
2 tablespoons milk
4 to 5 cups
   confectioners' sugar

Combine the eggs and vegetable oil in a large mixing bowl. Mix in the sugar, salt, baking soda, cinnamon and 1¹/₂ teaspoons of the vanilla. Fold in the undrained pineapple, bananas, pecans and flour. Spoon into 3 buttered and lightly floured 9-inch cake pans. Bake at 350 degrees for 45 minutes to 1 hour or until cake tests done. Cool in the pans for 20 minutes. Invert onto a wire rack to cool completely. Combine the cream cheese, milk, remaining 1 teaspoon vanilla and enough confectioners' sugar to make of spreading consistency in a mixing bowl. Beat until smooth and fluffy. Spread between the layers and over the top of the cooled cake. Chill until serving time. Yield: 12 to 14 servings.

Donna Jipp, Laureate Upsilon
Sioux Falls, South Dakota

TEXAS SHEET CAKE

2 cups sugar
2 cups flour
1 cup (2 sticks) margarine
4 tablespoons baking
   cocoa
1 cup water
¹/₂ cup buttermilk

2 eggs, beaten
1 teaspoon baking soda
1 teaspoon vanilla
   extract
1 teaspoon instant
   coffee granules
Cocoa Pecan Icing

Place the sugar and flour in a large bowl and mix well. Combine the margarine, baking cocoa and water in a saucepan; bring to a boil. Add the hot cocoa mixture to the flour mixture; mix well. Add the buttermilk, eggs, baking soda, vanilla and coffee granules; mix well. Pour into a buttered and floured 8×12-inch cake pan. Bake at 400 degrees for 20 minutes or until cake tests done. Spread Cocoa Pecan Icing over the warm cake. Yield: 15 servings.

COCOA PECAN ICING

¹/₂ cup (1 stick)
   margarine
4 tablespoons baking
   cocoa
6 tablespoons milk

1 (1-pound) package
   confectioners' sugar
1 teaspoon vanilla
   extract
1 cup chopped pecans

Combine the margarine, baking cocoa and milk in a saucepan; bring to a boil. Mix in the confectioners' sugar and vanilla. Stir in the pecans.

Connie Hogan, Preceptor Epsilon
Palmer, Alaska

SEAFOAM ICING

³/₄ to ⁷/₈ cup packed
   brown sugar
3 egg whites

3 tablespoons water
³/₄ cup light corn syrup

Place the brown sugar, egg whites, water and corn syrup in the top of a double boiler. Beat with an electric mixer over hot water for 7 to 10 minutes or until soft peaks form. Use to frost chocolate, white, angel food or just about any cake.
Yield: enough icing for 1 cake.

Doris Rohl, Preceptor Xi Kappa
Yorba Linda, California

Lois A. Boeyink, Laureate Gamma Zeta, Pella, Iowa, frosts an angel food cake cut into 3 layers by blending 1 cup confectioners' sugar with 1 cup sour cream, folding in 8 ounces whipped topping and an 8-ounce package of well-drained frozen raspberries and spreading the **Yummy Raspberry Fluff** *between the layers and on top.*

CHOCOLATE-CHOCOLATE CAKE

3/4 cup baking cocoa	3 eggs
2 1/4 cups flour	1 1/2 teaspoons vanilla
1 3/4 cups sugar	extract
1 1/2 cups buttermilk	1 1/4 teaspoons salt
1 cup vegetable oil	Chocolate Glaze
2 teaspoons baking soda	

Combine the baking cocoa, flour, sugar, buttermilk, vegetable oil, baking soda, eggs, vanilla and salt in a large mixing bowl and beat at low speed until blended, scraping bowl constantly. Beat at medium speed for 3 minutes, scraping bowl occasionally. Dust a buttered tube pan with additional baking cocoa. Spoon the batter into the prepared pan. Bake at 350 degrees for 50 minutes or until a wooden pick inserted in the center comes out clean. Cool in the pan for 10 minutes. Remove to a wire rack to cool completely. Place the cake on a serving plate. Spoon or pour the Chocolate Glaze over the top of the cake so the glaze flows evenly down the side. Refrigerate until the glaze is set. Yield: 16 servings.

CHOCOLATE GLAZE

6 (1-ounce) squares	2 tablespoons
semisweet baking	half-and-half
chocolate	2 tablespoons light corn
3 tablespoons butter	syrup

Break the chocolate into pieces and combine with the butter in a double boiler over hot water. Heat until melted, stirring occasionally until well blended. Remove from the heat. Add the half-and-half and corn syrup, blending until smooth and glossy.

ALL-AMERICAN THREE-LAYER CHOCOLATE CAKE

1 cup baking cocoa	1 cup (2 sticks) butter,
2 cups boiling water	softened
2 3/4 cups flour	2 1/2 cups sugar
2 teaspoons baking	4 eggs
soda	1 teaspoon vanilla
1/2 teaspoon baking	extract
powder	Chocolate Frosting or
1/2 teaspoon salt	Buttercream Frosting

Mix the baking cocoa and boiling water in a bowl; let stand until cool. Sift the flour, baking soda, baking powder and salt together. Cream the butter and sugar in a large mixing bowl until light and fluffy. Add the eggs and vanilla and mix well. Add the flour mixture alternately with the cocoa mixture, beating well after each addition. Butter three 9-inch cake pans and line the bottoms with waxed paper circles cut to fit. Butter the waxed paper and dust with flour.

Pour the batter evenly into the prepared pans. Bake at 350 degrees for 25 to 30 minutes or until surface springs back when pressed lightly. Cool in the pans for 10 minutes. Remove from pans and peel off the waxed paper. Cool completely on a wire rack. Frost with Chocolate Frosting or White Buttercream Frosting. Decorate with tiny cream puffs or rosettes of frosting if desired. Garnish with chocolate curls or sliced almonds if desired. Yield: 16 servings.

RICH CHOCOLATE FROSTING

12 ounces semisweet	1 1/2 cups (4 sticks) butter
chocolate, chopped	1 (1-pound) package
3/4 cup evaporated milk	confectioners' sugar,
or light cream	sifted

Combine the chocolate, evaporated milk and butter in a saucepan and cook over medium heat until melted and smooth, stirring constantly. Remove from heat and whisk in the confectioners' sugar until smooth. Place the saucepan in a bowl of ice and stir until frosting is of spreading consistency.

WHITE BUTTERCREAM FROSTING

1 1/2 cups butter-flavor	1 1/2 cups milk, scalded
shortening	3 egg whites, slightly
1 1/2 cups (3 sticks)	beaten
butter, softened	1 tablespoon vanilla
3 cups sugar	extract

Cream the shortening, butter and sugar in a mixing bowl until light and fluffy. Add the hot milk 3 tablespoons at a time, beating at high speed until smooth. Add the egg whites and vanilla; beat at high speed for 2 minutes.

DECORATING TIPS

Make your cake unique with one or more of the following suggestions:

- Frost the cake with either of the frostings.
- Arrange miniature cream puffs around the top of the cake.
- Pipe rosettes of the same or contrasting frosting over the top of the cake.
- Pat sliced almonds onto the side of the cake.
- Pat grated chocolate onto the frosted cake.
- Pipe a decorative design onto the frosted cake.
- Arrange colorful candies such as jelly beans or fresh or well-drained canned fruit on the cake.

Hint: If you have no pastry/icing bag, spoon a small amount of frosting into a small plastic bag, squeeze out the air and snip a tiny opening in the corner of the bag.

Pies & Pastries

ANGEL PIE

4 egg whites
Pinch of salt
3 cups milk
2¼ cups sugar
4 rounded tablespoons
   flour
2 tablespoons butter
2 teaspoons vanilla
   extract
2 baked (9-inch) pie
   shells

Beat the egg whites with the salt in a mixing bowl until stiff peaks form. Heat the milk in a large heavy saucepan over medium heat. Whisk in a mixture of the sugar and flour and cook until thickened, stirring constantly. Remove from heat. Stir in the butter and vanilla. Pour slowly over the beaten egg whites, stirring constantly. Pour into the pie shells. Let stand until cool. Top with whipped topping and sprinkle with coconut. Refrigerate leftovers. Yield: 6 to 8 servings.

Cindy Daniels, Laureate Gamma Kappa
Columbia, Missouri

DEEP-DISH APPLE PIE

This pie can be made without a pie shell, but it is delicious with one. It may also be baked in a 10×10-inch baking dish and cut into squares.

7 cups sliced peeled tart
   apples
1 unbaked (9-inch) pie
   shell
¾ cup flour
½ cup firmly packed
   brown sugar
½ cup granulated sugar
½ teaspoon nutmeg
½ teaspoon cinnamon
½ cup (1 stick) butter
1 pint vanilla ice cream
   or favorite whipped
   topping

Spread the apple slices in the pie shell. Combine the next 5 ingredients in a bowl. Cut in the butter until crumbly. Spread evenly over the apple layer. Bake at 350 degrees for 1 hour. Serve warm or cold with ice cream or whipped topping. Yield: 8 servings.

Rose Mary Coakes, Laureate Alpha Rho
Marshall, Michigan

SWEDISH APPLE PIE

1 (21-ounce) can apple
   pie filling
1 cup flour
⅔ cup sugar
1 teaspoon baking
   powder
¼ teaspoon salt
½ cup (1 stick) butter,
   softened
1 egg
½ cup chopped walnuts
2 tablespoons cinnamon
   sugar

Spread the pie filling in a buttered 10-inch deep-dish pie plate. Combine the flour, sugar, baking powder and salt in a bowl; stir to blend. Blend in the butter and egg, stirring to make a thick batter. Spoon the batter evenly over the pie filling. Sprinkle with walnuts and cinnamon sugar. Bake at 350 degrees for 45 minutes or until apples are bubbly and topping is browned. Serve warm with or without ice cream. Yield: 8 servings.

Dorothy Zientarski, Zeta Master
New Britain, Connecticut

FRENCH APPLE CREAM PIE

1 (21-ounce) can apple
   pie filling
¼ teaspoon cinnamon
¼ teaspoon nutmeg
1 egg
1 tablespoon lemon juice
1 teaspoon grated lemon
   zest
1 (2-crust) pie pastry
3 ounces cream cheese,
   softened
¼ cup sour cream

Combine the pie filling, cinnamon, nutmeg, egg, lemon juice and lemon zest in a bowl and mix well. Pour into a pastry-lined pie plate. Combine the cream cheese and sour cream in a mixing bowl and beat at medium speed until smooth. Pour evenly over the apples. Top with the remaining pastry, fluting edge and cutting vents. Sprinkle with cinnamon sugar. Bake at 425 degrees for 20 to 30 minutes or until bubbly and golden. Yield: 8 servings.

Jean C. Hove, Laureate Gamma Iota
Tallahassee, Florida

DRIED CHERRIES AND APPLE PIE

1 cup dried cherries	1/2 teaspoon cinnamon
4 cups thinly sliced peeled apples	1 (2-crust) 9-inch pie pastry
1 cup sugar	1 tablespoon butter
1/4 cup flour	

Combine the cherries, apples, sugar, flour and cinnamon in a large bowl and mix well. Let stand at room temperature for 15 to 20 minutes. Spread in a pastry-lined pie plate. Dot with butter. Top with the remaining pastry, fluting edge and cutting vents. Bake at 425 degrees for 40 to 50 minutes or until edge of crust is golden and apples are tender. Place foil strips around the edge if pastry browns too much before apples are tender. Yield: 8 servings.

Lillian Cook, Upsilon Master
Matheny, West Virginia

UPSIDE-DOWN APPLE PECAN PIE

To prevent spillage, place the pie plate on a baking sheet or a sheet of aluminum foil while baking.

1 cup chopped pecans	6 cups (6 medium) sliced peeled apples
1/2 cup firmly packed brown sugar	1/4 cup granulated sugar
1/3 cup butter or margarine, melted	2 tablespoons flour
1 (2-crust) pie pastry	1/2 teaspoon cinnamon
	1/8 teaspoon nutmeg

Mix the pecans, brown sugar and melted butter in a bowl. Spread evenly in a 9-inch pie plate. Prepare the pastry using the package directions for a 2-crust pie. Place the "bottom" pastry over the pecan mixture. Combine the apples, sugar, flour, cinnamon and nutmeg in a bowl and mix lightly. Spoon into the pastry-lined pie plate. Top with the remaining pastry, fluting edge and cutting vents. Bake at 375 degrees for 40 to 50 minutes or until crust is golden brown and apples are tender. Cool in the pie plate for 5 minutes. Place a serving plate over the top; invert. Remove the pie plate carefully. Some pecans may remain; use a knife to replace them on the pie. Cool for at least 1 hour before serving. Yield: 8 servings.

Jean McGuire, Laureate Tau
Worthing, South Dakota

MOCK APPLE PIE

36 butter crackers, coarsely broken (1 3/4 cups)	2 teaspoons cream of tartar
1 (2-crust) pie pastry	2 tablespoons lemon juice
2 cups water	Grated zest of 1 lemon
2 cups sugar	2 tablespoons margarine
	1/2 teaspoon cinnamon

Spread the crackers in a pastry-lined pie plate. Combine the water, sugar and cream of tartar in a saucepan over high heat; bring to a boil. Reduce heat and simmer for 15 minutes. Stir in the lemon juice and lemon zest. Let stand until cool. Pour the lemon mixture evenly over the crackers. Dot with margarine and sprinkle with cinnamon. Top with the remaining pastry, fluting edge and cutting vents. Bake at 425 degrees for 30 to 35 minutes or until crust is crisp and golden. Let stand until cool.
Yield: 6 servings.

Brenda Staggenborg, Preceptor Zeta
Marysville, Kansas

PERFECT APPLE PIE TOPPING

1 cup packed brown sugar	1/2 cup (1 stick) butter
1/2 cup flour	1/2 cup caramel ice cream topping
1/2 cup rolled oats or quick-cooking oats	1/2 cup chopped pecans

Combine the brown sugar, flour and oats in a bowl. Cut in the butter with a fork or pastry blender until mixture resembles coarse crumbs. Sprinkle over the top of a ready-to-bake double-crust apple pie and pat down lightly. Cover the pastry edge with small strips of foil. Bake at 375 degrees for 25 minutes. Remove the foil and bake for 25 to 30 minutes longer or until golden brown. Remove from oven. Drizzle with caramel topping and sprinkle with pecans.
Yield: 8 servings.

Jean Poynor, Epsilon Master
Eureka Springs, Arkansas

BANANA SPLIT PIE

You may use just a small amount of sugar or no sugar at all for the pie shell.

1 small package vanilla sugar-free instant pudding mix	1 (15-ounce) can crushed pineapple
2 cups low-fat milk	1 cup whipped topping
1 (9-inch) graham cracker pie shell	1/2 cup chopped pecans, chopped (optional)
2 medium bananas, sliced	

Combine the pudding mix and milk in a mixing bowl and beat until thickened. Pour into the pie shell. Arrange the banana slices over the pudding. Squeeze the pineapple to remove as much liquid as possible; layer over the bananas. Cover with whipped topping, sealing to the edge. Sprinkle with pecans. Chill, covered, until serving time. Yield: 8 servings.

Rita Orr, Laureate Delta Omicron
Kennett, Missouri

BLACKBERRY PIE WITH BLACKBERRY CHOCOLATE ICE CREAM

5 cups fresh or frozen blackberries	2 tablespoons lemon juice
4 tablespoons cornstarch	1 baked (9-inch) pie shell Blackberry Chocolate Ice Cream
1 cup sugar	

Crush half the blackberries with a fork and place the remaining blackberries in the freezer. Combine the cornstarch, sugar, lemon juice and crushed blackberries in a saucepan over medium-high heat. Cook for 4 to 6 minutes or until translucent and thick enough to hold a spoon straight up, stirring constantly. Fold in the remaining berries gently. Spoon into a pastry-lined pie plate. Chill, covered, until very cold. Serve with ice cream. Yield: 8 servings.

BLACKBERRY CHOCOLATE ICE CREAM

1 cup blackberries	1/2 cup dark chocolate chips
1 cup sugar	
2 cups half-and-half	1/2 cup chopped roasted almonds (optional)
2 teaspoons vanilla extract	

Purée the blackberries in a blender or food processor. Strain to remove the seeds. Stir in the sugar, half-and-half and vanilla; chill completely. Pour into an ice cream freezer container. Freeze using manufacturer's directions, adding chocolate chips and almonds as directed. Yield: 1 1/2 quarts.

Diana T. Aleo, Xi Zeta Psi
Wilkes-Barre, Pennsylvania

FRESH BLUEBERRY CREAM PIE

I have made this pie with many different fruits: strawberries, raspberries, or peaches, for example, or a combination of two.

1 cup sour cream	1 egg, beaten
2 tablespoons flour	2 1/2 cups fresh blueberries
3/4 cup sugar	
1 teaspoon vanilla extract	1 unbaked (9-inch) pastry shell
1/4 teaspoon salt	

Combine the sour cream, flour, sugar, vanilla, salt and egg in a mixing bowl and beat at medium speed until smooth. Fold in the blueberries. Pour into a pastry-lined pie plate. Bake at 400 degrees for 35 minutes or until set. Chill before serving. Yield: 8 servings.

Valerie Knickerbocker, Delta Gamma
Severna Park, Maryland

CRUNCHY BLUEBERRY SWIRL PIE

1/2 cup (1 stick) butter or margarine, melted	1 (3-ounce) package lemon gelatin
3/4 cup flour	1/2 cup boiling water
1/2 cup rolled oats	1 (21-ounce) can blueberry pie filling
1/2 cup chopped walnuts or pecans	1/2 cup sour cream
2 tablespoons sugar	

Combine the melted butter, flour, rolled oats, walnuts and sugar in a bowl and mix well. Press over the bottom and up the side of a 9-inch pie plate to form a shell. Bake at 400 degrees for 12 to 15 minutes or until golden. Cool. Dissolve the gelatin mix in the boiling water in a medium bowl. Stir in the blueberry pie filling. Chill, covered, until thickened. Pour into the cooled pie shell. Drop the sour cream by spoonfuls onto the pie filling. Use a knife to make light swirls in the sour cream and pie filling. Chill, covered, until serving time. Yield: 6 to 8 servings.

Mary Polvadore, Beta Epsilon Tau
Houston, Texas

BUTTERMILK PIE

1/2 cup (1 stick) butter or margarine	1 cup buttermilk
2 cups sugar	1 teaspoon vanilla extract
3 rounded tablespoons flour	1 unbaked (9-inch) pie shell
3 eggs, beaten	

Cream the butter and sugar in a mixing bowl until light and fluffy. Add the flour, eggs, buttermilk and vanilla and beat until well mixed. Pour into the pie shell. Bake at 350 degrees for 45 to 50 minutes or until brown on top. Serve at room temperature.
Yield: 6 to 8 servings.

Verla Ritchey, Preceptor Alpha Zeta
Toledo, Oregon

BUTTER TARTS

Pastry for tarts	2 eggs
1/2 cup (1 stick) butter, softened	2 tablespoons milk
1 cup packed brown sugar	1 teaspoon vanilla extract
1/2 cup maple syrup or corn syrup	1 cup raisins
	1/2 cup chopped pecans (optional)

Cut the pastry into circles and press into tart pans or muffin cups. Combine the butter, brown sugar, maple syrup, eggs, milk and vanilla in a food processor container or blender and process until smooth. Add the raisins and pecans and pulse to combine. Fill the pastry-lined tart pans 2/3 full. Bake at 375 degrees for 20 minutes or until set. Yield: 2 dozen.

Delma J. Waller, Laureate Delta Lambda
Waterloo, Ontario, Canada

CAPPUCCINO PIE

1 (4-ounce) package
   vanilla instant
   pudding mix
2 teaspoons instant
   coffee granules
1 1/2 cups milk
1 cup whipped topping
Chocolate sandwich
   cookie pie shell

Combine the pudding mix and coffee granules in a large bowl. Stir in the milk. Fold in half the whipped topping. Pour into the pie shell. Chill, covered, for at least 2 hours. Serve with remaining whipped topping. Yield: 6 to 8 servings.

Sharon J. Olson, Laureate Nu
Burnsville, Minnesota

CHEESECAKE PIE

1 1/4 cups cinnamon
   graham cracker
   crumbs
1/4 cup (1/2 stick) butter,
   melted
8 ounces cream cheese,
   softened
1 tablespoon lemon juice
1/2 cup plus
   2 tablespoons sugar
1 teaspoon vanilla
   extract
Dash of salt
2 eggs
1 cup sour cream

Mix the cracker crumbs and butter in a bowl. Press the mixture into a buttered pie plate. Place the cream cheese in a mixing bowl and beat until fluffy. Blend in the lemon juice, 1/2 cup sugar, 1/2 teaspoon of the vanilla and salt gradually. Beat in the eggs 1 at a time. Pour into the pie shell. Bake at 325 degrees for 25 to 30 minutes or until set. Combine the sour cream, the 2 tablespoons sugar and the remaining 1/2 teaspoon vanilla in a small bowl and whisk to blend. Spoon over the baked pie gently. Bake for 10 minutes longer. Cool and serve. Yield: 8 to 10 servings.

Lois Joyce, Xi Epsilon Zeta
Erie, Colorado

WHITE CHOCOLATE CHEESECAKE PIE

8 ounces cream cheese,
   softened
2 cups cold milk
2 (4-ounce) packages
   white chocolate
   instant pudding mix
8 ounces whipped
   topping
1 chocolate or graham
   cracker pie shell

Combine the cream cheese and 1/2 cup of the milk in a mixing bowl and beat until smooth. Stir in the remaining 1 1/2 cups milk and pudding mix. Beat at medium speed for 1 minute. Add the whipped topping; stir until smooth. Spoon into the pie shell. Chill, covered, for at least 4 hours before serving. Garnish with white chocolate curls. Yield: 5 to 7 servings.

Sarah Miller, Delta Mu Omega
Fortuna, California

CHERRY PIE

1 cup sugar
1/3 cup flour
1/4 teaspoon salt
4 cups drained pitted
   tart cherries, 1/2 cup
   juice reserved
1 tablespoon butter
10 drops almond extract
10 to 15 drops red food
   coloring
1 (2-crust) pie pastry

Combine the sugar, flour and salt in a saucepan and stir in 1/2 cup cherry juice. Cook over medium heat until thickened, stirring constantly. Cook for 2 minutes, stirring constantly. Remove from heat. Stir in the next 4 ingredients. Let stand for 10 to 15 minutes. Pour into a pastry-lined 9- or 10-inch pie plate. Top with the remaining pastry, fluting edge and cutting vents. Bake at 450 degrees for 10 minutes. Reduce oven temperature to 350 degrees and bake for 45 minutes. Yield: 8 to 10 servings.

Adalee Brenner, Xi Beta Xi
Manhattan, Kansas

FRENCH CHERRY PIE

3 egg whites
1 cup sugar
12 soda crackers, crushed
1 teaspoon white
   vinegar
1 teaspoon vanilla
   extract
1/2 cup chopped pecans
1 teaspoon baking
   powder
3 ounces cream cheese,
   softened
1/2 cup confectioners'
   sugar
1 teaspoon vanilla
   extract
1 cup whipping cream,
   partially whipped
1 (21-ounce) can cherry
   pie filling

Beat the egg whites in a mixing bowl until stiff peaks form. Fold in the sugar, crackers, vinegar, vanilla, pecans and baking powder. Spread in the bottom of a well-buttered pie plate. Bake at 350 degrees for 20 minutes. Let stand until cool. Combine the cream cheese, confectioners' sugar and vanilla in a mixing bowl and beat until smooth and creamy. Add the partially whipped cream and beat until stiff peaks form. Spoon into the pie crust. Layer the cherry pie filling over the top. Chill, covered, for 5 to 10 hours. Yield: 6 to 8 servings.

Barbara Henderson, Xi Eta Epsilon
Sugar Land, Texas

CHERRY CREAM PIE

8 ounces cream cheese,
softened
1 (14-ounce) can
sweetened condensed
milk

1/4 cup lemon juice
1 baked (9-inch) pie
shell
1 (21-ounce) can cherry
pie filling

Combine the cream cheese, condensed milk and lemon juice in a mixing bowl and beat until smooth. Pour into the pie shell. Chill, covered, for 4 hours. Spoon the cherry pie filling over the top. Chill for 1 hour longer before serving. Yield: 6 to 8 servings.

Carol Van Der Sluis, Omicron Chi
Milford, Iowa

PARTY CHERRY TORTE

3 egg whites
1 teaspoon vanilla
extract
Dash of salt
1 cup sugar
3/4 cup chopped pecans
1/2 cup saltine cracker
crumbs

1 teaspoon baking
powder
1 (21-ounce) can cherry
pie filling
1 cup whipping cream,
whipped

Beat the egg whites, vanilla and salt in a mixing bowl until foamy. Add the sugar gradually, beating constantly until stiff peaks form. Fold a mixture of the pecans, cracker crumbs and baking powder into the egg white mixture. Spread in a well-buttered 9-inch pie plate, building up the side to form a shell. Bake at 300 degrees for 40 minutes or until dry on the outside. Cool. Spread half the whipped cream in the shell. Layer the cherry pie filling over the whipped cream layer. Top with the remaining whipped cream. Chill until serving time. Yield: 6 servings.

Sybil Bruner, Alpha Master
Corpus Christi, Texas

BUTTERMILK CHESS PIE

1/2 cup (1 stick) butter,
melted
3 tablespoons flour
2 cups sugar
3 eggs

1 cup buttermilk
1 teaspoon vanilla
extract
1 unbaked (10-inch)
pie shell

Place the butter in a large bowl. Stir in a mixture of the flour and sugar. Blend in the eggs, buttermilk and vanilla. Pour into the pie shell. Bake at 325 degrees for 45 to 50 minutes or until set. Serve at room temperature. Refrigerate leftovers. Yield: 8 servings.

JoEddye Robinson, Laureate Omega
Cordova, Tennessee

❖ BUTTER CRUNCH CHOCOLATE PIE

Shredded coconut may be substituted for the nuts.

1/2 cup (1 stick) butter,
softened
1/4 cup packed brown
sugar
1 cup sifted flour
1/2 cup chopped pecans
or walnuts

1 (4-ounce) package
chocolate pudding
and pie mix
3 egg whites
1/4 teaspoon cream of
tartar
6 tablespoons sugar

Mix the butter, brown sugar, flour and pecans in a bowl with the hands. Spread in a 9×13-inch baking dish. Bake at 400 degrees for 15 minutes. Remove from oven and stir. Press 2 cups of the mixture over the bottom and up the side of a 9-inch pie plate. Prepare the chocolate pie filling using the package directions; pour into the pie shell. Beat the egg whites with the cream of tartar in a mixing bowl until foamy. Beat in the sugar 1 tablespoon at a time until dissolved and glossy peaks form. Spread over the pie filling, sealing to the edge. Bake at 400 degrees for 8 to 10 minutes. Let stand until cool. Sprinkle the remaining brown sugar mixture over the top. Yield: 6 to 8 servings.

Arlene Burken, Preceptor Zeta
Carthage, Missouri

OLD-FASHIONED CHOCOLATE PIE

1 1/2 cups sugar
3 rounded tablespoons
self-rising flour
3 tablespoons baking
cocoa
1 (5-ounce) can
evaporated milk

2 cups milk
3 eggs, beaten
3 to 4 tablespoons
butter
1 teaspoon vanilla
extract
2 baked (9-inch) pie shells

Combine the sugar, flour and baking cocoa in a large saucepan and stir to blend. Stir in the evaporated milk and milk. Mix in the eggs. Cook over medium heat until thickened, adding the butter and vanilla, stirring constantly. Remove from heat immediately. Pour into the pie shells. Chill, covered, until serving time. Top with whipped topping and serve. Yield: 12 to 16 servings.

Paige Robbins, Kappa Epsilon
Cartersville, Georgia

CARAMEL CHOCOLATE PIE

1 (14-ounce) package
caramels
1/4 cup plus 1/3 cup milk
1 baked (9-inch) graham
cracker pie shell

1 cup toasted chopped
pecans
8 ounces semisweet
chocolate

Combine the caramels and the ¼ cup milk in a glass bowl. Microwave on High for 2 minutes and stir until smooth. Pour into the pie shell and sprinkle with the pecans. Chill for 5 minutes. Place the chocolate and the ⅓ cup milk in a glass bowl and microwave on Medium for 2 minutes. Stir until smooth. Pour evenly over the caramel nut filling, spreading to the edge. Garnish with additional pecans. Chill, covered, until serving time. Yield: 8 servings.

Valerie McPherson, Xi Omicron
Calgary, Alberta, Canada

GERMAN CHOCOLATE PIE

4 ounces German's sweet chocolate	2 eggs
¼ cup (½ stick) butter	1 teaspoon vanilla extract
1 (12-ounce) can evaporated milk	1⅓ cups shredded coconut
1½ cups sugar	½ cup chopped pecans
3 tablespoons cornstarch	1 unbaked (10-inch) pie shell
⅛ teaspoon salt	

Combine the chocolate and butter in a saucepan over low heat. Cook until melted, stirring constantly. Remove from heat. Blend in the evaporated milk gradually. Place the sugar, cornstarch and salt in a mixing bowl and stir to blend. Beat in the eggs and vanilla until smooth. Blend in the chocolate mixture. Stir in the coconut and chopped pecans. Pour into the pie shell. Bake at 350 degrees for 45 to 50 minutes or until top puffs up. Serve warm or cold.
Yield: 8 to 10 small servings.

Sandy Waggoner, Xi Eta Tau
Joplin, Missouri

CHOCOLATE ANGEL PIE

2 egg whites	½ cup chopped walnuts or pecans
¼ teaspoon salt	1 (7-ounce) milk chocolate bar
⅛ teaspoon cream of tartar	3 tablespoons water
½ cup sugar	1 cup whipping cream, whipped
1½ teaspoons vanilla extract	

Place the egg whites, salt and cream of tartar in a mixing bowl and beat until foamy. Add the sugar 1 teaspoon at a time, beating well after each addition. Add the vanilla. Beat until stiff peaks form. Fold in the walnuts. Spread in a buttered pie plate to form a pie shell. Bake at 275 degrees for 50 to 60 minutes or until browned. Place the chocolate bar and water in a saucepan over low heat and cook until melted, stir-

ring constantly. Remove from heat. Cool. Fold the chocolate mixture into the whipped cream. Spoon into the meringue shell. Chill, covered, for 2 to 10 hours. Yield: 6 to 8 servings.

Marjorie Morcom, Laureate Iota
Lead, South Dakota

CHOCOLATE MOUSSE PIE

25 chocolate wafers, crumbled	5 ounces unsweetened chocolate
2 tablespoons butter, melted	6 tablespoons butter, softened
4 eggs, separated	¼ cup cold strong coffee
¾ cup plus 2 tablespoons sugar	¾ cup whipping cream, whipped
1 teaspoon vanilla extract	13 cordial cherries with stems
⅛ teaspoon salt	¼ cup brandy
1 ounce semisweet chocolate	

Line the bottom and side of a lightly buttered 8- or 9-inch springform pan with buttered waxed paper. Combine the chocolate wafer crumbs and melted butter in a small bowl and mix well. Press into the bottom of the prepared springform pan. Chill until ready to use. Combine the egg yolks, the ¾ cup sugar, brandy, vanilla and salt in the top of a double boiler. Cook over simmering water, beating with a hand mixer at high speed for about 8 minutes or until thick and pale yellow. Pour into a large bowl. Melt the semisweet chocolate and unsweetened chocolate in a bowl over simmering water. Remove bowl from heat. Beat in the butter 1 tablespoon at a time. Add the chocolate mixture to the egg yolk mixture gradually, beating until smooth and slightly thickened. Stir in the coffee. Place the egg whites in a large mixing bowl; beat at medium speed until foamy white. Add the remaining 2 tablespoons sugar gradually, beating until soft peaks form. Stir a small amount of the meringue into the chocolate mixture. Add the remaining meringue, folding in until no white streaks remain. Fold the whipped cream into the chocolate mixture. Pour into the prepared springform pan. Chill, covered, for 8 to 10 hours. Combine the cordial cherries and brandy. Freeze for at least a few hours. Pat dry with paper towels and dip into an additional melted 4 ounces semisweet chocolate. Arrange over the top of the pie.
Yield: 12 to 15 servings.

Karen Brown, Omicron
Trail, British Columbia, Canada

CHOCOLATE ALMOND PIE

2 (7-ounce) chocolate
candy bars with
almonds

3 cups whipping cream
1 baked (9-inch) pie
shell

Place the candy bars in the top of a double boiler. Melt over simmering water. Cool slightly. Beat the whipping cream until very, very stiff. Fold in the melted chocolate and pour into the pie shell. Chill, covered, until serving time. Yield: 6 to 8 servings.

Alice McClure, Xi Sigma
Vancouver, Washington

SNICKERS ICE CREAM PIE

20 chocolate sandwich
cookies, crushed
1/4 cup sugar
1/4 cup (1/2 stick) butter,
melted
4 or 5 (7-ounce) Snickers
bars, coarsely
chopped

1/2 gallon vanilla ice
cream, slightly
softened
1/2 cup fudge topping
1/2 to 3/4 cup caramel
topping
1 cup cocktail peanuts,
crushed

Combine the crushed cookies, sugar and melted butter in a small bowl and mix well. Press the mixture over the bottom and up the side of a deep 9-inch pie plate. Chill for 10 to 15 minutes. Place the candy bars and ice cream in a food processor container or blender and process just until mixed and creamy. Pour half the ice cream mixture in the pie shell. Freeze until firm. Layer the fudge topping, caramel topping and the remaining ice cream over the first ice cream layer. Freeze. Spread with a thin layer of whipped cream and sprinkle with the peanuts. Cover and freeze until serving time. Yield: 10 to 12 servings.

Janice Roth, Preceptor Beta Psi
Dodge City, Kansas

COCONUT CREAM PIE

2/3 cup sugar
1/4 cup cornstarch
1/2 teaspoon salt
3 cups milk
4 egg yolks
3/4 cup shredded coconut
2 tablespoons butter

2 teaspoons vanilla
extract
1 unbaked (9-inch) pie
shell
Whipped cream to taste
1/4 cup toasted shredded
coconut

Place the sugar, cornstarch, salt and 1 cup of the milk in a blender and process for 20 seconds. Add the remaining 2 cups milk and egg yolks; process until smooth. Pour into a saucepan over medium heat and cook until mixture thickens and boils, stirring constantly. Boil for 1 minute, stirring constantly. Remove

from heat. Add the 3/4 cup coconut, butter and vanilla and stir until melted and smooth. Pour into the pie shell. Chill, covered with plastic wrap, for 2 hours. Top with whipped cream and the 1/4 cup toasted coconut. Chill until serving time.
Yield: 6 to 8 servings.

Suzann Alstrin, Laureate Alpha Psi
Colorado Springs, Colorado

COCONUT CUSTARD PIE

1/2 cup (1 stick)
margarine
1 1/2 cups sugar
1/4 cup flour
1/2 teaspoon salt
2 eggs, beaten

1 1/2 cup milk
1 1/2 cups shredded
coconut
1 unbaked (9-inch) pie
shell

Cream the margarine and sugar in a mixing bowl until light and fluffy. Stir in a mixture of the flour and salt. Stir in a mixture of the eggs and milk. Finally, stir in the coconut. Pour into the pie shell and bake at 400 degrees for 10 minutes. Reduce oven temperature to 350 degrees and bake for 10 to 20 minutes longer or until set. Yield: 8 servings.

Ellen Howard, Xi Alpha Omega
Hazleton, Iowa

MAKES-ITS-OWN-CRUST COCONUT PIE

4 eggs
1 1/2 cups sugar
1/2 cup flour
1/4 cup (1/2 stick) butter,
melted

2 cups milk
1 1/2 cups shredded
coconut
1 teaspoon vanilla
extract

Combine the eggs, sugar, flour, butter, milk, coconut and vanilla in a mixing bowl in the order listed; mix well. Pour into a buttered 9-inch pie plate. Bake at 350 degrees for 45 minutes or until pie is set around the edge but still soft in the center. Cool and serve. Yield: 8 servings.

Beverly Long, Alpha Zeta Alpha
Lowry City, Missouri

COCONUT CRUNCH PIE

1 cup whipping cream
1/2 cup chopped pecans
1/2 cup confectioners'
sugar
1 cup crushed coconut
macaroons

1 teaspoon vanilla
extract
1/2 cup toasted shredded
coconut
1 baked vanilla wafer
pie shell

Beat the whipping cream in a chilled mixing bowl until stiff peaks form. Fold in the pecans, sugar, macaroons, vanilla and half the coconut. Spoon into the pie shell. Sprinkle with the remaining coconut. Chill, covered, until serving time. Yield: 6 to 8 servings.

Donna Ballard, Alpha Alpha Sigma
Lakeland, Florida

COCONUT CARAMEL PIE

1/4 cup (1/2 stick) butter
1 1/3 cups flaked coconut
1/2 cup chopped pecans
8 ounces cream cheese, softened
1 (14-ounce) can sweetened condensed milk

16 ounces whipped topping
2 baked (9-inch) pie shells
1 (12-ounce) jar caramel ice cream topping

Melt the butter in a large skillet over medium heat. Stir in the coconut and pecans and cook for 6 to 8 minutes or until coconut is golden, stirring constantly. Cool slightly. Place the cream cheese in a large mixing bowl and beat until smooth. Add the sweetened condensed milk gradually, beating at low speed. Fold in the whipped topping. Spoon about 1/4 of the mixture into each pie shell. Drizzle each with 1/4 of the caramel topping; sprinkle each with 1/4 of the coconut mixture. Repeat the layers. Cover and freeze until firm. Let stand at room temperature for 5 minutes before serving. Yield: 16 servings.

Kathy Foster, Xi Delta Upsilon
Great Bend, Kansas

COTTAGE CHEESE PIE

2/3 cup milk
2 tablespoons flour
1/2 cup sugar
1 egg yolk, beaten
2 tablespoons butter
1 cup cottage cheese

Juice and grated zest of 1 lemon
1 baked (9-inch) pie shell
1 recipe meringue

Heat the milk in the top of a double boiler over simmering water. Place the flour and sugar in a bowl and mix together. Add the hot milk to the flour mixture gradually, stirring constantly. Return the milk mixture to the top of the double boiler. Cook until thickened, stirring constantly. Add the egg yolk and cook until thickened, stirring constantly. Add the butter, cottage cheese and lemon juice and zest. Pour into the pie shell. Cover with meringue and brown in a slow oven. Yield: 6 to 8 servings.

Ruth Corley, Laureate Zeta Eta
Bryan, Texas

CRANBERRY CHERRY PIE

3/4 cup sugar
2 tablespoons cornstarch
2 cups cranberries

1 (21-ounce) can cherry pie filling
1 (2-crust) pie pastry

Combine the sugar and cornstarch in a large bowl. Stir in the cherry pie filling and cranberries. Pour into a pastry-lined pie plate. Top with the remaining pastry, fluting edge and cutting vents or cutting out stars with a star-shaped cookie cutter. Arrange the star cutouts over the top. Brush with milk and sprinkle with additional sugar. Cover the edge loosely with foil. Bake at 375 degrees for 55 to 60 minutes or until crust is golden brown and filling is bubbly. Cool in the pan on a wire rack. Yield: 6 to 8 servings.

Billy Jane Gabel, Xi Master
South Bend, Indiana

CRANBERRY PIE

2 cups fresh cranberries
1/3 cup Late Harvest wine or Grand Marnier
1 1/2 cups sugar
3/4 cup chopped walnuts

2 eggs, beaten
3/4 cup (1 1/2 sticks) butter, melted
1 cup flour
1 teaspoon almond extract

Combine the cranberries and wine in a small bowl and let stand at room temperature for several hours; drain. Spread the soaked cranberries in a buttered 10-inch pie plate. Sprinkle evenly with 1/2 cup of the sugar. Sprinkle evenly with the walnuts. Combine the remaining 1 cup sugar, eggs, melted butter, flour and almond extract in a bowl and mix well. Pour evenly over the walnut layer. Bake at 325 degrees for 35 to 45 minutes or until top is golden brown. Serve warm with whipped cream or vanilla ice cream. Yield: 8 to 12 servings.

Sara Neily, Alpha Chi
Phoenix, Arizona

CRANBERRY CHEESE PIE

8 ounces cream cheese, softened
1 cup sugar
2 teaspoons vanilla extract

1 (16-ounce) can whole cranberry sauce
12 ounces whipped topping
1 graham cracker pie shell

Cream the cream cheese and sugar in a mixing bowl until light and fluffy. Stir in the vanilla and cranberry sauce. Fold in the whipped topping. Pour into the pie shell. Cover and freeze. Remove from freezer 10 to 15 minutes before serving. Yield: 6 to 8 servings.

Jean Pessano, Laureate Pi
Ocean City, New Jersey

EGGNOG PIE

2 egg yolks	1/2 cup rum
1 cup sugar	3 egg whites
1/4 teaspoon nutmeg	1 baked (9-inch) pie
2 tablespoons	shell
unflavored gelatin	

Combine the egg yolks, 1/2 cup of the sugar and nutmeg in the top of a double boiler. Cook over simmering water until thick, stirring constantly. Cool. Dissolve the gelatin in 1/2 cup warm water and stir into the egg yolk mixture with the rum. Beat the egg whites in a small mixing bowl until stiff peaks form. Add the remaining 1/2 cup sugar gradually, beating constantly. Fold the egg white mixture gently into the rum mixture. Pour into the pie shell. Chill, covered, until serving time. Top with whipped cream and serve. Yield: 8 servings.

Louise B. Smith, Preceptor Xi Delta
Canyon Lake, Texas

FIG NUT PIE

I think of this as a variation on a pecan pie, as you get that same thick gooey filling. If you like figs, you'll love this pie.

6 eggs, beaten	1/2 teaspoon cinnamon
1 cup granulated sugar	1/2 teaspoon nutmeg
3 tablespoons lemon	1 1/2 cups chopped dried
juice	figs (9 ounces)
3 tablespoons butter,	1 cup chopped walnuts
melted	1 unbaked (9-inch) pie
1/4 teaspoon salt	shell

Combine the eggs, sugar, lemon juice, melted butter, salt, cinnamon and nutmeg in a mixing bowl and mix well. Stir in the figs and walnuts. Pour into the pie shell. Bake at 375 degrees for 40 minutes. Cool to room temperature. Yield: 8 servings.

Holly Ardrey, Xi Omicron Chi
Pleasant Hill, California

CHERRY PINEAPPLE FRUIT PIE

1 (21-ounce) can cherry	1 (3-ounce) package
pie filling	raspberry gelatin
3/4 cup sugar	1 cup chopped pecans
1 (20-ounce) can crushed	1 tablespoon butter
pineapple	(optional)
1 tablespoon cornstarch	4 to 6 bananas, sliced
1 teaspoon red food	2 baked (10-inch) pie
coloring	shells

Combine the cherry pie filling, sugar, undrained pineapple, cornstarch and red food coloring in a saucepan over medium-low heat. Cook for about 20 minutes until thickened, stirring frequently. Add the dry gelatin mix and stir until dissolved. Stir in the pecans and butter. Remove from heat and cool completely; mixture will thicken more. Spread the banana slices in the pie shells. Pour the cherry mixture evenly over the banana slices. Cover with whipped topping or whipped cream. Chill until serving time. Yield: 12 to 16 servings.

Shirley Kula, Tau
Fort Morgan, Colorado

TROPICAL FRUIT PIE

3 ounces cream cheese,	1 (3-ounce) package
softened	apricot gelatin
2 tablespoons apricot	3/4 cup boiling water
preserves	2 cups ice cubes
1 (8-inch) graham	1 cup whipping cream
cracker pie shell	1 teaspoon
1 medium banana, sliced	confectioners' sugar
Canned peaches, crushed	1 teaspoon vanilla
pineapple and	extract
mandarin oranges to	
make 2 cups	

Combine the cream cheese and apricot preserves in a mixing bowl and beat until smooth. Spread over the bottom and up the side of the pie shell. Layer the banana slices and mixed fruit over the cream cheese mixture. Dissolve the dry gelatin mix in the boiling water; add the ice cubes and let stand until slightly thickened, stirring constantly. Discard any unmelted ice cubes. Pour the gelatin over the mixed fruit layer. Chill until set. Beat the whipping cream with the confectioners' sugar and vanilla until soft peaks form. Serve the pie with the whipped cream.
Yield: 8 servings.

Dodie Botkins, Preceptor Chi
Covington, Virginia

GRAHAM CRACKER PIE

22 graham cracker	2 egg yolks, beaten
squares, crushed	4 tablespoons
2 tablespoons plus 1 cup	cornstarch
sugar	1/4 teaspoon salt
1/2 cup (1 stick) butter,	1 teaspoon vanilla
melted	extract
2 cups milk	2 egg whites

Combine the graham cracker crumbs, the 2 tablespoons sugar and butter in a small bowl and mix well. Reserve a small amount of the mixture. Press the remaining mixture into a buttered 9-inch pie plate. Bake at 375 degrees for 10 minutes. Heat the milk in a saucepan over medium-low heat. Combine

3/4 cup of the sugar, egg yolks, cornstarch and salt in a bowl; blend well. Add the egg yolk mixture to the hot milk and cook until thickened, stirring constantly. Stir in the vanilla. Pour into the pie shell. Beat the egg whites until stiff peaks form, adding the remaining 1/4 cup sugar gradually. Spread over the top of the pie, sealing to the edge. Sprinkle with the reserved crumbs. Bake at 425 degrees for 5 minutes. Chill until serving time. Yield: 8 to 10 servings.

Pat Gay, Preceptor Mu
Anchorage, Alaska

GRAPEFRUIT PIE

24 marshmallows
1/4 cup orange juice
1 cup whipping cream, whipped
2 grapefruit, peeled, membranes removed, cut into pieces
1 (9-inch) graham cracker pie shell

Place the marshmallows and orange juice in the top of a double boiler. Cook over simmering water until marshmallows melt and mixture is smooth, stirring frequently. Cool slightly. Fold in the whipped cream. Fold in the grapefruit pieces. Pour into the pie shell. Chill for at least 4 hours before serving. Yield: 6 to 8 servings.

Jeanne Caimano, Preceptor Pi
St. Petersburg, Florida

LEMON MERINGUE PIE

3 large egg yolks
7 tablespoons cornstarch
1 1/2 cups sugar
1/2 teaspoon salt
1 1/2 cups hot water
2 tablespoons butter
1 teaspoon grated lemon zest
1/2 cup fresh lemon juice
1 baked (9-inch) pie shell
Lemon Pie Meringue (optional)

Place the egg yolks in a medium bowl and beat slightly with a fork. Measure the cornstarch, sugar and salt into a heavy 2-quart saucepan and mix well with a wooden spoon. Add the hot water and stir until smooth. Place the saucepan over high heat. Bring to a boil, stirring constantly. When mixture begins to thicken, reduce to medium heat and let it bubble for 8 minutes, stirring constantly; mixture will be very thick. Remove from heat. Stir several spoonfuls of the hot mixture into the egg yolks and mix well. Stir egg yolk mixture into the hot sugar mixture in the saucepan, scraping the bowl with a spatula. Cook over medium heat for 5 minutes, stirring constantly. Mixture will be extremely thick.

Remove from heat. Stir in the butter and lemon zest. Add the lemon juice slowly and mix until smooth. Pour into a clean bowl and let stand until room temperature. Pour into the pie shell. Top with meringue, sealing to the edge. Bake in a preheated 350-degree oven for 12 minutes. Let stand for 2 to 3 hours before slicing. Yield: 6 to 8 servings.

LEMON PIE MERINGUE

1 tablespoon cornstarch
2 tablespoons cold water
1/2 cup boiling water
1 teaspoon fresh lemon juice
3 large egg whites, at room temperature
6 tablespoons sugar

Combine the cornstarch and cold water in a small heavy saucepan and whisk to blend. Stir in the boiling water. Place over medium heat and bring to a boil, stirring constantly. Simmer for 2 minutes or until thickened, stirring constantly. Remove from heat. Place the saucepan in a larger pan filled with cold water to hasten cooling. Add the lemon juice to the egg whites and beat until soft peaks form. Add the sugar 1 tablespoon at a time, beating well after each addition. Beat until stiff glossy peaks form. Add the cornstarch mixture all at once and beat well.

Beverly A. Raze, Preceptor Alpha Nu
Ontario, Ore

LEMON REFRIGERATOR PIE

1 (14-ounce) can sweetened condensed milk
3 eggs, separated
1/3 cup lemon juice
1 (9-inch) graham cracker pie shell
1/4 teaspoon cream of tartar
1/2 teaspoon vanilla extract
6 tablespoons sugar

Combine the condensed milk and egg yolks in a medium bowl; mix well until uniformly colored. Add the lemon juice and mix until thickened and uniform. Pour into the pie shell. Combine the egg whites, cream of tartar and vanilla in a glass or metal bowl and beat until soft peaks form. Add the sugar 1 tablespoon at a time, beating well after each addition. Beat until stiff peaks form. Spread over the lemon pie, sealing to the edge. Bake at 350 degrees until lightly browned. Cool slightly. Chill, in the refrigerator, before serving. Yield: about 8 servings.

Barbara Allen, Laureate Alpha
Boise, Idaho

LEMONADE PIE

1 (14-ounce) can
  sweetened condensed
  milk
1 (6-ounce) can frozen
  lemonade, thawed

8 ounces whipped
  topping
1 (9-inch) graham
  cracker pie shell

Combine the condensed milk, lemonade and whipped topping in a mixing bowl and mix well. Pour into the pie shell. Sprinkle with additional graham cracker crumbs if desired. Cover and freeze. Yield: 8 servings.

Patricia Herbert, Laureate Upsilon
Prescott, Arizona

LEMON CHESS PIE

1 unbaked (9-inch) pie
  shell
2 cups sugar
2 tablespoons cornmeal
1 tablespoon flour
1/2 cup (1 stick) butter,
  melted

1/4 cup milk
1 1/2 teaspoons vanilla
  extract
4 large eggs, beaten
1/3 cup lemon juice
2 teaspoons grated
  lemon zest

Partially bake the pie shell in a 425-degree oven for 5 to 7 minutes. Combine the sugar, cornmeal, flour, melted butter, milk and vanilla in a large bowl and blend well. Add the eggs, lemon juice and lemon zest; stir well. Pour into the cooled pie shell and bake at 350 degrees for 55 minutes. Let stand until cool. Yield: 6 to 8 servings.

Cynthia Thigpen, Alpha Rho Lambda
Farwell, Texas

KEY LIME PIE

4 eggs, separated
1 (6-ounce) can
  sweetened condensed
  milk
1/4 cup fresh Key lime
  juice

1 baked (9-inch) pie
  shell
1/2 teaspoon cream of
  tartar
6 tablespoons sugar

Combine the egg yolks, condensed milk and lime juice in a mixing bowl and blend well. Beat the egg whites until soft peaks form. Fold 1/4 of the beaten egg whites gently into the lime juice mixture. Pour into the pie shell. Add the cream of tartar to the remaining egg white mixture; add the sugar 1 tablespoon at a time, beating well after each addition until glossy peaks form. Spread over the top of the pie, sealing to the edge. Bake at 350 degrees for about 15 minutes or until lightly browned. Yield: 8 servings.

Laura Hennessey, Beta Alpha
Grants, New Mexico

TEX-MEX MARGARITA PIE

1 (14-ounce) can
  sweetened condensed
  milk
1/2 cup lime juice
  (Mexican lime juice if
  available)
1 (8-ounce) can crushed
  pineapple, drained
8 ounces whipped
  topping

1 teaspoon vanilla
  extract or almond
  extract
2 or 3 drops green food
  coloring (optional)
1 ready-to-use (10-inch)
  graham cracker pie
  shell

Combine the condensed milk and lime juice in a bowl and beat until slightly thickened. Fold in the pineapple. Fold in the whipped topping. Stir in the vanilla and food coloring. Pour into the pie shell. Garnish with grated lime zest. Chill until serving time. Yield: 6 to 10 servings.

Ruth M. Scoggins, Alpha Omicron Master
Harlingen, Texas

QUICK LIME PIE

1 (8-ounce) can frozen
  limeade, thawed
1 (14-ounce) can
  sweetened condensed
  milk
1 cup sour cream

8 ounces whipped
  topping
1 or 2 drops green food
  coloring
1 (9-inch) chocolate
  crumb pie shell

Combine the limeade, condensed milk, sour cream, whipped topping and green food coloring in a large bowl. Pour into pie shell. Chill for at least 1 hour before serving. Decorate with chocolate shavings or chocolate chips if desired. Yield: 6 to 8 servings.

Kathleen Priddy, Preceptor Beta Psi
Indio, California

ICE CREAM LIME PIE

1 (7-ounce) can lemon-
  lime soda
1 (3-ounce) package lime
  gelatin

1 pint vanilla ice cream,
  softened
1 (9-inch) graham
  cracker pie shell

Bring the lemon-lime soda to a boil in a small saucepan over medium heat. Remove from heat. Dissolve the lime gelatin in the heated soda. Cool slightly. Place the ice cream in a mixing bowl and beat well. Beat in the soda mixture. Pour into the pie shell. Chill, covered, for 3 to 4 hours or until set. Decorate the top with whipped topping and lime slices or a sprinkle of graham cracker crumbs. Yield: 6 to 8 servings.

Betty J. Orme, Laureate Iota
Maysville, Kentucky

ORANGE REFRIGERATOR PIE

1 (14-ounce) can
   sweetened condensed
   milk
1/2 cup sour cream

4 tablespoons orange
   drink mix
1 (9-inch) graham
   cracker pie shell

Combine the condensed milk, sour cream and orange drink mix in a bowl and blend well. Pour into the pie shell. Chill for at least 4 hours before serving. Garnish by drizzling with chocolate or top with whipped topping and orange slices. Yield: 8 servings.

Sandra E. White, Theta Chi
Steinhatchee, Florida

MANGO PIE

5 ripe mangoes, peeled
   and diced
1/3 cup flour
2/3 cup sugar
1 tablespoon lemon juice

1 (2-crust) pie pastry
2 tablespoons butter
2 tablespoons butter,
   melted

Combine the mangoes, flour, sugar and lemon juice in a bowl; stir with a spoon. Prepare the pastry using the package directions. Fit pastry into a 9-inch pie plate and trim edge. Prick the pastry shell all over with a fork. Fill with the mango mixture and dot with butter. Top with the remaining pastry, fluting edge and cutting vents. Brush top with melted butter. Bake in a preheated 425-degree oven for 45 to 50 minutes or until bubbly and lightly browned, loosely covering the pastry edge with foil for the first 20 minutes of baking time. Yield: 8 servings.

Sandra Hildebrand, Laureate Theta Lambda
Longview, Texas

VERMONT MAPLE PIE

1 cup medium or dark
   amber maple syrup
1 cup milk
2 tablespoons butter
3 egg yolks, beaten
1 teaspoon vanilla
   extract

3 tablespoons
   cornstarch
1 baked (10-inch) pie
   shell
3 egg whites
1/4 cup sugar

Warm the maple syrup, milk and butter in a saucepan over low heat. Stir in the egg yolks and vanilla. Dissolve the cornstarch in 1/4 cup cold water and stir gradually into the maple syrup mixture. Cook over medium heat until thickened, stirring constantly. Pour into the pie shell. Beat the egg whites in a mixing bowl until frothy. Add the sugar gradually, beating constantly until stiff peaks form. Spread over the maple pie, sealing to the edge. Bake at 400

degrees for 5 to 8 minutes. Serve the same day if possible. Yield: 8 servings.

Linda D. Fowler, Laureate Beta
Williston, Vermont

MINT CHIFFON PIE

1 envelope unflavored
   gelatin
2 ounces unsweetened
   chocolate, chopped
3 large eggs, separated
1 cup sugar

1/2 teaspoon peppermint
   extract
1/4 teaspoon salt
1 baked (9-inch) pie
   shell

Sprinkle the gelatin over 3/4 cup cold water in a saucepan; let stand for 1 minute. Heat over low heat, stirring constantly until dissolved. Remove from heat. Combine the chocolate and 1/4 cup water in a medium saucepan over medium-low heat. Heat until chocolate is melted, stirring frequently. Stir in the gelatin mixture. Beat the egg yolks in a small mixing bowl until pale yellow and increased in volume. Beat in 1/2 cup of the sugar, peppermint extract and salt. Add the egg yolk mixture to the chocolate mixture and bring to the boiling point. Chill, covered, until thickened. Beat the egg whites in a mixing bowl until soft peaks form. Add the remaining 1/2 cup sugar gradually, beating until stiff peaks form. Fold into the chocolate mixture. Spoon into the pie shell. Garnish with green-tinted whipped cream and chocolate mint squares. Yield: 6 to 8 servings.

Anne Boutilier, Omicron
Trail, British Columbia, Canada

CREME DE MENTHE PIE

16 chocolate sandwich
   cookies
3 tablespoons butter,
   melted
24 large marshmallows

3/4 cup evaporated milk
2 ounces crème de
   menthe
1 cup whipping cream,
   whipped

Place the cookies in a food processor container and process until crumbly. Pulse in the melted butter. Press the mixture into a 9-inch pie plate to form a shell. Melt the marshmallows with the evaporated milk in a saucepan over low heat or a microwave oven; stir until smooth. Let stand until completely cool. Stir in the crème de menthe. Fold the whipped cream into the evaporated milk mixture. Pour into the pie shell. Garnish with mint leaves or sprinkle with additional crushed cookies. Chill, covered, for 4 hours before serving. Yield: 8 to 10 servings.

Candace Harding, Xi Rho Omega
Livermore, California

CANDY CANE PIE

Bread dough loves to be handled, but pie dough hates to be handled, so roll out this dough only once!

3 cups flour	1 large package vanilla
1 teaspoon salt	sugar-free pudding
1¼ cups shortening	mix
5 tablespoons water	2 medium candy canes,
1 egg	crushed
1 tablespoon white	8 ounces fat-free
vinegar	whipped topping
2½ cups milk	

Combine the flour and salt in a bowl and cut in the shortening until mixture consists of pea-sized crumbs. Place the water, egg and vinegar in a small bowl and blend well. Add the egg mixture slowly to the flour mixture and stir gently until blended. Roll into 12-inch circles on a lightly floured surface. Fit into two 9-inch pie plates. Bake at 450 degrees for 12 minutes or until golden brown. Cool. Combine the milk and pudding mix in a bowl and blend well. Stir in the crushed candy canes. Pour into the cooled pie crusts. Top with whipped topping. Yield: 12 servings.

Linda Green, Preceptor Alpha Upsilon
Tacoma, Washington

SWEET GEORGIA PEACH PIE

6 to 8 large peaches,	1 cup sugar
peeled and sliced	2 tablespoons flour
1 unbaked (9-inch)	2 tablespoons melted
deep-dish pie shell	shortening
4 eggs, well beaten	

Arrange the peaches in the pie shell. Blend the eggs, sugar, flour and shortening in a mixing bowl. Pour evenly over the peaches. Bake at 400 degrees for 15 minutes. Reduce oven temperature to 325 degrees and bake for 40 minutes longer. Cool. Serve with ice cream if desired. Yield: 8 servings.

Tahnell Vogt, Laureate Pi
Highland Village, Texas

FRESH PEACH PIE

4 ripe peaches, peeled	2 tablespoons dry peach
1 baked (9-inch) pie	gelatin mix
shell	2 or 3 drops yellow food
1 cup sugar	coloring
2 tablespoons cornstarch	8 ounces whipped
1 cup water	topping

Slice the peaches into the pie shell. Combine the sugar, cornstarch and water in a saucepan over medium-low heat. Cook until thickened, stirring constantly. Stir in the dry gelatin mix and the yellow food coloring. Pour evenly over the peaches. Chill, covered, until set. Top with whipped topping. Yield: 6 servings.

Jeri Patterson, Omicron Master
Maryville, Missouri

SPICED PEACH PIE

1 (15-ounce) can sliced	4 ounces cream cheese,
peaches in syrup	softened
2 tablespoons brown	2 tablespoons butter or
sugar	margarine, softened
¼ teaspoon ginger	⅛ teaspoon nutmeg
1 (3-inch) cinnamon	1 baked (9-inch) pie
stick	shell
1 (3-ounce) package	8 ounces whipped
peach gelatin	topping

Drain the syrup from the peaches into a 2-cup measuring cup. Add enough water to make 1⅓ cups liquid. Chop the peaches. Combine the peach liquid mixture, brown sugar, ginger and cinnamon stick in a saucepan; bring to a boil. Reduce heat to medium and cook for 5 minutes, stirring constantly. Remove from heat. Discard the cinnamon stick. Stir the dry gelatin mix into the syrup mixture until dissolved. Stir in the peaches. Chill, covered, until partially set, about 40 minutes. Beat the cream cheese, butter and nutmeg in a mixing bowl until smooth. Spread over the bottom and up the side of the pie shell. Pour the gelatin mixture evenly into the cream cheese layer. Chill until serving time. Spread with whipped topping. Garnish with fresh mint. Yield: 6 to 8 servings.

Mary L. Daily, Preceptor Gamma Psi
Terre Haute, Indiana

PEANUT BUTTER CREAM PIE

3 cups miniature	3 ounces cream cheese,
marshmallows	softened
1 cup crunchy peanut	¾ cup plus 1 teaspoon
butter	confectioners' sugar
¼ cup (½ stick) plus 2	8 ounces whipped
tablespoons	topping
margarine	½ cup chocolate chips
4 cups cornflakes	2 tablespoons milk

Combine the marshmallows, ½ cup of the peanut butter and the ¼ cup margarine in a saucepan over medium-low heat; heat until melted, stirring until well mixed. Remove from heat. Stir in the cornflakes. Press into a 9-inch pie plate to make a shell. Combine the cream cheese, the remaining ½ cup peanut butter and the ¾ cup confectioners' sugar in a mixing bowl and mix well. Fold in the whipped topping. Spread in the pie shell. Chill, covered, until set. Combine the chocolate chips, the 2 tablespoons margarine, milk and the 1 teaspoon confectioners' sugar in a small saucepan; heat until melted, stirring until smooth. Spread evenly over the pie. Chill until serving time. Yield: 10 servings.

Paula Disterhaupt, Xi Gamma Nu
Garland, Texas

PEANUT BUTTER PIE IN COOKIE SHELL

24 peanut butter
  sandwich cookies,
  crushed
5 tablespoons butter,
  melted
8 ounces cream cheese,
  softened

1 cup smooth peanut
  butter
3/4 cup sugar
1 teaspoon vanilla
  extract
8 ounces whipped
  topping

Mix 2/3 of the crushed cookies and the butter in a small bowl. Press into a 9-inch pie plate to form a shell. Combine the cream cheese, peanut butter, sugar, vanilla and whipped topping in a mixing bowl and beat until smooth. Spread in the cookie shell. Sprinkle with the remaining crushed cookies. Freeze until ready to serve. Yield: 6 to 8 servings.

Julie A. Graber, Beta Eta
Hutchinson, Kansas

PEANUT BUTTER CANDY PIE

3 eggs, beaten
1/2 cup sugar
1 cup light corn syrup
1 teaspoon vanilla
  extract
1/2 cup smooth peanut
  butter

1/4 teaspoon salt
1 unbaked (9-inch) pie
  shell
1/2 cup semisweet
  chocolate chips
1/4 cup flaked coconut

Place the eggs in a mixing bowl. Beat in the sugar gradually; mix well. Add the corn syrup, vanilla, peanut butter and salt; mix well. Pour into the pie shell. Bake at 300 degrees for 40 to 45 minutes or until set. Arrange a circle of chocolate chips in the center of the hot pie; sprinkle the remaining chocolate chips around the outside edge. Sprinkle the rest of the pie top with coconut. Cool and serve. Yield: 8 servings.

Arline Bucksky, Xi Gamma Kappa
Weston, Ohio

PEANUT BUTTER PIE

8 ounces cream cheese,
  softened
1 cup confectioners' sugar
1 cup crunchy peanut
  butter

8 ounces whipped
  topping
1 (9-inch) graham
  cracker pie shell

Combine the cream cheese, confectioners' sugar and peanut butter in a mixing bowl and beat until well

blended. Fold in the whipped topping. Fill the pie shell. Cover, and chill or freeze until serving time. Yield: 6 to 8 servings.

Marilyn Kidd, Laureate Gamma Sigma
Bowling Green, Ohio

PEARS IN CREAM PIE

1 cup dry white wine
1/4 cup sugar
1/8 teaspoon ginger
4 firm ripe Anjou pears,
  peeled
1 cup heavy cream
1 tablespoon cornstarch
3 egg yolks, beaten

3 tablespoons sugar
2 teaspoons almond
  extract
1 baked (9- or 10-inch)
  pie shell
1/2 cup apricot jam
1 tablespoon hot water

Combine the wine, sugar and ginger in a saucepan and bring to a boil. Reduce heat and simmer for 3 minutes. Halve and core the pears. Poach them in the simmering wine mixture for 10 minutes. Drain, reserving the syrup. Boil the syrup down to 1 cup liquid or add water to make 1 cup liquid. Combine the cream and cornstarch in a small bowl and blend to make a smooth paste. Stir into the syrup; cook over low heat until thickened, stirring constantly. Combine the egg yolks, sugar and almond extract in a mixing bowl and beat until smooth. Stir the syrup into the egg yolk mixture gradually. Return to the saucepan and cook over low heat until thickened, stirring constantly. Cool slightly. Spread in the pie shell. Arrange pears over the filling round side up, pointed ends toward the center. Combine the apricot jam and hot water in a saucepan over low heat. Heat, stirring frequently; drizzle over the pears. Chill, covered, until serving time. Yield: 8 servings.

Mary A. Courten, Laureate Beta Omicron
North Fort Myers, Florida

CHOCOLATE PECAN PIE

3 eggs, slightly beaten
1 cup light corn syrup
1 cup granulated sugar
1/2 cup packed brown
  sugar
2 tablespoons butter,
  melted

1 teaspoon vanilla
  extract
1 cup chocolate chips
1 1/2 cups pecan pieces
1 unbaked (9-inch) pie
  shell

Combine the first 6 ingredients in a large bowl and stir to blend. Stir in the chocolate chips and pecans. Pour into the pie crust. Bake at 350 degrees for 55 minutes or until a knife inserted in the center comes out clean. Cool and serve. Yield: 8 servings.

Helen Karn, Alpha Master
Boise, Idaho

CHOCOLATE CHIP PECAN PIE

1 cup chocolate chips
1/2 cup (1 stick) butter, melted
1 cup chopped pecans
1 teaspoon vanilla extract
1/2 cup flour
1/2 cup granulated sugar
1/2 cup packed brown sugar
2 eggs, beaten
1 unbaked (9-inch) pie shell

Place the chocolate chips in a large bowl. Pour the warm melted butter over the chocolate chips and stir. Combine the pecans, vanilla, flour, granulated sugar, brown sugar and eggs in a separate bowl and mix well. Stir into the chocolate chip mixture. Pour into the pie shell. Bake at 350 degrees for 30 to 40 minutes or until a knife inserted in the center comes out clean. Yield: 6 servings.

Patricia L. Bailey, Laureate Mu
Angier, North Carolina

SOUTHERN PECAN PIE

1/4 cup (1/2 stick) butter
1 cup packed brown sugar
1/4 teaspoon salt
1 cup dark corn syrup
3 eggs, beaten
1 teaspoon vanilla extract
1 1/2 cups pecan halves
1 unbaked (9-inch) pie shell

Cream the butter and brown sugar in a mixing bowl until fluffy. Add the salt, corn syrup, eggs and vanilla and beat until smooth. Sprinkle the pecans evenly in the pie shell. Pour the egg mixture evenly over the pecans. Bake at 450 degrees for 10 minutes. Reduce oven temperature to 350 degrees and bake for 35 to 40 minutes longer or until edge is set and center is slightly soft; a wooden pick inserted in the center should come out clean. Serve warm. Top with vanilla ice cream. Yield: 8 servings.

Kathy Bennett, Preceptor Lambda
Davisville, West Virginia

PECAN PIE WITH BOURBON CREAM

1 cup pure maple syrup
1 cup granulated sugar
1/4 cup (1/2 stick) butter
4 large eggs
1 tablespoon vanilla extract
1 unbaked (9-inch) pie shell
1 1/2 cups pecan halves or pieces
1 cup whipping cream
2 tablespoons confectioners' sugar
1 to 2 tablespoons bourbon

Bring the first 3 ingredients to a boil in a 3-quart saucepan over medium heat. Reduce heat to medium-low and cook for 5 minutes, stirring constantly. Place the eggs in a large bowl and whisk slightly. Whisk in the hot syrup mixture gradually. Stir in the vanilla. Place the pie shell on a baking sheet. Spread the pecans in the pie shell and pour the syrup mixture evenly over the pecans. Bake at 350 degrees for 45 to 50 minutes or until set. Cool in the pan on a wire rack. Beat the cream with the confectioners' sugar and bourbon until soft peaks form. Serve pie with the whipped cream. Yield: 6 to 8 servings.

Sylvia Allen, Laureate Psi
Yorktown, Virginia

BUTTERMILK PECAN PIE

1/2 cup (1 stick) butter or margarine
2 cups sugar
5 eggs
2 tablespoons flour
2 tablespoons lemon juice
1 teaspoon vanilla extract
1/2 cup buttermilk
1 cup coarsely chopped pecans
1 unbaked (10-inch) pie shell

Cream the butter and sugar in a mixing bowl until light and fluffy. Add the eggs 1 at a time, mixing well after each addition. Add the flour, lemon juice, vanilla and buttermilk and blend well. Stir in the pecans. Pour into the pie shell. Bake at 325 degrees for 55 minutes. Yield: 8 servings.

I. Jane Holtsclaw, Alpha Beta
Oolitic, Indiana

CARAMEL PECAN PIE

1/2 pound (28) vanilla caramels
1/2 cup water
1/4 cup (1/2 stick) margarine
2 eggs, slightly beaten
3/4 cup sugar
1/4 teaspoon salt
1/2 teaspoon vanilla extract
1 cup chopped pecans
1 unbaked (8 1/2-inch) pie shell

Combine the vanilla caramels, water and margarine in the top of a double boiler. Heat over simmering water until caramels are melted and sauce is smooth, stirring frequently. Combine the eggs, sugar, salt and vanilla in a mixing bowl. Add the caramel sauce gradually, mixing well. Stir in the pecans. Pour into the pie shell. Bake at 400 degrees for 10 minutes. Reduce oven temperature to 350 degrees and bake for 20 minutes longer. Filling will firm as it cools. Yield: 6 to 8 servings.

Jayne Hornsby, Xi Alpha Xi
Hueytown, Alabama

LEMON PECAN PIE

3 whole eggs
1/3 cup butter, melted
1 1/2 cups granulated
    sugar
3/4 cup pecan pieces

1 teaspoon lemon
    extract
Juice of 1/2 lemon
1 unbaked (8-inch) pie
    shell

Beat the eggs lightly with a fork. Add the butter, granulated sugar, pecans, lemon extract and lemon juice; mix well. Pour into the pie shell. Bake at 300 degrees for about 45 minutes or until lightly browned. Yield: 6 to 8 servings.

Susan Mages, Preceptor Gamma Omicron
Durango, Colorado

PUMPKIN PECAN PIE

3 eggs, slightly beaten
1 cup canned pumpkin
1 cup sugar
1/2 teaspoon cinnamon
1/4 teaspoon ginger
1/8 teaspoon cloves
1 unbaked (10-inch)
    deep-dish pie shell

2/3 cup light corn syrup
2 tablespoons
    margarine, melted
1/2 teaspoon vanilla
    extract
1 cup pecans

Blend 1 of the eggs, pumpkin, 1/3 cup of the sugar, cinnamon, ginger and cloves in a mixing bowl. Spread evenly in the pie shell. Combine the remaining 2 eggs, corn syrup, the remaining 2/3 cup sugar, melted margarine and vanilla in a medium bowl and blend well. Stir in the pecans. Spoon over the pumpkin filling. Bake at 425 degrees for 15 minutes. Reduce oven temperature to 350 degrees and bake for 40 minutes longer or until set around the edge and puffed slightly in the center. Cool on a wire rack. Top with whipped topping. Yield: 6 to 8 servings.

Mary Ellen Hammontree, Preceptor Psi
Nevada, Missouri

MACADAMIA NUT CREAM PIE

1 cup plus 6 tablespoons
    sugar
6 tablespoons flour
1/2 teaspoon salt
1 cup cold milk
2 cups milk, scalded
3 eggs, separated
3 tablespoons butter

2 teaspoons vanilla
    extract
1/2 cup macadamia nuts,
    chopped
1 baked (9-inch) pie
    shall
1/4 teaspoon cream of
    tartar

Combine 1 cup sugar, flour, salt and cold milk in a saucepan over medium heat and whisk until smooth. Add the scalded milk; bring to a boil, stirring constantly. Remove from heat. Whisk a small amount of the hot milk mixture into the egg yolks in a bowl. Add the egg yolk mixture to the hot milk mixture and cook over medium heat until thickened, stirring constantly. Stir in the butter, vanilla and macadamia nuts. Cool slightly. Pour into the pie shell. Beat the egg whites in a mixing bowl until stiff peaks form. Add the cream of tartar. Add the 6 tablespoons sugar 1 tablespoon at a time, beating well until very stiff. Spread over the pie filling, sealing to the edge. Top with finely chopped macadamia nuts. Bake at 350 degrees for 12 to 15 minutes or until browned. Yield: 8 servings.

Sue Pickell, Preceptor Omicron
Las Vegas, Nevada

❖ OLDHAM PIE

Derby Pie, whose name is a registered trademark, is one of Kentucky's favorite desserts and is made by Kern's Kitchen Inc. of Louisville. The original Derby Pie was created by Walter and Leaudra Kern in 1954 as the specialty pastry of the Melrose Inn in Prospect, Kentucky. In Oldham County, where the Melrose Inn is located, legend has it that Oldham Pie is the original and that it came from Mrs. Kern, who shared it with her homemaker friends many years ago. The name may have changed, but cooks in the area claim this is the original recipe.

1/4 cup (1/2 stick)
    margarine
1 cup sugar
3 eggs
3/4 cup light corn syrup
1 teaspoon vanilla
    extract

1/4 teaspoon salt
1/2 cup chocolate chips
1/2 cup chopped black
    walnuts
2 tablespoons bourbon
1 unbaked (9-inch) pie
    shell

Cream the margarine and sugar in a mixing bowl until light and fluffy. Beat in the eggs and corn syrup. Add the vanilla and salt and mix well. Stir in the chocolate chips, black walnuts and bourbon. Pour into the pie shell. Bake at 350 degrees for 45 minutes. Serve warm with whipped cream. Yield: 8 servings.

Eugenia Wallace, Delta Master
Lexington, Kentucky

PINEAPPLE PIE

1 cup sour cream
1 (6-ounce) package
    vanilla instant
    pudding mix

1 (15-ounce) can crushed
    pineapple
1 (9-inch) graham
    cracker pie shell

Combine the first 3 ingredients in a large bowl and mix well. Spoon into the pie shell. Chill, covered, for at least 1 hour before serving. Top with whipped topping. Yield: 6 to 8 servings.

Mary Bennett, Eta Beta
Gainesville, Florida

MILLION-DOLLAR PINEAPPLE PIE

1 (14-ounce) can
  sweetened condensed
  milk
4 teaspoons lemon juice
1 (14-ounce) can coconut
  milk
1 cup pecans

1 (20-ounce) can crushed
  pineapple, drained
8 ounces whipped
  topping
2 graham cracker pie
  shells

Mix the condensed milk, lemon juice, coconut milk, pecans, pineapple and whipped topping in a large bowl. Pour into the pie shells. Chill, covered, until serving time. Yield: 12 to 16 servings.

Irene Greer, Laureate Delta Phi
Saint Augustine, Florida

PINEAPPLE COCONUT PIE

4 eggs
1 1/2 cups sugar
1 tablespoon
  cornmeal
1/4 cup (1/2 stick)
  margarine, melted

1 1/2 cups shredded
  coconut
1 (20-ounce) can crushed
  pineapple, drained
2 unbaked (9-inch) pie
  shells

Combine the eggs, sugar, cornmeal and margarine in a large bowl and mix well. Add the coconut and pineapple and stir to combine. Spoon into the pie shells. Bake at 350 degrees for 30 minutes. Serve warm or cold. Yield: 12 servings.

Lillian Liliensteins, Preceptor Beta Epsilon
Shelby, North Carolina

PINEAPPLE CRUMBLE PIE

3/4 cup plus
  3 tablespoons flour
1/2 cup plus 2/3 cup sugar
1/4 cup (1/2 stick) butter,
  softened
1/2 teaspoon salt
4 cups thinly sliced
  peeled apples

1 (9-ounce) can crushed
  pineapple
1 teaspoon cinnamon
1 frozen (9-inch) pie
  shell, thawed

Mix 3/4 cup flour, 1/2 cup sugar, butter and 1/4 teaspoon of the salt in a small bowl. Combine the apples and undrained pineapple in a large bowl. Add a mixture of 2/3 cup sugar, cinnamon and the 3 tablespoons flour and stir well. Spoon into the pie shell. Sprinkle the flour mixture over the filling. Bake at 350 degrees for 40 to 45 minutes or until apples are tender; use strips of foil to keep the crust edge from overbrowning if necessary. Yield: 6 to 8 servings.

Janice Brantley Adcock, Preceptor Beta
Shelbyville, Tennessee

PINEAPPLE GRITS PIE

If you think grits are good only for breakfast or as a holder of red-eye gravy, this delicious pie recipe will make you think again.

2 cups water
1/2 cup quick-cooking
  grits
1/4 teaspoon salt
1 (8-ounce) can crushed
  pineapple, drained
4 ounces cream cheese,
  softened

3 large eggs
1 cup sugar
1/2 cup milk
1 teaspoon vanilla
  extract
2 (9-inch) graham
  cracker pie shells

Bring the water to a boil in a saucepan. Add the grits and salt. Return to a boil and cover. Reduce heat to low and cook for 5 minutes, stirring occasionally. Remove from heat. Combine the grits mixture, pineapple and cream cheese in a blender and process until smooth, stopping once to scrape down the side. Add the eggs 1 at a time and the sugar, milk and vanilla slowly, processing constantly at high speed until smooth, stopping once to scrape down the side. Pour the pineapple mixture into the pie shells. Bake at 300 degrees for 1 hour. Serve at room temperature. Yield: 16 servings.

R. Gene Farley, Laureate Gamma Iota
Tallahassee, Florida

PINEAPPLE SOUR CREAM PIE

4 egg yolks, slightly
  beaten
1/2 cup plus 6
  tablespoons sugar
2 tablespoons flour
1 (20-ounce) can crushed
  pineapple

1 cup sour cream
1 baked (9-inch) pie shell
4 egg whites
1/4 teaspoon cream of
  tartar
1/2 teaspoon vanilla
  extract

Place the egg yolks in a large bowl. Combine the 1/2 cup sugar and flour in a 1 1/2-quart saucepan. Stir in the undrained pineapple and sour cream. Cook over medium heat until thickened and bubbly, stirring constantly. Reduce heat and cook for 2 minutes longer, stirring constantly. Stir 1 cup of the hot filling into the egg yolks gradually. Return to the saucepan and bring to a gentle boil; cook for 2 minutes, stirring constantly. Pour the hot filling into the pie shell. Combine the egg whites, cream of tartar and vanilla in a mixing bowl and beat at medium speed for 1 minute or until soft peaks form. Add the 6 tablespoons sugar 1 tablespoon at a time, beating well after each addition. Beat at high speed for about 4 minutes. Spread over the pie filling, sealing to the edge. Bake at 350 degrees for at least 15 minutes or until meringue is golden. Cool for 1 hour on a wire rack. Chill for 3 to 6 hours. Cover loosely for longer storage in the refrigerator. Yield: 8 servings.

Linda DeRosia, Laureate Delta Phi
Saint Augustine, Florida

PINEAPPLE MERINGUE PIE

1 cup sugar
1/4 cup cornstarch
1 (20-ounce) can crushed pineapple, drained, 1 cup juice reserved
3 egg yolks, lightly beaten
3 tablespoons butter or margarine
1 tablespoon lemon juice
1 baked (9-inch) pie shell
1 recipe meringue

Combine the sugar and cornstarch in a saucepan over medium heat. Stir in the 1 cup reserved pineapple juice and 1/2 cup water; cook until thickened and boiling, stirring constantly. Boil for 1 minute. Stir half the sugar mixture slowly into the egg yolks; return egg yolk mixture to the saucepan; boil for 1 minute longer, stirring constantly. Remove from heat; continue stirring until smooth. Blend in the butter and lemon juice; stir in the pineapple. Pour into the pie shell. Top with a meringue, sealing to the edge; swirl with a spoon or knife. Bake at 400 degrees for 8 to 10 minutes or until lightly browned. Yield: 6 to 8 servings.

Patricia Davis, Xi Gamma Theta
Redding, California

PUMPKIN CHIFFON PIE

1 envelope plain gelatin
1/4 cup cold water
1 cup sugar
3 eggs, separated
1 1/4 cups canned pumpkin
1/2 cup evaporated milk
1/2 teaspoon ginger
1/2 teaspoon nutmeg
1/2 teaspoon cinnamon
1 teaspoon vanilla extract
1/2 teaspoon salt
1 baked (8-inch) deep-dish pie shell

Soften the gelatin in the cold water. Combine 1/2 cup of the sugar, egg yolks, pumpkin, evaporated milk, ginger, nutmeg, cinnamon, vanilla and salt in a saucepan over low heat; cook until thickened and mixture begins to bubble, stirring constantly. Remove from heat. Stir in the gelatin mixture. Cool to room temperature. Beat the egg whites in a mixing bowl, adding the remaining 1/2 cup sugar gradually, beating just until thickened. Fold into the pumpkin mixture. Chill, covered, in the refrigerator. Spoon into the pie shell just before serving. Top with whipped cream or whipped topping. Yield: 6 to 8 servings.

Kathi Jeroue, Delta Epsilon
Twin Falls, Idaho

COCONUT PUMPKIN PIE

2 cups canned pumpkin
1 cup plus 2 tablespoons sugar
1 1/2 teaspoons ginger
1 teaspoon cinnamon
1 teaspoon salt
3 egg yolks, slightly beaten
2 cups sweetened condensed milk
1 cup flaked coconut
1/2 cup chopped pecans
1 teaspoon vanilla extract
3 egg whites, stiffly beaten
2 unbaked (9-inch) pie shells

Combine the pumpkin, sugar, ginger, cinnamon, salt, egg yolks, condensed milk, coconut, pecans and vanilla in a large bowl and mix well. Fold the egg whites carefully into the pumpkin mixture; do not beat. Pour into two pastry-lined 9-inch pie plates. Bake at 350 degrees for 50 minutes or until set and a wooden pick inserted in the center comes out clean. Serve with whipped cream, whipped topping or ice cream. Yield: 12 servings.

Judie M. Herbst, Alpha Mu Master
Cape Girardeau, Missouri

MINCEMEAT PUMPKIN HOLIDAY PIE

For an extra little kick, add 2 tablespoons rum to the mincemeat.

1 unbaked (9-inch) pie shell
1 cup (about) mincemeat
8 ounces cream cheese, softened
1 egg
1 cup sugar
1 teaspoon vanilla extract
2 cups canned pumpkin
1 teaspoon cinnamon
1/2 teaspoon ginger
1 cup milk or cream
2 eggs, beaten
Crushed peanut brittle

Cover the bottom of the pie shell with a generous layer of mincemeat. Place the cream cheese in a mixing bowl and beat until light and smooth; beat in the egg, 1/2 cup of the sugar and vanilla. Spread over the mincemeat layer. Combine the pumpkin, the remaining 1/2 cup sugar, cinnamon, ginger, milk and eggs in a mixing bowl and beat until smooth. Pour evenly over the cream cheese layer. Bake at 425 degrees for 10 minutes. Reduce oven temperature to 350 degrees and bake for 30 to 35 minutes or until set. Garnish cooled pie with a 1-inch-wide ring of whipped cream around the edge. Sprinkle with the peanut brittle pieces. Yield: 8 to 10 servings.

Barbara-Jo Clute, Laureate Alpha Eta
Belleville, Ontario, Canada

PUMPKIN PIE

1 cup packed brown sugar	1 cup canned pumpkin
1 tablespoon flour	1 cup creamy milk
1 teaspoon cinnamon	1 tablespoon molasses
1 scant teaspoon ginger	1 teaspoon vanilla extract
Pinch of salt	1 unbaked (9-inch)
2 eggs, beaten	deep-dish pie shell

Combine the brown sugar, flour, cinnamon, ginger and salt in a large bowl. Add the eggs, pumpkin, milk, molasses and vanilla and beat until smooth. Pour into the pie shell. Bake in a preheated 400-degree oven for 10 minutes. Reduce oven temperature to 350 degrees and bake for 30 minutes longer or until a knife inserted in the center comes out clean. Yield: 6 to 8 servings.

Charlene Roach, Xi Iota Beta
Jewell, Iowa

EASY PUMPKIN CREAM PIE

1 (15-ounce) can pumpkin	1 teaspoon pumpkin pie spice
1 (6-ounce) package vanilla instant pudding mix	6 ounces frozen whipped topping, thawed
1 cup milk	1 baked (9-inch) graham cracker pie shell

Combine the pumpkin, pudding mix, milk and pumpkin pie spice in a large mixing bowl; beat for 1 minute or until blended. Fold in 1½ cups of the whipped topping. Spoon into the pie shell. Freeze for at least 4 hours or until firm. Let stand in the refrigerator for 2 hours before serving. Garnish with the remaining whipped topping and with fresh raspberries if desired. Yield: 8 servings.

Ruth M. Burgess, Laureate Alpha Beta
Muskogee, Oklahoma

FRESH RASPBERRY PIE

4 cups raspberries	2 rounded tablespoons cornstarch
1 (8-inch) graham cracker pie shell	1 teaspoon lemon juice
1 cup cold water	1 (3-ounce) package raspberry gelatin
3/4 cup granulated sugar	

Spread the raspberries in the pie shell. Combine ½ cup of the water and sugar in a saucepan and bring to a boil. Mix the remaining ½ cup water and cornstarch and add to the boiling sugar water. Stir in the lemon juice. Cook until thickened, stirring constantly. Remove from heat. Stir in the dry gelatin mix and pour over the raspberry layer. Tap gently to eliminate bubbles. Chill, covered, for at least 4 hours

before serving. Top with additional fresh raspberries or whipped topping if desired. Yield: 8 servings.

Mary Novotny, Xi
Omaha, Nebraska

RASPBERRY MERINGUE PIE

1 cup flour	1 egg, beaten
1/3 cup plus 1/2 cup sugar	2 tablespoons milk
1/2 teaspoon baking powder	2 egg whites
1/4 teaspoon salt	2 cups unsweetened raspberries
2 tablespoons cold butter	

Combine the flour, the 1/3 cup sugar, baking powder and salt in a bowl. Cut in the butter until crumbly. Stir a mixture of the egg and milk into the flour mixture; dough will be sticky. Press over the bottom and up the side of a buttered 9-inch pie plate, forming a shell. Place the egg whites in a mixing bowl and beat at medium speed until soft peaks form. Add the 1/2 cup sugar 1 tablespoon at a time, beating until stiff peaks form. Fold in the raspberries. Spoon over the pie shell. Bake at 350 degrees for 30 to 35 minutes or until browned. Cool in the pie plate on a wire rack. Refrigerate leftovers. Yield: 6 to 8 servings.

Frances Kucera, Laureate Omicron
Eugene, Oregon

RASPBERRY MALLOW PIE

1/2 pound marshmallows	Pinch of salt
1/2 cup milk	2 cups fresh or frozen raspberries
1 cup whipping cream, whipped	1 baked (9-inch) pie shell
1/2 teaspoon vanilla extract	

Cook the marshmallows and milk in a saucepan over medium-low heat until the marshmallows are melted and the mixture is smooth, stirring frequently. Cool the marshmallow mixture in the refrigerator until it begins to mound. Fold in the whipped cream, vanilla, salt and raspberries. Spread in the pie shell. Chill, covered, until serving time. Yield: 6 servings.

Cathy Morris, Preceptor Epsilon Upsilon
Renfrew, Ontario, Canada

PINK LADY PIE

1½ cups crushed graham crackers	30 large marshmallows
1/4 cup (1/2 stick) margarine, softened	2 cups whipped topping or whipped cream
1/4 cup sugar	1 (10-ounce) package frozen raspberries, thawed
3/4 cup orange juice	

Place a mixture of the graham cracker crumbs, margarine and sugar in a 9-inch pie plate, pressing firmly to form a shell. Bake in a preheated 375-degree oven for 5 minutes. Let stand until cool. Chill until ready to use. Heat the orange juice in a heavy saucepan over medium heat. Add the marshmallows and cook until melted, stirring frequently. Chill until partially set. Fold in the whipped topping and the raspberries. Pour into the chilled crumb crust. Chill until serving time. Top with additional whipped topping. Yield: 8 servings.

Edith Zuidhof-Knoop, Gamma Iota
Edson, Alberta, Canada

WHITE CHOCOLATE RASPBERRY PIE

2 (6-ounce) containers white fat-free chocolate raspberry yogurt	*1 small package white chocolate fat-free sugar-free instant pudding mix*
8 ounces fat-free whipped topping	*1 ready-to-use graham cracker pie shell*

Combine the yogurt, whipped topping and pudding mix in a large bowl and mix well. Spread the mixture in the pie shell. Chill, covered, for 2 to 10 hours before serving. Refrigerate leftovers. Yield: 8 servings.

Millie Lockwood, Preceptor Pi
St. Pete Beach, Florida

BUTTER CRACKER PIE

4 egg whites	*22 butter crackers, crushed*
1 cup sugar	
1¹/₂ teaspoons vanilla extract	*1 cup whipping cream, whipped*
1 cup chopped pecans	*Sugar to taste*

Beat the egg whites in a mixing bowl, adding 1 cup sugar and 1 teaspoon of the vanilla gradually, beating until stiff peaks form. Stir in the pecans and crackers by hand. Spread in a buttered 10-inch pie plate. Bake at 325 degrees for 30 minutes or until lightly browned. Cool. Add the remaining ¹/₂ teaspoon vanilla and sugar to taste to the whipped cream and spread over the cooled pie. Chill, covered, until serving time. Yield: 8 to 10 servings.

Tommie Jenkins, Xi Delta Omega
Bartow, Florida

RHUBARB CHIFFON PIE

3 cups chopped rhubarb	*2 or 3 drops red food coloring (optional)*
1³/₄ cups sugar	
1 envelope unflavored gelatin	*¹/₄ teaspoon salt*
2 eggs, separated	*1 baked (10-inch) pie shell*

Combine the rhubarb, 1 cup of the sugar and 1 tablespoon cold water in a saucepan over medium heat. Simmer for 10 minutes or until rhubarb is tender; drain, reserving 1¹/₂ cups of the liquid. Discard the rhubarb. Soften the gelatin in 2 tablespoons cold water. Combine the egg yolks and ¹/₂ cup of the sugar in a saucepan over very low heat. Cook until thickened, stirring constantly. Stir in the gelatin mixture. Stir in the 1¹/₂ cups rhubarb liquid. Cool the mixture until thickened but not stiff. Stir in the red food coloring. Beat the egg whites in a mixing bowl with the salt until soft peaks form; add the remaining ¹/₄ cup sugar gradually, beating until stiff peaks form. Fold into the rhubarb mixture. Pour into the pie shell. Chill until firm, for about 2 hours. Yield: 8 servings.

Christina Carter, Xi Omicron
Whitefish, Montana

MULBERRY RHUBARB CREAM PIE

1¹/₂ cups plus ¹/₃ cup sugar	*2 cups mulberries or blackberries*
3 eggs	*1 unbaked (9- to 10-inch) pie shell*
1 cup flour	
³/₄ teaspoon nutmeg	*¹/₃ cup margarine*
2 cups chopped rhubarb	

Combine the 1¹/₂ cups sugar, eggs, ¹/₄ cup of the flour and nutmeg in a mixing bowl and mix until smooth. Fold in the rhubarb and mulberries. Pour into the pie shell. Combine the ¹/₃ cup sugar and the remaining ³/₄ cup flour in a bowl and mix well; cut in the margarine until crumbly. Dot the pie with additional margarine and sprinkle the flour mixture evenly over the top. Bake at 350 degrees for 1 hour. Yield: 8 servings.

Diane Hobson, Laureate Alpha Upsilon
Marshalltown, Iowa

RAISIN SPICE PIE

1 cup raisins	*2 eggs, beaten*
1 cup sour cream	*³/₄ cup sugar*
1 teaspoon cinnamon	*1 unbaked (8- or 9-inch) pie shell*
¹/₂ teaspoon nutmeg	
¹/₄ teaspoon ground cloves	

Combine the raisins, sour cream, cinnamon, nutmeg, cloves, eggs and sugar in a mixing bowl and mix well. Spread in the pie shell. Bake in a preheated 425-degree oven for 10 minutes. Reduce oven temperature to 350 degrees and bake for 30 minutes longer. Cool and serve. Yield: 6 servings.

Penni White, Omega Master
St. Louis, Michigan

EASY STRAWBERRY PIE

1¼ cups sugar
¼ cup cornstarch
1 cup water
1 (3-ounce) package
    strawberry gelatin

2 cups fresh
    strawberries, cut up
1 baked (9-inch) pie
    shell

Combine the sugar, cornstarch and water in a saucepan over low heat and cook until clear, stirring constantly. Remove from heat and add the dry gelatin mix, stirring until dissolved. Cool until mixture is slightly thickened. Stir in the strawberries. Pour into the pie shell. Chill, covered, until firm. Garnish with whipped topping. Yield: 6 to 8 servings.

Connie Snider, Xi Mu Upsilon
Shelbina, Missouri

FRESH STRAWBERRY PIE

10 saltine crackers
3 egg whites
½ teaspoon baking
    powder
1 cup sugar

½ cup chopped walnuts
    or pecans
1½ cups chopped or
    sliced strawberries

Crush the crackers into fine crumbs. Beat the egg whites in a mixing bowl until stiff peaks form. Beat in the baking powder. Add the sugar gradually, beating constantly. Fold in the cracker crumbs. Fold in the chopped nuts carefully. Pour into a well buttered 9-inch pie plate. Bake at 300 degrees for 30 minutes. Let stand until cool; pie will fall as it cools. Garnish with unsweetened strawberries and whipped topping. Yield: 6 to 8 servings.

Jaleigh Lashbrook, Chi Beta
Mount Carmel, Illinois

MILE-HIGH STRAWBERRY PIE

2 egg whites, at room
    temperature
1 cup sugar
1 tablespoon lemon
    juice
¼ teaspoon salt

1 (10-ounce) package
    frozen strawberries,
    thawed
1½ cups whipped
    topping
1 baked (8-inch) pie shell

Combine the egg whites, sugar, lemon juice, salt and strawberries in a large mixing bowl and beat at high speed for 15 minutes. Fold in the whipped topping. Spoon into the pie shell. Freeze, covered, until serving time. Yield: 8 servings.

Lila Couch, Preceptor Alpha Phi
Toccoa, Georgia

STRAWBERRY RIBBON PIE

1 (3-ounce) package
    strawberry gelatin
¼ cup sugar
1¼ cups boiling water
1 (10-ounce) package
    frozen strawberries
1 tablespoon lemon juice
1 cup whipping cream
⅓ cup confectioners'
    sugar

1 teaspoon vanilla
    extract
Dash of salt
3 ounces cream cheese,
    softened
1 baked (9-inch) pie
    shell or graham
    cracker pie shell

Dissolve the dry gelatin mix and sugar in the boiling water. Add the strawberries and lemon juice; stir gently until berries soften. Chill until partially set. Combine the cream, confectioners' sugar, vanilla and salt and beat until soft peaks form. Place the cream cheese in a large bowl. Add a small amount of the whipped cream mixture to the cream cheese and blend well. Fold in the remaining whipped cream mixture. Layer the cream cheese mixture and the strawberry mixture ½ at a time in the pie shell. Chill, covered, until serving time. Yield: 6 to 8 servings.

Judy McKeehan, Alpha Lambda
Cheney, Washington

STRAWBERRY DAIQUIRI PIE

8 ounces whipped
    topping
1 (6-ounce) can frozen
    strawberry daiquiri
    mix, thawed

1 (12-ounce) can
    evaporated milk
2 graham cracker pie
    shells

Combine the whipped topping, daiquiri mix and evaporated milk in a large mixing bowl and mix until smooth. Pour into the pie shells. Chill for at least 1 hour before serving. Yield: 16 servings.

Elizabeth Kendrick, Theta Psi
Cookeville, Tennessee

SOUR CREAM PIE

The recipe can be doubled to fill a deep-dish pie shell.

1 teaspoon baking soda
1 cup sour cream
1 teaspoon cinnamon
¼ teaspoon ground
    cloves
¼ teaspoon nutmeg
½ cup raisins
1 cup packed brown
    sugar

2 egg yolks
2 tablespoons
    cornstarch
1 baked (8-inch) pie
    shell
2 egg whites
2 tablespoons
    granulated sugar

Combine the baking soda and sour cream in the top of a double boiler over simmering water and bring to a boil; boil until foamy. Stir in the cinnamon, cloves, nutmeg, raisins, brown sugar, egg yolks and cornstarch; cook until thick, stirring constantly. Pour into the pie shell. Beat the egg whites and granulated sugar in a mixing bowl until stiff peaks form. Spread over the top of the pie, sealing to the edge. Broil 6 inches from the heat source until meringue is golden. Yield: 6 to 8 servings.

Sandy Korchinski, Alpha Gamma
Fort Saskatchewan, Alberta, Canada

WORLD'S GREATEST PIE PASTRY

If you're making a dessert pie, add 2 teaspoons of sugar to the crust recipe. If you're making a savory pie, sprinkle in some herbs and spices instead.

5 cups flour	1/4 cup ice water
1 teaspoon salt	1 tablespoon white
1 3/4 cups shortening	vinegar
1 egg, slightly beaten	

Combine the flour and salt in a mixing bowl and cut in the shortening until crumbly. Stir in the egg, ice water and vinegar. Divide the dough into 5 equal portions and roll into circles on a floured surface. Fit into pie plates. Wrap unbaked pastry and freeze until ready to use. Yield: 5 (1-crust) pastries.

Diane L. Pruett, Preceptor Alpha Upsilon
Tamaqua, Pennsylvania

PIE SHELL WITH VEGETABLE OIL

2 cups flour	1/2 cup vegetable oil
1 teaspoon salt	5 tablespoons ice water

Combine the flour, salt, vegetable oil and ice water in a bowl; cut and mix with a table knife. Mix by hand until a soft dough forms. Divide into halves and roll between sheets of waxed paper. Fit into pie plates. Bake at 400 degrees for 10 to 20 minutes. Yield: 2 (1-crust) pastries.

Darlene A. Freerksen, Xi Beta Epsilon
Woodward, Oklahoma

CRESCENT ORANGE GRANNY APPLES

1 (8-count) package	1 cup orange juice
crescent rolls	1 cup sugar
2 Granny Smith apples,	3/8 cup (3/4 stick) butter,
peeled and quartered	melted

Unroll the dough and separate into triangles. Wrap each apple quarter in a triangle. Arrange in an unbuttered glass or metal cake pan. Combine the orange juice, sugar and melted butter in a bowl and whisk until smooth. Drizzle the orange juice mixture over the dough. Bake at 250 degrees for 40 minutes. Serve warm. Yield: 8 servings.

Wanda Housteau, Xi Mu Lambda
Gainesville, Missouri

APPLE YULE LOGS

8 large cooking apples,	1 to 2 tablespoons plus
peeled and cored	1/2 cup Scotch whisky
1 cup soft bread crumbs	1/4 cup light corn syrup
1/2 cup finely chopped	1/4 cup dark corn syrup
seeded raisins	
1/4 cup packed brown	
sugar	

Arrange the apples in two rows in a large baking dish. Combine the bead crumbs, raisins, brown sugar and the 1 to 2 tablespoons whisky in a bowl and mix well. Spoon the mixture into the apple centers. Drizzle a mixture of the light corn syrup and dark corn syrup over the stuffed apples. Bake at 325 degrees for 30 to 40 minutes or until apples are tender, basting frequently. Pour the syrup into a small serving bowl. Warm the 1/2 cup whisky just before serving; pour it over the baked apples and ignite. Serve with the warm syrup. Yield: 8 servings.

Sonya Lee, Xi
Brandon, Mississippi

BUTTERSCOTCH PULL-APARTS

1 pound frozen bread	1 (4-ounce) package
dough, thawed	butterscotch instant
1 cup packed light	pudding mix
brown sugar	3/4 cup melted butter
1 cup chopped pecans	1 cup granulated sugar
1 teaspoon cinnamon	

Pinch the dough into pieces and roll into egg-size balls until all dough is used. Sprinkle 1/2 cup of the brown sugar and 1/2 cup of the chopped pecans in the bottom of a buttered bundt pan. Combine the cinnamon, dry pudding mix and the remaining 1/2 cup brown sugar in a bowl and mix well. Roll each dough ball in melted butter; roll in the pudding mixture to coat. Arrange in the prepared pan. Combine 1/2 cup of the melted butter and granulated sugar in a saucepan over medium heat; heat until warm, stirring frequently. Remove from heat and cool slightly. Drizzle the butter mixture over the dough in the pan. Let rise in a warm place until doubled in bulk. Bake at 350 degrees for 35 to 40 minutes or until golden brown. Invert onto a serving plate immediately. Yield: 12 servings.

Elaine Huber, Xi Sigma
Vancouver, Washington

CARAMEL BISCUIT RING

3/4 cup packed brown
  sugar
1/2 cup chopped walnuts
  or pecans

1/3 cup margarine
2 tablespoons water
2 (8-count) cans biscuits

Place the brown sugar, chopped nuts, margarine and water in a small saucepan and heat until margarine is melted; stir to combine. Unroll the dough and separate into 20 biscuits. Cut each biscuit into quarters and place in a large bowl. Pour the brown sugar mixture over the biscuits and toss lightly to coat evenly. Spoon the biscuit mixture into a fluted tube pan. Bake at 400 degrees for 20 to 30 minutes or until golden brown. Let stand for 3 minutes. Invert onto a serving plate. Serve warm. Yield: 10 servings.

Marcia Crawford, Laureate Delta Omicron
Kennett, Missouri

CINNAMON TWISTS

5 cups flour
1 cup sugar
1 teaspoon salt
2 envelopes dry yeast
3/4 cup milk
1/2 cup water
1/2 cup shortening or
  margarine

2 eggs, at room
  temperature
1/2 cup (1 stick) butter or
  margarine, melted
1 teaspoon cinnamon

Measure 1 3/4 cups of the flour into a large mixing bowl. Stir in 1/2 cup of the sugar, salt and yeast. Heat the milk, water and shortening in a saucepan to 120 to 130 degrees. Pour into the flour mixture. Add the eggs and beat at low speed for 30 seconds. Beat at high speed for 3 minutes. Stir in the remaining flour; dough will be soft and rather sticky. Knead until smooth, about 3 minutes. Cover the dough with plastic and a towel; let stand for 30 minutes. Roll 1/2 inch thick into an 8-inch-wide rectangle on a floured surface. Cut into 3/4-inch-wide strips. Pour the melted butter into a bowl. Mix the remaining 1/2 cup sugar and cinnamon together in a separate bowl. Dip each dough strip in the butter and then in the cinnamon mixture to coat. Tie in a knot. Arrange the knots in a buttered 10×15-inch cake pan with sides touching, 20 to a pan. Let rise until double in bulk. Bake at 350 degrees for 15 to 20 minutes or until golden brown. Cool slightly. Remove to a wire rack to cool completely. Yield: 20 servings.

Libbie Wilkie, Laureate Pi
Worland, Wyoming

CINNAMON CREAM ROLL-UPS

1 (1-pound) loaf
  sandwich bread,
  crusts trimmed
8 ounces cream cheese,
  softened

1 egg yolk
1 1/4 cups sugar
1 tablespoon cinnamon
1/4 cup (1/2 stick) butter,
  melted

Flatten the bread slices with a rolling pin. Combine the cream cheese, egg yolk and 1/4 cup of the sugar in a small mixing bowl; mix well. Spread cream cheese over each slice to within 1/2 inch of the edges. Roll up diagonally, from point to point. Combine the cinnamon and remaining 1 cup sugar in a shallow bowl and mix well. Place the melted butter in a separate bowl. Dip the roll-ups in melted butter; roll to coat in the cinnamon mixture. Arrange in an unbuttered 10×15-inch cake pan. Bake at 350 degrees for 16 to 19 minutes or until lightly browned. Remove to a wire rack to cool. Yield: 8 to 10 servings.

Darlene Ebeling, Xi Beta Epsilon
Woodward, Oklahoma

EGGNOG PUFFS

1 cup water
1/2 cup (1 stick) butter
1 cup flour
4 eggs
1 cup milk
1 teaspoon rum flavoring

1 teaspoon nutmeg
1/4 teaspoon ginger
1 (4-ounce) package
  vanilla instant
  pudding mix
2 cups whipping cream

Bring the water to a boil in a 1-quart saucepan; add the butter. Reduce heat to low and add the flour, stirring vigorously for 1 minute or until mixture forms a ball. Remove from heat. Add the eggs and beat until smooth. Drop 1/4-cup measures of dough 3 inches apart onto an unbuttered baking sheet. Bake in a preheated 400-degree oven until puffed and golden. Cool completely. Slice off the tops of the puffs and remove any filaments of soft dough. Combine the milk, rum flavoring, nutmeg, ginger and dry pudding mix in a large mixing bowl and beat at low speed until blended. Add the whipping cream and beat at high speed for 1 or 2 minutes or until soft peaks form. Fill the puffs with the whipped cream mixture and replace the tops. Sprinkle with confectioners' sugar before serving. Yield: 12 servings.

Suzi L. B. Crapson, Epsilon Nu
Moses Lake, Washington

CREAM PUFFS

1 cup hot water
1/2 cup shortening
1/4 teaspoon salt
1 cup sifted flour

4 eggs
Whipped topping or
  vanilla pudding
  to fill puffs

Combine the hot water, shortening and salt in a saucepan; bring to a rolling boil. Add the flour all at once, stirring constantly until mixture forms a smooth ball that leaves the pan clean. Before the shortening seeps out, place the mixture in a mixing bowl. Mix in 1 egg at a time; dough will be thick and glossy. Spoon by tablespoons 2 inches apart onto an unbuttered baking sheet. Bake in a preheated 450-degree oven for 15 minutes. Reduce oven temperature to 350 degrees and bake for 20 to 30 minutes longer or until golden brown. Let stand until cool. Cut off the tops. Fill with whipped topping or vanilla pudding. Sprinkle with confectioners' sugar. Yield: 10 to 12 servings.

Daire Ochs, Alpha Theta
Fallon, Nevada

CZECH PASTRIES

1 cake yeast	1 teaspoon grated lemon
1/2 cup very warm (not	zest
hot) water	1 cup (2 sticks) butter,
1/2 teaspoon plus 1/4 cup	softened
sugar	3 egg yolks, beaten
4 cups flour	1 cup heavy cream
1 teaspoon salt	

Crumble the yeast over the warm water in a bowl. Stir in the 1/2 teaspoon sugar. Let stand for a few minutes. Mix the flour, 1/4 cup sugar, salt and lemon zest in a large mixing bowl. Mix in the butter. Add the yeast mixture and a mixture of the egg yolks and cream; mix until the dough leaves the side of the bowl. Let stand in the refrigerator, covered, for 8 to 10 hours. Roll into 3/8-inch thickness on a floured surface. Cut out 2 1/4-inch rounds and arrange on an unbuttered baking sheet. Let rise, covered, in a warm place until doubled in bulk. Make a depression with a finger in the center of each pastry and fill with 3/4 teaspoon of a filling such as prune, cherry, apricot or cheese. Bake at 375 degrees for 12 minutes or until golden. Yield: 4 dozen.

Mary J. Weidman, Laureate Epsilon Kappa
Mt. Bethel, Pennsylvania

PUMPKIN PASTRIES

2 tablespoons vegetable	1 tablespoon baking
oil	powder
1 cup milk	1/4 teaspoon salt
2 eggs, well beaten	1/2 cup sugar
1 cup canned pumpkin	1 teaspoon cinnamon
3 cups flour	Vegetable oil for
1/4 teaspoon nutmeg	deep-frying

Combine 2 tablespoons vegetable oil, milk, eggs and pumpkin in a large bowl and mix well. Add a mix-ture of the next 6 ingredients; mix well. Dough will be sticky; it may be refrigerated for a few days before frying. Drop by rounded teaspoonfuls into 375-degree oil and deep-fry until brown on both sides. Drain on paper towels. Roll in a mixture of sugar and cinnamon. Yield: about 40 small round pastries.

Ruth Dalton, Preceptor Eta Beta
Gainesville, Florida

PINEAPPLE-FILLED CREAM PUFFS

1 cup water	1 cup flour
1/2 cup (1 stick) butter	4 eggs
1/4 teaspoon salt	Pineapple Filling

Bring water, butter and salt to a full boil in a large saucepan. Remove from the heat and add the flour all at once. Beat with a wooden spoon. Return to the heat and cook until the mixture forms a ball, beating constantly. Remove from the heat and add the eggs 1 at a time, beating until smooth and shiny after each addition. Drop by tablespoonfuls 2 inches apart onto an ungreased baking sheet. Bake at 400 degrees for 45 minutes or until puffed and golden brown. Let stand until cool. Cut off and reserve the tops. Scoop out and discard any doughy centers. Fill with Pineapple Filling and replace the tops. Yield: 8 servings.

PINEAPPLE FILLING

1/4 cup minute tapioca	1/2 cup pineapple juice
3 tablespoons sugar	2 1/2 cups milk
1/2 teaspoon salt	2 egg whites, stiffly
1 teaspoon vanilla or	beaten
almond extract	1 (8-ounce) can crushed
2 egg yolks	pineapple, drained

Mix the tapioca, sugar, salt, vanilla and egg yolks in a large saucepan. Stir in the pineapple juice and milk. Cook over medium heat until thickened, stirring constantly. Remove from the heat and fold in the egg whites and pineapple. Let stand until cool.

Marcia Rickman, Laureate Theta
Billings, Montana

Edna Mogk, Laureate Omega, Guelph, Ontario, Canada, prepares **Pears in a Nest** *by cutting filo into 6-inch squares and stacking 4 sheets at a time, brushing each with melted butter. She nestles a drained canned-in-triple-sec pear in the center of each stack, folds the filo over to enclose the pear and pinches to seal. Brush with butter. Bake at 375 degrees for 15 minutes or until golden brown and serve warm drizzled with chocolate sauce.*

RAISIN TARTS

1 cup raisins
2 tablespoons butter
1 cup packed brown
  sugar
1 egg, beaten

1/2 teaspoon vanilla
  extract
1 dozen unbaked pastry
  shells

Place the raisins in a kettle. Add enough water to cover. Simmer until raisins are plump; drain. Place the hot raisins in a bowl and stir in the butter and brown sugar at once. Cool completely. Stir in the egg and vanilla. Fill the pastry shells. Bake at 400 degrees for 20 minutes or until tops are slightly browned. Yield: 1 dozen.

Eleanor Frandsen, Xi Lambda
Edmonton, Alberta, Canada

PAVLOVA

Pavlova is a great Australian dessert named for the great Russian ballerina.

6 egg whites
1 cup fine or granulated
  sugar
1 1/2 teaspoons white
  vinegar
1/2 teaspoon vanilla
  extract
Pinch of salt

1 1/2 teaspoons
  cornstarch
2 cups whipping cream
Fruit such as
  strawberries,
  kiwifruit, bananas,
  peaches, passion
  fruit, any berries

Preheat the oven to 250 degrees. Beat the egg whites in a mixing bowl until soft peaks form. Add the sugar gradually, beating until stiff peaks form. Beat in the vinegar, vanilla and salt. Add the cornstarch and beat until glossy; do not overbeat. Tip the mixture onto a baking sheet and nudge into a circle or oval or any shape as long as the mound remains 2 to 3 inches high. Bake in the center of the oven for 1 hour. Turn off the oven and let stand until oven is cold. Cut into wedges. Top with whipped cream and fruit to serve. Yield: 8 large servings.

Glenda Sewell, Gamma Iota
Edson, Alberta, Canada

PRALINE CRESCENT DESSERT

1/3 cup butter
1/2 cup packed brown
  sugar
3 tablespoons sour
  cream
1 cup crisp rice cereal
1/2 cup chopped pecans
  or other nuts

1 (8-count) can crescent
  rolls
3 ounces cream cheese,
  softened
1 tablespoon
  confectioners' sugar

Melt the butter in a saucepan over medium-low heat. Add the brown sugar and cook for 2 minutes, stirring constantly. Add the sour cream and cook for 4 minutes, stirring occasionally. Remove from heat. Stir in the cereal and chopped nuts. Unroll the dough and separate into 8 triangles. Fit a dough triangle into each of 8 muffin cups, pressing to cover the bottom and side. Combine the cream cheese and confectioners' sugar in a bowl and blend well. Spoon 1 teaspoon of the cream cheese mixture into each dough cup. Divide the cereal mixture among the dough cups. Bake at 375 degrees for 11 to 16 minutes or until golden brown. Serve warm or cold. Top with whipped cream. Yield: 8 servings.

A. Virginia Koerner, Xi Beta Epsilon
Ocean Pines, Maryland

✤ IRISH PUFF PASTRIES

2 sheets frozen puff
  pastry
8 ounces whipped
  topping

1 (12-ounce) jar black
  currant jam
1/4 to 1/2 cup
  confectioners' sugar

Thaw pastry sheets at room temperature for 30 min. Unfold the pastry on a lightly floured surface. Cut into 2×4-inch pieces. Arrange on a baking sheet. Bake at 400 degrees for 15 minutes or until golden. Let stand until cool. Cut each piece in half. Spread a large tablespoon of whipped topping and 1 teaspoon jam in the center of each of half the squares. Cover with the remaining pieces. Sift confectioners' sugar over the top. Chill, covered, for at least 1 hour before serving. Yield: about 20 pastries.

Cheryl L. Conway, Xi Gamma Rho
Clinton, Iowa

WELSH CAKES

2 cups flour
2/3 cup sugar
1/2 teaspoon salt
1 tablespoon baking
  powder
1/2 cup (1 stick) butter or
  margarine

1/2 cup currants, washed
  and dried
2 eggs, beaten
1 teaspoon vanilla
  extract

Sift the flour, sugar, salt and baking powder into a bowl. Cut in the butter until mixture resembles coarse crumbs. Stir in the currants. Add the eggs and vanilla. Mix until well blended, forming a ball; mixture will be very dry. Knead about 15 strokes on a generously floured flat surface. Roll 1/4 inch thick and cut into circles. Bake on a 320- to 325-degree electric griddle for about 5 minutes per side until golden brown on both sides, turning once. Cool on paper towels. These cakes freeze well. Yield: 3 to 3⅓ dozen.

Olive Hall, Eta Master
Burnaby, British Columbia, Canada

ECCLES CAKES

I'm from England, and I miss the bakeries that one finds everywhere in the small villages. Eccles are made differently in different regions—this recipe is the closest to the ones from my home area, Norfolk.

6 ounces margarine	1 teaspoon cinnamon
1½ cups flour	½ teaspoon freshly
Pinch (generous) of salt	grated nutmeg
⅓ to ½ cup cold water	Grated zest of 1 large
3 ounces butter	orange
⅔ cup soft brown sugar	2 ounces finely chopped
5 ounces currants	orange peel

Wrap the margarine in foil and let stand in the freezer for 30 minutes. Sift the flour and salt into a bowl. Remove the margarine from the freezer. Holding it with the foil, dip it into the flour and grate it on a coarse grater placed in the bowl over the flour. Continue dipping the margarine in the flour to make it easier to grate. When finished, there will be a lump of grated margarine resting in the middle of the flour. Use a palette knife (not the hands) to cut the margarine into the flour until mixture is crumbly. Add cold water 1 tablespoon at a time, mixing with the hands until the mixture forms a ball. Chill in the main part of the refrigerator, wrapped in plastic wrap or a sealable plastic bag, for 30 minutes. Melt the butter in a small saucepan and remove from heat. Stir in the brown sugar, currants, cinnamon, nutmeg, orange zest and orange peel; mix well. Cool to lukewarm. Roll the chilled dough to ⅛-inch thickness on a lightly floured surface. Cut into circles with a 3½-inch cutter. Place a teaspoon of the currant mixture in the center of each circle. Brush the edges of half the pastry circle with water and pull up the other side to enclose the filling; press to seal. Pull up the corners over the center and pinch to seal. Turn over the sealed pastry parcel so seam faces down. Gently roll it flat to about ¼ inch thick; pat into a round shape. Arrange all on a buttered baking sheet. Cut 3 diagonal slashes in the top of each with a sharp knife. Brush with milk and sprinkle with extra-fine sugar. Bake in a preheated 425-degree oven for 15 minutes or until golden brown. Remove to a wire rack to cool. Yield: 18 to 20 cakes.

Diana O'Conor, Alpha Zeta
Wallkill, New York

SPUDNUTS

I was raised on my grandmother's farm, and she made these as an after-school treat. The family grew potatoes, so we enjoyed potatoes cooked many ways. This was my favorite.

4 cakes yeast	3½ teaspoons vanilla
3 medium potatoes,	extract
cooked and mashed	Vegetable oil for deep-
5 cups cold milk	frying
1½ cups sugar	Sifted flour to make a
1 teaspoon salt	dough
½ cup (1 stick) butter,	2 (1-pound) packages
softened	confectioners' sugar
3 large eggs	

Dissolve the yeast in 1 cup lukewarm water. Combine the potatoes, 4 cups of the cold milk, sugar, salt, butter, eggs, 1 teaspoon of the vanilla and yeast mixture in a large bowl and mix well. Add enough flour to make a soft dough. Let rise, covered, in a warm place until doubled in bulk. Punch the dough down. Roll to 1-inch thickness on a floured surface. Cut into doughnut shapes. Fry until golden brown on both sides. Drain on paper towels. Roll hot doughnuts in a mixture of the confectioners' sugar, the remaining 1 cup cold milk and the remaining 2 teaspoons vanilla. Yield: 12 servings.

Joycee Davis, Laureate Alpha Epsilon
Lowell, Arkansas

APPLE CRISP PIZZA

1 (1-crust) pie pastry	⅓ cup packed brown
⅔ cup granulated sugar	sugar
3 tablespoons plus	⅓ cup rolled oats
½ cup flour	¼ cup (½ stick) butter,
2 teaspoons cinnamon	softened
4 medium apples, peeled,	¼ to ½ cup caramel ice
cut into ½-inch slices	cream topping

Roll the pastry to fit a 12-inch pizza pan and fit in the pan. Mix the sugar, the 3 tablespoons flour and 1 teaspoon of the cinnamon together in a bowl. Add the apples and toss to coat. Arrange the coated apples in a single layer in a circular pattern to cover the pastry completely. Combine the ½ cup flour, brown sugar, oats and the remaining 1 teaspoon cinnamon in a bowl. Cut in the butter until crumbly. Sprinkle evenly over the apple layer. Bake at 350 degrees for 35 to 40 minutes or until golden brown. Remove from oven and drizzle with caramel topping immediately. Serve warm with ice cream. Yield: 12 servings.

Jo Prusha, Preceptor Gamma
Omaha, Nebraska

Bars & Brownies

ALMOND SQUARES

2 cups flour
1 cup sugar
Pinch of salt
1 cup unsalted butter,
    softened
1 teaspoon cinnamon

1 cup finely chopped
    almonds
3 egg yolks
$^1/_2$ to $^3/_4$ cup raspberry
    jam

Combine the flour, sugar, salt, butter, cinnamon, almonds and egg yolks in a bowl and mix well. Press $^2/_3$ of the mixture in a nonstick 9×13-inch baking pan. Spread raspberry jam evenly over the flour layer. Sprinkle the remaining flour mixture over the top. Bake at 350 degrees for 30 to 40 minutes or until golden brown. Cut into squares or diamonds.
Yield: 2 dozen.

Laura Fisher, Theta Master
New Westminster, British Columbia, Canada

ALMOND BARS

2 cups (4 sticks) butter
    or margarine, at
    room temperature
$^3/_4$ cup granulated sugar
$^1/_2$ teaspoon salt
$^3/_4$ teaspoon almond
    extract
1 egg

$2^3/_4$ cups flour
1 cup packed brown
    sugar
$^1/_3$ cup honey
$^1/_4$ cup heavy cream
1 pound almonds, sliced
    (about $5^1/_4$ cups)

Line a 10×15-inch cake pan with foil. Cream 1 cup of the butter, $^1/_2$ cup of the sugar, salt and almond extract in a mixing bowl until light and fluffy. Beat in the egg. Beat in the flour. Press the dough over the bottom and up the sides of the prepared pan. Chill until ready to bake. Preheat the oven to 375 degrees. Prick the dough all over with a fork and bake for 10 minutes. Combine the brown sugar, honey, the remaining 1 cup butter and the remaining $^1/_4$ cup sugar in a saucepan over low heat. Cook until sugar dissolves, stirring occasionally. Bring to a boil with-

out stirring; boil for 3 minutes. Remove from heat. Stir in the cream and almonds. Spread evenly over the crust. Bake for 15 minutes or until hot and bubbly. Cool and cut into bars.
Yield: 75 (1×2-inch) pieces.

Arlene Poplewko, Laureate Alpha Epsilon
Longmont, Colorado

APPLE SLICES

$2^1/_2$ cups flour
1 tablespoon plus 1 cup
    sugar
1 teaspoon salt
1 cup shortening or
    margarine
1 egg, separated
$^2/_3$ cup crushed
    cornflakes

5 cups sliced peeled
    apples
1 teaspoon cinnamon
1 cup confectioners'
    sugar
Lemon juice to make a
    glaze

Sift the flour, the 1 tablespoon sugar and salt together into a bowl. Cut in the shortening until crumbly. Place the egg yolk in a measuring cup and add enough milk to reach the $^2/_3$ cup line. Stir into the flour mixture. Roll half the dough into a ball and roll into a rectangle the size of a large baking sheet on a lightly floured flat surface. Fit the dough into the baking sheet. Layer the cornflakes and apple slices evenly over the rectangle. Sprinkle a mixture of the 1 cup sugar and cinnamon over the apples. Roll the remaining dough into a ball; roll into a rectangle and place over the sugared apple layer. Press the edges to enclose the apple filling. Beat the egg white until stiff peaks form and spread over the top dough layer. Bake at 400 degrees for 40 minutes. Mix the confectioners' sugar and enough lemon juice to make a thin glaze. Drizzle over the hot pastry. Cool and cut into rectangles of desired size. Yield: variable.

Kathy Brogard, Preceptor Nu Xi
Anderson, California

WORKING WOMAN APPLE BARS

2 eggs
1 cup flour
1¼ cups sugar
2 cups diced peeled tart
  apples
¼ teaspoon salt

2 teaspoons baking
  powder
1 cup chopped pecans
1 teaspoon vanilla
  extract

Combine the eggs, flour, sugar, apples, salt, baking powder, pecans and vanilla in a large bowl and mix well. Spread in a buttered 9×13-inch baking pan. Bake at 350 degrees for 30 minutes. Top with ice cream or whipped cream if desired.
Yield: 12 servings.

Patty Greene, Phi Alpha Delta
Gaffney, South Carolina

APRICOT BARS

1 cup (2 sticks) butter,
  softened
1 cup sugar
2 egg yolks

2 cups flour
1 (12-ounce) jar apricot
  preserves

Cream the butter and sugar in a mixing bowl until light and fluffy. Stir in the egg yolks. Stir in the flour. Press half the dough into a nonstick 9×13-inch baking pan. Spread the apricot preserves evenly over the dough. Crumble the remaining dough over the top and press lightly. Bake at 325 degrees for 35 minutes. Cool and cut into squares. Yield: 16 to 20 servings.

Janet Perkins, Preceptor Gamma Psi
Terre Haute, Indiana

FROSTED BANANA BARS

You may frost with cream cheese frosting, but these bars are very good without frosting, too.

½ cup (1 stick) butter or
  margarine, softened
2 cups sugar
3 eggs
3 medium bananas,
  mashed

1 teaspoon vanilla
  extract
2 cups flour
1 teaspoon baking soda
Pinch of salt

Cream the butter and sugar in a mixing bowl until light and fluffy. Beat in the eggs, bananas and vanilla. Add a mixture of the flour, baking soda and salt; mix well. Spread in a buttered 10×15-inch cake pan. Bake at 350 degrees for 20 to 25 minutes. Frost with cream cheese frosting if desired. Yield: 12 servings.

Karla Grant, Preceptor Alpha Upsilon
Hayden, Idaho

❖ BANANAS FOSTER CHEESECAKE SQUARES

2 cups vanilla wafer
  crumbs
½ cup chopped pecans
¾ cup packed brown
  sugar
¼ cup (½ stick) butter
  or margarine, melted
24 ounces cream cheese,
  softened
2 teaspoons rum extract
  (optional)

3 eggs
½ cup mashed ripe
  banana
2 bananas, sliced
2 teaspoons lemon juice
25 candy caramels,
  unwrapped
2 tablespoons milk
½ cup pecan halves

Combine the crumbs, chopped pecans, ¼ cup of the brown sugar and butter in a small bowl and mix well. Press in a 9×13-inch baking pan. Combine the cream cheese, remaining brown sugar and rum extract in a mixing bowl and beat at medium speed until well blended. Beat in the eggs 1 at a time. Stir in the mashed banana. Pour over the crumb layer. Bake at 350 degrees for 25 minutes or until center is almost set. Cool. Chill, covered, for 3 to 10 hours. Toss the sliced bananas with the lemon juice and arrange over the chilled cheesecake. Combine the caramels and milk in a microwave-safe bowl; microwave on High for 2 minutes. Stir until smooth and drizzle evenly over the cheesecake. Sprinkle with the pecan halves and cut into squares. Yield: 2 dozen.

Beverly McDaniel, Laureate Beta Theta
Blue Spring, Missouri

CARAMEL CRUNCHIES

2 cups flour
¾ cup packed light
  brown sugar
1 egg, beaten
¾ cup (1½ sticks)
  margarine, softened
¾ cup chopped walnuts
  or pecans

24 unwrapped candy
  caramels
1 (14-ounce) can
  sweetened condensed
  milk

Preheat the oven to 350 degrees. Mix the flour, brown sugar and egg in a bowl. Mix in ½ cup of the margarine. Stir in the chopped nuts. Reserve 2 cups of the flour mixture; press the remaining flour mixture firmly over the bottom of a buttered 9×13-inch baking pan. Bake for 15 minutes. Melt the caramels with the remaining ¼ cup margarine and condensed milk. Pour over the prepared crust. Top with the remaining flour mixture. Bake for 20 minutes or until bubbly. Cool and cut into squares. Yield: 2 dozen.

Elizabeth Glass, Delta Delta
Dublin, Georgia

CHUNKY OATMEAL CARAMELITAS

1 cup plus 3 tablespoons
   flour
1 cup quick-cooking oats
3/4 cup firmly packed
   brown sugar
1/4 teaspoon salt
1/2 teaspoon baking soda
3/4 cup (1 1/2 sticks) butter
   or margarine, melted
   and cooled

1 cup semisweet
   chocolate chips
1/2 cup chopped pecans
   (optional)
3/4 cup caramel ice cream
   topping
3/4 to 1 cup chopped milk
   chocolate English
   toffee bars (optional)

Preheat the oven to 350 degrees. Combine the 1 cup flour, oats, brown sugar, salt, baking soda and melted butter in a large mixing bowl and beat at low speed until mixture resembles coarse crumbs. Press half the crumbs in a nonstick 9×11-inch baking pan. Bake for 10 minutes. Remove from oven and sprinkle with the chocolate chips and pecans. Combine the caramel topping with the 3 tablespoons flour in a small bowl and blend well. Drizzle evenly over the chips and nuts. Sprinkle the remaining crumbs evenly over the top. Bake for 15 to 20 minutes. Sprinkle the chopped candy over the top. Cool. Chill, covered, for 1 to 2 hours. Cut into bars. Yield: 20 to 24 servings.

Angie Berzina, Iota
Rapid City, South Dakota

CHESS BARS

1 (18-ounce) package
   yellow cake mix
4 eggs
1/2 cup (1 stick)
   margarine, softened

1 (1-pound) package
   confectioners' sugar
8 ounces cream cheese,
   softened

Mix the dry cake mix, 1 of the eggs and margarine in a bowl. Pat into a buttered 9×13-inch baking pan. Combine the remaining 3 eggs, confectioners' sugar and cream cheese in a mixing bowl and beat until smooth. Pour evenly over the cake layer. Bake at 350 degrees for 45 minutes. Yield: 20 bars.

Delinda Pinson, Xi Gamma Delta
Aurora, Colorado

---

*Mildred Sharp, Kappa Master, McClave, Colorado, makes **Butterscotch Bars** by mixing a butter pecan cake mix with 1/2 cup butter and 1 egg until crumbly and pressing half the mixture into the bottom of a 9×13-inch pan. Bake at 350 degrees for 10 minutes and drizzle a 12-ounce jar of caramel topping over the baked layer. Top with the remaining crumb mixture and bake for 20 to 25 minutes or until golden brown. Cool completely before cutting.*

CHOCOLATE CHIP CHEESECAKE BARS

1 roll chocolate chip
   cookie dough,
   softened
1/2 cup sugar

1 egg
8 ounces cream cheese,
   softened

Pat half the cookie dough evenly in a 9×9-inch baking pan that has been sprayed with nonstick cooking spray. Combine the sugar, egg and cream cheese in a mixing bowl and mix until smooth. Pour the cream cheese mixture evenly over the cookie dough layer in the prepared pan. Crumble the remaining cookie dough over the top and press into the cream cheese layer. Bake at 350 degrees for 15 to 20 minutes or until firm. Yield: 9 to 12 servings.

Linda C. Madden, Laureate Omicron
Elberton, Georgia

CHEESY CRESCENT BARS

2 (8-count) cans crescent
   rolls
8 ounces cream cheese,
   softened
1 egg, separated

1 cup sugar
1 teaspoon vanilla
   extract
1/2 cup chopped walnuts
   or pecans

Unroll the dough, pressing perforations to seal. Fit half the dough into an unbuttered 9×13-inch baking pan. Combine the cream cheese, egg yolk, 3/4 cup of the sugar and vanilla in a bowl and mix well. Spread the cream cheese mixture evenly over the dough layer. Place the remaining dough over the cream cheese layer. Beat the egg white and brush over the top. Sprinkle with the remaining 1/4 cup sugar and chopped nuts. Bake at 350 degrees for 30 minutes. Cool and cut into bars. Yield: 1 dozen.

Susan Bradford, Xi Upsilon Kappa
Bakersfield, California

SWEET CHOCOLATE COCONUT BARS

1/2 cup (1 stick)
   margarine
1 cup graham cracker
   crumbs
1 cup shredded coconut
1 cup butterscotch
   morsels

1 cup chocolate chips
1 cup peanuts
1 (14-ounce) can low-fat
   sweetened condensed
   milk

Melt the margarine in a 9×13-inch baking pan. Layer the graham cracker crumbs, coconut, butterscotch morsels, chocolate chips and peanuts in the baking pan. Drizzle the condensed milk over the top. Bake at 325 degrees for 35 minutes. Yield: 2 dozen.

Sharon Rayner, Preceptor Psi
Shelby Township, Michigan

FUDGY CHOCOLATE OATMEAL BARS

1 cup (2 sticks) butter
2 cups packed brown
  sugar
2 eggs
4 teaspoons vanilla
  extract
3 cups quick-cooking
  oats
2¹/2 cups flour
1 teaspoon baking soda
1 (14-ounce) can
  sweetened condensed
  milk
1 cup each semisweet
  and milk chocolate
  chips

Remove 2 tablespoons of butter from the cup and reserve. Cream the remaining butter and brown sugar in a mixing bowl until light and fluffy. Add the eggs and 2 teaspoons of the vanilla and beat well. Add a mixture of the oats, flour and baking soda and beat well. Combine the 2 tablespoons butter, condensed milk and chocolate chips in a saucepan. Heat until melted and smooth, stirring constantly. Stir in the remaining 2 teaspoons vanilla. Pat half the flour mixture in a buttered 9×13-inch baking pan. Bake in a preheated 350-degree oven for 10 minutes. Pour the chocolate mixture evenly over the crust. Layer the remaining flour mixture over the chocolate layer. Bake for 25 to 30 minutes longer or until top is lightly browned. Cool and cut into bars. Yield: 2 dozen.

Rebecca Leidy, Xi Delta Chi
Sidney, New York

PEBBLE-TOP CHOCOLATE BARS

1¹/2 cups shredded
  coconut
2 tablespoons melted
  butter
2 tablespoons plus
  ¹/2 cup sugar
¹/4 cup graham cracker
  crumbs
¹/2 cup (1 stick) butter,
  softened
¹/4 cup firmly packed
  brown sugar
1 egg
1 teaspoon vanilla
  extract
2 tablespoons milk
1 cup flour
¹/2 teaspoon salt
¹/2 teaspoon baking soda
¹/2 cup chopped pecans
1 cup chocolate chips
8 ounces dried cherries
  or other dried fruit

Place the coconut, melted butter, the 2 tablespoons sugar and graham cracker crumbs in a 9×9-inch baking pan. Mix well and pat evenly over the bottom of the pan. Place ¹/2 cup butter, brown sugar, egg, vanilla, milk, flour, salt, baking soda and ¹/2 cup sugar in a mixing bowl; mix until smooth. Stir in the pecans and chocolate chips. Spoon evenly over the crumb layer. Scatter the cherries over the top. Bake at 350 degrees for 35 to 40 minutes or until lightly browned. Cool and cut into squares.
Yield: 16 squares.

Lu Ann Petty, Lambda Tau
Meriden, Kansas

CHOCOLATE CAKE BARS

1 (2-layer) package
  chocolate cake mix
2 eggs
¹/3 cup vegetable oil
¹/3 cup butter
2 cups chocolate chips
1 (14-ounce) can
  sweetened condensed
  milk
1 cup fresh or frozen
  cranberries, halved

Combine the cake mix, eggs and vegetable oil in a mixing bowl and mix well. Place the butter, chocolate chips, condensed milk and cranberries in a microwave-safe bowl. Microwave on High for about 2 minutes and stir until well mixed. Press half the cake mix mixture in an oiled 9×13-inch glass baking dish. Pour the chocolate chip mixture over the cake mix layer and spread evenly. Crumble the remaining cake mix mixture evenly over the top. Bake at 325 degrees for 20 minutes. Cool and cut into bars. Yield: 2 dozen.

Karen Crook, Preceptor Laureate Alpha Eta
Moses Lake, Washington

FUDGE NUT BARS

1 cup semisweet
  chocolate chips
¹/2 cup sweetened
  condensed milk
1 tablespoon butter
¹/4 teaspoon salt
¹/2 cup chopped walnuts
1 teaspoon vanilla
  extract
1¹/4 cups flour
¹/2 teaspoon baking soda
¹/2 teaspoon salt
¹/2 cup butter (1 stick),
  softened
1 cup packed brown
  sugar
1 egg
1 teaspoon vanilla
  extract
1¹/2 cups rolled oats
¹/4 cup chopped walnuts

Combine the chocolate chips, condensed milk, 1 tablespoon butter and ¹/4 teaspoon salt in the top of a double boiler over boiling water. Heat until chocolate is melted, stirring until smooth. Remove from heat. Stir in ¹/2 cup walnuts and 1 teaspoon of the vanilla. Sift the flour, baking soda and ¹/2 teaspoon salt together. Cream the ¹/2 cup butter and brown sugar in a mixing bowl until fluffy. Add the egg and 1 teaspoon vanilla and blend well. Stir in the rolled oats and the flour mixture. Press ²/3 of the mixture in a buttered 9×13-inch baking pan. Spread the chocolate mixture evenly over the oats layer. Crumble the remaining oats mixture over the top. Sprinkle with ¹/4 cup chopped walnuts. Bake at 350 degrees for 25 to 30 minutes or until lightly browned.
Yield: 2 to 3 dozen.

Sharon Peine, Pi Iota
Shawnee, Kansas

AMAZON BARS

1/2 cup (1 stick) butter	1 cup semisweet
24 graham crackers	chocolate chips
1 (14-ounce) can	1 cup chopped Brazil
sweetened condensed	nuts
milk	1/2 cup chopped cashews
1 (7-ounce) package	
flaked coconut	

Melt the butter in a 9×13-inch baking pan. Crush the graham crackers. Sprinkle the graham cracker crumbs evenly over the melted butter and press evenly into the pan to form a crust. Drizzle the sweetened condensed milk over the crust and spread evenly with a spatula. Sprinkle the coconut and chocolate chips evenly over the condensed milk and cover with the Brazil nuts and cashews. Bake at 350 degrees for 30 minutes. Cool in the pan on a wire rack. Cut into bars. Serve at room temperature or slightly chilled. Yield: 2 dozen.

Linda Derby, Eta Beta
Gainesville, Florida

SPEEDY LITTLE DEVILS

1 (2-layer) package	3/4 cup creamy peanut
devil's food cake mix	butter
1/2 cup (1 stick)	1 (8-ounce) jar
margarine, melted	marshmallow creme

Combine the dry cake mix and margarine in a bowl and mix well. Remove 1 cup of the mixture and reserve. Press the remaining cake mixture in a greased 9×13-inch baking pan. Spread a mixture of the peanut butter and marshmallow creme evenly over the cake layer. Crumble the reserved cake mixture over the top. Bake at 350 degrees for 20 minutes. Cool and cut into squares. Yield: 12 to 16 servings.

Dolores Brown, Tau Master
Martinsburg, West Virginia

CHOCOLATE MELTAWAYS

1 (2-layer) package	1/2 cup chopped walnuts
devil's food cake mix	or pecans
1/4 cup water	1 (8-ounce) package
2 eggs	creamy white frosting
1/4 cup (1/2 stick) butter	mix
or margarine	3 ounces unsweetened
1/4 cup packed brown	chocolate, melted
sugar	

Combine half the dry cake mix, water, eggs, butter and brown sugar in a mixing bowl and mix well. Blend in the remaining cake mix. Stir in the chopped nuts. Spread in a buttered and floured 10×15-inch cake pan. Bake at 375 degrees for 20 to 25 minutes or until edges are firm. Cool. Prepare the frosting mix using the package directions and spread over the cooled cake. Spread the melted chocolate evenly over the frosting. Chill for 1 hour. Cut into 1 1/2-inch squares before chocolate is completely firm. Chill, covered, until serving time. Yield: 5 1/2 dozen.

Ann Marie Phillips, Delta Gamma
Jamestown, New York

GERMAN CHOCOLATE CAKE MIX BARS

1 (2-layer) package	1/2 cup (1 stick)
German chocolate	margarine, melted
cake mix	50 caramels
2/3 cup milk	1 cup chocolate chips

Prepare the cake mix using the package directions, substituting 1/3 cup of the milk for the water and the 1/2 cup margarine for the oil. Spread 2/3 of the cake mixture in a buttered 9×13-inch baking pan. Bake at 350 degrees for 10 minutes. Melt the caramels with the remaining 1/3 cup milk in a saucepan or microwave; stir to blend. Layer the chocolate chips evenly over the cake layer. Drizzle the caramel mixture evenly over the chocolate chips. Crumble the remaining cake mixture over the caramel layer. Bake for 20 minutes. Cool and cut into bars. Yield: 2 dozen.

MaryAnn Navratil, Omicron Omega
Bettendorf, Iowa

TURTLE CAKES

1 (2-layer) package	40 caramels
German chocolate	1/2 to 1 cup pecan pieces
cake mix	1/2 to 1 cup chocolate
1 cup evaporated milk	chips
3/4 cup (1 1/2 sticks) butter	
or margarine	

Combine the dry cake mix, half the evaporated milk and butter in a mixing bowl and mix well. Pour half the cake mixture evenly into a buttered 9×13-inch baking pan. Bake in a preheated 350-degree oven for 5 to 6 minutes; batter will puff up a little but will remain gooey. Melt the caramels with the remaining 1/2 cup evaporated milk and stir to blend. Pour evenly over the top of the cake. Sprinkle with pecans and chocolate chips. Drop the remaining cake mixture by tablespoons over the top. Bake for 18 to 20 minutes. Cool and cut into bars. Keep refrigerated during hot weather. Yield: 2 dozen.

Betty L. Muhleman, Preceptor Nu Delta
Penn Valley, California

DOUBLE CHOCOLATE MINT BARS

1 cup flour	2 cups confectioners'
1 cup sugar	sugar
1 cup plus 6 to	1 tablespoon water
9 tablespoons butter,	1/2 teaspoon peppermint
softened	extract
1 teaspoon vanilla	3 drops green food
extract	coloring
4 eggs	2 cups semisweet
1 (16-ounce) can	chocolate chips
chocolate syrup	

Combine the flour, sugar, 1/2 cup of the butter, vanilla, eggs and chocolate syrup in a mixing bowl and beat until smooth. Pour into a buttered 9×13-inch baking pan. Bake at 350 degrees for 25 to 30 minutes or until top springs back when lightly pressed. Cool completely. Combine the confectioners' sugar, 1/2 cup butter, water, peppermint extract and green food coloring in a mixing bowl and blend well. Spread over the cooled chocolate layer. Chill, covered, until very cold. Melt the remaining butter and chocolate chips and drizzle evenly over the mint layer. Chill and serve. Yield: 1 1/2 to 2 dozen.

Melissa Schmitt, Epsilon Sigma
Early, Iowa

CREME DE MENTHE SQUARES

1 1/4 cups butter	2 cups graham cracker
1/2 cup baking cocoa	crumbs
3 1/2 cups sifted	1/3 cup green crème de
confectioners' sugar	menthe
1 egg, beaten	1 1/2 cups semisweet
1 teaspoon vanilla	chocolate chips
extract	

Combine 1/2 cup of the butter and baking cocoa in a saucepan over medium-low heat. Cook until butter melts, stirring frequently to blend. Remove from heat. Stir in 1/2 cup of the confectioners' sugar, egg and vanilla. Add the graham cracker crumbs and mix well. Press into an unbuttered 9×13-inch baking pan. Melt another 1/2 cup of the butter and pour into a mixing bowl. Stir in the crème de menthe. Beat in the remaining 3 cups confectioners' sugar at low speed until smooth. Spread over the chocolate layer. Chill for 1 hour. Combine the remaining 1/4 cup butter and chocolate chips in a saucepan over low heat. Cook until melted, stirring frequently to blend. Spread over the crème de menthe layer. Chill for 1 to 2 hours. Cut into small squares. Chill, covered, until serving time. Keep leftovers refrigerated. Yield: 8 dozen.

Mary Ellen Grossman, Laureate Beta Nu
Laurenceburg, Indiana

CRANBERRY SQUARES

1 1/2 cups flour	2 eggs, beaten
1 1/2 cups sugar	2 cups whole cranberries
1 cup (2 sticks)	1 cup chopped walnuts
margarine, melted	or pecans

Mix the first 4 ingredients in a mixing bowl. Stir in the cranberries and nuts. Spread in a buttered 9×13-inch baking pan. Bake at 325 degrees for 45 to 60 minutes. Cool and cut into squares. Yield: 2 dozen.

Dianna E. Maffucci, Preceptor Beta Gamma
Center Harbor, New Hampshire

CRANBERRY LEMON SQUARES

1/2 cup frozen lemonade	1 egg
concentrate, thawed	1 1/2 cups flour
1/2 cup sugar or	1/2 teaspoon baking soda
spoonable sugar	1/2 teaspoon salt
substitute	2 teaspoons grated
1/4 cup (1/2 stick)	lemon rind
margarine, softened	1/2 cup dried cranberries

Combine the lemonade concentrate, sugar, margarine and egg in a bowl and mix well. Add a mixture of the flour, baking soda and salt and mix well. Stir in the lemon rind and dried cranberries. Pour into a greased 8-inch square baking pan. Bake at 375 degrees for 20 minutes or until light brown. Cool in the pan on a wire rack. Cut into squares. Yield: 16 squares.

Carole Stokes, Preceptor Alpha Beta
Portage, Michigan

DATE ORANGE SQUARES

2 cups chopped dates	1 teaspoon lemon juice
3/4 cup cold water	1 1/2 cups large-flake
1 teaspoon grated	rolled oats
orange zest	1 1/2 cups flour
2 tablespoons plus 1 cup	1/8 teaspoon salt
packed brown sugar	1 teaspoon baking soda
2 tablespoons orange	1 cup (2 sticks) butter or
juice	margarine, softened

Cook the dates, water, orange zest and 2 tablespoons brown sugar in a saucepan over medium heat until thickened, stirring until smooth. Remove from heat. Stir in the orange juice and lemon juice. Cool completely. Mix the oats, flour, 1 cup brown sugar, salt and baking soda in a bowl. Cut in the butter until crumbly. Press half the flour mixture in a buttered 9×9-inch baking pan. Spread with the date filling. Top with remaining flour mixture. Bake at 375 degrees for 20 minutes or until golden brown. Cool; cut into squares. Yield: 1 1/3 dozen.

Rhoda Dickson, Alpha Beta
Fort Frances, Ontario, Canada

GUMDROP SQUARES

1 cup sifted flour	1 cup spiced gumdrops,
1/4 teaspoon salt	chopped
1/4 cup (1/2 stick) butter	1 teaspoon vanilla
or margarine	extract
1 cup packed light	1 1/2 cups chopped
brown sugar	walnuts or pecans
1 egg, well beaten	

Sift the flour and salt together. Cream the butter and brown sugar in a mixing bowl until light and fluffy. Stir in the egg, gumdrops, vanilla and nuts. Add the flour mixture gradually, stirring after each addition. Spread in a buttered 8×8-inch pan. Bake at 350 degrees for 20 to 30 minutes or until a knife inserted in the center comes out clean; do not overbake. Cut into squares. Cool and serve. Yield: 25 cookies.

Debbi Gwynn, Xi Delta Rho
Miami, Florida

FRUIT PUNCH BARS

2 1/4 cups sugar	2 1/4 cups flour
1/2 cup (1 stick) butter	1 (17-ounce) can fruit
1 1/2 teaspoons vanilla	cocktail
extract	2 1/2 teaspoons baking
1/4 cup evaporated milk	soda
1 cup chopped walnuts	1/2 teaspoon salt
2 eggs	1 1/3 cups flaked coconut

Combine 3/4 cup of the sugar, butter, 1/2 teaspoon of the vanilla and evaporated milk in a saucepan over medium-high heat; bring to a boil. Boil for 2 minutes, stirring constantly. Remove from heat and stir in 1/2 cup of the walnuts. Set glaze aside. Mix the eggs, flour, remaining 1 1/2 cups sugar, undrained fruit cocktail, baking soda, salt and the remaining 1 teaspoon vanilla in a bowl. Pour into a buttered 8 1/2×11-inch baking pan. Sprinkle with coconut and the remaining 1/2 cup walnuts. Bake at 350 degrees for 20 to 25 minutes or until beginning to set. Drizzle warm glaze over hot baked layer. Yield: 2 dozen.

M. Connie Frye, Laureate Alpha Eta
Moses Lake, Washington

---

*Adrienne Lander, Preceptor Phi, Mesa, Arizona, makes **Easy Angel Dessert Bars** by combining a package of angel food cake mix with a 22-ounce can of crushed pineapple, mixing well and spreading in a lightly greased 10x15-inch baking pan. Bake at 350 degrees for 15 to 20 minutes or until light brown.*

OLD-WORLD JAM BARS

2 1/4 cups flour	1 egg
1 cup sugar	1 cup chopped pecans
1 cup (2 sticks) butter,	1 (10-ounce) jar
softened	raspberry jam

Combine the flour and sugar in a mixing bowl. Add the butter and egg and beat at low speed until well mixed. Mix in the pecans. Reserve 1 1/2 cups of the mixture. Press the remaining mixture into an 8-inch square baking pan. Spread with the jam to within 1/2 inch of the edge. Crumble the reserved mixture over the top. Bake at 350 degrees for 42 to 50 minutes or until light brown. Cool and cut into bars.
Yield: 1 to 2 dozen.

Carole Toomey, Preceptor Alpha Tau
Massena, New York

BABY FOOD BARS

3 eggs	1 (3-ounce) jar baby
2 cups sugar	food, applesauce
2 cups flour	4 cups confectioners'
1/4 cup vegetable oil	sugar
1 teaspoon salt	8 ounces cream cheese,
2 teaspoons baking soda	softened
2 teaspoons cinnamon	1 tablespoon vanilla
1 (3-ounce) jar baby	extract
food, carrots	1/2 cup (1 stick)
1 (3-ounce) jar baby	margarine, softened
food, apricots	

Combine the eggs, sugar, flour, vegetable oil, salt, baking soda, cinnamon and all baby food in a large bowl and mix well. Spread in a lightly buttered 10×15-inch cake pan. Bake at 350 degrees for 25 to 30 minutes or until beginning to brown. Cool. Frost with a mixture of the confectioners' sugar, cream cheese, vanilla and margarine. Cut into bars.
Yield: 2 to 3 dozen.

Ellen Otten, Alpha Gamma
Marshalltown, Iowa

✤ CARIBBEAN BARS

1/2 cup (1 stick) butter or	1 teaspoon rum extract
margarine	2 tablespoons flour
1/4 cup sugar	1/2 teaspoon baking
1 1/4 cups flour	powder
1/2 cup crushed pineapple	1 1/2 cups confectioners'
2 eggs, slightly beaten	sugar
1 cup packed brown	3 tablespoons butter,
sugar	softened
1 cup shredded coconut	1/2 teaspoon rum extract
1/3 cup chopped candied	
cherries	

Combine ¹/₂ cup butter, sugar and 1¹/₄ cups flour in a bowl and mix until crumbly. Press into an unbuttered 9×9-inch baking pan. Bake at 350 degrees for 15 minutes. Drain the pineapple, reserving the juice. Combine the eggs, brown sugar, pineapple, coconut, candied cherries, 1 teaspoon rum extract, 2 tablespoons flour and baking powder in a mixing bowl and mix until smooth. Spread over the baked layer. Bake for 25 to 30 minutes or until set and medium brown. Combine the confectioners' sugar, 3 tablespoons butter, ¹/₂ teaspoon rum extract and 1¹/₂ tablespoons of the reserved pineapple juice in a mixing bowl. Beat until of spreadable consistency, adding more pineapple juice if necessary. Spread over the pineapple layer. Let stand for ¹/₂ hour before cutting into bars. Yield: 3 dozen.

Sally Reiter, Preceptor Delta Gamma
Aldergrove, British Columbia, Canada

HOMEMADE GINGERBREAD

1 cup Blackburn's Syrup	2 cups self-rising flour
1 cup liquid shortening	1 teaspoon baking soda
1 cup buttermilk	1 teaspoon salt
1 cup sugar	4 teaspoons cinnamon
2 eggs	¹/₈ teaspoon nutmeg

Combine the syrup, shortening, buttermilk, sugar and eggs in a large mixing bowl and mix well. Combine the flour, baking soda, salt, cinnamon and nutmeg in another large mixing bowl and blend well. Pour the liquid ingredients over the dry ingredients and mix well. Pour into a buttered 9×13-inch baking pan. Bake at 350 degrees for 35 to 45 minutes or until gingerbread tests done. Yield: 3 dozen.

Jean Smith Sanders, Xi Alpha Nu
Natchez, Mississippi

SPICE BARS

1 cup granulated sugar	1 teaspoon baking soda
1 egg	1 teaspoon cinnamon
³/₄ cup vegetable oil	¹/₄ teaspoon salt
¹/₄ cup honey	1 cup sifted
1 cup chopped pecans	confectioners' sugar
1 teaspoon white	1 tablespoon water
vinegar	1 tablespoon
2 cups sifted flour	mayonnaise

Combine the granulated sugar, egg, vegetable oil and honey in a mixing bowl and mix well. Stir in the pecans and vinegar. Sift the flour, baking soda, cinnamon and salt together and stir into the honey mixture; dough will be very stiff. Spread in a buttered 10×15-inch cake pan. Bake at 350 degrees for

20 minutes; do not overbake. Place the confectioners' sugar in a bowl. Blend the water and mayonnaise together and stir into the confectioners' sugar. Spread over the warm cake. Cool and cut into bars. Yield: 3 dozen (2-inch) bars.

Angela Fannin, Alpha Mu Chi
Madisonville, Texas

GLAZED HONEY BARS

1 cup sugar	1 cup chopped walnuts
¹/₄ cup honey	or pecans
1 egg	1 cup confectioners'
³/₄ cup vegetable oil	sugar
2 cups flour	2 tablespoons real
1 teaspoon baking soda	mayonnaise
1 teaspoon cinnamon	1 teaspoon water
¹/₂ teaspoon salt	
2 teaspoons vanilla	
extract	

Combine the sugar, honey, egg, vegetable oil, flour, baking soda, cinnamon, salt and half the vanilla in a bowl and mix well. Mix in the chopped nuts. Press into an 11×17-inch baking pan that has been sprayed with nonstick cooking spray. Bake at 350 degrees for 12 to 15 minutes. Glaze hot cake with a mixture of the confectioners' sugar, the remaining 1 teaspoon vanilla, mayonnaise and water. Cool and cut into bars. Yield: about 3 dozen.

Linda Humphrey, Xi Beta Epsilon
Woodward, Oklahoma

LEMON SQUARES

1 cup (2 sticks) butter or	¹/₄ cup lemon juice
margarine	1 teaspoon baking
2 cups plus ¹/₄ cup flour	powder
¹/₂ cup plus 2 cups sugar	1 teaspoon lemon
4 eggs	extract

Cut the butter into chunks. Combine the butter, the 2 cups flour and the ¹/₂ cup sugar in a food processor container and process until crumbly, for about 20 seconds. Press in a lightly buttered 9×13-inch baking pan. Bake at 350 degrees for 20 minutes. Combine the eggs, lemon juice, the 2 cups sugar, the ¹/₄ cup flour, baking powder and lemon extract in the food processor. Process until blended, about 10 seconds. Pour evenly over the base. Bake for 25 minutes longer. Cool and cut into small squares. May be frozen. Yield: 4 dozen.

Val Wilmot, Laureate Gamma Beta
Victoria, British Columbia, Canada

CARAMEL OATMEAL BARS

3¹/₂ cups Cookie Mix	1 cup chocolate chips
¹/₂ cup sugar	¹/₂ jar caramel ice cream
¹/₂ cup melted butter	topping

Combine the Cookie Mix, sugar and butter in a bowl and mix well. Press half the mixture into an ungreased 9×13-inch baking pan. Bake at 350 degrees for 10 minutes. Sprinkle with the chocolate chips and drizzle with the caramel ice cream topping. Sprinkle with the remaining oatmeal mixture and press lightly. Bake for 15 minutes longer. Cool in the pan on a wire rack and cut into bars. Yield: 32 bars.

COOKIE MIX

3 cups flour	1 cup packed brown
3¹/₂ teaspoons baking	sugar
powder	1¹/₂ cups shortening
1¹/₂ teaspoons salt	3 cups rolled oats
¹/₂ cup sugar	

Combine the first 5 ingredients in a large bowl. Cut in the shortening until crumbly. Mix in the oats. Store, tightly covered, in a cool dry place for up to 10 to 12 weeks.

Stephanie Strand, Beta Phi
Challis, Idaho

OATMEAL BUTTERSCOTCH BARS

1 cup shortening or	4 cups flour
butter	4 teaspoons baking
4 cups packed brown	powder
sugar	1 teaspoon salt
¹/₂ cup evaporated milk	4 teaspoons cinnamon
4 eggs	2 cups rolled oats
4 teaspoons vanilla	
extract	

Melt the shortening and brown sugar in a saucepan. Cook until bubbly, stirring occasionally. Blend in the evaporated milk and set aside until cool. Beat in the eggs 1 at a time. Beat in the vanilla. Mix the flour, baking powder, salt and cinnamon together. Mix in the oats. Add to the egg mixture and mix well. Spread in a well-greased 9×13-inch baking pan. Bake at 350 degrees for 35 to 45 minutes or until golden brown. Cool slightly and cut into bars. Yield: 2 to 3 dozen.

VARIATIONS:

- Reduce flour to 3¹/₂ cups and add 1 cup wheat germ.
- Omit cinnamon and oats; add 3 to 4 cups coconut.

Milly Stevens, Xi Epsilon Nu
Colorado Springs, Colorado

OATMEAL BARS

1 cup (2 sticks)	Dash of salt
margarine	1 cup flour
1 cup packed brown	1 cup rolled oats
sugar	4 (7-ounce) chocolate
1 cup granulated sugar	candy bars
2 eggs	

Cream the margarine and sugars in a mixing bowl until light and fluffy. Add the eggs, salt, flour and oats and mix well. Press in a buttered 9×13-inch baking pan. Bake at 350 degrees for 30 minutes. Remove from oven and place the candy bars over the top immediately. Let stand for a few minutes to melt. Spread like frosting. Cool and cut into bars. Yield: 20 bars.

Diane Ponzio, Xi Delta Kappa
Alpharetta, Georgia

ORANGE SLICE BARS

1 pound candied orange	4 eggs, beaten
slices, chopped	1 teaspoon vanilla
2 cups sifted flour	extract
¹/₂ teaspoon salt	1 cup chopped walnuts
3 cups packed light	or pecans
brown sugar	Granulated sugar

Place the chopped candy and flour in a large bowl and toss to combine. Add the salt, brown sugar, eggs, vanilla and chopped nuts and mix well. Spread in a buttered 10×15-inch cake pan. Bake at 350 degrees for 35 minutes. Cool and cut into bars. Separate the bars and roll in granulated sugar. Yield: 4 dozen.

Helen Easterly, Xi Iota Rho
Joshua Tree, California

SALTED PEANUT CHEWS

1 (2-layer) package	²/₃ cup light corn syrup
yellow cake mix	2 teaspoons vanilla
¹/₃ cup plus ¹/₄ cup butter	extract
or margarine	1 (10-ounce) package
1 egg	peanut butter chips
3 cups miniature	2 cups crisp rice cereal
marshmallows	2 cups salted peanuts

Combine the dry cake mix, ¹/₃ cup butter and egg in a large mixing bowl; beat at low speed until crumbly. Press in a nonstick 9×13-inch baking pan. Bake at 325 degrees for 12 to 18 minutes or until golden brown. Remove from oven and sprinkle with marshmallows immediately. Bake for 1 to 2 minutes longer or until marshmallows puff. Cool. Combine the corn syrup, the ¹/₄ cup butter, vanilla and peanut butter chips in a saucepan over medium heat. Heat until melted, stirring constantly. Remove from heat and stir in the cereal and peanuts. Spread over the marshmallow layer. Chill for 1 hour or until firm. Cut into bars. Store in an airtight container. Yield: 4 dozen.

Anita Prescott, Preceptor Beta Tau
Dallas, Texas

PEANUT BUTTER CARAMEL BARS

1 (2-layer) package yellow cake mix	*2 tablespoons cornstarch*
1/2 cup (1 stick) butter, softened	*1/4 cup smooth peanut butter*
1 egg	*1 cup caramel topping*
20 miniature peanut butter cups, chopped	*1 cup salted peanuts*
	1 (16-ounce) can milk chocolate frosting

Combine the dry cake mix, butter and egg in a mixing bowl and beat for 3 minutes until uniformly mixed. Stir in the peanut butter cups. Press in a buttered 9×13-inch baking pan. Bake at 350 degrees for 18 to 22 minutes or until lightly browned. Cool slightly. Combine the cornstarch, peanut butter and caramel topping in a saucepan over low heat and stir until smooth. Cook for about 25 minutes or until it comes to a boil, stirring occasionally. Boil gently for 2 minutes longer, stirring constantly. Remove from heat. Stir in half the peanuts. Spread over the warm crust. Bake at 350 degrees for 6 to 7 minutes. Cool. Spread the frosting over the top and sprinkle with the remaining peanuts. Chill for at least 1 hour. Keep refrigerated. Yield: 3 dozen.

Jeanette Petersen, Laureate Beta Gamma
Clinton, Iowa

TEN-MINUTE PEANUT BARS

1/4 cup butter or margarine	*1 (10-ounce) package miniature marshmallows*
1 (10-ounce) package peanut butter chips	*1 (16-ounce) jar dry-roasted peanuts*
1 (14-ounce) can sweetened condensed milk	

Combine the butter and peanut butter chips in a microwave-safe bowl. Microwave on High for 2 minutes. Stir until melted and smooth. Stir in the condensed milk and microwave for 30 seconds longer. Stir in the marshmallows to coat; they should not melt. Layer half the peanuts in a 9×13-inch baking pan that has been sprayed with nonstick cooking spray. Pour the marshmallow mixture over the peanuts and spread evenly. Layer the remaining peanuts over the top and press firmly. Cut into bars when cool. Yield: 1 1/2 to 2 dozen.

Gwendolyn R. Anthony, Beta Phi
Wilber, Nebraska

PEANUTTY CHOCOLATE BARS

2 cups chocolate graham cracker crumbs	*1 2/3 cups peanut butter and milk chocolate morsels*
1/2 cup (1 stick) butter, melted	*1 teaspoon vanilla extract*
1/3 cup granulated sugar	*1 cup coarsely chopped peanuts*
1 (14-ounce) can sweetened condensed milk	

Combine the crumbs, butter and sugar and mix well. Press the mixture into an unbuttered 9×13-inch baking pan. Combine condensed milk, 1 cup of the morsels and vanilla in a medium microwave-safe bowl. Microwave on High for 1 minute and stir. Continue to microwave until melted, stirring at 10- to 20-second intervals until smooth. Pour evenly over the crumb layer. Sprinkle the remaining morsels and chopped peanuts over the top. Bake at 350 degrees for 20 to 30 minutes or until bubbly. Cool in the pan on a wire rack. Cut into bars. Yield: 2 dozen.

Mildred L. Johnson, Laureate Gamma Upsilon
Ellensburg, Washington

PEANUT BUTTER MARSHMALLOW BARS

1 cup packed brown sugar	*2 large egg whites*
1/2 cup reduced-fat peanut butter	*1 1/2 cups self-rising flour*
2 tablespoons butter, softened	*1 (7-ounce) jar marshmallow creme*
1/2 teaspoon vanilla extract	*1/4 cup chopped roasted peanuts*
	2/3 cup semisweet chocolate chips

Combine the brown sugar, peanut butter, butter, vanilla and egg whites in a mixing bowl; beat at medium speed until uniformly mixed. Spoon the flour lightly into dry measuring cups and level with a knife; stir into the peanut butter mixture. Press the mixture into a 9×13-inch baking pan that has been coated with nonstick cooking spray. Spread the marshmallow creme over the dough. Sprinkle evenly with peanuts and chocolate chips. Bake at 350 degrees for 20 to 22 minutes or until edges are firm. Cool and cut into bars. Yield: 28 bars.

Sue Seggebruch, Preceptor Alpha Chi
Watseka, Illinois

BABY RUTH BARS

1 cup sugar	*2 cups cornflakes*
1¹/₂ cups light corn syrup	*1 cup Spanish peanuts*
1 cup packed brown	*2 cups chocolate chips*
* sugar*	*3 tablespoons smooth*
1 cup smooth peanut	* peanut butter*
* butter*	

Combine the sugar, corn syrup and brown sugar in a saucepan over medium-high heat and bring to a boil. Boil for 1 minute, stirring frequently. Remove from heat. Stir in 1 cup peanut butter. Combine the peanut butter mixture, cornflakes and Spanish peanuts in a bowl and mix well. Spread in a buttered 11×15-inch baking pan. Melt the chocolate chips and 2 tablespoons peanut butter in a small saucepan, stirring until smooth. Spread over the peanut butter layer. Cut the warm cake into bars. Yield: 3 dozen.

Myrna Wells, Alpha Gamma Psi
Aurora, Missouri

CHOCOLATE CHIP PECAN PIE BARS

1¹/₂ cups flour	*2 tablespoons melted*
¹/₄ cup packed brown	* butter*
* sugar*	*1 teaspoon vanilla*
¹/₂ cup (1 stick) butter	* extract*
3 eggs	*1³/₄ cups semisweet*
³/₄ cup light corn syrup	* chocolate chips*
³/₄ cup granulated sugar	*1¹/₂ cups chopped pecans*

Combine the flour and brown sugar in a bowl. Cut in the butter until crumbly. Press into an unbuttered 9×13-inch baking pan. Bake at 350 degrees for 12 to 15 minutes. Combine the eggs, corn syrup, granulated sugar, the 2 tablespoons melted butter, vanilla, chocolate chips and pecans in a bowl and mix well. Spread evenly over the crust. Bake for 25 to 30 minutes or until a knife inserted near the center comes out clean. Cool completely and cut into bars. Yield: 2 dozen.

Luella Nelson, Zeta Master
Superior, Wisconsin

HONEY PECAN BARS

¹/₂ cup butter, softened	*1¹/₂ cups flour*
¹/₂ cup packed brown	*¹/₄ cup honey*
* sugar*	*¹/₂ cup heavy cream*
1 egg yolk	*4 cups chopped pecans*
¹/₂ cup butter, softened	
1 cup packed brown	
* sugar*	

Line a 9×13-inch baking pan with foil. Butter the foil. Cream ¹/₂ cup butter and ¹/₂ cup brown sugar in a mixing bowl until fluffy. Add the egg yolk and mix well. Mix in the flour gradually; mixture will be dry. Press into the prepared pan. Bake at 350 degrees for 15 minutes or until golden brown. Combine 1 cup brown sugar, the remaining ¹/₂ cup butter and honey in a saucepan over medium heat; bring to a gentle boil. Simmer for 3 minutes, stirring constantly. Remove from heat. Stir in the cream and pecans. Pour evenly over the crust. Bake for 30 minutes or until hot and bubbly. Cool in the pan on a wire rack. Use the foil to lift the baked layer from the pan and place on a cutting board. Remove the foil carefully. Cut into bars. Yield: 2 dozen.

Gloria Fenter, Xi Nu Zeta
Newhall, California

PECAN DREAMS

Use half of an 18-ounce package of cake mix if you cannot find the smaller package.

¹/₂ cup (1 stick) butter or	*2 egg whites*
* margarine*	*¹/₂ cup sugar*
1 (9-ounce) package	*¹/₂ cup pecan pieces*
* white cake mix*	
1 teaspoon vanilla	
* extract*	

Cut the butter into the cake mix until crumbly; mix in half the vanilla. Press into a 9×9-inch baking pan. Bake at 350 degrees for 20 minutes; it will rise, but it will fall when removed from the oven. Beat the egg whites in a mixing bowl until soft peaks form. Add the sugar and the remaining ¹/₂ teaspoon vanilla gradually, beating until stiff peaks form. Spread over the warm cake. Sprinkle with the pecans. Bake for 8 minutes longer. Cool for 5 minutes and cut into bars. Remove warm bars from the pan. Yield: 25 pieces.

Patricia A. Gee, Preceptor Alpha Theta
Deale, Maryland

PECAN PIE BARS

This dessert is easier than pecan pie and just as good.

1¹/₂ cups flour	*¹/₄ cup beaten egg (1 or*
¹/₃ cup confectioners'	* 2 large eggs)*
* sugar*	*1 teaspoon vanilla*
³/₄ cup (1¹/₂ sticks)	* extract*
* butter, softened*	*1¹/₂ to 2 cups pecans*
1 (14-ounce) can	
* sweetened condensed*	
* milk*	

Adjust oven rack to center position. Combine the flour and confectioners' sugar in a large mixing bowl and blend. Add the butter and mix well. Press firmly into a buttered 9×13-inch baking pan. Bake in a preheated 325-degree oven for 15 minutes. Combine the condensed milk, egg and vanilla in a mixing bowl and mix well. Stir in the pecans. Spread over the crust and bake for 25 minutes longer or until golden brown. Cool and cut into bars. Yield: 2 to 3 dozen.

Dianne Nichols, Preceptor Beta Nu
Placentia, California

BUTTER PECAN BARS

1 (2-layer) package butter pecan cake mix	8 ounces cream cheese, softened
1 egg	2 eggs
1 cup (2 sticks) butter or margarine, melted	1/4 to 1/2 cup chopped pecans
3 1/2 cups confectioners' sugar	

Combine the dry cake mix, 1 egg and half the butter in a mixing bowl and mix until crumbly. Pat into a buttered 9×13-inch baking pan. Combine the confectioners' sugar, cream cheese, the remaining melted butter and 2 eggs in a mixing bowl and mix well. Pour evenly over the baked layer. Sprinkle with pecans. Bake at 350 degrees for 55 minutes. Cool and cut into bars. Yield: 1 to 3 dozen.

Barbara Stuart, Laureate Gamma Pi
Mexico, Missouri

EASY PRALINE BARS

12 graham cracker squares	1/2 teaspoon vanilla extract
1/2 cup packed brown sugar	1/2 to 3/4 cup chopped pecans
1/2 cup (1 stick) butter	

Arrange the graham crackers in a single layer in an unbuttered 10×15-inch cake pan. Combine the brown sugar and butter in a saucepan over medium-high heat and bring to a boil. Boil for 1 minute, stirring constantly. Remove from heat and stir in the vanilla. Spread evenly over the graham cracker layer. Sprinkle with pecans. Bake in a preheated 350-degree oven for 6 to 8 minutes or until bubbly. Cool slightly. Cut into 2 1/4×1 1/4-inch bars. Yield: 4 dozen.

Sue Moulton, Laureate Epsilon Kappa
Ridgecrest, California

MIXED NUT BARS

1 1/2 cups flour	1 (11-ounce) can mixed nuts
3/4 cup packed brown sugar	1 cup butterscotch chips
1/4 teaspoon salt	1/2 cup light corn syrup
1/2 cup plus 2 tablespoons cold butter or margarine	

Combine the flour, brown sugar and salt in a bowl. Cut in the 1/2 cup butter until mixture resembles coarse crumbs. Press into a buttered 9×13-inch baking pan. Bake at 350 degrees for 10 minutes. Remove from oven and sprinkle with the mixed nuts. Combine the butterscotch chips, corn syrup and the 2 tablespoons butter in a saucepan over medium-low heat and cook until melted, stirring constantly. Pour evenly over the mixed nuts layer. Bake for 10 minutes longer; do not overbake. Cool and cut into bars. Yield: 3 dozen.

Nancy J. Baker, Laureate Omega
Beatrice, Nebraska

PECAN CREAM CHEESE BARS

1 (2-layer) package yellow cake mix	1 cup packed brown sugar
3/4 cup chopped pecans	3/4 cup chopped pecans
3/4 cup melted margarine	
16 ounces cream cheese, softened	

Combine the cake mix and 3/4 cup pecans in a bowl and mix well. Add the margarine and mix well. Press evenly into the bottom of a 9×13-inch baking pan. Blend the cream cheese and brown sugar in a bowl. Spread evenly over the cake mix mixture and sprinkle with the remaining 3/4 cup pecans. Bake at 350 degrees for 25 to 30 minutes or until the edges are brown and the cream cheese mixture is set. Cool in the pan on a wire rack. Cut into bars. Store in the refrigerator. Yield: 2 dozen.

Beth Roberson, Beta Kappa
Meeteetse, Wyoming

Phyllis Shurb, Chi, Brandon, Manitoba, Canada, makes **Christmas Shortbread Bars.** *Cream 1 cup softened margarine with 1/4 cup sugar. Mix in 2 cups flour until crumbly. Pat into a greased 9-inch square pan. Bake at 350 degrees for 20 minutes. Combine 2/3 cup chopped red or green cherries, 1/4 cup raisins, 1 1/2 cups coconut and 1/3 cup chopped walnuts in a bowl. Stir in a can of sweetened condensed milk. Spread over the baked layer and bake for 35 minutes. Cool completely before cutting into squares.*

PUMPKIN BARS

2 cups wheat or rice
  flour
1½ cups sugar
2 teaspoons baking
  powder
2 teaspoons cinnamon
1 teaspoon baking soda
¼ teaspoon salt
¼ teaspoon ground
  cloves

¼ teaspoon pumpkin pie
  spice
¼ teaspoon nutmeg
4 eggs, beaten
1 (16-ounce) can
  pumpkin
1 cup vegetable oil
Cream Cheese Frosting

Place the flour, sugar, baking powder, cinnamon, baking soda, salt, cloves, pumpkin pie spice and nutmeg in a large bowl and stir to combine. Stir in the eggs, pumpkin and vegetable oil. Spread the batter in an unbuttered 9×13-inch baking pan. Bake at 350 degrees for 25 to 30 minutes or until a wooden pick inserted in the center comes out clean. Cool for 2 hours. Spread with Cream Cheese Frosting and cut into bars. Yield: 2 dozen.

CREAM CHEESE FROSTING

3 ounces cream cheese,
  softened
¼ cup (½ stick) butter
  or margarine,
  softened

1 teaspoon vanilla
  extract
2½ cups confectioners'
  sugar, sifted

Combine the cream cheese, butter and vanilla in a mixing bowl and beat until light and fluffy. Add the confectioners' sugar gradually, beating well until the mixture is of spreading consistency.

Phyllis Kraich, Laureate Beta Epsilon
Akron, Colorado

RASPBERRY BARS

1 cup packed dark
  brown sugar
1¼ cups old-fashioned
  rolled oats
1¼ cups flour

½ teaspoon salt
¾ to 1 cup (2 sticks)
  butter, melted
Raspberry jam to taste

Place the brown sugar, rolled oats, flour and salt in a bowl and combine. Add the butter and mix well. Pat half the mixture in an unbuttered 9×11-inch baking pan. Spread raspberry jam over the top. Layer the remaining flour mixture over the raspberry jam and pat down firmly. Bake at 350 degrees for 30 minutes or until lightly browned. Cool and cut into bars. Yield: 10 to 12 servings.

Julie Van Etten, Laureate Theta Chi
Pleasanton, California

PUFFY CARAMEL WALNUT BARS

1½ cups flour
1 teaspoon baking
  powder
½ cup (1 stick) butter or
  margarine, softened
1 cup sugar
2 egg yolks
2 tablespoons milk

1 teaspoon vanilla
  extract
2 egg whites
1 cup packed light
  brown sugar
1 cup coarsely chopped
  walnuts

Sift the flour and baking powder together. Cream the butter, sugar and egg yolks in a bowl until light and fluffy. Add the milk, vanilla and flour mixture and beat until well-blended. Spread in a greased 9-inch square baking pan. Bake at 350 degrees for 20 minutes. Beat the egg whites in a mixing bowl until stiff. Beat in the brown sugar gradually. Stir in the walnuts. Spread over the warm baked layer. Bake for 20 minutes or until puffed and lightly browned. Cool for about 15 minutes. Cut into bars. Yield: 16 bars.

Griff Jappé, Laureate Delta Xi
Lehigh Acres, Florida

SPECIAL-K BARS

A platter of these bars made by my 82-year-old mother sold for seventy dollars at an auction to raise money to rebuild our church which had burned!

1 cup light corn syrup
1 cup sugar
1 cup peanut butter
5 cups Special-K cereal

2 cups butterscotch
  chips
1 cup chocolate chips

Combine the corn syrup and sugar in a saucepan over medium-low heat; heat until sugar is dissolved, stirring constantly. Remove from heat. Add the peanut butter and Special-K cereal and mix well. Spread in a buttered 10×15-inch cake pan. Melt the butterscotch chips and chocolate chips in the microwave or in a saucepan and stir to blend. Spread evenly over the Special-K layer. Let stand until set. Cut into bars. Yield: 3 dozen.

Brenda Johnson, Gamma Beta
Oak Grove, Missouri

---

*Kelly Henderson, Xi Eta, Truro, Nova Scotia, Canada, makes a delicious **No-Bake Chocolate Marshmallow Crisp Delight** by melting 4 Mars candy bars with 1 cup small marshmallows and ¼ cup butter in a saucepan and stirring in 2 cups crisp rice cereal. She presses the mixture into a greased 8×8-inch pan and chills until firm. Melt 1 cup chocolate chips with 2 tablespoons butter to spread over the top and chill before cutting into squares.*

CORNFLAKE BARS

3/4 cup (1 1/2 sticks) butter
30 marshmallows
1 cup flaked coconut

1 cup sliced almonds, toasted
3 1/2 cups cornflakes

Combine the butter and marshmallows in a medium saucepan over medium heat. Cook until melted, stirring occasionally. Remove from heat. Stir in the coconut, almonds and cornflakes. Press into an unbuttered 9×13-inch baking pan. Let stand for 30 minutes and cut into bars. Yield: 20 bars.

Shirley Grudzinski, Omicron Master
Grand Island, Nebraska

HELLO DOLLY BARS

1/4 cup (1/2 stick) butter
  or margarine, melted
1 cup crushed graham
  crackers

1 cup chocolate chips
1 cup butterscotch chips
1 (12-ounce) can
  evaporated milk

Spread the butter evenly in an 8×8-inch baking pan. Layer the graham cracker crumbs, chocolate chips and butterscotch chips in the pan. Drizzle the evaporated milk evenly over the top. Bake at 350 degrees for 35 minutes or until bubbly. Cool to room temperature and cut into small squares.
Yield: about 3 dozen.

Nancy O'Neill, Xi Beta Phi
Kingman, Arizona

CHOCOLATE COCONUT BARS

1/2 cup (1 stick) butter
1 1/2 cups graham cracker
  crumbs
1 cup semisweet
  chocolate chips
1 cup sweetened
  shredded coconut

1/2 cup chopped walnuts
  or pecans
1 (14-ounce) can
  sweetened condensed
  milk

Melt the butter in a 9×13-inch baking pan and tilt to coat the bottom. Press the crumbs firmly in the pan. Layer the chocolate chips, coconut and walnuts over the crumbs. Drizzle evenly with condensed milk. Bake at 350 degrees for 25 to 30 minutes or until bubbly. Chill and cut into bars. Yield: 2 dozen.

Rhonda Fogle, Alpha Zeta Alpha
Liberty, Missouri

CRUNCHY COCONUT SNACK BARS

2 eggs
1 cup sugar
3/4 cup (1 1/2 sticks) butter
1/2 cup graham cracker
  crumbs

2 cups miniature
  marshmallows
1 cup shredded coconut
1 cup chopped pecans

Combine the eggs, sugar and butter in a saucepan over medium heat. Cook until thickened, stirring constantly. Remove from heat. Stir in the remaining ingredients. Press into a buttered 9×13-inch baking pan. Chill, covered, in the refrigerator. Cut into squares. Yield: 2 to 3 dozen.

Jenny Knight, Preceptor Alpha Zeta
Toledo, Oregon

PEANUT BUTTER OATMEAL BARS

1 cup brown sugar
4 cups rolled oats
1/2 cup light corn
  syrup
1 cup (2 sticks) butter,
  melted
1/2 cup (1 stick) butter,
  softened

2 cups confectioners'
  sugar
2 tablespoons vanilla
  instant pudding mix
3 tablespoons milk
1 cup peanut butter
2 cups milk chocolate
  chips

Combine the brown sugar, oats, corn syrup and melted butter in a bowl and mix well. Pat into an unbuttered 9×13-inch baking pan. Bake in a preheated 400-degree oven for 10 minutes. Cool. Combine the softened butter, confectioners' sugar, pudding mix and milk in a mixing bowl and beat until fluffy. Spread over the crust. Cool for 1 hour. Melt the peanut butter and chocolate chips in a saucepan over low heat, stirring frequently until smooth. Spread over the top. Chill, covered, until serving time. Yield: 2 to 3 dozen.

Shery A. Kaskie, Epsilon Eta
Hawarden, Iowa

OATMEAL RAISIN BARS

1 cup (2 sticks) butter
1 1/2 cups packed brown
  sugar
1 1/2 cups plus 2
  tablespoons flour
1 1/2 cups rolled oats

1 1/2 teaspoons vanilla
  extract
Pinch of salt
1 cup raisins
1/2 cup granulated sugar
1 cup water

Cream the butter and brown sugar in a mixing bowl until fluffy. Stir in the 1 1/2 cups flour, oats, 1 teaspoon of the vanilla and salt. Pat half the mixture in an unbuttered 9×13-inch baking pan. Combine the raisins, 2 tablespoons flour, granulated sugar, water and the remaining 1/2 teaspoon vanilla in a saucepan over medium-low heat. Cook until thickened, stirring constantly. Spread over the flour mixture in the baking pan. Layer the remaining flour mixture over the top and press. Bake at 350 degrees for 30 minutes or until lightly browned. Cool and cut into bars. Yield: 15 servings.

Dollris Hanson, Zeta Master
Tioga, North Dakota

ORANGE COCONUT DREAM BARS

3/4 cup (1 1/2 sticks) plus 3 tablespoons butter, softened
3 tablespoons plus 2 3/4 cups packed brown sugar
1 1/2 cups plus 3 tablespoons flour
1 1/2 cups shredded coconut
3/4 cup chopped walnuts or pecans
3 eggs, beaten
3/4 teaspoon vanilla extract
1 1/2 cups confectioners' sugar
3 tablespoons orange or lemon juice

Combine the 3/4 cup butter, the 3 tablespoons brown sugar and the 1 1/2 cups flour in a mixing bowl and beat until well mixed. Press into a buttered 9×13-inch baking pan. Bake at 350 degrees for 5 to 10 minutes or until light brown. Mix the 2 3/4 cups brown sugar, coconut, chopped nuts, eggs, the 3 tablespoons flour and vanilla in a mixing bowl. Pour over the crust and bake for 20 to 30 minutes or until bubbly. Combine the confectioners' sugar, orange juice and the 3 tablespoons butter in a small mixing bowl and beat until smooth. Spread over the warm coconut layer. Cut into bars before completely cool. Cool and serve.
Yield: 1 to 3 dozen.

Mary Ann Dale, Laureate Eta
Gadsden, Alabama

MARSHMALLOW SQUARES

2 eggs, beaten
1 cup granulated sugar
1/2 cup (1 stick) butter
1 teaspoon vanilla extract
1/4 cup dried shredded coconut
2 cups graham cracker crumbs
1 cup miniature marshmallows
1/2 cup chopped walnuts (optional)
Butter Frosting

Combine the eggs, granulated sugar and butter in the top of a double boiler over simmering water. Cook until thickened, stirring constantly. Cool to room temperature. Stir in the next 5 ingredients. Press with a spatula into an unbuttered 9×9-inch or 10×10-inch baking pan. Chill until set. Frost with Butter Frosting.
Yield: 3 dozen.

BUTTER FROSTING

1 1/2 cups confectioners' sugar
1/2 cup (1 stick) butter, softened
1 egg
1 teaspoon vanilla extract

Combine all the ingredients in a small mixing bowl and beat for 3 minutes until spreadable consistency.

Wanda Rathbone, Alpha Iota Master
Sault Ste. Marie, Ontario, Canada

BUTTER CRACKER SQUARES

1 (14-ounce) can sweetened condensed milk
1/2 (16-ounce) package butter crackers, crushed
1 (8-ounce) package English toffee bits
1/4 cup (1/2 stick) butter, softened
1 1/2 cups confectioners' sugar
Pinch of salt
1 teaspoon vanilla extract
1 to 2 tablespoons milk

Combine the condensed milk, butter crackers and English toffee bits in a bowl, reserving a few bits for garnish; mix well. Press into a buttered 8×8-inch baking pan. Bake at 350 degrees for 15 minutes or until golden brown. Cool completely. Combine the butter, confectioners' sugar, salt, vanilla and milk in a mixing bowl and beat until spreadable consistency. Frost the baked layer and sprinkle with the reserved English toffee bits. Cut into 1-inch squares.
Yield: about 5 dozen.

Anita Hebblethwaite, Gamma Zeta
Swastika, Ontario, Canada

OLD-FASHIONED CAKELIKE BROWNIES

1 cup (2 sticks) butter or margarine
2 cups sugar
4 eggs
1 1/2 cups flour
2/3 cup baking cocoa
1 cup chopped pecans

Cream the butter and sugar in a mixing bowl until light and fluffy. Add the eggs 1 at a time, beating at medium speed after each addition. Add the flour and baking cocoa and beat until smooth. Stir in the pecans. Spread in a 9×13-inch baking pan that has been sprayed with nonstick cooking spray. Bake at 350 degrees for 30 minutes or until edges are firm.
Yield: 2 dozen.

Demitra Green, Xi Mu Upsilon
Mundelein, Illinois

MARSHMALLOW CREME BROWNIES

2 cups sugar
1/2 cup (1 stick) butter, softened
1/2 cup milk
1 cup chopped walnuts or pecans
1 1/2 cups flour
2 ounces unsweetened chocolate, melted
1 tablespoon light corn syrup
4 eggs, beaten
1 teaspoon vanilla extract
Pinch of salt
1 (8-ounce) jar marshmallow creme

Combine the sugar, butter, milk, chopped nuts, flour, melted chocolate, corn syrup, eggs, vanilla and salt in the order listed in a mixing bowl, mixing at medium speed after each addition. Spread in a buttered 9×13-

inch baking pan. Bake at 350 degrees for 18 to 20 minutes or until edges are firm. Spread the marshmallow creme over the warm brownies. Frost with chocolate frosting. Cool and cut into squares.
Yield: 2 to 4 dozen.

Wanda Rutherford, Kappa Xi
Purcell, Oklahoma

FROSTED BROWNIES

1/2 cup (1 stick) butter,	*1 (16-ounce) can*
softened	*chocolate syrup*
1 cup sugar	*1 cup flour*
4 eggs	*1 cup chopped walnuts*
1 teaspoon vanilla	*or pecans*
extract	*Brownie Frosting*
Dash of salt	

Combine the butter, sugar, eggs, vanilla, salt, chocolate syrup and flour in a mixing bowl and mix well. Stir in the chopped nuts. Spread in a buttered 8×8-inch baking pan. Bake at 350 degrees for 25 to 30 minutes or until edges are firm. Cool. Frost with Brownie Frosting. Cut into squares.
Yield: 15 to 20 brownies.

BROWNIE FROSTING

11/2 cups sugar	*1 cup chocolate chips*
6 tablespoons milk	*1 teaspoon vanilla*
6 tablespoons butter	*extract*

Combine the sugar, milk and butter in a saucepan over medium-high heat and bring to a boil, stirring constantly. Boil for 1 minute without stirring. Remove from heat. Stir in the chocolate chips and vanilla; beat well until spreading consistency.

Lucille Finn, Iota Master
Salem, Oregon

CHOCOLATE CHIP BROWNIES

1 (4-ounce) chocolate	*1 cup chocolate chips*
instant pudding mix	*Low-fat whipped*
2 cups skim milk	*topping (optional)*
1 (2-layer) package	
chocolate cake mix	

Combine the pudding mix and milk in a large mixing bowl. Add the chocolate cake mix and beat at medium speed until well blended. Stir in the chocolate chips. Spread in a buttered and floured 10×15-inch baking pan. Bake at 350 degrees for 20 minutes. Cool and cut into squares. Serve with whipped topping. Yield: 2 dozen.

Sue Kerouac, Preceptor Zeta Nu
Springfield, Illinois

GOOEY BROWNIES

11/4 cups sifted flour	*2 cups sugar*
1 teaspoon salt	*1 teaspoon vanilla*
1 cup (2 sticks) butter	*extract*
2 ounces bittersweet	*4 eggs*
chocolate	
4 ounces unsweetened	
chocolate	

Sift the flour and salt together. Melt the butter, bittersweet chocolate and unsweetened chocolate in a saucepan over low heat. Add 1 cup of the sugar and cook for 2 minutes, stirring constantly. Remove from heat and stir in vanilla. Place the eggs and the remaining 1 cup sugar in a bowl and whisk to combine. Stir half the egg mixture slowly into the chocolate mixture. Add the sugar to the remaining egg mixture and beat at medium speed for about 4 minutes or until light and thickened; fold into the chocolate mixture. Fold in the flour mixture. Scrape into an unbuttered 8×8-inch glass baking dish. Bake at 350 degrees for about 43 minutes or until barely set. Cool and cut into 21/2×11/2-inch bars.
Yield: 15 brownies.

Melanie Phealt, Lambda Lambda
Emporia, Kansas

CARAMEL BROWNIES

1 (44-count) package	*3/4 cup (11/2 sticks)*
caramels	*margarine, melted*
2/3 cup (5 ounces)	*1 teaspoon vanilla*
evaporated milk	*extract*
1 (2-layer) package	*1 cup milk chocolate*
German chocolate	*chips*
cake mix	

Unwrap the caramels and place in a microwave-safe bowl. Microwave on Low for 2 minutes. Continue to microwave for 2 minutes at a time until caramels are melted. Stir in 1/3 cup of the evaporated milk and continue to microwave, stirring occasionally until well blended. Combine the dry cake mix, margarine, the remaining 1/3 cup evaporated milk and vanilla in a bowl; stir by hand until a soft dough forms. Press a little more than half the dough into a lightly buttered 9×13-inch baking pan. Bake at 350 degrees for 8 minutes. Remove from oven and layer the chocolate chips over the top. Pour the warm caramel mixture evenly over the chips. Flatten pieces of the remaining dough and arrange over the top. Bake for 15 to 20 minutes longer or until brownies test done.
Yield: 2 to 3 dozen.

Cathy Gilliland, Alpha Kappa
Rose Hill, Iowa

CHEESECAKE BROWNIES

1 (22-ounce) package fudge brownie mix	1 tablespoon cornstarch
1/2 cup shredded coconut	1 (14-ounce) can sweetened condensed milk
1/2 cup milk chocolate chips	1 egg
1/2 cup chopped walnuts or pecans	2 teaspoons vanilla extract
8 ounces cream cheese, softened	1 (16-ounce) can chocolate frosting
2 tablespoons butter	

Prepare the brownie mix using the package directions; stir in the coconut, chocolate chips and chopped nuts. Spread in a well-buttered 9×13-inch baking pan. Combine the cream cheese, butter and cornstarch in a small mixing bowl and beat until fluffy. Add the condensed milk gradually, beating well. Add the egg and the vanilla, beating until smooth. Pour evenly over the brownie batter. Bake at 350 degrees for 45 minutes or until edges are firm. Cool and frost with the chocolate frosting. Cut into bars. Store in an airtight container in the refrigerator. Yield: 2 to 3 dozen.

Tammy Jens
Grand Junction, Colorado

CHOCOLATE CRUNCH BROWNIES

1 cup (2 sticks) butter or margarine	1/2 teaspoon salt
2 cups sugar	1 (7-ounce) jar marshmallow creme
4 eggs	1 cup creamy peanut butter
6 tablespoons baking cocoa	2 cups semisweet chocolate chips
1 cup flour	3 cups crisp rice cereal
2 teaspoons vanilla extract	

Cream the butter and sugar in a mixing bowl until light and fluffy. Add the eggs 1 at a time, beating well after each addition. Stir in the baking cocoa, flour, vanilla and salt. Pat into a greased 9×13-inch baking pan. Bake at 350 degrees for 20 to 25 minutes. Do not overbake. Cool. Spread marshmallow creme over the cooled layer. Combine the peanut butter and chocolate chips in a saucepan over low heat and cook until melted, stirring constantly. Stir in the cereal. Spread over the marshmallow creme layer. Chill before cutting into squares. Store in the refrigerator. Yield: about 45 servings.

Sharmis Emig, Rho Beta
Goodland, Kansas

CHOCOLATE MARSHMALLOW BROWNIES

1 1/4 cups margarine, softened	1 (16-ounce) package miniature marshmallows
2 cups sugar	1/2 cup evaporated milk
4 eggs	1 (1-pound) package confectioners' sugar
1 1/2 cups flour	1/2 cup chopped pecans
2/3 cup baking cocoa	
2 teaspoons vanilla extract	

Cream 1 cup of the margarine and sugar in a mixing bowl until light and fluffy. Add the eggs 1 at a time, beating well after each addition. Stir in the flour, 1/3 cup of the baking cocoa and 1 teaspoon of the vanilla. Spread in a buttered and floured 9×13-inch baking pan. Bake at 350 degrees for 30 minutes. Layer the marshmallows over the top of the hot cake. Bake for 10 or 15 minutes longer or until marshmallows are puffed and golden brown. Cool and frost with a mixture of the remaining 1/4 cup margarine, evaporated milk, confectioners' sugar, the remaining 1/3 cup baking cocoa, the remaining 1 teaspoon vanilla and pecans. Cut into small squares. Yield: 2 to 3 dozen.

Judy Rounkles, Preceptor Sigma
Excelsior Springs, Missouri

BUTTERSCOTCH AND MARSHMALLOW BROWNIES

1 cup butterscotch chips	1/2 teaspoon salt
1/2 cup (1 stick) margarine	2 teaspoons baking powder
2 eggs	2 cups miniature marshmallows
1 teaspoon vanilla extract	2 cups chocolate chips
2/3 cup packed brown sugar	1/2 cup chopped walnuts or pecans
1 1/2 cups flour	

Melt the butterscotch chips and margarine in a saucepan and stir to blend. Remove from heat. Combine the eggs and vanilla in a mixing bowl and beat well. Beat in the brown sugar. Sift the flour, salt and baking powder together. Add to the egg mixture alternately with the butterscotch mixture. Stir in the marshmallows, chocolate chips and chopped nuts. Spread in a buttered 9×13-inch baking pan. Bake at 350 degrees for 20 to 25 minutes or until edges are firm; do not overbake. Yield: 2 to 3 dozen.

Marilyn Shaw, Laureate Gamma Zeta
Pella, Iowa

PECAN PIE BROWNIES

2³/₄ cups flour
1¹/₄ cups packed brown
   sugar
1¹/₄ cups butter
4 eggs
1 cup light corn syrup
2 tablespoons vanilla
   extract
¹/₄ teaspoon salt
1¹/₂ cups chopped pecans

Combine the flour and ¹/₄ cup of the brown sugar in a bowl and mix well. Cut in 1 cup of the butter until mixture resembles coarse crumbs. Press firmly into an unbuttered 9×13-inch baking pan. Bake at 350 degrees for 12 to 15 minutes or until lightly browned. Melt the remaining ¹/₄ cup butter. Combine the eggs and the remaining 1 cup brown sugar in a mixing bowl and mix well. Stir in the remaining ingredients. Pour evenly over the crust. Bake for 25 to 30 minutes or until set. Cool and then chill in the refrigerator. Cut into small pieces. Yield: 4 to 5 dozen.

Colleen Burrichter, Laureate Sigma
Ottawa, Kansas

IRISH WHISKEY BROWNIES

2 cups milk chocolate
   chips
¹/₂ cup (1 stick) butter
¹/₂ cup sugar
1 teaspoon vanilla
   extract
2 eggs
2 teaspoons instant
   coffee granules
2 tablespoons Irish
   whiskey
1 cup flour

Melt 1 cup of the chocolate chips and butter in a saucepan over low heat, stirring frequently. Remove from heat. Beat the sugar, vanilla and eggs in a mixing bowl until smooth. Beat in the chocolate mixture. Dissolve the coffee granules in the Irish whiskey and stir into the sugar mixture. Stir in the flour gradually. Pour into a buttered 8×8-inch baking pan. Bake at 350 degrees for 30 minutes or until edges are firm. Sprinkle with the remaining chocolate chips, spreading chips as they melt. Yield: 16 to 25 servings.

Mary Ann Borrmann, Preceptor Omega
Beaufort, South Carolina

BEST CHOCOLATE BROWNIES

1 cup flour
³/₄ cup granulated sugar
¹/₄ cup packed brown
   sugar
¹/₂ teaspoon baking soda
¹/₄ cup buttermilk
¹/₄ cup (¹/₂ stick) butter
¹/₄ cup shortening
¹/₂ cup brewed coffee
2 tablespoons baking
   cocoa
1 large egg
1 teaspoon coffee liqueur
   or vanilla extract
Chocolate Frosting

Mix the flour, granulated sugar and brown sugar in a large mixing bowl. Dissolve the baking soda in the buttermilk. Bring the butter, shortening, coffee and baking cocoa to a boil in a heavy saucepan over medium-high heat, stirring constantly. Pour the coffee mixture over the flour mixture. Stir in the buttermilk mixture, egg and liqueur with a wooden spoon. Pour into a buttered 9×11-inch baking pan. Bake at 375 degrees for 20 minutes or until edges are firm. Cool and frost with Chocolate Frosting. Yield: 16 servings.

CHOCOLATE FROSTING

9 ounces semisweet
   chocolate
3 tablespoons butter
⁵/₈ cup milk
3 cups confectioners'
   sugar

Combine the chocolate and butter in a microwave-safe bowl and microwave on High for 1 to 2 minutes, stirring occasionally until melted. Stir in the milk and confectioners' sugar.

Linda McGovern, Delta Theta
Batesville, Indiana

❖ KAHLUA COLADA BROWNIES

3 eggs, lightly beaten
³/₄ cup granulated sugar
¹/₂ cup packed brown
   sugar
¹/₄ cup vegetable oil
²/₃ cup plus 2
   tablespoons Kahlúa
1¹/₂ cups flour
1¹/₂ teaspoons baking
   powder
1 (20-ounce) can crushed
   pineapple, drained
1 cup flaked coconut
1 cup chopped
   macadamia nuts

Combine the eggs, granulated sugar, brown sugar, vegetable oil and Kahlúa in a mixing bowl and mix well. Stir in a mixture of the flour and baking powder gradually. Fold in the pineapple, ³/₄ cup of the coconut and macadamia nuts. Pour into a buttered 9×13-inch baking pan. Sprinkle with the remaining ¹/₄ cup coconut. Bake at 350 degrees for 30 to 35 minutes or until edges are firm. Cool in the pan and cut into bars. Yield: 2 dozen.

Patricia R. Soard, Theta Psi
Cookeville, Tennessee

Aliene Gribas, Zeta Master, Havre, Montana, makes **Zucchini Brownies** *by creaming ¹/₂ cup margarine ¹/₂ cup vegetable oil and 1³/₄ cups sugar in a bowl until light. Stir in 2 eggs, ¹/₂ cup buttermilk and ¹/₂ teaspoon vanilla extract. Add a sifted mixture of 2¹/₂ cups flour, ¹/₂ teaspoon baking powder, 1 teaspoon baking soda and ¹/₄ cup baking cocoa and mix well. Stir in 2 cups shredded zucchini, 1 cup chocolate chips and ¹/₂ cup chopped walnuts. Pour into a buttered 10×15-inch baking pan. Bake at 325 degrees for 20 to 25 minutes. Cool and cut into bars.*

Cookies & Candy

APPLE COOKIES WITH CREAMY CARAMEL FROSTING

1/2 cup shortening	*1/4 cup apple juice*
1 1/2 cups packed light brown sugar	*1 cup finely chopped peeled apples*
1 egg	*1 cup chopped walnuts*
2 cups flour	*1 cup raisins*
1 teaspoon baking soda	*Creamy Caramel Frosting*
1/2 teaspoon nutmeg	
3/4 teaspoon cinnamon	

Cream the shortening and brown sugar in a mixing bowl until smooth and fluffy. Add the egg and mix well. Add a mixture of the flour, baking soda, nutmeg and cinnamon alternately with the apple juice, mixing well after each addition. Stir in the apples, walnuts and raisins. Drop by scant tablespoonfuls 2 inches apart onto a buttered cookie sheet. Bake at 400 degrees for 11 to 14 minutes or until lightly browned. Cool and frost. Store in airtight containers. Yield: 3 dozen.

CREAMY CARAMEL FROSTING

1/3 cup margarine	*3/4 teaspoon vanilla extract*
3/4 cup packed brown sugar	*1 1/2 to 2 cups confectioners' sugar*
3 tablespoons milk	

Melt the margarine in a saucepan. Stir in the brown sugar and cook over low heat for 2 minutes. Remove from heat and cool slightly. Add the milk, vanilla and confectioners' sugar; beat until creamy.

Maggie Ballentine, Laureate Eta
Elida, Ohio

BANANA COOKIES

2 1/2 cups flour	*1 cup sugar*
1/2 teaspoon baking soda	*2 eggs*
1/2 teaspoon salt	*1 teaspoon vanilla extract*
1/2 cup (1 stick) butter or margarine	*2/3 cup mashed banana*

Sift the flour, baking soda and salt together. Cream the butter and sugar in a mixing bowl until light and fluffy. Add the eggs and beat until creamy. Beat in the vanilla. Add the banana alternately with the flour mixture, stirring after each addition until smooth. Drop by teaspoonfuls 2 inches apart onto a buttered cookie sheet. Bake at 400 degrees for 8 to 10 minutes or until puffy and golden. Remove immediately to a wire rack or paper towel to cool. Yield: 3 dozen.

Nancy Mattison-Trevino, Psi Delta
Plainfield, Illinois

TWICE-BAKED COOKIES (BISCOTTI)

6 medium eggs, or 3 extra-large eggs	*3/4 cup (1 1/2 sticks) margarine, melted*
1 1/2 cups sugar	*1 tablespoon baking powder*
1/2 teaspoon vanilla extract or lemon extract	*5 cups flour*

Combine all the ingredients in a large bowl and mix well. Divide dough in half and roll each half into a 12-inch-long log. Place on 2 cookie sheets. Bake at 375 degrees for 30 minutes. Let stand for 10 minutes. Cut into 1-inch slices and lay the slices flat on the cookie sheets. Return to the oven and bake for 16 to 20 minutes longer or until lightly browned on each side, turning once halfway through the baking time. Yield: 2 to 3 dozen.

Sarah Basile, Nu Eta
West Middlesex, Pennsylvania

CHEESECAKE COOKIES

8 ounces cream cheese, softened	*1 (18-ounce) package yellow cake mix*
1/4 cup (1/2 stick) margarine, softened	*Red or green candied cherries or both, halved*
1 egg	*Pecan halves*
1/2 teaspoon vanilla extract	

Combine the cream cheese, margarine, egg and vanilla in a mixing bowl and beat until smooth and fluffy. Add the dry cake mix and mix well. Drop by teaspoonfuls 2 inches apart onto a buttered cookie sheet. Top each with a cherry half or pecan half. Bake at 350 degrees for 10 minutes; do not overbake. Remove at once to a wire rack to cool. Yield: about 6 dozen.

Sallie Belperche, Laureate Mu
Winter Park, Florida

CARROT CAKE COOKIES WITH LEMON GLAZE

1¹/₂ cups unbleached flour	5 tablespoons milk
¹/₂ cup whole wheat flour	¹/₄ cup maple syrup
¹/₂ cup packed brown sugar	1 egg
1 cup freshly grated carrots	¹/₂ cup canola oil
2 teaspoons baking powder	1 tablespoon melted butter
1 teaspoon cinnamon	1¹/₂ cups confectioners' sugar
¹/₂ teaspoon salt	2¹/₂ tablespoons fresh lemon juice
	1 tablespoon grated lemon zest

Combine the unbleached flour, whole wheat flour, brown sugar, carrots, baking powder, cinnamon and salt in a large mixing bowl and mix well. Add the milk, maple syrup, egg and canola oil and beat at low speed just until blended. Drop (2-tablespoon) spoonfuls of dough 2 inches apart onto a cookie sheet that has been coated with nonstick cooking spray. Bake at 350 degrees for 10 minutes; cool on a wire rack. Combine the melted butter, confectioners' sugar, lemon juice and lemon zest in a mixing bowl and beat until smooth. Frost the cooled cookies. Let stand until frosting is set. Yield: about 3 dozen.

Diana Hersey, Xi Rho Beta
Duncanville, Texas

CHERRY DATE SKILLET COOKIES

1 cup (2 sticks) butter	3 cups crisp rice cereal
1 cup firmly packed brown sugar	4 cups flaked coconut
1 (8-ounce) package chopped dates	¹/₂ cup chopped maraschino cherries
1 egg	1 tablespoon vanilla extract

Melt the butter in a 10-inch skillet over medium-low heat. Stir in the brown sugar and dates; remove from heat. Stir in the egg. Return to heat and cook over medium heat for about 4 to 6 minutes or until mixture comes to a full boil, stirring constantly. Boil for 1 minute, stirring constantly. Remove from heat. Add the cereal, 1 cup of the coconut, maraschino cherries and vanilla and stir until moistened. Let stand for 10 minutes. Roll into 1-inch balls. Roll the balls in the remaining coconut. Yield: 5 dozen.

Ardene MacLeod, Upsilon Kappa
Turlock, California

CHOCOLATE THUMBPRINTS

1 cup (2 sticks) butter, melted	3 cups flour
2 cups sugar	¹/₂ teaspoon baking soda
2 eggs	¹/₄ cup (¹/₂ stick) butter, softened
1 cup baking cocoa	¹/₃ cup milk
1 tablespoon vanilla extract	¹/₄ cup baking cocoa
¹/₂ teaspoon baking powder	1 (1-pound) box confectioners' sugar

Combine the melted butter, sugar and eggs in a large mixing bowl and mix well. Add 1 cup baking cocoa, vanilla and a mixture of the baking powder, flour and baking soda; mix well. Roll into 1-inch balls and arrange on a nonstick cookie sheet. Bake at 350 degrees for 5 minutes. Press with your thumb to make a depression in the center of each cookie. Let stand until cool. Combine the butter, milk, ¹/₄ cup baking cocoa and confectioners' sugar in a mixing bowl and beat until smooth and fluffy. Drop 1 tablespoon into each thumbprint. Yield: 3 dozen.

Lashauna Kelley, Zeta Xi
Clovis, New Mexico

STOVETOP FUDGE COOKIES

³/₄ cup butter	2 tablespoons water
1¹/₂ cups packed brown sugar	2¹/₂ cups flour
2 cups semisweet chocolate chips	1¹/₄ teaspoons baking soda
2 eggs	¹/₂ teaspoon salt

Melt the butter in a large saucepan over low heat. Add the brown sugar and 1¹/₂ cups of the chocolate chips and cook until melted and smooth, stirring frequently. Remove from heat. Add the eggs and stir until well mixed. Add the water and a mixture of the flour, baking soda and salt; stir until smooth. Stir in the remaining chocolate chips. Drop by teaspoonfuls 2 inches apart onto an unbuttered cookie sheet. Bake at 350 degrees for 8 to 12 minutes; cookies will appear cracked and very moist. Let stand for 2 minutes before removing from the cookie sheet. Yield: about 3 dozen.

Jill Czuczman, Zeta Theta
Brooklin, Ontario, Canada

CHOCOLATE OATMEAL SANDWICH COOKIES

These cookies are remembered and treasured by all who eat them.

1¹/₂ cups (3 sticks) butter, softened	2 cups flour
1 cup sugar	2 cups semisweet chocolate chips
¹/₄ cup orange juice	2 tablespoons olive oil
3 cups quick-cooking oats	

Cream the butter and sugar in a mixing bowl until light and fluffy. Blend in the orange juice. Add a mixture of the oats and flour; mix well. Chill, covered, for 10 minutes. Roll into 1-inch balls. Arrange on an unbuttered cookie sheet and press into 2-inch circles. Bake at 350 degrees for 10 to 12 minutes or until edges are firm. Remove to a wire rack to cool. Combine the chocolate chips and olive oil in a microwave-safe bowl. Microwave on High for 1 minute and stir. Microwave for 1 minute longer; stir until smooth. Spread 2 tablespoons of the chocolate mixture over the flat side of each of half the cookies; top with the remaining cookie halves. Drizzle with the remaining chocolate mixture. Yield: 2¹/₂ dozen.

Michelle Triano, Eta
Oviedo, Florida

CHOCOLATE MARSHMALLOW COOKIES

³/₄ cup (1¹/₂ sticks) margarine	1³/₄ cups flour
2 cups sugar	¹/₂ cup baking cocoa
1 egg	¹/₂ teaspoon baking soda
1 teaspoon vanilla extract	10 to 20 marshmallows, halved
¹/₂ cup milk	¹/₂ cup chocolate chips

Cream ¹/₂ cup of the margarine and 1 cup of the sugar in a mixing bowl until light and fluffy. Add the egg, vanilla and ¹/₄ cup of the milk and mix well. Stir in a mixture of the flour, baking cocoa and baking soda. Drop by teaspoonfuls onto a buttered cookie sheet. Bake at 350 degrees for 8 minutes; do not overbake. Press a marshmallow half cut side down over each cookie. Bake for 2 minutes longer. Combine ¹/₄ cup margarine, the remaining 1 cup sugar and the remaining ¹/₄ cup milk in a saucepan; bring to a boil. Add the chocolate chips; stir until heat melts the chocolate chips and the mixture begins to thicken. Frost the cooled cookies. Yield: 20 to 30 cookies.

Aleda Caudle, Preceptor Sigma
Rockford, Illinois

FUDGY BONBONS

Use mint-flavored chocolate chips, Hugs, or Kisses if you desire and if you can find them.

2 cups semisweet chocolate chips	2 cups flour
¹/₄ cup (¹/₂ stick) margarine	1 teaspoon vanilla extract
1 (14-ounce) can sweetened condensed milk	24 Hershey's Hugs chocolates
	24 Hershey's Kisses chocolates

Place the chocolate chips and margarine in a microwave-safe bowl. Microwave until melted. Stir in the condensed milk. Stir in the flour and vanilla. Shape the flour mixture around the Hugs and Kisses, forming slightly flattened balls. Arrange 1 inch apart on an unbuttered cookie sheet. Bake at 350 degrees for 6 to 8 minutes; do not overbake or cookies will be dry; cookies should be soft and shiny and will firm as they cool. Dust with confectioners' sugar when cool. Yield: about 4 dozen.

Kristine DeMarinis, Xi Beta Xi
Fairfax, Virginia

CHOCOLATE COOKIES WITH PEPPERMINT FILLING

These cookies melt in your mouth. You may tint the filling pink or green if you like, depending on the holiday.

¹/₂ cup shortening	¹/₂ teaspoon baking powder
¹/₂ cup sugar	
1 egg	3 tablespoons heavy cream
2 ounces unsweetened chocolate, melted and cooled	¹/₄ teaspoon peppermint extract
1³/₄ cups flour	2 cups confectioners' sugar
1 teaspoon salt	

Combine the shortening, sugar and egg in a mixing bowl and mix until smooth. Blend in the chocolate. Stir in a mixture of the flour, salt and baking powder. Shape into a smooth roll 2 inches in diameter. Chill, wrapped in waxed paper, for several hours. Slice the dough into ¹/₈-inch-thick circles with a sharp knife. Arrange on a lightly buttered baking sheet. Bake in a preheated 400-degree oven for about 7 minutes or until edges are firm. Blend the cream, peppermint extract and the confectioners' sugar in a bowl and spread generously between the cookies to make sandwich cookies. Yield: 2¹/₂ to 3 dozen.

Corky Egendoenfer, Beta Eta
Bryant, Arkansas

CHOCOLATE CHIP COOKIES

2/3 cup shortening
2/3 cup (1 1/3 sticks) butter, softened
1 cup granulated sugar
1 cup packed brown sugar
2 eggs
2 teaspoons vanilla extract
3 1/2 cups flour
1 teaspoon baking soda
1 teaspoon salt
2 cups semisweet chocolate chips

Combine the shortening, butter, granulated sugar, brown sugar, eggs and vanilla in a large bowl and mix well. Mix in a mixture of the flour, baking soda and salt. Stir in the chocolate chips. Drop by rounded teaspoonfuls 2 inches apart onto an unbuttered cookie sheet. Bake at 375 degrees for 8 to 10 minutes or until light brown. Cool slightly before removing from the cookie sheet to a wire rack. Yield: 7 dozen.

Carla McDaniel, Preceptor Delta
Centralia, Illinois

CHOCOLATE CHIP PUDDING COOKIES

1 cup shortening
1 1/2 cups margarine, softened
1 1/2 cups packed brown sugar
1 1/2 cups granulated
4 teaspoons vanilla extract
4 eggs
1 1/3 cups dry vanilla instant pudding mix
2 teaspoons salt
2 teaspoons baking soda
6 cups flour
3 cups chocolate chips

Combine the shortening, margarine, brown sugar, granulated sugar, vanilla, eggs and a mixture of the dry pudding mix, salt, baking soda and flour in a large bowl; mix well. Stir in the chocolate chips. Drop by teaspoonfuls 2 inches apart onto an unbuttered cookie sheet. Bake at 375 degrees for 8 to 10 minutes or until light brown. Yield: 6 dozen.

Sharon Lorentz, Xi Alpha Nu
Berryville, Arkansas

FRESH PUMPKIN CHOCOLATE CHIP COOKIES

2 cups puréed cooked fresh pumpkin
1 cup sugar
1/2 cup vegetable oil
1 egg
1 teaspoon baking soda dissolved in 1 teaspoon milk
1 teaspoon vanilla extract
2 cups flour
2 teaspoons baking powder
1 teaspoon cinnamon
1/4 teaspoon five-spice powder
1/2 teaspoon salt (optional)
1 cup semisweet chocolate chips or milk chocolate chips

Combine the pumpkin, sugar, vegetable oil, egg, baking soda mixture and vanilla in a large mixing bowl and mix until smooth. Add a mixture of the flour, baking powder, cinnamon, five-spice powder and salt and mix well. Stir in the chocolate chips. Drop by teaspoonfuls 1 inch apart onto a nonstick cookie sheet. Bake at 375 degrees for 10 to 12 minutes or until set. Yield: 2 dozen.

Larrianne Rodriguez, Delta Epsilon
Twin Falls, Idaho

PEANUT CHOCOLATE CHIP COOKIES

1 cup crunchy peanut butter
2 eggs
1 cup shortening
1 cup packed brown sugar
1 cup granulated sugar
1 cup chocolate chips
2 cups flour
2 teaspoons baking soda
1/4 teaspoon salt

Combine the first 6 ingredients and a mixture of the flour, baking soda and salt in a large bowl; mix well until mixture forms a large ball. Drop by teaspoonfuls 2 inches apart onto a buttered cookie sheet and flatten with a fork. Bake at 375 degrees for 10 to 12 minutes. Cool on the cookie sheet before removing to a wire rack. Yield: 6 dozen.

Ghislaine Regaudie, Preceptor Alpha Delta
Sudbury, Ontario, Canada

CINNAMON STICKS

1/3 cup (2/3 stick) butter or margarine, softened
1 1/2 cups flour
1/2 cup granulated sugar
1/2 cup packed brown sugar
1 egg
1 teaspoon cinnamon
1/2 teaspoon vanilla extract
1/4 teaspoon salt
1/2 cup finely chopped walnuts or pecans

Line a 5×9×3-inch loaf pan with foil and spray with nonstick cooking spray. Place the butter in a large mixing bowl and beat at medium speed for 30 seconds. Add 3/4 cup of the flour, granulated sugar, brown sugar, egg, cinnamon, vanilla and salt and beat until well mixed. Add the remaining flour and mix well. Stir in the chopped nuts. Press the mixture into the prepared loaf pan; smooth the surface with the back of a spoon. Chill, covered, for 8 to 10 hours. Lift the dough from the pan. Cut crosswise (parallel to the short sides) into 1/4-inch-thick slices. Cut in half lengthwise, making 2 sticks from each slice. Arrange on a buttered cookie sheet. Bake at 350 degrees for 10 minutes or until firm. Yield: 72 pieces.

Elaine Sills, Beta Gamma Master
El Paso, Texas

DATE PINWHEEL COOKIES

8 ounces dates, chopped
1/2 cup water
1 cup granulated sugar
1/2 cup (1 stick) butter, softened
1/2 cup firmly packed brown sugar
1 egg, well beaten
1/2 teaspoon vanilla extract
2 cups sifted flour
1/2 teaspoon baking soda
1/2 teaspoon salt
1 cup pecans, chopped

Combine the dates, water and granulated sugar in a saucepan over medium heat. Cook for about 3 minutes or until thickened, stirring constantly. Let stand until cool. Cream the butter and brown sugar in a mixing bowl until light and fluffy. Add the egg and beat well. Beat in the vanilla. Sift the flour, baking soda and salt together. Add to the creamed mixture; stir until smooth. Chill, wrapped in plastic wrap, for 2 hours or longer. Combine the date mixture and chopped pecans in a bowl and mix well. Divide the dough into 2 portions (for smaller cookies, divide into 3 portions). Roll 1/4 inch thick on a floured surface. Spread with the pecan mixture. Roll as for a jelly roll to enclose the filling. Wrap in waxed paper and freeze until baking time. Cut into 1-inch slices. Place cut side down on a nonstick cookie sheet. Bake in a preheated 400-degree oven for 8 to 10 minutes. Cool on the cookie sheet for 1 minute and remove to a wire rack to cool completely. Yield: 3 dozen.

Marcine Bolsins, Beta Kappa Mu
Hilltop Lakes, Texas

DATE PECAN COOKIES

1 cup margarine, softened
1 1/2 cups sugar
3 egg yolks
1 teaspoon vanilla extract
1/8 teaspoon salt
1 teaspoon baking soda
1/4 teaspoon cloves
1 teaspoon cinnamon
2 tablespoons buttermilk
2 1/2 cups self-rising flour
1 pound chopped dates
4 cups chopped pecans
1 (15-ounce) package raisins

Cream the margarine and sugar in a mixing bowl until light and fluffy. Add the egg yolks, vanilla, salt, baking soda, cloves, cinnamon and buttermilk and beat until smooth. Beat in 2 cups of the flour. Toss the dates, pecans and raisins with the remaining 1/2 cup flour. Add to the batter and stir by hand; batter will be stiff. Chill, covered, for 1 hour or longer. Roll into 1-inch balls. Bake at 325 degrees for about 10 to 15 minutes or until lightly browned. Yield: 5 dozen.

Martha Stiles, Laureate Alpha Gamma
Knoxville, Tennessee

FRUITCAKE COOKIES

16 ounces mixed candied fruit
1 small citron, chopped
1 (10-ounce) package currants
1 (15-ounce) package golden raisins
1/4 cup rum
3 cups chopped pecans, walnuts and filberts
3 cups sifted flour
1 cup vegetable oil
1 1/2 cups packed brown sugar
4 eggs, beaten
1 teaspoon each baking powder, salt, ground cloves, nutmeg and cinnamon
2 teaspoons allspice
1 cup orange juice

Combine the candied fruit, citron, currants and golden raisins in a large bowl and mix well. Drizzle the rum over the mixture and let stand in the refrigerator for 8 to 10 hours. Stir in the chopped nuts and 1 cup of the flour. Combine the vegetable oil, brown sugar, eggs, the remaining 2 cups flour, baking powder, salt, cloves, nutmeg, cinnamon, allspice and orange juice in a large bowl; mix well. Mix the egg mixture into the fruit mixture. Drop by tablespoonfuls 2 inches apart onto a buttered cookie sheet and decorate with red and green cherries. Bake at 325 degrees for about 15 minutes, watching carefully to make sure cookies don't burn. Remove to a wire rack to cool. Store in airtight containers. Yield: 9 dozen.

Lillian Minor, Tau Master
Jefferson City, Missouri

SWEDISH GINGER COOKIES

1 cup packed brown sugar
1 egg
1 cup molasses
1/2 cup shortening
1/2 cup heavy cream
Grated zest of 1 orange
5 cups sifted flour
1 teaspoon each baking soda, ginger and cinnamon
1/2 teaspoon ground cloves, allspice and salt
1/4 teaspoon white pepper

Combine the brown sugar, egg and molasses in a large mixing bowl and blend well. Beat in the shortening, cream and orange zest. Add a mixture of the flour, baking soda, ginger, cinnamon, cloves, allspice, salt and white pepper; mix well. Chill, covered, in the refrigerator for at least 3 hours. Roll 1/8 to 1/4 inch thick on a lightly floured surface. Cut into desired shapes. Arrange 1 inch apart on a lightly buttered cookie sheet. Bake at 375 degrees for 8 to 10 minutes or until no imprint remains when pressed lightly with a finger. Spread with thin confectioners' sugar icing if desired. Yield: 8 dozen.

Phoebe Richards, Laureate Mu
Montclair, California

❖ DIPPED GINGERSNAPS

2 cups sugar	1 teaspoon ginger
1¹/₂ cups vegetable oil	2 teaspoons cinnamon
2 eggs	¹/₂ teaspoon salt
¹/₂ cup molasses	4 cups vanilla baking
4 cups flour	chips
4 teaspoons baking soda	¹/₄ cup shortening

Combine the sugar and vegetable oil in a mixing bowl and mix well. Add the eggs 1 at a time, beating well after each addition. Stir in the molasses. Mix the next 5 ingredients together. Add to the molasses mixture gradually, mixing well after each addition. Roll into ³/₄-inch balls and roll in additional sugar. Place 2 inches apart on an unbuttered cookie sheet. Bake at 350 degrees for 10 to 12 minutes or until cookie springs back when touched lightly. Remove to a wire rack to cool. Melt the vanilla chips with the shortening in a small saucepan over low heat, stirring frequently. Remove from heat. Dip half of each cooled cookie into the vanilla mixture and shake off the excess. Place on waxed paper to harden. Yield: 12 to 14 dozen.

Rita Montgomery, Preceptor Eta
Wichita, Kansas

MOLASSES COOKIES

1 cup (2 sticks) butter	2 eggs
1 cup sugar	1 tablespoon baking
1 cup molasses	soda
¹/₂ cup boiling water	1 tablespoon ginger
1 tablespoon vanilla	1 tablespoon cinnamon
extract	3 to 4 cups flour

Combine the butter, sugar, molasses and boiling water in a large bowl and mix well. Add the vanilla, eggs, baking soda, ginger and cinnamon and mix well. Add the flour gradually, mixing well after each addition; use the larger amount of flour for a thicker cookie. Drop a spoonful of dough onto a nonstick cookie sheet; bake a test cookie at 350 degrees for 8 to 12 minutes. If desired thickness and doneness, drop by teaspoonfuls 2 inches apart onto a buttered cookie sheet and bake. Yield: 2 to 3 dozen.

Shelly Eaton, Preceptor Pi
Douglas, Wyoming

SHERBET MACAROONS

2 cups sherbet, softened	2 teaspoons almond
1 (2-layer) package	extract
white cake mix	6 cups shredded coconut

Combine the sherbet, dry cake mix and flavoring in a mixing bowl and mix well. Stir in the coconut. Drop by tablespoonfuls 2 inches apart onto a buttered

cookie sheet. Bake at 350 degrees for 12 to 15 minutes or until edges are golden brown. Yield: 5 to 6 dozen.

Shirley A. Collingwood, Preceptor Iota
Springfield, Oregon

LEMON-FILLED COOKIES

1 cup (2 sticks) butter or	1 teaspoon cream of
margarine, softened	tartar
1¹/₄ cups packed brown	2 teaspoons ginger
sugar	¹/₄ teaspoon salt
2 eggs, beaten	6 to 7 tablespoons
1 teaspoon lemon	confectioners' sugar
extract	1 tablespoon grated
3¹/₂ cups flour	lemon zest
1 teaspoon baking soda	Lemon juice to taste

Combine the butter, brown sugar, eggs, lemon extract and a mixture of the flour, baking soda, cream of tartar, ginger and salt in a large mixing bowl; mix well. Let stand, covered, in the refrigerator for 8 to 10 hours. Roll into walnut-size balls and arrange 2 inches apart on a nonstick cookie sheet. Flatten with a fork, pressing at two angles. Bake at 325 degrees for 10 to 12 minutes or until edges are brown. Remove to a wire rack to cool completely. Combine the confectioners' sugar, lemon zest, lemon juice and additional lemon extract if desired in a mixing bowl. Mix until smooth. Spread between cookies to make sandwich cookies. Yield: 2 dozen.

Myrna Hardy, Preceptor Kappa
Swan River, Manitoba, Canada

CHOCOLATE MACAROONS

6 large egg whites	1 cup sugar
2¹/₄ teaspoons vanilla	³/₈ cup flour
extract	1¹/₃ cups chocolate chips
1 (14-ounce) package	¹/₄ cup (¹/₂ stick) butter
sweetened flaked	or margarine
coconut	1 tablespoon amaretto

Beat the egg whites in a mixing bowl until frothy peaks form. Add the next 4 ingredients and mix well. Drop by teaspoonfuls 2 inches apart onto a greased and floured cookie sheet. Bake at 325 degrees for 20 to 25 minutes or just until golden brown. Melt the chocolate chips and butter with the amaretto in a saucepan over low heat, stirring frequently. Remove from heat and let stand until completely cooled. Dip half of each macaroon in the cooled amaretto mixture. Spread dipped macaroons on a tray and freeze until very cold. Store in sealable plastic bags in the refrigerator or freezer. Yield: 2 dozen.

Carole Michael, Delta Nu Alpha
Mariposa, California

MERINGUE COOKIES

4 egg whites, at room
    temperature
1/4 teaspoon cream of
    tartar
3/4 cup sugar
1/2 teaspoon vanilla
    extract
2 cups chocolate chips

Beat the egg whites with the cream of tartar in a small mixing bowl at high speed until soft peaks form. Add the sugar 2 tablespoons at a time, beating until sugar is dissolved after each addition. Beat in the vanilla. Fold in the chocolate chips gently. Drop by teaspoonfuls 2 inches apart onto a large lightly buttered and floured cookie sheet. Bake at 200 degrees for 1 hour and 45 minutes. Turn off the oven; let cookies stand in the oven for 30 minutes longer. Remove to waxed paper to cool. Store in an airtight container. Yield: about 100.

Jean Van Stelten, Epsilon Master
Manchester, New Hampshire

OATMEAL COOKIES

7 cups rolled oats
1 cup granulated sugar
1 cup packed brown
    sugar
2 cups raisins
2 cups flour
2 cups chopped walnuts
    or pecans
1/2 teaspoon ground
    cloves
1/2 to 1 teaspoon nutmeg
3 to 4 teaspoons
    cinnamon
2 cups vegetable oil
1 teaspoon baking soda
4 eggs, well beaten
1 teaspoon vanilla
    extract
1/2 teaspoon salt

Combine the oats, granulated sugar, brown sugar, raisins, flour, chopped nuts, cloves, nutmeg and cinnamon in a large bowl and mix well. Add the vegetable oil and mix well. Let stand at room temperature, covered, for 8 to 10 hours. Dissolve the baking soda in 1/2 cup lukewarm water and add to the oats mixture. Add the eggs, vanilla and salt and mix well. Drop by teaspoonfuls 2 inches apart onto a buttered cookie sheet. Bake at 375 degrees for 10 to 12 minutes or until edges begin to brown. Yield: 6 dozen.

Bobbi Shannon, Laureate Lambda
Port St. Lucie, Florida

OATMEAL PEANUT BUTTER COOKIES

2 tablespoons cocoa
    powder
1/2 cup (1 stick) butter
1/2 cup milk
2 cups sugar
2 teaspoons vanilla
    extract
1/2 cup peanut butter
2 1/2 cups quick-cooking
    oats
1 cup graham cracker
    crumbs

Combine the cocoa powder, butter, milk, sugar and vanilla in a large saucepan and bring to a boil, stirring constantly. Boil gently for 1 minute, stirring constantly. Mix in the peanut butter, oats and graham cracker crumbs. Remove from heat. Drop by teaspoonfuls onto waxed paper immediately. Let stand until cool. Yield: 1 to 1 1/2 dozen.

Myra Smith, Epsilon
Stuttgart, Arkansas

OATMEAL CRANBERRY WHITE CHOCOLATE CHUNK COOKIES

2/3 cup (1 1/3 sticks) butter
    or margarine
2/3 cup packed brown
    sugar
2 large eggs
1 1/2 cups old-fashioned
    rolled oats
1 1/2 cups flour
1 teaspoon baking soda
1/2 teaspoon salt
1 (6-ounce) package
    craisins
2/3 cup white chocolate
    chunks

Cream the butter and brown sugar in a mixing bowl until smooth and fluffy. Add the eggs and mix well. Mix the oats, flour, baking soda and salt together. Add to the butter mixture gradually, mixing well after each addition. Stir in the craisins and white chocolate. Drop by teaspoonfuls 2 inches apart onto an unbuttered cookie sheet. Bake at 375 degrees for 10 to 12 minutes or until edges begin to brown. Yield: 3 dozen.

Pat Trantham, Alpha Delta Rho
Chillicothe, Missouri

EASY PEANUT BUTTER COOKIES

1 cup sugar
1 cup peanut butter
1 egg
1/2 teaspoon vanilla
    extract

Combine the sugar, peanut butter, egg and vanilla in a bowl and mix well. Drop by teaspoonfuls 2 inches apart onto a nonstick cookie sheet. Bake at 325 degrees for 10 to 15 minutes or until edges are firm. Yield: 2 to 2 1/2 dozen.

Bette Grant, Gamma Master
Omaha, Nebraska

PEANUT BUTTER AND JELLY SANDWICH COOKIES

1/3 cup margarine
1/4 cup creamy peanut
    butter
3/4 cup packed brown
    sugar
1 egg
1 teaspoon vanilla
    extract
1 3/4 cups flour
1/2 teaspoon baking soda
Grape jelly or
    strawberry jam

Cream the margarine, peanut butter and brown sugar in a mixing bowl until light and fluffy. Mix in the egg and vanilla. Add a mixture of the flour and baking soda; mix well. Roll into 1-inch balls. Arrange on an unbuttered cookie sheet. Flatten with a fork. Bake at 350 degrees for 9 minutes or until firm. Remove to a wire rack to cool completely. Spread 1 teaspoon jelly on the flat side of each of half the cookies; top with the remaining cookie halves to make sandwich cookies. Yield: 28 cookies.

Darlene Gumfory, Laureate Alpha Sigma
Iola, Kansas

PEANUT BUTTER CHOCOLATE COOKIES

1 cup (2 sticks) margarine, softened	2 eggs
1 cup peanut butter	2 cups flour
1 cup granulated sugar	1 teaspoon baking soda
1 cup packed brown sugar	1 cup chocolate chips
	1 cup chopped walnuts or pecans (optional)

Combine the margarine and peanut butter in a mixing bowl and mix until smooth. Add the sugars and beat until light and fluffy. Add the eggs 1 at a time, beating well after each addition. Sift the flour and baking soda together and add to the peanut butter mixture. Beat at low speed until well blended. Stir in the chocolate chips and chopped nuts. Drop by tablespoonfuls 2 inches apart onto a greased cookie sheet. Bake at 325 degrees for 12 to 15 minutes or until edges are firm. Yield: 6 dozen.

Judy Runge, Xi Delta Theta
Taylorville, Illinois

PEANUT BUTTER TEMPTATIONS

A tassie pan is like a muffin pan except the cups are smaller.

1/2 cup (1 stick) butter	1 1/4 cups flour
1/2 cup creamy peanut butter	3/4 teaspoon baking soda
1/2 cup granulated sugar	1/2 teaspoon salt
1/2 cup packed brown sugar	1 (10-ounce) package miniature peanut butter cups, unwrapped
1 egg	
1/2 teaspoon vanilla extract	

Cream the butter, peanut butter, granulated sugar and brown sugar in a mixing bowl until light and fluffy. Beat in the egg and vanilla. Add a mixture of the flour, baking soda and salt; mix well. Roll into 1-inch balls. Place in unbuttered tassie cups. Bake at 375 degrees for 8 to 10 minutes or until light brown. Remove from the oven and press peanut butter cups in the centers immediately. Yield: 40 cookies.

Lillian K. Van Natta, Xi Lambda Psi
Englewood, Florida

UNCOOKED PEANUT BUTTER COOKIES

2 cups sugar	2 cups quick-cooking oats
1/2 cup milk	
3 tablespoons baking cocoa	1/2 cup peanut butter
1/4 cup (1/2 stick) butter or margarine	1 teaspoon vanilla extract

Combine the sugar, milk, baking cocoa and butter in a saucepan and bring to a boil. Boil for 1 minute, stirring constantly. Remove from heat. Add the oats, peanut butter and vanilla; stir until well mixed. Drop by teaspoonfuls onto waxed paper; cookies will harden as they stand. Yield: variable.

Christine Dutcher, Xi Phi Chi
Del Rio, Texas

PECAN PRALINE COOKIES

Wonderful, especially for people who can't have chocolate.

1/2 cup (1 stick) butter or margarine, softened	1 1/2 teaspoons baking powder
2 cups firmly packed brown sugar	1/2 teaspoon salt
1 teaspoon vanilla extract	1/4 cup half-and-half
	1 cup confectioners' sugar
1 egg	1/2 cup chopped pecans
1 1/2 cups flour	

Cream the butter and 1 1/2 cups of the brown sugar in a mixing bowl until smooth and fluffy. Add the vanilla and egg and mix well. Stir in a mixture of the flour, baking powder and salt; mix well. Drop by rounded teaspoonfuls 2 inches apart onto a buttered cookie sheet. Bake at 350 degrees for 9 to 11 minutes or until light golden brown. Cool for 1 minute before removing to a wire rack. Combine the remaining 1/2 cup brown sugar and half-and-half in a small saucepan over medium heat; bring to a boil. Boil gently for 2 minutes, stirring constantly. Remove from heat. Stir in the confectioners' sugar and beat until smooth. Stir in the pecans quickly. Drizzle over the cooled cookies. Let stand for at least 20 minutes before serving or storing. Yield: 3 dozen.

Kim Steinle, Xi Beta Sigma
Hutchinson, Kansas

ROSETTES

2 eggs, beaten	1 cup flour
2 teaspoons sugar	1 tablespoon lemon
1/8 teaspoon salt	extract
1 cup milk	

Combine the eggs, sugar, salt, milk, flour and lemon extract in a mixing bowl and beat well to form a thin pancake-like batter. Heat a rosette iron in hot vegetable oil and dip into the batter. Return the iron to the oil; rosette will drop off the iron into the oil. Fry for 1 to 2 minutes or until crisp and golden brown. Cool slightly. Dust with confectioners' sugar. Yield: 4 dozen.

Barbara Beran, Preceptor Delta Chi
Hays, Kansas

POTATO CHIP COOKIES

1 cup (2 sticks) butter, softened	1 3/4 cups flour
1/2 cup sugar	1/2 cup crushed potato chips
1 teaspoon vanilla extract	1/2 cup chopped pecans

Cream the butter and sugar with the vanilla in a mixing bowl until light and fluffy. Stir in the flour, potato chips and pecans. Roll into 1-inch balls. Arrange on an unbuttered cookie sheet. Flatten with a glass dipped lightly in flour. Bake at 350 degrees for 12 to 14 minutes or until edges are golden. Yield: 2 1/2 dozen.

Pam Thomas, Laureate Alpha Pi
Canon City, Colorado

BUTTER CRISP POTATO COOKIES

1 cup (2 sticks) butter, soft	1 egg
1 cup granulated sugar	2 tablespoons water
1 cup packed brown sugar	2 1/3 cups flour
1 teaspoon vanilla extract	1/2 teaspoon salt
	1 teaspoon baking soda
	1 cup potato flakes
	1 cup shredded coconut

Cream the butter, granulated sugar and brown sugar with the vanilla in a mixing bowl until light and fluffy. Beat in the egg and water. Add a mixture of the flour, salt, baking soda, potato flakes and coconut; mix well. Roll into 1-inch balls and arrange on a buttered cookie sheet. Flatten with a glass dipped in sugar. Bake at 325 degrees for 6 to 8 minutes or until light brown. Yield: 2 to 3 dozen.

Sharon New, Preceptor Beta Lambda
Cottage Grove, Oregon

PUMPKIN COOKIES

1 cup sugar	1/2 cup unsweetened applesauce
2 cups flour	
1 teaspoon baking powder	1 cup canned pumpkin
1 teaspoon baking soda	1/2 cup (1 stick) butter, softened
1 teaspoon cinnamon	1 1/2 teaspoons vanilla extract
1/4 teaspoon salt	
1 cup quick-cooking oats	1 cup raisins
1/4 cup chopped walnuts or pecans	1 cup chocolate chips

Combine the sugar, flour, baking powder, baking soda, cinnamon, salt, oats and chopped nuts in a large bowl and mix well. Combine the applesauce, pumpkin, butter and vanilla in a separate mixing bowl and mix until smooth. Add the applesauce mixture to the flour mixture and mix well. Stir in the raisins and chocolate chips. Drop by tablespoonfuls 2 inches apart onto a cookie sheet that has been sprayed with nonstick cooking spray. Bake at 375 degrees for 12 to 15 minutes or until lightly browned. Yield: 2 1/2 to 3 dozen.

Judith Irion, Preceptor Zeta Theta
Chico, California

SOUR CREAM RAISIN DROPS

1/2 cup (1 stick) margarine, softened	1/3 cup sour cream
	1 cup raisins
3/4 cup sugar	1/2 cup (1 stick) margarine, softened
1 egg	
1/2 teaspoon vanilla extract	1 teaspoon grated orange zest
1 1/2 cups flour	2 cups sifted confectioners' sugar
1/2 teaspoon baking soda	
1/4 teaspoon salt	4 teaspoons milk

Cream 1/2 cup margarine and sugar in a mixing bowl until light and fluffy. Mix in the egg and vanilla. Mix the flour, baking soda and salt together. Add to the egg mixture alternately with the sour cream, mixing well after each addition. Stir in the raisins. Drop by rounded teaspoonfuls 2 inches apart onto an unbuttered cookie sheet. Bake at 375 degrees for 8 to 10 minutes or until edges are brown. Remove to a wire rack and cool completely. Beat 1/2 cup margarine in a mixing bowl until fluffy. Blend in the orange zest. Add the sugar alternately with the milk, beating until light and fluffy after each addition. Spread frosting over cookies. Yield: 5 dozen.

Berniece Luthy, Laureate Alpha Alpha
Phillips, Nebraska

SHORTBREAD

1 cup (2 sticks) butter, softened	1 egg yolk
1 teaspoon vanilla extract	2 cups flour
	3/4 cup sugar
	1/4 teaspoon salt

Combine the butter, vanilla and egg yolk in a bowl and blend until smooth. Mix the flour, sugar and salt together. Add the flour mixture to the butter mixture and knead by hand gently until well blended. Divide the dough into 2 portions. Pat into two unbuttered 9-inch pie plates. Prick the dough all over with a fork. Bake at 375 degrees for 10 minutes. Dust with confectioners' sugar and cut into wedges. Yield: 2 dozen.

Marjorie Hadsell, Laureate Zeta
Tonawanda, New York

GINGER SHORTBREAD

1/2 cup (1 stick) butter (no substitute), softened	1/3 cup sugar
	1 cup flour
	1 teaspoon ginger

Combine the butter, sugar, flour and ginger in a bowl and mix well, using the hands if necessary. Pat into a pie plate. Score into 8 wedges. Bake at 350 degrees for 30 minutes. Cut almost all the way through where the dough was scored. Cool slightly on a wire rack. Separate the pieces. Do not wait until it's completely cold before separating the shortbread or it will crumble and stick to the plate. Yield: 8 servings.

Ardyce Cibuzar, Beta Master
Minneapolis, Minnesota

ROLLED SUGAR COOKIES

1 cup shortening	1 teaspoon lemon extract
1 cup granulated sugar	
1 cup packed brown sugar	4 1/2 cups flour
2 eggs	1 teaspoon baking soda
1 cup milk	1 teaspoon salt
1 teaspoon vanilla extract	1 teaspoon nutmeg
	1 tablespoon baking powder

Beat the first 3 ingredients in a mixing bowl until creamy. Add the eggs and mix well. Beat in the milk, vanilla and lemon extract. Mix the flour, baking soda, salt, nutmeg and baking powder together. Add to the sugar mixture gradually, mixing well after each addition. Shape into a log. Chill, tightly wrapped, in the refrigerator. Cut into 1/8- to 1/4-inch slices. Place on a buttered cookie sheet. Bake at 400 degrees for 10 to 12 minutes or until edges are firm. Yield: variable.

Amy L. Kelley, Preceptor Beta Nu
Wayland, New York

SPICY WALNUT COOKIES

2 cups walnut pieces	2 egg whites, whisked until frothy
1/3 cup sugar	
1 teaspoon cinnamon	

Combine the walnuts, sugar and cinnamon in a food processor container or blender and process until finely ground. Blend in the egg whites. Drop by teaspoonfuls 2 inches apart onto an oiled cookie sheet. Bake at 350 degrees for 15 minutes. Do not overbake; cookies will be soft. Yield: 15 cookies.

Norma Jean Jones, Epsilon Master
Broken Arrow, Oklahoma

BEST COOKIE RECIPE EVER

1 cup butter-flavor shortening	1 teaspoon vanilla extract
1 cup sugar	1/2 teaspoon salt
1 whole egg	2 1/2 cups flour
1 egg yolk	

Cream the shortening and sugar in a mixing bowl until light and fluffy. Add the egg, egg yolk, vanilla and salt and blend well. Mix in the flour. Divide the dough into 2 portions and shape into logs. Wrap in plastic wrap. Chill for 30 minutes or double-wrap and freeze for up to 2 months. Cut the chilled logs into 1/4-inch-thick slices and arrange 1/2 inch apart on a parchment paper-lined baking sheet. Bake in a preheated 375-degree oven for 12 to 14 minutes or until edges are firm. Cool for 2 minutes on the cookie sheet. Remove to a wire rack to cool completely. Store cookies up to 1 week in an airtight container. Yield: 6 dozen.

VARIATIONS:

Cherry Almond Cookies: Add 1/4 teaspoon almond extract to the dough and roll a log in a mixture of 1/2 cup chopped dried cherries and 3/4 cup chopped toasted almonds.

Chocolate Chip Hazelnut Cookies: Roll a log in a mixture of 1/2 cup chopped chocolate chips and 1/2 cup chopped toasted hazelnuts.

Currant Pine Nut Cookies: Add 2 teaspoons rosemary to the dough and roll a log in a mixture of 1/2 cup chopped currants and 3/4 cup chopped pine nuts.

Orange Pecan Cookies: Add 1/2 teaspoon grated orange zest to the dough and roll a log in 1/2 cup chopped pecans.

Coconut Lime Cookies: Add 1 teaspoon grated lime zest to the dough and roll a log in 3/4 cup flaked coconut.

Laura Hannan, Xi Eta Theta
Wamego, Kansas

ALMOND-FLAVORED FAIRY DUSTERS

1 cup (2 sticks) butter	2 eggs
1 cup confectioners' sugar	4¹/2 cups flour
1 cup granulated sugar	1 teaspoon baking soda
2 teaspoons almond extract	1 teaspoon cream of tartar
1 cup vegetable oil	1 teaspoon salt

Cream the butter, confectioners' sugar and sugar in a mixing bowl until light and fluffy. Add the almond extract, vegetable oil and eggs and beat until smooth. Add a mixture of the flour, baking soda, cream of tartar and salt gradually, mixing well after each addition. Chill, covered, for 30 minutes. Roll into 1-inch balls and arrange on a buttered cookie sheet. Flatten with a glass dipped in sugar or leave plain to frost after baking. Bake at 350 degrees for 10 minutes or until edges are firm. Yield: 4¹/2 to 5 dozen.

Leslie Rainey, Xi Xi
Peoria, Arizona

CRISP GRAHAM COOKIES

¹/2 cup butter-flavor shortening	3 tablespoons creamy peanut butter
¹/2 cup packed brown sugar	1¹/2 cups flour
1 egg	1 cup graham cracker crumbs
1 (14-ounce) can sweetened condensed milk	1 teaspoon baking soda
	1 teaspoon salt
1¹/2 teaspoons vanilla extract	2 cups plain "M & M's" Chocolate Candies
	¹/2 cup chopped pecans

Cream the shortening and brown sugar in a mixing bowl until smooth and fluffy. Beat in the egg. Blend in the next 3 ingredients. Mix the flour, cracker crumbs, baking soda and salt together. Mix into the creamed mixture. Stir in the chocolate candies and chopped nuts. Drop by teaspoonfuls 2 inches apart onto an unbuttered cookie sheet. Bake at 350 degrees for 10 to 12 minutes or until golden brown. Cool on a wire rack. Yield: 7 dozen.

Heidi Wicks, Xi Theta Xi
Spirit Lake, Iowa

*Valerie Rankin, Preceptor Epsilon Theta, Pinellas Park, Florida, makes **Chocolate Peppermint Balls** by creaming ¹/2 cup shortening with 1 egg yolk and ¹/2 teaspoon peppermint extract and adding a devil's food cake mix. Shape into small balls and arrange 2 inches apart on an ungreased cookie sheet. Bake at 375 degrees for 10 minutes and roll the warm cookies in confectioners' sugar.*

CHEWY CAKE MIX COOKIES

1 (18-ounce) package cake mix of choice	1 cup chopped walnuts or pecans (optional)
2/3 cup butter-flavor shortening	1 cup chocolate chips (optional)
3 eggs	1 cup peanut butter chips (optional)
1 teaspoon poppy seeds (optional)	1 cup shredded coconut (optional)
1 cup raisins (optional)	

Combine the dry cake mix, shortening and eggs in a large mixing bowl and mix until smooth. Stir in optional ingredients of your choice. Drop by rounded teaspoonfuls 2 inches apart onto a buttered cookie sheet. Bake at 350 degrees for 10 to 11 minutes or until edges are firm. Cool slightly before removing from the cookie sheet. Suggested combinations: lemon cake with poppy seeds; spice cake with raisins and nuts; chocolate cake with chocolate chips and nuts; chocolate cake with peanut butter chips and nuts; German chocolate cake with coconut. Yield: about 3 dozen.

Lila Logan, Xi Zeta Lambda
Ponca City, Oklahoma

COCONUT NO-BAKE SANDWICH COOKIES

4 ounces shredded coconut	2 tablespoons chocolate syrup
2 or 3 drops green food coloring	2 cups crisp rice cereal
10 large marshmallows	40 vanilla wafers
	White frosting

Toss the coconut with the food coloring in a bowl or jar until tinted and set aside. Melt the marshmallows in a double boiler over hot water. Remove from the heat and blend in the chocolate syrup. Add the cereal and mix until coated. Spread a teaspoon of the mixture on the bottoms of half the vanilla wafers. Sprinkle with tinted coconut. Spread the bottoms of each of the remaining vanilla wafers with about ¹/2 teaspoon frosting. Press the frosted wafers onto the coconut-filled wafers to make cookie sandwiches. Yield: 20 cookies.

JoAnn Gruber, Laureate Theta
Hagerstown, Maryland

BOURBON BALLS

¹/2 cup chopped pecans	1 (1-pound) package confectioners' sugar
Enough bourbon to cover pecans	Pinch of salt
¹/2 cup (1 stick) margarine, softened	4 to 8 ounces semisweet chocolate, melted

Place the pecans in a bowl and add the bourbon. Let stand at room temperature, covered, for 24 to 48 hours; drain. Combine the pecans, margarine, confectioners' sugar and salt in a bowl and mix well. Roll into 3/4-inch balls. Dip in melted chocolate. Store in the refrigerator. Yield: 2 to 3 dozen.

Anne C. Wade, Alpha Master
Lexington, Kentucky

BONBONS

1/2 cup sweetened
  condensed milk
2/3 cup confectioners'
  sugar
2 tablespoons unsalted
  butter, at room
  temperature
2 2/3 cups flaked coconut

1/4 cup finely chopped
  almonds
2 tablespoons vanilla
  extract
8 ounces semisweet
  chocolate, coarsely
  chopped

Combine the condensed milk, confectioners' sugar, butter, coconut, almonds and vanilla; mix well. Chill, covered, in the refrigerator for 1 hour. Roll into pecan-size balls. Line a baking sheet with waxed paper or parchment pepper. Melt the chocolate in the top of a double boiler over simmering water. Use 2 wooden picks to dip each coconut ball in the melted chocolate, coating evenly. Place on the prepared baking sheet. Chill until set. Keep refrigerated. Yield: 2 dozen.

Wilma Webber, Laureate Gamma Xi
Columbus, Ohio

CHOCOLATE TRUFFLES

1/2 cup walnuts
3 ounces semisweet
  chocolate
2 tablespoons heavy
  cream
2/3 cup confectioners'
  sugar

1 tablespoon Grand
  Marnier, Cointreau or
  rum
1/3 cup chocolate
  sprinkles

Place the walnuts in a food processor container or blender and process until finely ground. Line the bottom of a 5×9×3-inch loaf pan with waxed paper. Combine the chocolate and cream in a small heavy saucepan over low heat. Heat just until melted. Remove from heat. Place the walnuts and confectioners' sugar in a medium bowl and stir with a wooden spoon. Add the chocolate mixture and Grand Marnier; mix well. Spread in the prepared loaf pan. Chill until firm. Roll into thirty 3/4-inch balls. Roll in chocolate sprinkles to coat. Keep in the refrigerator, covered, until ready to serve. Yield: 30 truffles.

Rita Beaver, Xi Alpha Sigma
Ashland, Ohio

PEANUT BUTTER BALLS

1 cup light corn syrup
1 cup sugar
2 cups peanut butter
1 teaspoon vanilla
  extract

Pinch of salt
4 cups Special-K
1 cup chopped pecans
1 cup shredded coconut

Combine the corn syrup and sugar in a saucepan over medium heat and bring to the boiling point; do not boil. Remove from heat and stir in the peanut butter, vanilla and salt. Combine the next 3 ingredients in a large bowl and mix well. Add the hot peanut butter mixture and mix well. Roll the hot mixture into 1-inch balls. Cool; store in an airtight container. Yield: 3 to 4 dozen.

Pat Mitchell, Theta Phi
Terrell, Texas

BUCKEYES

2 (16-ounce) jars creamy
  peanut butter
2 cups (4 sticks) butter,
  at room temperature

3 (1-pound) packages
  confectioners' sugar
4 cups chocolate chips
1/2 bar paraffin

Combine the peanut butter, butter and confectioners' sugar in a large mixing bowl and beat until smooth. Roll into balls the size of "buckeyes" or large marbles. Chill, covered, for at least 1 hour. Combine the chocolate chips and paraffin in the top of a double boiler over simmering water and melt slowly; stir until smooth. Use a wooden pick to dip each chilled buckeye in the chocolate mixture until 2/3 covered. Let dry on waxed paper. Yield: about 160 candies.

Karen Deutsch, Epsilon Xi
Marshall, Missouri

STRAWBERRY MACAROON CANDIES

2 (3-ounce) packages
  strawberry gelatin
1 tablespoon sugar
2 to 4 drops red food
  coloring

2 cups sweetened
  shredded coconut
1 cup sweetened
  condensed milk
Green gumdrops

Blend 1 tablespoon of the dry gelatin mix and sugar in a small bowl. Stir in the food coloring. Mix the coconut, condensed milk and the remaining dry gelatin mix in a bowl. Shape into 1- to 1 1/2-inch strawberry shapes. Add condensed milk 1 tablespoon at a time if too dry; add coconut 1 tablespoon at a time if mixture is too sticky. Roll each "strawberry" in the tinted gelatin mixture. Cut the gumdrops into 1/8-inch slices and use as leaves. Yield: 3 to 4 dozen.

Virginia Petersen, Laureate
Story, Wyoming

CARAMEL CHEWS

28 caramels
3 tablespoons margarine
1 (3-ounce) can chow
  mein noodles
1 cup peanuts
1 cup semisweet
  chocolate chips

Combine the caramels, margarine and 2 tablespoons water in a saucepan over low heat; cook until melted, stirring occasionally until smooth. Remove from heat. Add the noodles and peanuts; toss to coat. Drop by rounded teaspoonfuls onto a buttered baking sheet. Melt the chocolate chips and another 2 tablespoons water in a saucepan over low heat, stirring occasionally until smooth. Drizzle over the chews; chill until firm. Yield: 2^1/$_2$ dozen.

Sarah Strope, Alpha Epsilon Psi
Linn, Missouri

QUICK CHOCOLATE CANDY

1 cup sugar
2 tablespoons baking
  cocoa
^{1}/$_4$ cup shortening
^{1}/$_4$ cup milk
^{1}/$_4$ teaspoon salt
1 cup shredded coconut
1 cup rolled oats
1 teaspoon vanilla
  extract

Combine the sugar, baking cocoa, shortening, milk and salt in the top of a double boiler over boiling water; bring to a boil. Add the coconut, oats and vanilla, stirring constantly. Drop by teaspoonfuls onto a waxed paper-lined baking sheet. Let stand until cool. Yield: 2 to 3 dozen.

Karen Sturdy, Alpha Nu Master
Goderich, Ontario, Canada

PECAN CHRISTMAS CANDY

3 (4-ounce) bars
  German's sweet
  chocolate
1 (14-ounce) can
  sweetened condensed
  milk
4 cups pecan halves
1 teaspoon vanilla
  extract

Melt the chocolate with the condensed milk in the top of a double boiler over simmering water; stir until smooth. Add the pecans and vanilla, stirring to coat the pecans. Drop by teaspoonfuls onto waxed paper. Let stand for 8 to 10 hours to dry. Store in an airtight container. Freeze leftovers to prevent molding. Yield: 1 quart.

Sandy White, Xi Nu Phi
Cuero, Texas

POTATO CANDY

^{1}/$_4$ cup hot mashed
  potatoes
1 teaspoon butter or
  margarine, melted
1^3/$_4$ cups confectioners'
  sugar
1^1/$_2$ cups flaked coconut
Dash of salt
^{1}/$_4$ teaspoon grated
  lemon or orange zest
^{1}/$_2$ teaspoon vanilla
  extract

Combine the potatoes and butter in a medium mixing bowl. Add the confectioners' sugar gradually, beating until well blended. Add the coconut, salt, lemon zest and vanilla; mix well. Drop by teaspoonfuls onto waxed paper. Let stand until firm. Yield: 2 dozen.

Edna Faye Williams, Delta Omicron
Kennett, Missouri

CRUNCHY PEANUT CLUSTERS

^{1}/$_2$ cup peanut butter,
  creamy or crunchy
2 cups milk chocolate
  chips
2 cups dry-roasted
  peanuts, coarsely
  chopped

Melt the peanut butter and chocolate chips in the top of a double boiler over hot water; stir to blend well. Stir in the peanuts and remove from heat. Drop by teaspoonfuls into foil-lined 2-inch baking cups; or drop onto foil or waxed paper. Chill until firm. Cover and store in the refrigerator. Yield: 40 pieces.

Evelyn Oberlander, Rho Master
Allison Park, Pennsylvania

WHITE CHOCOLATE PEANUT BUTTER CANDY

2 pounds almond bark,
  melted
1^3/$_4$ cups peanut butter
2^1/$_2$ cups miniature
  marshmallows
2 cups dry-roasted
  peanuts
1 cup shredded coconut
3 cups crisp rice cereal

Combine the almond bark, peanut butter, marshmallows, peanuts, coconut and crisp rice cereal in a large bowl and mix well. Drop by teaspoonfuls onto waxed paper. Chill until firm. Yield: 10 to 12 dozen.

Penelope K. Tippy, Xi Alpha Pi
West Frankfort, Illinois

BUTTERSCOTCH CHOCOLATE CLUSTERS

2 cups chocolate
  chips
2 cups butterscotch
  chips
2 (12-ounce) packages
  salted peanuts
1 (12-ounce) can chow
  mein noodles

Melt the chocolate chips and butterscotch chips in a saucepan over medium-low heat, stirring constantly; remove from heat. Add the peanuts and chow mein noodles, stirring until well coated. Drop quickly by teaspoonfuls onto a waxed paper-lined baking sheet. Chill for 10 to 15 minutes or until set. They freeze well. Yield: 4 to 5 dozen.

Bonnie Greenlee, Preceptor Delta Gamma
Surrey, British Columbia, Canada

BUTTERSCOTCH PEANUT CRUNCHIES

1 (12-ounce) can salted peanuts
1 (7-ounce) can potato sticks

3 cups butterscotch chips
3 tablespoons peanut butter

Combine the peanuts and potato sticks in a large mixing bowl and mix well. Microwave the butterscotch chips and peanut butter in a microwave-safe bowl on High for 1 to 2 minutes or until melted, stirring every 30 seconds. Add to the peanut mixture and stir to coat evenly. Drop by rounded tablespoons onto waxed paper-lined baking sheets. Chill until set, about 5 minutes. Store in an airtight container. Yield: 4 1/2 dozen.

Nadine E. Thomas, Xi Epsilon
Hoquiam, Washington

MINT CHOCOLATES

1/2 cup (1 stick) butter, softened
1 1/2 cups confectioners' sugar
2 eggs (may use egg substitute)

2 cups semisweet chocolate chips
2 teaspoons vanilla extract
1 1/2 teaspoons peppermint extract

Cream the butter and confectioners' sugar in a mixing bowl until light and fluffy. Beat in the eggs. Melt the chocolate chips in a saucepan and stir into the sugar mixture. Add the vanilla and mix well. Add the peppermint; mix until smooth. Drop by teaspoonfuls onto waxed paper. Chill and serve. Yield: 4 dozen.

Marie A. Ried, Alpha Eta Master
Gig Harbor, Washington

MICROWAVE DIVINITY

This candy will not fail—it is fast and delicious.

1/2 cup cold water
2 cups sugar
1 teaspoon white vinegar
1 large egg white, or 2 small

1 teaspoon vanilla extract
1 cup pecans, chopped

Combine the water, sugar and vinegar in a 4-quart microwave-safe dish. Cover with plastic wrap (do not use a glass lid). Microwave on High for 12 to 15 minutes. After 12 minutes, if the mixture forms a hard ball in cold tap water, it is ready; if not, microwave for 3 minutes longer. Beat the egg white in a mixing bowl until stiff peaks form. Add the hot syrup to the beaten egg white gradually, beating constantly. Beat in the vanilla. Continue beating; when the sheen has left the mixture, fold in the pecans. Continue folding until thick enough to drop by teaspoonfuls; work fast, as it sets up in a hurry. Drop by teaspoonfuls onto waxed paper. Yield: 3 dozen.

Syble A. Shoults, Xi Mu
Bessemer, Alabama

TRADITIONAL DIVINITY

2 egg whites, at room temperature
3 cups sugar
1/2 cup water
1/2 cup light corn syrup

1 teaspoon vanilla extract
3 cups pecans (pieces, chopped or whole)

Place the egg whites in a mixing bowl. Lay 2 large sheets of waxed paper on a flat surface. Combine the sugar, water and corn syrup in a saucepan over medium heat. Bring to the boiling point. At that moment, begin to beat the egg whites at medium speed; continue beating while cooking the syrup. Cook the syrup to 234 to 240 degrees on a candy thermometer, soft-ball stage. Egg whites should be stiff by now. Pour half the syrup over the egg whites slowly as beaters continue to beat. Return the remaining syrup to the heat. Cook over medium heat to 250 to 268 degrees on a candy thermometer, hard-ball stage. Pour it over the beating egg white mixture slowly. Add the vanilla and continue beating until very thick. Stop the mixer and tip back the beaters. When the mixture keeps its shape when it drips off the beaters into the bowl, remove the bowl from the mixer; do not underbeat. Stir in the pecans with a large wooden spoon. Place the bowl on the flat surface between the sheets of waxed paper. Another person should help you at this stage. Take 2 teaspoons and fill one with the mixture, using the other to scrape the mixture onto waxed paper. If the spoonful of mixture spreads, it is not ready; do not spoon out the remaining mixture. Keep stirring with the large wooden spoon, testing every minute or two. When the mixture holds its shape, spoon it out quickly with your assistant's help; it will harden very quickly. Yield: 50 to 60 pieces.

Juanita Burleigh, Gamma Master
Lafayette, Louisiana

CREAMY CARAMELS

1 cup sugar
1 cup dark corn syrup
1 cup (2 sticks) butter or
  margarine
1 (14-ounce) can
  sweetened condensed
  milk

1 teaspoon vanilla
  extract

Line an 8×8-inch pan with foil and butter the foil. Combine the sugar, corn syrup and butter in a 3-quart saucepan over medium heat. Bring to a boil, stirring constantly. Boil slowly for 4 minutes without stirring. Remove from heat. Stir in the condensed milk. Cook over medium-low heat to 238 degrees on a candy thermometer, soft-ball stage, stirring constantly. Remove from heat. Stir in the vanilla. Pour into the prepared pan; cool to room temperature. Remove from the pan and cut into 1-inch squares. Wrap individually in waxed paper. Yield: 64 pieces.

Lisa Morford, Mu
Dakota Dunes, South Dakota

PECAN CARAMEL CANDY

1 cup sugar
3/4 cup dark corn syrup
1/2 cup (1 stick) butter
1 cup heavy cream

1/2 teaspoon vanilla
  extract
2 cups pecan halves

Combine the sugar, corn syrup, butter and 1/2 cup of the cream in a saucepan; bring to a boil, stirring constantly with a wooden spoon. Add the remaining 1/2 cup cream; do not stir after blending in the cream. Cook over medium heat to 245 degrees on a candy thermometer, firm-ball stage. Remove from heat and stir in the vanilla and pecans. Pour into a buttered 9×12-inch pan. Let stand until cool. Cut the cooled candy into pieces. Wrap in plastic wrap or store in snack-size sealable plastic bags.
Yield: about 25 pieces.

Peggy Brittain, Alpha Master
Corpus Christi, Texas

RICH FUDGE

1 cup (2 sticks)
  margarine
5 cups sugar
1 (12-ounce) can
  evaporated milk

Dash of salt
3 cups semisweet
  chocolate chips
1 teaspoon vanilla
  extract

Melt the margarine in a saucepan over medium heat. Add the sugar, evaporated milk and salt, stirring constantly until dissolved. Bring to a boil. Boil for 6 minutes, stirring constantly. Remove from heat. Stir

in the chocolate chips and vanilla. Beat at medium speed until stiff. Pour into a buttered 10×10-inch pan. Chill, covered, in the refrigerator until firm. Cut into small squares. Yield: 20 to 30 pieces.

Anna E. Lewis, Xi Omicron Mu
Ridgecrest, California

FAST-AND-EASY FUDGE

1 (14-ounce) can
  sweetened condensed
  milk
2 cups semisweet
  chocolate chips

1 (11-ounce) package
  butterscotch chips
1/2 teaspoon vanilla
  extract
1 cup walnuts, chopped

Heat the condensed milk in a medium saucepan over medium heat until warm. Add the chocolate chips and butterscotch chips, stirring until smooth. Remove from heat. Stir in the vanilla and walnuts. Pour into a lightly buttered 8×8-inch or 9×9-inch pan. Let stand in the refrigerator until set. Cut into 2-inch squares. Yield: 16 to 20 pieces.

Donna Speer, Sigma Mu
Golconda, Illinois

WHITE CHOCOLATE FUDGE

2 cups sugar
1 cup evaporated milk
1/2 cup (1 stick) butter
8 ounces white almond
  bark
1 cup miniature
  marshmallows

1/2 cup flaked coconut
1/2 cup chopped walnuts
  or pecans
1 teaspoon vanilla
  extract

Butter the side of a 3-quart saucepan. Combine the sugar, evaporated milk and butter in the prepared saucepan. Cook over medium heat to 234 degrees on a candy thermometer, soft-ball stage, stirring frequently. Remove from heat. Add the almond bark and marshmallows and beat until melted and well blended. Stir in the coconut, chopped nuts and vanilla quickly. Pour into a buttered 6×10-inch pan. Cool to room temperature. Cut into squares; garnish each square with a walnut or pecan. Yield: 20 pieces.

Laurie Lambert, Kappa
Coats, Kansas

Mary Ellen Sansone, Laureate Nu, Wallingford, Connecticut, cuts an 18-ounce roll of refrigerator chocolate chip cookie dough into 9 slices and quarters each slice. Place each piece in a muffin cup. Bake at 350 degrees for 6 minutes and push a miniature peanut butter cup into each cookie. Bake for 2 minutes longer for **Chocolate Chip Surprises.**

CRANBERRY WALNUT WHITE FUDGE

2 cups white vanilla
  chips
1/2 cup confectioners'
  sugar
3 ounces cream cheese,
  softened
1/2 cup creamy vanilla
  frosting

3/4 cup chopped walnuts
1 teaspoon grated
  orange zest
2/3 cup sweetened dried
  cranberries

Line a 9×9-inch pan with foil, extending foil beyond the edges. Spray lightly with nonstick cooking spray. Melt the vanilla chips in a small saucepan over low heat, stirring until smooth. Remove from heat. Combine the confectioners' sugar, cream cheese and frosting in a bowl; mix well. Stir in the melted chips, walnuts, orange zest and cranberries. Spread in the prepared pan. Chill for 1 hour or until firm. Remove from the pan by lifting the foil; remove the foil. Cut into squares. Serve at room temperature.
Yield: 3 dozen.

Anita Milligan, Beta Beta
Bethany, Missouri

CHERRY PECAN FUDGE

1 (14-ounce) can
  sweetened condensed
  milk
1 (3-ounce) package
  cherry gelatin
Pinch of salt

2 cups semisweet
  chocolate chips
1/2 to 1 cup crushed
  pecans
1/2 teaspoon vanilla
  extract

Combine the condensed milk, dry gelatin mix and salt in the top of a double boiler over simmering water; heat until gelatin is dissolved. Add the chocolate chips, stirring as they melt. Remove from heat when melted completely and well blended. Stir in the pecans and vanilla. Pour the chocolate mixture into a waxed paper-lined 8×8-inch pan; smooth the top with a spatula. Chill, covered, for at least 2 hours. Remove from the pan and cut into small squares.
Yield: 64 squares.

Sara McHone, Xi Delta Rho
Arden, North Carolina

CREAMY PEANUT BUTTER FUDGE

1 1/2 cups sugar
1/2 cup (1 stick) butter
2/3 cup evaporated milk
1 (7-ounce) jar
  marshmallow creme
2 cups peanut butter
  chips

1/2 teaspoon vanilla
  extract
1/2 cup creamy peanut
  butter

Combine the sugar, butter and evaporated milk in a heavy saucepan and bring to a boil. Boil rapidly for 5 minutes, stirring constantly. Remove from the heat. Add the marshmallow creme, peanut butter chips, vanilla and peanut butter and stir until the peanut butter chips melt and the mixture is smooth. Spread in a lightly buttered 8×12-inch shallow pan. Let stand until set. Cut into 1-inch squares. Yield: 8 dozen.

Freda Bush, Preceptor Gamma Kappa
Chesapeake, Virginia

PUMPKIN FUDGE

2/3 cup evaporated milk
2 1/2 cups sugar
3/4 cup canned pumpkin
1 teaspoon cinnamon
1 (7-ounce) jar
  marshmallow creme

2 tablespoons butter
1 cup white chocolate
  chips
1 teaspoon vanilla
  extract

Line a 9×9-inch pan with foil. Combine the evaporated milk and sugar in a 3-quart saucepan over medium heat. Bring to a boil, stirring occasionally with a wooden spoon. Mix in the pumpkin and cinnamon; bring to a boil. Stir in the marshmallow creme and butter; bring to a rolling boil. Cook for 18 minutes, stirring occasionally. Remove from heat. Stir in the white chocolate chips and vanilla and stir until the mixture is creamy. Pour into the prepared pan. Let stand at room temperature until cool and firm. Remove from the pan and cut into squares. Store in a cool dry place. Yield: 16 servings.

Belinda Holland, Xi Zeta Lambda
Fort Stockton, Texas

CHEWY PECAN PRALINES

1 cup sugar
1 cup light corn syrup
1 cup (2 sticks) butter or
  margarine

1 cup heavy cream
1 teaspoon vanilla
  extract
4 cups chopped pecans

Combine the sugar and corn syrup in a saucepan over medium heat. Cook to 250 degrees on a candy thermometer, hard-ball stage. Remove from the heat and add the butter; stir until melted. Add the cream gradually, stirring constantly. Return to the heat and cook to 242 degrees on a candy thermometer, firm-ball stage, stirring constantly. Remove from the heat and add the vanilla and pecans; stir until well mixed. Drop by spoonfuls of the preferred size onto foil. Let stand until cool. Wrap pieces individually in plastic wrap. Yield: variable.

Barbara Kaiser, Xi Upsilon Psi
Yoakum, Texas

CREAMY CAJUN PRALINES

3/4 cup packed brown sugar	*1 tablespoon butter*
3/4 cup granulated sugar	*1 cup pecan halves*
1/2 cup evaporated milk	*1/4 teaspoon vanilla extract*

Combine the brown sugar, granulated sugar, evaporated milk and butter in a medium saucepan; bring to a boil. Reduce heat. Cook over medium heat for about 5 minutes to 234 to 240 degrees on a candy thermometer, soft-ball stage. Remove from heat and beat by hand until creamy. Stir in the pecans and vanilla. Drop by teaspoonfuls quickly in a buttered dish. Let stand until firm. Yield: 20 pieces.

Jeanne L. Phillips, Laureate Sigma
Garland, Texas

CHOCOLATE ALMOND BUTTER CRUNCH

1 tablespoon light corn syrup	*1 cup chocolate dipping wafers or chocolate*
1 1/4 cups sugar	*chips (semisweet*
1 cup (2 sticks) butter	*chocolate or milk*
1/4 cup water	*chocolate)*
1 1/4 cups toasted slivered almonds	

Combine the corn syrup, sugar, butter and water in a large heavy saucepan over medium heat. Cook for about 20 minutes to 300 degrees on a candy thermometer, hard-crack stage; do not stir. Remove from heat. Add the almonds and stir well. Spread in an unbuttered 10×15-inch cake pan. Sprinkle immediately with chocolate dipping wafers. Spread the chocolate evenly over the candy as the chocolate melts. Sprinkle with chopped almonds if desired. Cool in the refrigerator or freezer. Break into pieces. Yield: variable.

Barbara Henson, Iota Master
Calgary, Alberta, Canada

ENGLISH TOFFEE

1/4 to 3/4 cup chopped walnuts or pecans	*1 cup (2 sticks) butter (no substitute)*
4 to 5 (7-ounce) chocolate candy bars	*3 tablespoons water*
1 1/2 cups sugar	*1 tablespoon vanilla extract*

Butter an 8×12 or a 9×13-inch pan and sprinkle the chopped nuts in the pan. Break the candy bars into pieces. Combine the sugar, butter, water and vanilla in a heavy saucepan. Cook over medium heat to 280 degrees on a candy thermometer or until brown; it will began to have a faint burned odor. Pour into the prepared pan. Lay the candy bar pieces over the top and spread evenly when melted. Sprinkle with additional chopped nuts. Let stand until cool. Break into pieces. Yield: variable.

Judy A. Ramsey, Preceptor Alpha Omega
Albuquerque, New Mexico

CHOCOLATE-COVERED TOFFEE

36 saltine crackers	*2 cups milk chocolate*
1 cup (2 sticks) butter	*chips*
1 cup packed brown sugar	*1 cup chopped walnuts*

Preheat the oven to 375 degrees. Line a 10×15-inch cake pan with foil. Butter the foil with soft butter. Spread the saltine crackers over the buttered foil. Combine the butter and brown sugar in a saucepan over medium-high heat and bring to a boil. Boil for 4 minutes, stirring constantly. Spread the mixture over the cracker layer. Bake in the oven for 5 minutes. Layer the chocolate chips over the top; spread evenly over the top as they melt. Sprinkle the walnuts over the chocolate layer. Chill until cool. Break into pieces. Yield: variable.

Norma Mathis, Beta Nu Master
Hanford, California

ALMOND TOFFEE WAFERS

Graham crackers to line a baking sheet	*1 cup (2 sticks) butter*
1 cup packed brown sugar	*6 ounces sliced almonds*
	3 tablespoons sesame seeds

Line a baking sheet with graham crackers. Combine the brown sugar and butter in a heavy saucepan over medium heat and bring to a boil. Stir in the almonds and sesame seeds; bring to a boil. Cover the graham cracker layer with the almond mixture. Bake at 350 degrees for 10 minutes or until brown. Break into pieces immediately. Yield: about 50 pieces.

Phyllis Graham, Preceptor Beta Nu
Placentia, California

PEANUT BRITTLE

2 teaspoons baking soda	*1/2 cup water*
2 cups granulated sugar	*1 pound raw peanuts*
1 cup light corn syrup	

Crush the baking soda in the hand so there are no lumps; set aside. Combine the sugar, corn syrup and water in a large kettle. Cook over medium heat to 250 degrees on a candy thermometer, hard-ball stage. Add the peanuts and cook to 290 degrees, soft-crack stage. Remove from heat and stir in the baking soda;

the mixture will foam up quickly increasing greatly in volume. Spread in a buttered 12×18-inch rimmed pan. Let stand until cool. Break into pieces. Yield: more than 1 pound.

Patricia Thomas, Preceptor Gamma Epsilon
Marion, Ohio

PECAN BRITTLE

1 cup sugar
¼ cup water
¼ cup light corn syrup

1 cup chopped pecans
½ teaspoon baking soda

Combine the sugar, water and corn syrup in a saucepan and bring to a boil. Add the pecans. Cook over medium heat to 300 to 310 degrees on a candy thermometer, hard-crack stage. Remove from heat and stir in the baking soda. Spread over a buttered platter while still foaming. Let stand until cool. Break into pieces. Yield: variable.

Barbara Melton, Eta Beta
Stonewall, Louisiana

TOFFEE DELIGHTS

1 (12-ounce) package
*   butter crackers*
1 (10- to 12-ounce)
*   package toffee bits*

1 (14-ounce) can
*   sweetened condensed*
*   milk*
1½ cups chocolate chips

Crush the crackers into medium crumbs and place in a large bowl. Add the toffee bits and toss with the crumbs to mix well. Add the condensed milk and stir until well mixed. Press the mixture into a buttered 9-inch square pan. Sprinkle the chocolate chips evenly over the top and press in lightly. Bake at 350 degrees for 8 minutes; do not overbake. Cool completely before cutting into squares. Yield: 2 dozen.

Karen Mayner, Alpha Gamma
Fort Saskatchewan, Alberta, Canada

CINNAMON NUTS

1 cup sugar
⅓ cup evaporated milk
½ teaspoon cinnamon
½ teaspoon salt

½ teaspoon vanilla
*   extract*
2 cups walnuts, whole
*   or halved*

Combine the sugar, evaporated milk, cinnamon and salt in a saucepan over low heat. Cook to 234 to 240 degrees on a candy thermometer, soft-ball stage. Remove from heat and stir in the vanilla and walnuts. Spread over waxed paper quickly. Separate into pieces with a fork. Store in an airtight container. Serve in candy dishes. Yield: 2 cups.

Sandra Duncan Hoyt, Alpha Alpha Master
Grants Pass, Oregon

JUBILEE PIECES

12 to 24 graham
*   crackers*
1 cup packed brown
*   sugar*

1 cup (2 sticks) butter
1 cup coarsely chopped
*   pecans*

Cover the bottom of a baking sheet with graham crackers. Combine the brown sugar and butter in a saucepan and bring to a boil; boil for 1 minute. Stir in the pecans. Pour the boiling mixture over the graham cracker layer. Bake at 350 degrees for 10 minutes. Remove from oven. Turn the warm candy onto waxed paper. Cool and cut or break into pieces. Store in an airtight container. Yield: variable.

Carol Heath, Xi Psi
Crestview, Florida

GRAHAM ALMOND BARS

Graham crackers to line
*   a cake pan*
1 cup (2 sticks) butter
*   (no substitute)*

½ cup packed brown
*   sugar*
1 (4-ounce) package
*   sliced almonds*

Line a 10×15-inch cake pan with foil; line the foil-lined pan with a single layer of graham crackers. Combine the butter, brown sugar and almonds in a saucepan and bring to a boil. Boil vigorously for 2 minutes, stirring constantly. Pour the hot mixture evenly over the graham cracker layer. Bake at 325 to 350 degrees for 8 minutes. Cool in the pan. Break into pieces. Yield: variable.

Elda Petrich, Preceptor Mu Kappa
Yoakum, Texas

BROWN SUGAR CANDY

Add nuts or 1 cup peanut butter to this simple candy if desired.

3 cups packed brown
*   sugar*
1 cup evaporated
*   milk*
½ cup (1 stick) butter or
*   margarine*

3 tablespoons corn
*   syrup*
1 cup marshmallow
*   creme*
1 teaspoon vanilla
*   extract*

Combine the brown sugar, evaporated milk, butter and corn syrup in a saucepan and bring to a boil. Cook over medium heat to 234 to 240 degrees on a candy thermometer, soft-ball stage. Remove from heat and stir in the marshmallow creme and vanilla. Beat until creamy. Pour into a buttered 9×9-inch pan. Let stand until cool. Yield: variable.

Sherri Blair, Zi Alpha Phi
Paintsville, Kentucky

CREAM CHEESE CANDY

2 cups pecans
2 tablespoons butter
6 ounces cream cheese,
   softened

1 (1-pound) package
   confectioners' sugar
1 teaspoon vanilla
   extract

Place the pecans and butter in a large shallow pan. Bake at 350 degrees for 15 minutes or until pecans are toasted, stirring occasionally. Melt the cream cheese in the top of a double boiler over simmering water. Add the confectioners' sugar and vanilla gradually, stirring well. Stir in the pecans. Spread over a baking sheet. Let stand until cool. Cut into squares. Yield: variable.

Glendola King, Xi Gamma Omicron
Pryor, Oklahoma

CHOCOLATE NUT BARK

This candy offers a wonderful blend of flavors, buttery sweet chocolate with crunchy salted nuts. Substitute 2 cups of mixed nuts for the listed nuts if desired.

1 (8-ounce) can salted
   cashews
1 (8-ounce) package
   salted pistachios
1/2 cup walnuts

1/2 cup almonds
2 cups dark chocolate
   chips
2 tablespoons butter

Line a baking sheet with foil. Combine the cashews, pistachios, walnuts and almonds in a bowl and mix well. Spread the nut mixture over the prepared baking sheet. Melt the chocolate chips and butter with 1/2 cup water in the top of a double boiler over simmering water. Drizzle the chocolate mixture evenly over the nuts. Chill for 2 hours. Cut into 1-inch squares. Yield: 40 pieces.

Rhonda Moore, Preceptor Gamma Delta
Monument, Colorado

TIGER BUTTER

1 pound white chocolate
   almond bark
1 (12-ounce) jar crunchy
   peanut butter

1 cup chocolate chips,
   melted

Spray a 9×13-inch pan with nonstick cooking spray and line with waxed paper. Melt the white chocolate and peanut butter in a microwave oven, stirring occasionally until well blended. Pour into the prepared pan. Drizzle the melted chocolate chips over the peanut butter mixture and swirl in with a knife. Chill until firm. Cut into squares. Refrigerate leftovers. Yield: variable.

Bertha Cooley, Delta Kappa
Ellisville, Mississippi

PEANUT BUTTER CANDY BARS

2 cups graham cracker
   crumbs
1 (1-pound) package
   confectioners' sugar
1 (18-ounce) jar peanut
   butter, softened

1 cup (2 sticks) butter or
   margarine, melted
1 cup chocolate chips
1/4 cup (1/2 stick) butter
   or margarine

Combine the graham cracker crumbs and confectioners' sugar in a bowl and mix well with a fork. Add the peanut butter and the 1 cup melted butter; mix well. Spread in an unbuttered 10×15-inch cake pan. Melt the chocolate chips and the 1/4 cup butter together; spread over the peanut butter layer. Chill until firm. Remove from refrigerator and bring to room temperature. Cut into bars. Yield: 4 dozen.

Mary Kennedy, Preceptor Upsilon
South Windsor, Connecticut

EASY CHOCOLATE PEANUT BUTTER CANDY

1 pound white chocolate
1 (12-ounce) jar crunchy
   peanut butter

1 cup semisweet
   chocolate chips

Break the white chocolate into pieces and place in a 1 1/2-quart microwave-safe bowl. Microwave on High for 3 minutes or until melted. Add the peanut butter. Microwave on High for 2 minutes longer and stir to blend. Spread the mixture in a waxed paper-lined 10×15-inch cake pan. Place the chocolate chips in a 2-cup glass measuring cup. Microwave on High for about 2 minutes or until chocolate is melted (stir to see if it has melted). Drizzle over the peanut butter mixture and swirl with a knife. Chill until set. Cut into squares. Yield: 2 pounds.

Laurie Center, Preceptor Alpha Rho
Phillipsburg, New Jersey

ROCKY ROAD

A great dessert in minutes!

2 1/3 cups chocolate chips
1 cup miniature
   marshmallows

1 cup creamy peanut
   butter
1 cup peanuts

Place the chocolate chips in a microwave-safe bowl. Microwave until melted. Stir in the marshmallows, peanut butter and peanuts. Scrape into a buttered shallow pan and smooth the top. Chill, covered, until serving time. Yield: variable.

Shauna Spees, Beta Upsilon
Medford, Oregon

❖ MAMA HARPER'S CREAMY CHOCOLATE CANDY

4¹/₂ cups sugar
1 (12-ounce) can
   evaporated milk
1 cup (2 sticks) butter or
   margarine
3 cups chocolate chips

1 (7-ounce) jar
   marshmallow creme
2 tablespoons vanilla
   extract
2 cups walnut halves

Combine the sugar, evaporated milk and butter in a saucepan over medium heat and bring to a boil. Boil for 9 to 12 minutes. Add the chocolate chips, marshmallow creme and vanilla; do not stir. Remove from the heat and let stand until cooled to 110 degrees. Beat until smooth and stir in the walnuts. Pour into a buttered 9×13-inch dish. Let stand until firm and cut into squares. Yield: about 5 pounds.

Jan C. Nelson, Preceptor Delta Phi
Twain Harte, California

❖ HOMEMADE THREE MUSKETEERS

3 egg whites
3 cups sugar
³/₄ cup light corn syrup
³/₄ cup water
¹/₈ teaspoon salt

¹/₃ cup semisweet
   chocolate chips
4 cups milk chocolate
   chips

Place the egg whites in a large bowl and beat until stiff peaks form. Combine the sugar, corn syrup, water and salt in a large saucepan over medium heat; bring to a boil, stirring constantly. Cook to 270 degrees on a candy thermometer, soft-crack stage. Remove from heat and pour in a thin stream over the egg whites, beating constantly at low speed. Continue to mix until the mixture begins to harden to the consistency of dough; this may take as long as 20 minutes. Stir in the semisweet chocolate chips until well mixed. Press the mixture into a buttered 9×9-inch pan. Chill until firm, about 30 minutes. Cut the candy in half down the center of the pan with a sharp knife. Cut across into 7 segments to make 14 bars; cut again to make 28. Place the milk chocolate chips in a microwave-safe bowl. Microwave on Medium for 2 minutes or until melted, stirring halfway through the heating time; do not overheat. Resting a bar on a fork, and using your fingers if necessary, dip each bar into the melted chocolate to coat completely. Place each coated bar on waxed paper. Cool to room temperature until firm, about 1 or 2 hours. Yield: 28 pieces.

Mary Ann Williams, Chi Iota
Summerfield, Illinois

OH HENRY BARS

1 cup light corn syrup
1 cup sugar
1¹/₂ cups peanut butter
6 cups Special-K

1 cup chocolate chips
2 cups butterscotch
   chips

Combine the corn syrup and sugar in a large kettle over medium hat and bring to a boil. Stir in the peanut butter and remove from heat. Add the Special-K and mix well; spread the mixture quickly in a buttered 9×13-inch pan. Combine the chocolate chips and butterscotch chips in a 2-cup glass measuring cup. Microwave on High for 2 minutes; stir until smooth. Spread evenly over the Special-K layer. Let stand until cool. Cut into squares and serve. Yield: 4 dozen.

Ellen Althaus-Day, Gamma Pi
Wellsville, New York

MARS BARS DELIGHTS

4 Mars Bars
1 cup miniature
   marshmallows
¹/₄ cup (¹/₂ stick) plus
   2 tablespoons butter

2 cups crisp rice cereal
1 cup chocolate chips

Combine the Mars Bars, marshmallows and the ¹/₄ cup butter in a saucepan over medium-low heat. Heat until melted, stirring occasionally. Stir in the crisp rice cereal. Spread the mixture in a buttered 8×8-inch pan. Let stand in the refrigerator while completing the recipe. Combine the chocolate chips and the 2 tablespoons butter in a saucepan over medium-low heat. Heat until melted, stirring occasionally. Drizzle over the cereal layer. Chill, covered, for at least 2 hours. Cut and serve. Yield: 16 to 25 squares.

Kelly Henderson, Xi Eta
Truro, Nova Scotia, Canada

PEANUT BUTTER FINGERS

1 cup crunchy peanut
   butter
1 cup confectioners'
   sugar

1¹/₂ cups crisp rice cereal
¹/₄ cup chopped walnuts
   or pecans (optional)
¹/₄ cup melted butter

Combine the peanut butter, confectioners' sugar, crisp rice cereal, chopped nuts and melted butter in a bowl and mix well. Shape spoonfuls into finger-size logs. Roll in confectioners' sugar, chopped nuts or shredded coconut. Chill until serving time. Yield: about 20 pieces.

Joanne Buckel, Kappa Alpha
Petawawa, Ontario, Canada

Refrigerator Desserts

APRICOT NECTAR DESSERT

1 prepared angel food
    cake, broken into
    small pieces
1 (46-ounce) can apricot
    nectar
1¹/2 cups sugar
7 rounded tablespoons
    cornstarch
8 ounces whipped
    topping

Spread the angel food pieces in a 9×13-inch baking dish. Combine the next 3 ingredients in a kettle over medium heat and cook until thickened, stirring constantly. Cool slightly. Pour over the cake and chill, covered. Spread whipped topping over the top and sprinkle with chopped walnuts. Yield: 12 servings.

Lueann Schisler, Alpha Delta
Macon, Missouri

BLUEBERRY DESSERT

8 ounces cream cheese,
    softened
1 cup confectioners'
    sugar
8 ounces whipped
    topping
1 angel food cake, cut in
    1-inch cubes
1¹/2 teaspoons grated
    orange zest
2 (21-ounce) cans
    blueberry pie filling

Mix the cream cheese and confectioners' sugar in a mixing bowl until smooth. Fold in the next 3 ingredients. Spread in an unbuttered 9×13-inch baking dish. Layer the blueberry pie filling over the top. Chill, covered, for at least 2 hours. Yield: 15 servings.

Margaret E. Grindley, Eta Master
Seattle, Washington

Donna McCormick, Delta Master, Douglas, Alaksa, makes **Cranberries à la Alaska.** *She grinds a package of cranberries, mixes in 1 cup sugar and lets stand for 1 hour. Add a package of miniature marshmallows and 2 cups whipping cream and let stand for 1 hour. Mix in 1 cup drained crushed pineapple and ¹/2 cup chopped walnuts and chill overnight.*

CARAMEL ANGEL FOOD DESSERT

3 ounces cream cheese,
    softened
¹/4 cup confectioners'
    sugar
8 ounces whipped
    topping
1 (10-inch) prepared
    angel food cake
1 cup half-and-half
³/4 cup granulated sugar
¹/2 cup light corn syrup
¹/4 cup (¹/2 stick) butter
    (no substitute)
Pinch of salt
¹/2 teaspoon vanilla
    extract

Combine the cream cheese and confectioners' sugar in a mixing bowl and beat until smooth. Fold in the whipped topping. Slice the cake horizontally into 2 layers. Place the bottom layer on a serving plate and spread evenly with the cream cheese mixture. Replace the top of the cake and chill, covered, in the refrigerator. Combine ³/4 cup of the half-and-half, granulated sugar, corn syrup, butter and salt in a saucepan. Cook and stir over medium heat to 234 degrees on a candy thermometer, soft-ball stage. Add the remaining ¹/4 cup half-and-half slowly, and cook until mixture returns to 234 degrees, soft-ball stage. Remove from heat and stir in the vanilla. Cool slightly and drizzle over the filled cake. Store in the refrigerator. Yield: 12 servings.

Kathy Young, Laureate Beta Beta
Cave Junction, Oregon

❖ CHOCOLATE MOCHA TRIFLE

1 (20-ounce) package
    brownie mix
1³/4 cups milk
1 (4-ounce) package
    vanilla instant
    pudding mix
4 teaspoons instant
    coffee granules
¹/4 cup warm water
2 cups whipped topping
3 (2-ounce) chocolate
    candy bars

Prepare and bake the brownie mix using the package directions; cool completely. Pour the milk into a large bowl. Whisk the pudding mix into the milk; continue to whisk until mixture begins to thicken. Dissolve the coffee granules in the warm water and add to the pudding mixture; mix well. Fold in the whipped topping. Cut the cooled brownies into 1-inch cubes. Chop the candy bars into small bits. Layer the brownie cubes, pudding and chopped candy bars ⅓ at a time in a serving bowl or trifle bowl. Chill, covered, for 25 to 30 minutes before serving. Yield: 12 servings.

Dena Stewart, Gamma Theta
Wetaskiwin, Alberta, Canada

CHOCOLATE ANGEL FOOD DESSERT

4 eggs, separated
2 cups chocolate chips
½ cup sugar
Dash of salt
2 cups whipping cream
2 teaspoons vanilla
  extract
1 prepared angel food
  cake

Beat the egg yolks slightly. Melt the chocolate chips with the sugar and salt in the top of a double boiler over simmering water; stir until smooth. Add the egg yolks and cook for 5 minutes longer, stirring well. Remove from heat and let stand until cool. Beat the whipping cream in a chilled bowl until stiff peaks form. Beat the egg whites in a separate bowl until stiff peaks form. Fold into the whipped cream. Add 1 cup of the whipped cream mixture to the chocolate mixture and beat until smooth. Fold the chocolate mixture into the remaining whipped cream mixture; mix well. Stir in the vanilla. Tear the angel food cake into 1-inch pieces and layer in a buttered 9×13-inch baking dish. Pour the chocolate mixture evenly over the cake layer and poke it down through the cake pieces. Chill, covered, for 24 hours. Yield: 16 servings.

Kim Spreacker, Laureate Gamma Zeta
Pella, Iowa

PUNCH BOWL CAKE

1 (2-layer) package
  butter cake mix
2 (6-ounce) packages
  vanilla instant
  pudding mix
5 cups milk
8 ounces cream cheese,
  softened
1 cup confectioners'
  sugar
20 ounces whipped
  topping
3 to 5 cups mixed fresh
  or canned fruits, well
  drained
1 cup shredded coconut
1 cup chopped walnuts
  or pecans

Prepare and bake the cake mix using the package directions for a 9×13-inch cake pan. Cool completely and cut or break into small pieces. Combine the pudding mix and milk in a mixing bowl and mix well. Combine the cream cheese, confectioners' sugar and 12 ounces of the whipped topping in a separate mix-

ing bowl and mix well. Layer cake pieces, pudding mixture and mixed fruit ⅓ at a time in a punch bowl. Cover with the remaining whipped topping. Sprinkle with coconut and nuts. Chill, covered, in the refrigerator for 8 to 10 hours. Yield: 15 to 20 servings.

Barbara Cole, Preceptor Gamma
Beckley, West Virginia

LEMON ANGEL PARTY CAKE

1 (10-inch) prepared
  angel food cake
6 eggs, separated
1½ cups sugar
¾ cup lemon juice
1½ teaspoons grated
  lemon zest
1 envelope unflavored
  gelatin (1 tablespoon)
¼ cup cold water
4 drops yellow food
  coloring
Sweetened whipped
  cream

Trim the crusts from the cake and save for another purpose. Tear the cake into small pieces. Beat the egg yolks. Combine the egg yolks, ¾ cup of the sugar, lemon juice and lemon zest in the top of a double boiler over hot, not boiling, water. Cook until the mixture coats a metal spoon, stirring constantly. Remove from heat. Soften the gelatin in the cold water and add to the lemon mixture. Stir in the food coloring. Cool until partially set. Beat the egg whites until foamy; beat with the remaining ¾ cup sugar until stiff peaks form. Fold into the lemon mixture. Layer the cake pieces and lemon mixture alternately in a 10-inch tube pan until all of the ingredients are used, ending with the lemon mixture. Chill, covered, for 8 to 10 hours. Invert into a serving plate and fill the center with whipped cream. Frost with additional whipped cream if desired. Yield: 12 to 14 servings.

Heather A. Murray, Lambda Master
North Bay, Ontario, Canada

TRIPLE ORANGE FLUFF

1 small package
  orange sugar-free
  gelatin
1 cup boiling water
1 pint orange sherbet,
  softened
8 ounces reduced-fat
  whipped topping
1 (16-ounce) prepared
  angel food cake
1 (15-ounce) can
  mandarin oranges

Dissolve the gelatin in the boiling water in a large bowl. Stir in the sherbet. Chill until partially set. Fold in the whipped topping. Tear the cake into bite-size pieces and spread in a 9×13-inch baking dish. Layer the mandarin oranges over the cake. Pour the gelatin mixture evenly over the top. Chill, covered, for at least 4 hours. Yield: 15 servings.

Dorothy M. Donay, Laureate Xi
Coldwater, Michigan

RASPBERRY BANANA TRIFLE

1 (4-ounce) package
   vanilla cook-and-
   serve pudding mix
1 (3-ounce) package
   raspberry gelatin
2 (10-ounce) packages
   frozen raspberries in
   syrup, thawed
6 ounces raspberry
   preserves

1 prepared pound cake
1/4 to 1/2 cup cream
   sherry or dark rum
1 banana, sliced
1 cup whipping cream,
   whipped, or 8 ounces
   whipped topping
12 whole fresh
   raspberries

Prepare the pudding mix using the package directions; chill until set. Prepare the gelatin using the package directions; chill until set. Drain the raspberries, reserving 1/2 cup of the syrup. Combine the reserved syrup and raspberry preserves in a small bowl and mix well. Cut the pound cake into 1/2-inch-thick slices and use to line the bottom of an 8-inch-diameter 5-inch-deep flat-bottomed glass bowl. Drizzle with the sherry and spread with 1/4 cup of the preserves mixture. Layer the banana slices and thawed raspberries over the top. Pour the cooled gelatin mixture evenly over the top and chill until set. Spread with whipped cream and garnish with the whole strawberries. Yield: 15 servings.

Viktoria Lawson, Epsilon Pi
Longmont, Colorado

SHERRY TRIFLE

1/2 pound cake
6 to 10 tablespoons
   sherry
1 (16-ounce) can fruit
   cocktail, drained
1 (3-ounce) package
   strawberry gelatin
1 cup boiling water
1 cup cold water

1 (4-ounce) package
   vanilla instant
   pudding mix
8 ounces whipped
   topping
1 (11-ounce) can
   mandarin oranges,
   drained
Maraschino cherries

Cut the pound cake into cubes. Place in a trifle bowl or large glass bowl and drizzle with the sherry to soak. Cover with the fruit cocktail. Place the gelatin in a bowl and add the boiling water; mix well. Stir in the cold water. Drizzle the gelatin mixture over the fruit cocktail. Chill until firm. Prepare the pudding mix using the package directions and pour evenly over the gelatin layer. Spread the whipped topping over the top. Decorate with mandarin oranges and cherries. Yield: 12 to 15 servings.

Sharron deMontigny, Xi Kappa
Corvallis, Oregon

PINK STRAWBERRY CLOUD

1 (16-ounce) package
   angel food cake mix
2 (3-ounce) packages
   strawberry-banana
   gelatin
2 cups boiling water
2 (10-ounce) packages
   frozen strawberries

2 cups whipping cream
1/4 cup confectioners'
   sugar
1/2 cup chopped walnuts
   or pecans

Prepare and bake the angel food cake mix using the package directions; cool. Place the dry gelatin mix in a bowl; add the boiling water and stir to dissolve. Add the frozen strawberries and stir to break up the frozen fruit; chill in the refrigerator for about 5 minutes to thicken. Combine the whipping cream and confectioners' sugar and beat until stiff peaks form. Fold into the thickened gelatin. Tear the cooled cake into small pieces. Layer the cake pieces and gelatin mixture 1/2 at a time in a 9×13-inch baking dish. Chill, covered, for at least 2 hours. Yield: 15 servings.

Judy K. Diede, Xi Eta
Bismarck, North Dakota

STRAWBERRY TRIFLE

1 (16-ounce) package
   angel food cake mix
1/2 envelope whipped
   topping mix
1 pint strawberries,
   sliced

2 (6-ounce) cartons
   nonfat strawberry
   yogurt
3 kiwifruit, sliced
1/4 cup slivered almonds,
   toasted

Prepare and bake the cake mix using the package directions; cool. Cut into halves vertically; freeze one half for another purpose. Tear the remaining half into 3/4-inch pieces. Prepare the whipped topping mix using the package directions, substituting skim milk for the milk. Layer the cake pieces, whipped topping, strawberries, yogurt and kiwifruit 1/2 at a time in a 2-quart serving bowl. Sprinkle with almonds. Garnish with whole strawberries if desired. Chill until firm, for at least 2 hours. Yield: 12 servings.

Cindy Dix, Laureate Gamma Nu
Lancaster, California

STRAWBERRY BLUEBERRY TRIFLE

3 cups cold fat-free milk
2 small packages white
   chocolate sugar-free
   instant pudding mix
1 prepared angel food
   cake, cut into 1-inch
   pieces

3 cups sliced
   strawberries
3 cups blueberries
8 ounces reduced-fat
   whipped topping

Combine the milk and pudding mix in a large mixing bowl and beat at low speed for 2 minutes. Layer the cake, pudding, strawberries, blueberries and whipped topping 1/3 at a time in the order given in a trifle bowl or 3 1/2-quart glass bowl. Chill, covered, until serving time. Yield: 18 servings.

Annette M. Hoch, Preceptor Beta Epsilon
Topeka, Kansas

LADYFINGER CROWN

2 (3-ounce) packages
  ladyfingers
1/4 cup rum or brandy
  (optional)
2 cups whipping cream
1/2 cup sugar

1 teaspoon vanilla
  extract
8 ounces cream cheese,
  softened
1 (21-ounce) can pie
  filling of choice

Separate the ladyfingers and brush the flat side of each with rum. Line the bottom and side of a 9-inch springform pan with the ladyfingers, sides touching, rounded sides against the pan. Beat the cream with the sugar in a mixing bowl until stiff peaks form. Blend in the vanilla and cream cheese. Spread half the cream cheese mixture in the ladyfinger-lined pan. Layer the remaining ladyfingers and the remaining cream cheese mixture over the cream cheese layer. Chill, covered, in the refrigerator for 2 to 10 hours. Spoon the pie filling carefully over the top. Chill until serving time. Remove the side of the pan and place dessert on a serving plate. Yield: 10 to 12 servings.

Anne Stone, Laureate Phi
Montgomery, New York

NEW-NEW TIRAMISU

8 ounces cream cheese,
  softened
1/2 cup sugar
1/4 cup sour cream
2 1/2 cups whipped
  topping
1 tablespoon instant
  coffee granules

1 cup hot water
2 tablespoons coffee
  liqueur
2 (3-ounce) packages
  ladyfingers
2 tablespoons baking
  cocoa

Combine the cream cheese, sugar and sour cream in a mixing bowl and beat at low speed until creamy. Fold in the whipped topping gently. Stir the coffee granules into the hot water in a small bowl; stir in the liqueur. Split the ladyfingers and arrange 1/4 of the ladyfinger halves in the bottom of a 3-quart bowl. Drizzle with 1/4 of the coffee mixture. Spoon 1/3 of the cream cheese mixture over the top. Layer 1/4 of the ladyfingers and 1/4 of the coffee mixture over the cream cheese layer. Repeat the cream cheese, ladyfinger and coffee mixture layers twice. Sprinkle evenly

with the baking cocoa. Chill, covered, for at least 3 hours before serving. Yield: 10 to 12 servings.

Elsie Samet, Kappa Eta
Woodstock, Virginia

CREAMY CHERRY DELIGHT

1 1/4 cups graham cracker
  crumbs
3 tablespoons
  granulated sugar
1/2 cup (1 stick)
  margarine, melted
2 envelopes whipped
  topping mix

8 ounces cream cheese,
  softened
1 cup confectioners'
  sugar
1 (21-ounce) can cherry
  pie filling

Press a mixture of the graham cracker crumbs, granulated sugar and melted margarine into a 9×13-inch baking dish. Prepare the whipped topping using the package directions. Combine the cream cheese and confectioners' sugar in a separate mixing bowl and beat until smooth. Mix the cream cheese mixture into the whipped topping and spread in a 9×13-inch baking dish. Spoon the cherry pie filling evenly over the top. Chill, covered, until serving time.
Yield: 10 to 12 servings.

Ann Blaser, Xi Zeta Rho
Lamar, Missouri

MINT DAZZLER

2 cups vanilla wafer or
  graham cracker
  crumbs
6 tablespoons butter,
  melted
1 1/2 cups confectioners'
  sugar
1/2 cup butter, softened
3 eggs
3 ounces baking
  chocolate, melted

1 cup whipping cream,
  whipped, or 2 cups
  nondairy whipped
  topping
3 1/2 cups miniature
  marshmallows
1/4 cup crushed pillow
  mints

Mix the crumbs and melted butter together in a bowl. Press the crumb mixture into a 9×13-inch baking dish. Combine the confectioners' sugar and softened butter in a mixing bowl and beat until light and fluffy. Beat in the eggs 1 at a time. Add the chocolate and beat until smooth and fluffy. Spoon over the crumb layer. Chill for at least 30 minutes. Place the whipped cream in a bowl and fold in the marshmallows gently. Spread the marshmallow mixture over the chocolate layer. Sprinkle with crushed mints. Chill, covered, for at least 3 hours. Yield: 18 to 20 servings.

Doris M. Swinehart, Xi Alpha Omicron
Necedah, Wisconsin

❖ WHITE AND DARK CHOCOLATE ICEBOX CAKE

1 cup white chocolate chips	1 cup whipping cream
1/3 cup whipping cream	1 tablespoon confectioners' sugar
1 cup dark chocolate chips	1 tablespoon dark rum
1/2 cup whipping cream	1 cup chocolate wafer cookie crumbs or
2 tablespoons confectioners' sugar	chocolate sandwich cookie crumbs
1 tablespoon Grand Marnier	1 1/3 cups whipping cream

Line a 5×9-inch loaf pan or 8 individual loaf pans with plastic wrap, leaving a 2-inch overhang. Combine the white chocolate chips and 1/3 cup cream in a small microwave-safe bowl. Microwave on Medium for 1 minute and stir. Microwave for 30 seconds longer or until chocolate is softened; stir until smooth and set aside to cool. Combine the dark chocolate chips and 1/2 cup cream in a small bowl. Microwave on Medium for 1 minute and stir. Microwave for 30 seconds longer or until chocolate is softened; stir until smooth and set aside to cool. Place 1 cup of the cream in a medium bowl and beat at medium speed until soft peaks form. Add 2 tablespoons confectioners' sugar and the Grand Marnier and beat until stiff peaks form. Stir about 1/3 of the Grand Marnier mixture into the cooled white chocolate mixture to lighten the texture. Fold in the remaining Grand Marnier mixture and place in the refrigerator. Place another cup of the whipping cream in a medium bowl and beat at medium speed until soft peaks form. Add 1 tablespoon of the confectioners' sugar and dark rum and beat until stiff peaks form. Fold about 1/3 of the dark rum mixture into the cooled dark chocolate mixture to lighten the texture. Fold in the remaining rum mixture and place in the refrigerator. Spread 1/3 cup of the cookie crumbs in the prepared loaf pan. Spread the white chocolate mixture evenly over the crumbs and sprinkle with another 1/3 cup cookie crumbs. Spread the dark chocolate mixture over the white chocolate layer and sprinkle with the remaining 1/3 cup cookie crumbs. Cover with plastic wrap and chill for at least 6 hours. Whip the remaining 1 1/3 cups cream. Invert the loaf onto a serving platter carefully and peel off the plastic wrap. Spread the whipped cream over the top and around the bottom edge of the cake. Garnish with fresh raspberries or strawberries.
Yield: 8 to 10 servings.

Vickie Looney, Xi Alpha Alpha Lambda
Sugar Land, Texas

CHOCOLATE STRAWBERRY LAYERED DESSERT

1/2 cup plus 2 tablespoons butter (no substitute)	1 cup sour cream
2 cups chocolate graham cracker crumbs (about 26 squares)	1 (4-ounce) package chocolate instant pudding mix
1/4 cup sugar	1 pint strawberries, sliced
12 ounces whipped topping	1 ounce semisweet chocolate

Melt the 1/2 cup butter in a saucepan or microwave oven. Combine the cracker crumbs, melted butter and sugar in a bowl and mix well. Press over the bottom and 1 1/2 inches up the side of a buttered 9-inch springform pan. Place in the refrigerator. Combine the whipped topping, sour cream and pudding mix in a mixing bowl and blend well. Spread half the pudding mixture in the graham cracker shell. Arrange the strawberries over the pudding layer. Spread the remaining pudding mixture over the top. Melt the semisweet chocolate and the 2 tablespoons butter in the microwave oven; stir until smooth. Let stand until cool and drizzle over the pudding layer. Chill, covered, for at least 4 hours.
Yield: 10 to 12 servings.

Joyce Auger, Laureate Omega
Guelph, Ontario, Canada

ECLAIR CAKE

2 (4-ounce) packages vanilla instant pudding mix	3 tablespoons margarine
1 (12-ounce) can evaporated milk	2 teaspoons light corn syrup
2 cups milk	2 teaspoons vanilla extract
8 ounces whipped topping	1 to 1 1/2 tablespoons milk
1 (16-ounce) package graham crackers	1 1/2 cups confectioners' sugar
2 ounces German's chocolate	1 cup chopped pecans

Combine the pudding mix, evaporated milk and 2 cups milk in a large bowl and stir until smooth and slightly thickened. Stir in the whipped topping and let stand until thick. Line a buttered 9×13-inch baking dish with a single layer of graham crackers. Pour half the pudding mixture evenly over the graham crackers. Layer graham crackers, the remaining pudding mixture and a final layer of graham crackers over the pudding layer. Chill, covered, until firm, about 1 hour. Melt the German's chocolate with the margarine and corn syrup in a saucepan or microwave oven. Stir in the vanilla. Beat in the confectioners' sugar and 1 tablespoon milk. Spread over the top of the layered dessert. Sprinkle with pecans. Chill, covered, until serving time. Yield: 12 servings.

Sandra Jones, Gamma Phi Master
Amarillo, Texas

GHOSTS IN THE GRAVEYARD CHOCOLATE DESSERT

3¹/₂ cups cold milk
2 (4-ounce) packages chocolate instant pudding mix
12 ounces whipped topping
1 (16-ounce) package chocolate sandwich cookies, crumbled

Pour the cold milk into a large bowl. Add the pudding mix and beat with a wire whisk for 2 minutes. Blend in ³/₄ of the whipped topping and half the cookie crumbs. Spoon into a 9×13-inch baking dish. Sprinkle with the remaining cookie crumbs. Chill, covered, for at least 1 hour. Decorate with tombstone-shaped cookies. Write "boo" and "RIP" on cookies with a frosting tube and stand the cookies upright in various places over the dessert. Drop tablespoons of whipped topping onto the dessert to resemble ghosts; use frosting to make eyes, noses. Sprinkle the dessert with corn candies and pumpkin candies if desired. Yield: 15 servings.

June Hamann, Laureate Beta Delta
Pasco, Washington

MOCK FRENCH PASTRIES

1 (4-ounce) package vanilla cook-and-serve pudding mix
1 (16-ounce) package honey graham crackers
1 cup whipping cream, whipped
2 cups confectioners' sugar
2 tablespoons margarine, softened
¹/₂ cup semisweet chocolate chips

Prepare the pudding mix using the package directions; cool. Line a 9×13-inch baking dish with whole graham crackers. Layer the cooled pudding and whipped cream over the graham crackers. Top with whole graham crackers. Combine the confectioners' sugar and margarine in a mixing bowl and beat until smooth; beat in a little water to make a thin icing. Spread over the graham cracker layer. Melt the chocolate chips and stir in a little hot water to thin.

Drizzle the chocolate mixture in a V shape from side to side. Run a knife gently from end to end to make a chevron pattern. Chill, covered, for 8 to 10 hours. Yield: 12 servings.

Carolyn Chirrey, Xi Beta Upsilon
Decatur, Alabama

COCONUT CREAM DESSERT

60 butter crackers, crushed
¹/₂ cup (1 stick) butter, melted
¹/₂ gallon vanilla ice cream, softened
1¹/₄ cups milk
2 (4-ounce) packages coconut cream instant pudding mix
8 ounces whipped topping

Combine the cracker crumbs and melted butter in a bowl and mix well. Set aside ¹/₂ cup of the crumb mixture for the topping. Press the remaining crumb mixture into a 9×13-inch baking dish. Combine the ice cream, milk and pudding mix in a large bowl and mix well. Pour the ice cream mixture evenly over the crumb layer. Chill, covered, for 3 to 10 hours. Cover with whipped topping and sprinkle with reserved crumb mixture just before serving.
Yield: 15 to 20 servings.

Ann Lipps, Preceptor Theta
Williamson, West Virginia

LEMON FLUFF

1 (12-ounce) can evaporated milk
1 (6-ounce) package lemon gelatin
1³/₄ cups boiling water
¹/₄ cup lemon juice
¹/₂ cup sugar
2¹/₂ cups vanilla wafer crumbs
12 maraschino cherries, halved

Chill unopened can of evaporated milk in the refrigerator until very cold, about 3 or 4 hours. Dissolve the gelatin mix in the boiling water in a mixing bowl; chill until partially set. Whip the gelatin mixture until light and fluffy. Beat in the lemon juice and sugar. Whip the chilled evaporated milk in a mixing bowl until stiff peaks form. Fold into the gelatin mixture. Reserve ¹/₄ cup of the wafer crumbs for garnish. Line the bottom of a 9×13-inch baking dish with the remaining wafer crumbs. Pour the gelatin mixture evenly over the crumbs. Top with the reserved crumbs. Chill, covered, until firm. Cut into squares and top each square with a maraschino cherry half. Yield: 12 servings.

Barbara A. Willson, Xi Omega
Highlands Ranch, Colorado

LEMON PINEAPPLE DESSERT

¹/3 cup butter
1²/3 cups crushed graham
   crackers
1¹/4 cups sugar
4 eggs, separated

1 (8-ounce) can crushed
   pineapple
1 (3-ounce) package
   lemon gelatin

Melt the butter in a 9×13-inch baking dish. Add the graham cracker crumbs and ¹/4 cup of the sugar; mix well and spread over the bottom of the dish. Combine the egg yolks, ¹/2 cup of the sugar and undrained pineapple in a saucepan over medium heat and bring to a boil, stirring constantly. Boil gently until thickened. Add the dry gelatin mix and stir until dissolved. Cool. Place the egg whites in a mixing bowl and beat until foamy. Add the remaining ¹/2 cup sugar gradually, beating until stiff peaks form. Fold into the egg yolk mixture and pour gently over the graham cracker layer. Chill, covered, for at least 2 hours. Cut into squares and serve with whipped topping. Yield: 12 to 15 servings.

Ruth E. Cook, Alpha Theta Master
Lakewood, Colorado

TWENTY-FOUR-HOUR PINEAPPLE DELIGHT

¹/2 cup (1 stick) butter,
   softened
1 (12-ounce) package
   vanilla wafers,
   crushed
16 ounces cream cheese,
   softened
2 eggs

1 (1-pound) package
   confectioners' sugar
3 (20-ounce) cans
   crushed pineapple,
   well drained
2 envelopes whipped
   topping mix

Combine the butter and wafer crumbs in a bowl and mix well. Pat ³/4 of the crumb mixture into a 9×13-inch baking dish. Combine the cream cheese, eggs and confectioners' sugar in a mixing bowl and beat until smooth; spread over the crumb layer. Layer the pineapple over the cream cheese layer and sprinkle with the remaining crumb mixture. Cover with foil and chill for 24 hours. Yield: 12 servings.

Joyce Klupp, Xi Gamma Rho
Gassville, Arkansas

PINEAPPLE PUDDING

3 eggs, separated
1 (8-ounce) can crushed
   pineapple
²/3 cup sugar
¹/2 (3-ounce) package
   lemon gelatin

18 whole graham
   crackers, crushed
¹/4 cup (¹/2 stick)
   margarine, melted

Combine the egg yolks, undrained pineapple and ¹/3 cup of the sugar in a saucepan over low heat. Cook until thickened, stirring constantly. Remove from heat and stir in the dry gelatin mix. Let stand until cool. Combine the graham crackers and melted margarine in a bowl and mix well. Press half the crumb mixture into a 9×9-inch baking dish. Beat the egg whites in a mixing bowl until stiff peaks form. Add the remaining ¹/3 cup sugar and beat for several minutes longer. Fold into the pineapple mixture; pour evenly over the crumb layer. Chill, covered, for 3 hours or until set. Yield: 9 servings.

Kari Schultz, Preceptor Delta Chi
Hays, Kansas

PISTACHIO DESSERT

2 sleeves butter crackers,
   crushed
³/4 cup (1¹/2 sticks)
   margarine, melted
3 (4-ounce) packages
   pistachio instant
   pudding mix
2¹/4 cups milk
1¹/2 quarts vanilla ice
   cream, softened

2 or 3 drops green food
   coloring
12 ounces whipped
   topping
1 (7-ounce) chocolate
   candy bar, frozen,
   crushed

Combine the cracker crumbs and margarine in a bowl. Spread the crumb mixture in a 9×13-inch baking dish and press firmly. Combine the dry pudding mix and milk in a large mixing bowl and mix well. Add the ice cream and food coloring and beat at low speed until smooth. Pour into the prepared baking dish and let stand in the refrigerator until set. Spread whipped topping over the pudding layer and sprinkle with the crushed candy. Chill, covered, for 3 to 10 hours. Freeze if desired. Yield: 12 to 15 servings.

Irene G. Berghoff, Pi Master
Bethalto, Illinois

ICE CREAM PUDDING DESSERT

75 butter crackers,
   crushed
¹/2 cup sugar
¹/2 cup (1 stick)
   margarine,
   melted
2 cups milk

2 (4-ounce) packages
   vanilla instant
   pudding mix
1 quart vanilla ice
   cream, softened
8 ounces whipped
   topping

Combine the cracker crumbs, sugar and melted margarine in a bowl and mix well. Reserve ¹/2 cup of the crumb mixture for garnish. Press the remaining mixture into a 9×13-inch baking dish. Combine the milk and dry pudding mix in a large mixing bowl and mix well. Add the ice cream and mix until smooth. Pour evenly over the crumb layer. Chill in the refrigerator for 20 to 30 minutes. Spread whipped topping over the top and sprinkle with the reserved 1/2 cup crumb mixture. Yield: 15 to 20 servings.

Berlita Anderson, Laureate Kappa
Beatrice, Nebraska

CHOCOLATE PUDDING

6 tablespoons cornstarch	3³/4 cups water
3 tablespoons baking cocoa	2 teaspoons vanilla extract
Dash of salt	2 tablespoons butter
1¹/3 cups nonfat dry milk powder	Artificial sweetener equal to 1 cup sugar

Combine the cornstarch, baking cocoa, salt and dry milk powder in a glass bowl and mix well. Add the water slowly, stirring until blended. Microwave on High for 3 minutes, 2 minutes and 1 minute, stirring well at each interval. Pudding should be smooth and thick. Stir in the vanilla, butter and artificial sweetener. Pour into dessert dishes and chill until serving time. Yield: 6 to 8 servings.

Mary S. Beamer, Xi Delta Xi
Oakridge, Oregon

OLD-FASHIONED ORANGE PUDDING

3 cups milk	1 egg (optional)
4¹/2 tablespoons cornstarch	³/4 teaspoon vanilla extract
³/4 cup sugar	2 oranges, peeled, cut into chunks
1/2 teaspoon salt	

Scald 2¹/2 cups of the milk in the top of a double boiler over simmering water. Combine the cornstarch, sugar, salt, egg and the remaining 1/2 cup milk in a mixing bowl and mix until smooth. Blend in a little of the scalded milk. Add the cornstarch mixture to the remaining scalded milk gradually, stirring constantly until smooth. Cook, covered, for 25 minutes, stirring occasionally to prevent lumping. Remove from heat. Stir in the vanilla and cool. Stir in the oranges. Chill, covered, until serving time. Yield: 6 servings.

Linda Anderson, Laureate Alpha Iota
Greely, Ontario, Canada

PEANUT BUTTER PUDDING

1 cup sugar	3 tablespoons vanilla extract
1/2 cup flour	
4 cups boiling water	1/2 cup butter
2 cups peanut butter	

Combine the first 3 ingredients in a saucepan over medium heat. Cook until thickened, stirring constantly. Stir in the peanut butter, vanilla and butter. Remove from heat and beat with an electric mixer at high speed until smooth. Chill, covered, until serving time. Serve on graham crackers. Yield: 6 servings.

Debbie Holmes, Theta Theta
Clintwood, Virginia

POTS DE CREME

1¹/4 cups heavy cream	2 egg yolks, at room temperature
1¹/4 cups dark chocolate buttons	

Scald the cream in a heavy saucepan over medium-low heat. Combine the chocolate buttons and egg yolks in a blender. Add the scalded cream in a fine stream, processing constantly until chocolate is melted and mixture is smooth. Spoon the chocolate mixture into "cream pots" or very small cups. Chill, covered, for at least 3 hours. Serve with tiny spoons. Top with dollops of whipped cream. Yield: 6 to 8 servings.

Penny Sabath, Preceptor Iota
Eugene, Oregon

FROSTY CHOCOLATE MOUSSE

1¹/2 cups whipping cream	1/2 teaspoon vanilla extract
1/2 cup sugar	1/2 cup sifted baking cocoa
1/2 teaspoon rum extract	

Combine the cream, sugar, rum extract, vanilla and baking cocoa in a mixing bowl and beat until mixture is smooth and mounds softly. Spoon into dessert dishes. Cover and freeze for at least 2 hours before serving. Yield: 4 servings.

Nancy Ingman, Laureate Iota Delta
Encinitas, California

PUMPKIN MOUSSE

8 ounces cream cheese, softened	1 (29-ounce) can pumpkin
1 cup sour cream	Cinnamon and nutmeg to taste
1 (16-ounce) can vanilla frosting	1 cup whipped topping

Combine the cream cheese, sour cream and vanilla frosting in a mixing bowl and mix well. Add the pumpkin and mix until smooth. Mix in the cinnamon and nutmeg. Mix in the whipped topping. Spoon into individual dessert dishes. Chill, covered, for at least 1 hour before serving. Yield: 8 to 10 servings.

Sandra Scholfield Plunkett, Preceptor Nu Nu
Brawley, California

LEMON MOUSSE

4 egg yolks, beaten
1 teaspoon grated lemon
  zest
1/4 cup lemon juice
1/2 cup plus 2
  tablespoons sugar
4 egg whites
1 cup whipped cream

1 (4-ounce) package
  vanilla instant
  pudding mix
1 cup miniature
  marshmallows
1/2 cup chopped walnuts
  or pecans

Combine the egg yolks, lemon zest, lemon juice and the 1/2 cup sugar in a saucepan over medium-low heat. Cook until thickened, stirring constantly. Cover and chill. Beat the egg whites in a mixing bowl until foamy. Add the 2 tablespoons sugar and beat until stiff peaks form. Fold in the whipped cream. Prepare the pudding mix using the package directions; stir in the marshmallows and chopped nuts. Fold into the lemon mixture. Chill, covered, until serving time. Spoon into dessert cups and serve. Yield: 6 servings.

Doris J. Bain, Xi Epsilon
Chattanooga, Tennessee

RUSSIAN CREME

1³/4 cups half-and-half
1 cup plus 2 tablespoons
  sugar
2 tablespoons
  unflavored gelatin
1/2 cup cold water
1¹/2 cups thick sour
  cream

1 teaspoon vanilla
  extract
1 (10-ounce) package
  frozen raspberries,
  thawed

Combine the half-and-half and the 1 cup sugar in a saucepan and heat until very hot. Remove from heat. Soften the gelatin in the cold water and whisk into the hot half-and-half mixture. Whisk the sour cream and fold into the half-and-half mixture. Stir in the vanilla. When mixture begins to thicken, pour into individual molds or brandy snifters. Chill, covered, until serving time. Sweeten the thawed raspberries with the 2 tablespoons sugar; spoon over the gelled mixture and serve. Yield: 8 servings.

Judith Gale, Theta Phi
Terrell, Texas

TANGY CITRUS CREAM

24 ounces whipped
  topping
1 (14-ounce) can
  sweetened condensed
  milk

1/2 cup lemon juice
1/2 cup grapefruit juice

Combine the whipped topping and condensed milk in a large mixing bowl and mix well. Mix in the lemon juice and grapefruit juice gradually, blending well. Spoon into a pretty bowl or individual serving dishes. Garnish with fresh fruit and serve.
Yield: 10 servings.

Mary Ruth Tasler, Laureate Theta Epsilon
Port Lavaca, Texas

APRICOT GELATIN DESSERT

This refreshing dessert may also be served as a salad.

2 (3-ounce) packages
  apricot gelatin (or
  orange or lemon
  gelatin)
1 (8-ounce) can crushed
  pineapple, or 2 or
  3 (11-ounce) cans
  mandarin oranges

1 (16-ounce) can apricot
  halves
1/2 cup sugar
3 rounded tablespoons
  flour
1 egg, beaten
12 ounces whipped
  topping

Dissolve the dry gelatin mix in 2 cups boiling water in a bowl. Stir in 1 cup cold water. Drain the pineapple and apricots, reserving the juice. Apricots may be cut into smaller pieces if desired. Stir the apricots and pineapple into the gelatin mixture. Chill until set. Combine the sugar and flour with a small amount of reserved fruit juice in a saucepan over medium-low heat. Add the remaining juice and the egg gradually; cook until very thick, stirring constantly. Remove from heat and let stand until cool. Add the whipped topping and beat until smooth. Spread the egg mixture over the gelatin layer. Sprinkle a few shreds of Cheddar cheese over the top to garnish if desired. Yield: 12 servings.

Pam Zorens, Theta Eta
St. Louis, Missouri

FRUITED GELATIN

2 (3-ounce) packages
  cherry gelatin
2 cups boiling water
1 (20-ounce) can crushed
  pineapple

1 (21-ounce) can cherry
  pie filling
8 ounces whipped
  topping

Combine the dry gelatin mix and boiling water in a bowl and stir to dissolve. Stir in the undrained pineapple. Stir in the cherry pie filling and mix well. Pour into a 9×13-inch baking dish. Chill until firm. Spread whipped topping over the top and serve. Yield: 15 to 20 servings.

Dorothy Spears, Preceptor Beta Sigma
Niagara Falls, New York

FROSTED SALAD

1 small package orange sugar-free gelatin	1 medium banana, sliced
1 small package lemon sugar-free gelatin	2 cups miniature marshmallows
2 cups boiling water	2 tablespoons flour
1 (20-ounce) can crushed pineapple	1/2 cup sugar
	1 egg, beaten
	1 cup whipped cream

Combine the orange and lemon gelatins in a large bowl. Add the boiling water and stir until completely dissolved. Stir in 1 1/2 cups cold water and let stand to cool. Drain the pineapple, reserving 1 cup juice. Stir the pineapple, banana slices and marshmallows into the gelatin and pour into a 9×13-inch baking dish. Chill, covered, for 8 to 10 hours. Combine the reserved pineapple juice, flour, sugar and egg in a saucepan and bring to a boil, stirring constantly. Reduce heat and simmer until very thick, stirring constantly. Remove from heat. Let stand until cool. Blend the whipped cream into the cool pineapple juice mixture. Spread over the gelatin 1 hour before serving. Serve each gelatin square over a leaf of lettuce with a scoop of orange (or other flavor) sherbet over the top. Yield: 12 to 16 servings.

Laurie Raeshel Irion
Grand Junction, Colorado

STRAWBERRY PRETZEL GELATIN

3 (3-ounce) packages strawberry gelatin	3 tablespoons sugar
3 cups boiling water	8 ounces cream cheese, softened
2 (10-ounce) packages frozen strawberries	1/2 cup sugar
3 cups crushed pretzels	8 ounces whipped topping
1/2 cup (1 stick) butter, softened	

Dissolve the gelatin in boiling water in a large bowl. Add the strawberries and stir to break up. Chill in the refrigerator until soft set. Combine the pretzels, butter and 3 tablespoons sugar in a bowl and mix well. Press the mixture into a 9×13-inch baking dish. Bake at 400 degrees for 8 minutes. Let stand until cool. Combine the cream cheese and 1/2 cup sugar in a mixing bowl and beat until smooth and fluffy; stir in the whipped topping. Spread the mixture over the cooled pretzel crust. Layer the soft-set gelatin over the cream cheese layer. Chill, covered, until firm. Yield: 15 servings.

Christine Novicky, Upsilon Alpha
Erie, Pennsylvania

BROKEN GLASS GELATIN DESSERT

1 (3-ounce) package blueberry gelatin	1/2 cup (1 stick) margarine, melted
1 (3-ounce) package cherry gelatin	1/2 cup packed brown sugar
1 (3-ounce) package lemon gelatin	1 envelope unflavored gelatin
4 1/2 cups boiling water	1 cup pineapple juice
2 cups graham cracker crumbs	12 ounces whipped topping

Place each package of flavored gelatin mix in a separate bowl. Add 1 1/2 cups boiling water to each bowl and stir to dissolve. Pour each into a separate shallow dish to cool. Chill, covered, for 8 to 10 hours. Combine the graham cracker crumbs, margarine and brown sugar in a bowl; mix well. Pat half the crumbs into a 9×13-inch baking dish. Combine 1/4 cup cold water, the unflavored gelatin and pineapple juice in a saucepan over medium heat and cook until very warm, stirring occasionally. Remove from heat and let stand until cool. Fold the whipped topping into the cooled pineapple mixture. Cut the firm gelatin into small cubes and fold into the pineapple mixture. Spoon over the graham cracker layer and sprinkle with the remaining crumbs. Chill, covered, for at least 5 hours. Yield: 15 servings.

Mary Ellen Bradley, Preceptor Kappa
Landisville, Pennsylvania

THIRTEEN-LAYER GELATIN DESSERT

It takes time and patience, but it always gets raves.

6 (3-ounce) packages gelatin in different flavors	3 cups sour cream
	18 tablespoons boilng water
6 cups boiling water	1 cup whipped topping

Dissolve each package of gelatin in a separate bowl using 1 cup boiling water. Divide each gelatin into 2 portions and blend 1/2 cup of the sour cream into 1 portion of each flavor. Stir 3 tablespoons boiling water into each gelatin that does not contain sour cream. Pour 1 of the clear gelatins into a 9×13-inch baking dish. Chill for 20 to 30 minutes and spread the the same flavor sour cream mixture over the top. Chill for 20 to 30 minutes. Repeat the layers with the remaining gelatin flavors. Spread with whipped topping to make the thirteenth layer. Chill and serve. Yield: 15 to 20 servings.

Bert Ondak, Laureate Delta Gamma
Lee's Summit, Missouri

RAINBOW FLUFF

1 (3-ounce) package lime
   gelatin
8 ounces Key lime pie
   fat-free yogurt
32 ounces whipped
   topping
1 (3-ounce) package
   blueberry gelatin
8 ounces peach fat-free
   yogurt

1 (3-ounce) package
   orange gelatin
8 ounces blueberry
   fat-free yogurt
1 (3-ounce) package
   strawberry gelatin
8 ounces strawberry
   fat-free yogurt

Dissolve the lime gelatin in 1 cup boiling water in a bowl, stirring well. Let stand for 10 minutes. Stir in the Key lime pie yogurt and let stand for 10 minutes. Stir in 1/4 of the whipped topping. Pour into a 10-inch springform pan. Chill for about 20 minutes or until firm. Repeat the procedure for each gelatin flavor, layering in the order listed. Chill until serving time. Just before serving, run a warm knife around the side of the pan and remove the side. Cut into wedges. Garnish each serving with whipped topping. Yield: 8 to 10 servings.

Rita Romagnoli, Xi Eta Eta
Greensburg, Pennsylvania

QUICK FRUIT SALAD

1 (20-ounce) can
   pineapple chunks in
   juice
1 (15- or 29-ounce) can
   sliced peaches in
   light syrup
1 (16-ounce) can pear
   halves in juice

1 (22-ounce) can
   mandarin oranges
1 (6-ounce) package
   cook-and-serve
   pudding mix
2 bananas, sliced

Drain all the cans of fruit, reserving all the juices. Prepare the pudding using the package directions, substituting fruit juices for the milk; cool. Cut the fruit into bite-size pieces. Layer the bananas in a large serving bowl. Add the pineapple, peaches, pears and mandarin orange and mix gently. Layer the pudding over the fruit. Chill, covered, until serving time. Yield: variable.

Jennifer Kelly, Kappa Epsilon
Cartersville, Georgia

FRUIT COCKTAIL DESSERT

1 (15-ounce) can light
   fruit cocktail,
   drained
1 cup light strawberry
   yogurt

8 ounces light whipped
   topping
1 (2-ounce) package
   slivered almonds

Place the fruit cocktail, yogurt and whipped topping in a bowl and fold until well combined. Sprinkle with almonds. Serve from the bowl or from individual dessert cups. Yield: 6 servings.

Judy Gillerlain, Alpha Sigma
Mobile, Alabama

HOLIDAY CRANBERRY DESSERT

1 (20-ounce) can crushed
   pineapple
1 (6-ounce) package
   cran-raspberry
   gelatin mix
1 cup shredded coconut

2 cups buttermilk
1 cup pecan pieces
   (optional)
12 ounces whipped
   topping

Place the undrained pineapple in a saucepan over medium-high heat and bring to a boil. Remove from heat and stir in the dry gelatin mix until dissolved; cool. Stir in the coconut, buttermilk and pecans. Fold in the whipped topping. Pour into a 9×13-inch baking dish. Chill until firm. Yield: 15 servings.

Irene E. Rau, Laureate Nu
Albany, Oregon

FLOWER POT CHOCOLATE DESSERT

2 cups cold milk
1 (4-ounce) package
   chocolate instant
   pudding mix
8 ounces whipped
   topping

1 (16-ounce) package
   chocolate sandwich
   cookies, crushed

Pour the milk into a large bowl. Add the dry pudding mix and beat with a wire whisk for 1 or 2 minutes or until well blended. Let stand for 5 minutes. Stir in the whipped topping. Layer the cookie crumbs and pudding mixture alternately in a new flower pot until all the ingredients are used, ending with a cookie layer. Place an artificial flower in the center if desired and bury gummy worms around the flower. Serve with a trowel. Yield: 6 to 10 servings.

Sandra J. Hale, Xi Theta
Staunton, Virginia

FROZEN RASPBERRY BANANA DESSERT

1/4 cup honey
8 ounces cream cheese,
   softened
12 ounces whipped
   topping
1 cup sliced bananas

2 cups small
   marshmallows
2 (10-ounce) packages
   frozen raspberries,
   thawed

Combine the honey, cream cheese and whipped topping in a large bowl and mix until smooth. Add the bananas, marshmallows and raspberries and mix well. Pour into a 9×13-inch baking dish and freeze. Thaw for about 30 minutes before serving. Yield: 15 servings.

Eva Darlene Greenwell, Gamma Nu
Adrian, Missouri

FROZEN ANGEL FOOD FRUIT DESSERT

1 prepared angel food cake	1 cup blueberries
1/2 gallon vanilla ice cream, softened	1 (3-ounce) package lime gelatin
1 (11-ounce) can mandarin oranges, drained	1 1/2 cups sliced strawberries
1 (3-ounce) package orange gelatin	1 (3-ounce) package strawberry gelatin

Tear the cake into small pieces. Press 1/4 of the cake pieces in the bottom of a 10-inch tube pan. Layer 1/4 of the ice cream and the mandarin oranges over the cake layer. Sprinkle evenly with the dry orange gelatin mix. Layer 1/4 of the cake pieces, 1/4 of the ice cream and the blueberries over the orange gelatin; sprinkle evenly with the dry lime gelatin mix. Layer 1/4 of the cake pieces, 1/4 of the ice cream and the strawberries over the lime gelatin; sprinkle evenly with the dry strawberry gelatin mix. Layer the remaining cake pieces and remaining ice cream over the top. Freeze until serving time. Invert onto a serving plate and cut into slices. Yield: 12 servings.

Judy Behnke, Xi Gamma Alpha
Norfolk, Nebraska

MACAROON SHERBET DESSERT

18 macaroons, crumbled	1/2 cup chopped English walnuts
2 cups whipping cream, whipped	1 pint lemon sherbet
1 teaspoon vanilla extract	1 pint lime sherbet
3 tablespoons confectioners' sugar	1 pint orange sherbet

Combine the macaroons, whipped cream, vanilla, confectioners' sugar and walnuts in a bowl and mix well. Spread half the macaroon mixture in a 9×13-inch baking dish. Arrange scoops of sherbet over the mixture, alternating flavors. Layer the remaining macaroon mixture over the top. Freeze for at least 2 hours before serving. Yield: 12 servings.

Millie Myers, Laureate Sigma
Elyria, Ohio

ICED LEMON CREAM

1 cup thick cream	Juice and grated zest of 2 lemons
1 3/4 cups sugar	
2 cups milk	

Pour the cream into a chilled bowl and whisk until soft peaks form. Stir in the sugar, milk, lemon juice and lemon zest and mix well. Pour into a 5-cup plastic container. Cover and freeze for 6 hours. Cut into chunks and place in a food processor container; process until smooth and creamy. Pour into a freezer-safe serving dish or ramekins and return to the freezer until time to serve. Yield: 10 servings.

Claire Swinhoe, Preceptor Beta
Los Alamos, New Mexico

FROZEN STRAWBERRY DESSERT

1/4 cup light brown sugar	1 cup granulated sugar
1/2 cup (1 stick) butter, softened	1 tablespoon lemon juice
1 cup flour	1 (10-ounce) package frozen strawberries, or 1 pint fresh
1 cup ground or finely chopped walnuts or pecans	8 ounces whipped topping
3 egg whites	

Mix the brown sugar, butter, flour and walnuts in a bowl. Pat the mixture into a deep 9×13-inch baking dish. Bake at 325 degrees for 20 to 30 minutes or until lightly browned. Cool and break into pieces. Reserve 3/4 cup of the mixture for the topping and spread the remaining mixture over the bottom of the dish. Combine the next 5 ingredients in a large mixing bowl and mix at high speed for 15 minutes; do not use a hand mixer. Fold in the whipped topping. Spread the mixture over the crust and sprinkle with the reserved crumbs. Cover with plastic wrap and freeze until serving time. Yield: 12 servings.

Cindy Strecker, Xi Alpha Omega
Oelwein, Iowa

FROZEN KOOL-AID DESSERT

1 cup sugar	2 cups milk
1 envelope drink mix, any flavor	1 cup whipping cream

Dissolve the sugar and drink mix in the milk in a bowl. Pour into a freezer container. Freeze for 1 hour or until slushy. Beat the cream in a mixing bowl until stiff peaks form. Add the drink mix mixture and stir just until combined. Return to the freezer container. Freeze for at least 2 hours or until solid. Yield: 4 cups.

Gloria M. Avilucea, Preceptor Delta
Las Cruces, New Mexico

PEANUT ICE CREAM DESSERT

The dry-roasted peanuts may be salted or unsalted.

1¼ cups graham cracker crumbs	½ cup light corn syrup
¼ cup sugar	⅓ cup chunky peanut butter, softened
6 tablespoons margarine, melted	1 quart vanilla ice cream, softened
1 cup dry-roasted peanuts, chopped	

Combine the graham cracker crumbs, sugar and melted margarine in a bowl and mix well. Press the mixture into a 9×9-inch baking pan and freeze for 30 minutes. Combine ⅔ cup of the chopped peanuts, corn syrup and peanut butter in a bowl and mix well. Spoon half the softened ice cream evenly over the chilled crumb layer. Layer the corn syrup mixture and remaining ice cream over the ice cream layer. Sprinkle with the remaining chopped peanuts. Cover and freeze until firm. Let stand at room temperature for 10 to 15 minutes before serving. Cut into 3-inch squares. Yield: 9 servings.

Madalyn Fae Fazzolari, Preceptor Beta
Clackamas, Oregon

KAHLUA ICE CREAM BALLS

Coffee ice cream	Whipped topping
Flaked coconut, toasted	(optional)
Kahlúa	

Scoop the ice cream into small to medium balls. Roll each ice cream ball in the toasted coconut and arrange on a plastic wrap-lined baking sheet. Freeze until firm. Store in a plastic bag until serving time. Place each ice cream ball in a champagne goblet and drizzle with 1 to 1½ ounces Kahlúa. Let stand for 5 minutes before serving. Top with a dab of whipped topping. Yield: variable.

Shirley M. Erickson, Xi Beta Mu
Conway, South Carolina

❖ FROZEN MOCHA LOAF

2 cups crushed chocolate sandwich cookies	1 teaspoon vanilla extract
3 tablespoons melted butter or margarine	2 tablespoons instant coffee granules
8 ounces cream cheese, softened	½ cup chocolate syrup
1 (14-ounce) can sweetened condensed milk	2 cups whipping cream, whipped

Press a mixture of the cookie crumbs and melted butter into a foil-lined loaf pan. Combine the cream cheese, condensed milk and vanilla in a mixing bowl and mix well. Dissolve the coffee granules in 1 tablespoon hot water and add to the cream cheese mixture. Add the chocolate syrup and blend well. Fold in the whipped cream until marbleized. Spoon into the loaf pan over the cookie layer and cover with plastic wrap. Freeze for 8 to 10 hours. Thaw for about 15 minutes before serving. Lift from the pan and remove the foil. Cut into slices. Yield: 12 servings.

Diane Hill, Xi Alpha Gamma
Valley City, North Dakota

HOT FUDGE ICE CREAM DESSERT

1 (16-ounce) can chocolate syrup	12 ounces whipped topping
¾ cup peanut butter	1 cup salted peanuts, chopped
19 ice cream sandwiches	

Pour the chocolate syrup into a medium microwave-safe bowl. Microwave on High for 2 minutes; do not let it boil. Add the peanut butter, stirring until smooth. Let stand until room temperature. Line the bottom of a deep 9×13-inch baking dish with 9½ ice cream sandwiches. Layer half the whipped topping, half the chocolate mixture and half the peanuts over the ice cream sandwich layer. Layer the remaining ice cream sandwiches, whipped topping, chocolate mixture and peanuts over the peanut layer. Freeze until firm. Cut into squares. Yield: 18 servings.

Diane Stephens, Preceptor Beta Sigma
Oklahoma City, Oklahoma

BROWNIES AND CREAM

1 (20-ounce) package walnut brownie mix	1 cup flaked coconut
½ cup (1 stick) margarine	½ gallon vanilla ice cream, softened
	½ cup chocolate syrup

Place the dry brownie mix in a bowl and cut in the margarine until crumbly. Stir in the coconut. Spread in an unbuttered 9×13-inch baking dish. Bake at 350 degrees for 20 minutes, stirring once after 10 minutes. Stir to crumble; cool. Reserve 1½ cups of the crumbs for the topping. Combine the remaining crumbs and ice cream in a large bowl and mix well. Return to the baking dish and press firmly. Sprinkle the reserved 1½ cups crumbs over the top and drizzle with chocolate syrup. Freeze, covered, for 12 hours. Yield: 20 or more servings.

Cookie Register, Xi Beta Upsilon
Decatur, Alabama

COOKIES AND CREAM DESSERT

1 (18-ounce) package
    chocolate sandwich
    cookies
1/2 gallon vanilla ice
    cream, softened

12 ounces whipped
    topping
1 cup finely chopped
    pecans

Crumble the cookies into small pieces. Combine the crumbled cookies, ice cream, whipped topping and pecans in a large bowl and mix well. Spread in a 9×13-inch baking dish or freezer container. Freeze until serving time. Serve with a dab of whipped topping and chopped pecans or shredded chocolate if desired. Yield: 12 or more servings.

Barbara Gerami, Eta Master
Lafayette, Louisiana

OREO ICE CREAM DESSERT

24 chocolate sandwich
    cookies, crushed
1/2 cup (1 stick)
    margarine, melted
1/2 gallon vanilla ice
    cream, softened
4 ounces German's
    chocolate
1/2 cup (1 stick)
    margarine

2/3 cup sugar
1 (5-ounce) can
    evaporated milk
1 teaspoon vanilla
    extract
1/8 teaspoon salt
8 ounces whipped
    topping

Spread the cookie crumbs over the bottom of a 9×13-inch baking dish. Drizzle the melted margarine over the cookie layer. Spread the ice cream over the crumbs. Freeze for at least 2 hours. Combine the German's chocolate, margarine, sugar, evaporated milk, vanilla and salt in a saucepan and bring to a boil. Boil gently for 4 minutes, stirring frequently; cool. Pour evenly over the top of the ice cream layer. Return to the freezer until serving time. Top with whipped topping. Sprinkle with chopped walnuts or pecans if desired. Yield: 10 to 12 servings.

Anita Vaughan, Preceptor Beta Gamma
Peachtree City, Georgia

COCOA KRISPIES ICE CREAM DESSERT

3 1/4 cups crisp cocoa rice
    cereal
1/2 cup light corn syrup
1/2 cup creamy peanut
    butter

1/2 gallon vanilla ice
    cream
1/2 cup chocolate sauce
1/2 cup chopped walnuts
    or pecans (optional)

Combine the cereal, light corn syrup and creamy peanut butter in a bowl and mix well. Spread in a 9×13-inch baking dish. Spread the ice cream over the cereal layer and drizzle with chocolate sauce.

Sprinkle with chopped nuts. Freeze, covered, until serving time. Yield: 18 servings.

Patricia Jacks, Alpha Nu
Knoxville, Iowa

DIRT CAKE

2 (16-ounce) packages
    chocolate sandwich
    cookies
8 ounces cream cheese,
    softened
1 cup confectioners'
    sugar
1/4 cup (1/2 stick) butter,
    softened

3 1/2 cups cold milk
2 (4-ounce) packages
    chocolate instant
    pudding mix
16 ounces whipped
    topping
Assorted gummy worms
    and spiders

Place the cookies in a food processor container and process until finely crumbled. Press half the cookie crumbs firmly into a 9×13-inch baking dish. Combine the cream cheese, confectioners' sugar and butter in a large mixing bowl and beat until smooth and fluffy. Add the milk and pudding mix and blend well. Fold in the whipped topping. Spread the pudding mixture over the cookie crumbs in the dish and top with the remaining cookie crumbs. Decorate with gummy bugs or artificial flowers. Freeze, covered, for 8 to 10 hours. Thaw for several hours before serving. Yield: 8 to 12 servings.

Lisa Ross, Xi Beta Psi
Apex, North Carolina

CHOCOLATE MINT ICE CREAM DESSERT

24 chocolate sandwich
    cookies, crushed
1/4 cup (1/2 stick) butter
    or margarine, melted
1/2 gallon chocolate mint
    ice cream

1 (16-ounce) jar hot
    fudge topping
12 ounces whipped
    topping

Combine the cookies and melted butter in a bowl and mix well. Press the cookie mixture into a 9×13-inch baking dish, reserving 3 tablespoons of the mixture for the topping. Let the ice cream stand at room temperature for 20 minutes to soften. Slice or scoop the ice cream over the cookie layer. Freeze, covered, for at least 30 minutes. Spoon the fudge topping over the top and smooth with a spatula. Freeze for at least 30 minutes longer. Spread whipped topping over the top and sprinkle with the reserved cookie mixture. Freeze. Thaw for 20 minutes before serving. Yield: 16 servings.

Terri K. Baldwin, Preceptor Gamma Mu
Lakewood, Colorado

TOFFEE ICE CREAM DESSERT

1 (10-ounce) package
  butter cookies,
  crushed
1/2 cup (1 stick) butter or
  margarine, melted
2 (3-ounce) packages
  vanilla instant
  pudding mix

1 cup cold milk
1 quart vanilla ice
  cream, softened
8 ounces whipped
  topping
2 (7-ounce) chocolate-
  covered toffee candy
  bars, crushed

Combine the cookie crumbs and butter in a bowl and mix well. Press the mixture into a 9×13-inch baking dish. Chill for at least 1 hour. Combine the dry pudding mix and milk in a bowl and whisk for 2 minutes. Fold in the ice cream. Spread over the chilled cookie layer. Top with whipped topping. Cover and freeze for at least 2 hours. Sprinkle with crushed candy bars before serving. Yield: 12 to 15 servings.

Bonnie Shepherd, Xi Beta Epsilon
Woodward, Oklahoma

BUTTER PECAN ICE CREAM

1 1/2 cups pecans
1/2 cup (1 stick) butter
8 eggs
1/2 cup granulated sugar
1 (1-pound) package
  brown sugar

3 tablespoons flour
1 tablespoon vanilla
  extract
2 cups heavy cream
Milk, 2% or whole

Combine the pecans and butter in a shallow baking pan and bake at 350 degrees until browned, stirring occasionally. Combine the eggs and granulated sugar in a mixing bowl and beat well. Add the brown sugar, flour and vanilla and mix well. Stir in the roasted pecans and cream. Pour into an ice cream freezer container; add milk to the fill line. Freeze using manufacturer's directions. Yield: 8 servings.

Denise Jordan, Preceptor Gamma Phi
Amarillo, Texas

CHOCOLATE ICE CREAM

1 (12-ounce) can
  evaporated milk
1 1/3 cups chocolate syrup
2 cups half-and-half

6 eggs
1/2 cup sugar
Salt to taste
Vanilla extract to taste

Combine all the ingredients in a large mixing bowl and beat until smooth. Pour into an ice cream freezer container; add milk to the fill line. Freeze using manufacturer's directions. Yield: 8 servings.

Donna Melton, Preceptor Zeta Tau
Granbury, Texas

RUM RAISIN ICE CREAM

1 cup dark raisins
1/4 cup dark Jamaican
  rum
1 envelope unflavored
  gelatin
2 tablespoons cold
  water

2 cups half-and-half
1 cup sugar
2 cups heavy cream
1/2 cup evaporated milk
2 teaspoons rum extract
Pinch of salt

Soak the raisins in the dark rum for 8 to 10 hours. Soften the gelatin in the cold water. Place the half-and-half in a saucepan over low heat and bring to a boil slowly, stirring constantly. Add the sugar and gelatin mixture; stir to dissolve. Cool. Stir in the cream, evaporated milk, rum extract and salt. Chill, covered, in the refrigerator for at least 2 hours. Pour into an ice cream freezer container and add the undrained raisins. Add milk to the fill line. Freeze using manufacturer's directions. Yield: 2 quarts.

Carol J. Harper, Alpha Delta Phi
Lowry City, Missouri

STRAWBERRY ICE CREAM

2 eggs
2 cups milk
1 1/4 cups sugar
1 cup miniature
  marshmallows
1 cup half-and-half

1/2 cup heavy cream
2 cups puréed
  unsweetened
  strawberries
1 teaspoon vanilla
  extract

Combine the eggs and milk in a heavy saucepan; stir in the sugar. Cook over medium-low heat for about 14 minutes until the mixture reaches 160 degrees or coats a metal spoon with a thin film, stirring constantly. Remove from heat; add the marshmallows and stir until melted by the heat. Place the saucepan in a bowl of ice and stir the mixture for 5 to 10 minutes or until cool. Stir in the half-and-half, cream, strawberries and vanilla. Chill, covered, for 8 to 10 hours. Pour into an ice cream freezer container; add milk to the fill line. Freeze using manufacturer's directions. Yield: 2 quarts.

Ruby Jeanette Beard, Gamma Nu
Adrian, Missouri

FROZEN RUM TORTONI

1 cup chopped almonds
1 cup chopped
  maraschino cherries
1 cup shredded coconut

2 quarts vanilla ice
  cream, softened
2 tablespoons rum
  extract

Spread the almonds and maraschino cherries in a shallow baking dish. Bake in a 350-degree oven until almonds are lightly toasted, stirring occasionally. Let stand until cool. Combine the almond mixture, coconut, ice cream and rum extract in a large bowl and mix well. Pour into a container and freeze for 8 to 10 hours. Scoop into individual serving bowls. Yield: 8 servings.

Patricia R. Conrath, Alpha Lambda
Cheney, Washington

ELEGANT SORBET

Purchased sorbet, flavor
of choice
Sliced bananas

Fresh raspberries
Fresh pineapple, cut into
chunks

Place 1 or 2 scoops of sorbet in each of desired number of individual china or crystal dishes. Garnish with banana slices, whole raspberries and pineapple chunks. Yield: variable.

Jackie Hoskins, Preceptor Gamma Eta
Merritt Island, Florida

HOT FUDGE SAUCE

2 ounces unsweetened
chocolate
1 tablespoon butter

2 cups sugar
²/₃ cup evaporated milk

Melt the chocolate and butter in the top of a double boiler over simmering water. Add the sugar and mix well. Stir in the evaporated milk. Cook until mixture is consistency of heavy cream, stirring frequently. Serve as topping for ice cream or as fondue for cake and fruit dippers. Yield: about 1 cup.

Kay Levanti, Xi Alpha Pi
West Frankfort, Illinois

LATE-NIGHT CHOCOLATE SAUCE

4 ounces semisweet
chocolate
2 tablespoons
butter
2 tablespoons milk

1 (14-ounce) can
sweetened condensed
milk
1 teaspoon vanilla
extract

Melt the chocolate in the top of a double boiler over simmering water. Stir in the butter and heat until melted. Add the milk and condensed milk gradually, stirring constantly. Remove from heat and stir in the vanilla. Serve over ice cream. It will keep in the refrigerator for 4 to 6 weeks. Yield: about 2 cups.

Irene Moore, Phi Master
Annandale, Virginia

HOT FUDGE TOPPING

1¹/₂ cups sugar
¹/₄ teaspoon salt
1¹/₂ cups hot water
¹/₂ cup baking cocoa

¹/₄ cup cornstarch
¹/₄ cup cold water
1 teaspoon vanilla
extract

Combine the sugar, salt, hot water and baking cocoa in a saucepan over medium heat and bring to a boil. Boil gently for 5 minutes. Add a mixture of the cornstarch and cold water gradually to the boiling mixture, stirring constantly. Continue to stir until thickened. Remove from heat and stir in the vanilla. Yield: 6 servings.

Bonnie J. Hula, Omicron
Clarksville, Arizona

WILD RICE BLUEBERRY DESSERT SAUCE

2 cups blueberries
¹/₄ teaspoon salt
¹/₂ cup sugar
2 tablespoons cornstarch

1 tablespoon lemon
juice
³/₄ cup cooked wild rice

Combine the blueberries, ³/₄ cup water and salt in a saucepan over medium heat. Combine the sugar, cornstarch and ¹/₄ cup cold water; stir into the blueberry mixture. Cook until thickened and translucent. Stir in the lemon juice. Stir in the wild rice. Serve over ice cream. Yield: about 3¹/₂ cups.

Joyce Stillwell, Eta Master
Swift Current, Saskatchewan, Canada

PLUMA MOOS

Pluma Moos is a Russian fruit soup. Serve alone or over cake or ice cream for a truly decadent dessert.

1 cup pitted prunes
1 cup seedless raisins
¹/₂ cup dried apricots, or
¹/₄ cup dried apricots
plus ¹/₄ cup dried
peaches

2 quarts water
¹/₂ cup sugar
6 tablespoons flour
¹/₂ teaspoon salt
1 cup heavy cream
1 teaspoon cinnamon

Chop the fruit. Combine the prunes, raisins, apricots and water in a large saucepan over medium-high heat and bring to a boil. Reduce heat and simmer until fruit is tender; stir in the sugar. Combine the flour, salt, cream and cinnamon in a small bowl and mix into a paste. Add the flour paste to the simmering fruit mixture gradually, stirring constantly. Cook until slightly thickened. Add more cream or water if desired. Serve warm. Yield: 12 large servings.

Joanne Watts, Preceptor Lambda
Kitchener, Ontario, Canada

More Desserts

APPLE CHEESECAKE

1 cup flour	*1 egg*
2/3 cup plus 1/4 cup sugar	*1 teaspoon cinnamon*
1/2 cup margarine	*2 apples, peeled and*
1 teaspoon vanilla	*sliced*
extract	*1/2 cup slivered almonds*
8 ounces cream cheese,	*(optional)*
softened	

Combine the flour and 1/3 cup of the sugar in a bowl. Cut in the margarine with 1/2 teaspoon of the vanilla until crumbly. Press in the bottom of a buttered 9-inch springform pan. Cream the cream cheese and the 1/4 cup sugar in a mixing bowl until light and fluffy. Beat in the egg and the remaining 1/2 teaspoon vanilla. Pour evenly over the cheesecake base. Combine the 1/3 cup sugar and cinnamon in a sealable plastic bag. Add the apples and toss to coat. Layer the apple mixture over the cream cheese layer. Top with almonds. Bake in a preheated 450-degree oven for 10 minutes. Reduce oven temperature to 400 degrees and bake for 25 minutes longer. Cool in the pan for 10 minutes. Loosen the cake from the side of the pan and cool completely. Remove the side of the pan and serve. Yield: 6 to 8 servings.

Maxine Inglis, Preceptor Gamma Omicron
Terrace, British Columbia, Canada

INDIVIDUAL CHERRY CHEESECAKES

2 eggs	*24 vanilla wafers*
3/4 cup sugar	*1 (21-ounce) can cherry*
16 ounces cream cheese,	*pie filling*
softened	
1 teaspoon vanilla	
extract	

Combine the eggs, sugar, cream cheese and vanilla in a mixing bowl and beat until creamy. Line 24 muffin cups with paper liners. Place a vanilla wafer in each liner. Fill cups 3/4 full with cream cheese mixture. Bake at 350 degrees for 20 minutes. Cool. Top each cheesecake with a spoonful of cherry pie filling. Chill, covered, until serving time. Yield: 2 dozen.

Doris Galbraith, Alpha Theta
Crete, Nebraska

SPUMONI CHEESECAKE

1 cup graham cracker	*3 eggs*
crumbs	*3 tablespoons flour*
2 tablespoons plus 11/2	*3/4 cup chopped*
cups sugar	*maraschino cherries*
1/4 cup melted butter	*Red and green food*
24 ounces cream cheese,	*coloring to taste*
softened	*1/2 (4-ounce) package*
1/3 cup sour cream	*pistachio instant*
1/2 teaspoon vanilla	*pudding mix*
extract	

Combine the graham cracker crumbs, the 2 tablespoons sugar and melted butter in a small bowl and mix well. Press over the bottom and 1/2 inch up the side of a 9-inch springform pan. Bake at 350 degrees for 8 to 10 minutes. Cool. Combine the cream cheese, the 11/2 cups sugar, sour cream, vanilla, eggs and flour in a mixing bowl and mix well. Divide the cream cheese mixture evenly among 3 bowls (about 2 cups mixture in each bowl). Stir the undrained cherries and red food coloring into 1 portion; add additional flour to thicken if necessary. Pour evenly over the cooled crust. Stir the pistachio pudding mix and green food coloring into the second portion; pour carefully over the cherry layer. Pour the remaining portion evenly over the pistachio layer. Bake in a preheated 400-degree oven for 10 minutes. Reduce oven temperature to 350 degrees and bake for 60 minutes longer or until center is almost set. Cool in the pan for 30 minutes. Loosen the cake from the side of the pan. Cool to room temperature. Chill, covered, for 3 to 10 hours. Remove the side of the pan. Store in the refrigerator. Yield: 12 servings.

Connie Dodson, Laureate Delta Tau
Defiance, Ohio

LEMON CHEESECAKE

18 graham crackers, crushed
1/2 cup (1 stick) butter, melted
11 ounces cream cheese, softened
1 teaspoon vanilla extract
1 cup sugar
1 (3-ounce) package lemon gelatin
1 cup boiling water
1 (12-ounce) can evaporated milk, chilled

Combine the graham crackers and melted butter in a bowl and mix well. Pat into a 9×13-inch baking dish. Combine the cream cheese, vanilla and sugar in a bowl and mix well. Dissolve the gelatin in the boiling water. Let stand until cool. Whip the evaporated milk until stiff peaks form. Add the whipped milk and cooled gelatin mixture to the cream cheese mixture. Pour evenly over the graham cracker layer. Chill and serve. Yield: 12 to 15 servings.

Karen Brunia, Mu Tau
Huxley, Iowa

LEMON-GLAZED CHEESECAKE

1 3/4 cups butter, melted
1 cup crushed graham crackers
1 1/2 tablespoons plus 3/4 cup plus 3 tablespoons sugar
24 ounces cream cheese, softened
3 eggs
1/4 cup lemon juice
2 teaspoons grated lemon zest
3 teaspoons vanilla extract
2 cups sour cream
Lemon Glaze

Combine the melted butter, graham cracker crumbs and the 1 1/2 tablespoons sugar in a small bowl and mix with a fork. Press into a 9- to 10-inch springform pan. Combine the cream cheese and the 3/4 cup sugar in a mixing bowl and mix well. Add the eggs 1 at a time, beating well after each addition. Beat in the lemon juice, lemon zest and 2 teaspoons of the vanilla. Pour over the graham cracker layer. Bake at 350 degrees for 35 minutes. Combine the sour cream, the 3 tablespoons sugar and the remaining 1 teaspoon vanilla in a bowl and blend well. Spread evenly over the cheesecake. Bake for 12 minutes longer. Let stand until cool. Spread slightly cooled Lemon Glaze over the cheesecake. Chill, covered, for 8 to 10 hours. Yield: 12 to 15 servings.

LEMON GLAZE

1/2 cup sugar
2 tablespoons cornstarch
1 egg yolk
1/3 cup lemon juice
3/4 cup water
1 teaspoon grated lemon zest
1 tablespoon butter

Combine the sugar and cornstarch in a saucepan and mix well. Place the egg yolk in a coffee cup and beat well. Beat in the lemon juice and water. Add the egg yolk mixture and lemon zest to the cornstarch mixture. Cook over medium heat until thickened and boiling, stirring constantly. Add the butter. Remove from heat .

Loretta Samuelson, Alpha Iota Master
Yakima, Washington

ZESTY LEMON CHEESECAKE

24 slices zwieback (6 ounces)
1/2 cup sifted confectioners' sugar
3 teaspoons grated lemon zest
1/2 cup (1 stick) butter or margarine, softened
1 3/4 cups sugar
3 tablespoons flour
40 ounces (2 1/2 pounds) cream cheese, softened
1/2 teaspoon vanilla extract
5 eggs, slightly beaten
2 egg yolks
1/4 cup heavy cream

Butter the bottom and side of a 9-inch springform pan. Crush the zwieback into fine crumbs. Place the zwieback crumbs, confectioners' sugar and 1 1/2 teaspoons of the lemon zest in a bowl. Cut in the butter with a fork. Reserve 3/4 cup of the crumbs for garnish. Spread the remaining crumbs in the prepared springform pan; press firmly and evenly with fingers or back of spoon across the bottom and up the side of the pan. Combine the sugar, flour, cream cheese, the remaining 1 1/2 teaspoons lemon zest and vanilla in a mixing bowl and beat until smooth and fluffy. Beat in the eggs and egg yolks 1 at a time. Blend in the cream. Pour into the crumb-lined pan. Sprinkle the top with the reserved crumbs. Bake at 350 degrees for 1 hour. Turn off the oven. Let the cheesecake stand in the oven for 1 hour until center is firm. Remove to a wire rack to cool for 4 to 6 hours. Chill, in the refrigerator, for several hours. Yield: 16 servings.

Verna Raney, Preceptor Alpha Kappa
Ozark, Arkansas

---

*Lorraine Johnson, Laureate Beta Iota, Tempe, Arizona, makes **Crunchy Chocolate Sauce** by melting 1 ounce unsweetened chocolate with 1/4 cup milk and adding 3/4 cup brown sugar, 1/4 cup crunchy peanut butter and 1/4 teaspoon vanilla. Serve warm on cake or ice cream and top with toffee bits.*

LIME CHEESECAKE

1 cup shredded coconut	1/4 cup lime juice
2 tablespoons flour	1 teaspoon grated lime
2 tablespoons melted	zest
margarine	3 to 5 drops green food
1 envelope unflavored	coloring
gelatin	1 cup whipping cream,
3 eggs, separated	whipped
3/4 cup sugar	
16 ounces cream cheese,	
softened	

Combine the coconut, flour and margarine in a bowl and mix well. Press into a 9-inch springform pan. Bake at 350 degrees for 10 to 12 minutes; let stand until cool. Soften the gelatin in 1/4 cup cold water. Beat the egg whites in a mixing bowl until stiff peaks form. Combine the egg yolks, 3/4 cup water and sugar in a saucepan over medium heat. Cook for 5 minutes, stirring constantly. Add the gelatin mixture and stir until dissolved. Combine the egg yolk mixture and cream cheese in a mixing bowl and blend well. Stir in the lime juice, lime zest and food coloring. Fold in the whipped cream and stiffly beaten egg whites. Pour over the cooled crust. Chill until firm.
Yield: 10 to 12 servings.

Darlene J. Jeffries, Laureate Upsilon
Chico, California

PEACH CHEESECAKE

3/4 cup flour	1/2 cup milk
1 teaspoon baking	1 (16-ounce) can sliced
powder	peaches, drained,
1 (4-ounce) package	juice reserved
vanilla instant	8 ounces cream cheese,
pudding mix	softened
3 tablespoons butter or	1/2 cup plus 1 tablespoon
margarine, softened	sugar
1 egg	1/2 teaspoon cinnamon

Combine the first 6 ingredients in a mixing bowl and beat at medium speed for 2 minutes; batter will be stiff. Pour into a buttered 9-inch pie plate. Arrange the peach slices over the batter. Combine the cream cheese, the 1/2 cup sugar and 3 tablespoons of the peach juice in a mixing bowl and beat for 2 minutes or until fluffy. Spoon the cream cheese mixture over the peach slices to within 1 inch of the edge. Mix the 1 tablespoon sugar and cinnamon and sprinkle over the top. Bake at 350 degrees for 25 minutes or until almost set. Remove from oven and cool. Store leftovers in refrigerator. Yield: 6 to 8 servings.

Vicki Cavins, Delta Theta Nu
Batesville, Indiana

CHOCOLATE-GLAZED CHEESECAKE

1 cup crushed chocolate	2 eggs
sandwich cookies (10	1 cup semisweet
or 11 cookies)	chocolate chips
1 tablespoon melted	1 cup caramel topping
margarine	or butterscotch
24 ounces cream cheese,	topping
softened	Chopped walnuts or
3/4 cup sugar	pecans
1/4 cup plus	
2 tablespoons heavy	
cream	

Combine the crushed cookies and margarine; mix well and press into a foil-lined 9-inch cake pan. Bake at 325 degrees for 8 minutes. Place the cream cheese in a large mixing bowl and beat until smooth. Beat in the sugar, the 1/4 cup cream and eggs. Pour over the crust. Bake at 325 degrees for 30 to 45 minutes or until center is set. Cool. Melt the chocolate chips with the 2 tablespoons cream in a small saucepan over low heat, stirring occasionally. Spread evenly over the cheesecake. Chill, covered, for 3 or more hours. Lift the foil-lined cheesecake from the pan; remove the foil. Top with caramel topping and chopped nuts.
Yield: 10 servings.

Pat Toth, Xi Gamma Psi
Clifton Park, New York

CHOCOLATE SWIRL CHEESECAKE

1 cup semisweet	16 ounces cream cheese,
chocolate chips	softened
1 1/4 cups plus 2	1/2 cup sour cream
tablespoons sugar	1 teaspoon vanilla
1 1/4 cups graham cracker	extract
crumbs	4 eggs
1/4 cup (1/2 stick) butter	
or margarine, melted	

Combine the chocolate chips and 1/2 cup of the sugar in the top of a double boiler over hot, not boiling, water. Cook until chocolate is melted and mixture is smooth, stirring constantly. Remove from heat. Combine the graham cracker crumbs, the 2 tablespoons sugar and melted butter in a small bowl and mix well. Pat the crumb mixture firmly over the bottom and 1/2 inch up the side of a 9-inch springform pan. Place the cream cheese in a large bowl and beat until light and fluffy. Beat in the remaining 3/4 cup sugar gradually. Mix in the sour cream and vanilla. Add the eggs 1 at a time, beating well after each addition. Pour half the cream cheese mixture into a small bowl. Blend in the melted chocolate. Spoon into the prepared pan. Pour the remaining cream cheese mixture over the chocolate layer. Use a rubber spatula to zigzag lightly through both layers, being careful not to blend too well. Bake at 325 degrees for 50 minutes or until set except for a 2- or 3-inch circle in the center. Cool in the pan. Chill, in the refrigerator, until serving time. Yield: 12 to 16 servings.

Maxine Brown, Alpha Master
Lexington, Kentucky

OREO CHEESECAKES

24 ounces cream cheese, softened	2 ounces unsweetened chocolate, melted
3/4 cup sugar	8 ounces whipped topping
3 eggs	
12 to 14 chocolate sandwich cookies	

Combine the cream cheese and sugar in a mixing bowl and beat until smooth. Add the eggs 1 at a time, beating well after each addition. Place a chocolate sandwich cookie in each of 12 to 14 paper-lined muffin cups. Drop a large spoonful of cream cheese mixture over each cookie. Cool completely. Chill, covered, in the refrigerator for 1 to 10 hours. Drizzle with melted chocolate and dollops of whipped topping and serve. Yield: 12 to 14 servings.

Sue McClellan, Xi Beta Upsilon
Decatur, Alabama

AMARETTO CHEESECAKE

2 cups graham cracker crumbs	1 cup sugar
1/4 cup finely chopped almonds	3 eggs
	1 cup sour cream
1/3 cup margarine, melted	1/2 cup heavy cream
	1/3 cup amaretto
16 ounces cream cheese, softened	1/2 teaspoon almond extract
	Amaretto Topping

Mix the graham cracker crumbs, almonds and melted margarine in a medium bowl. Press over the bottom and 1 1/2 inches up the side of an unbuttered 10-inch springform pan. Combine the cream cheese and sugar in a large mixing bowl and beat until light and fluffy. Add the eggs 1 at a time, beating well after each addition. Add the sour cream, heavy cream, amaretto and almond extract; blend well. Pour into the prepared pan. Fill a shallow pan half full of water and place on the lower oven rack. Bake the cheesecake on a center rack at 350 degrees for about 1 hour or until set; arrange the Amaretto Topping in a circle around the edge during the last 15 minutes of baking time. Cool in the pan for 15 minutes. Remove the side of the pan and cool completely. Chill, covered, for at least 2 hours before serving. Yield: 16 servings.

AMARETTO TOPPING

1/2 cup sugar	1 cup sliced almonds
1/2 cup water	1 1/2 teaspoons amaretto

Combine the sugar and water in a small saucepan and bring to a boil. Boil gently for 2 minutes without stirring. Remove from heat. Stir in the almonds and amaretto. Remove the coated almonds to waxed paper with a slotted spoon. Separate with a fork. Cool.

Eileen Hill, Xi Zeta Psi
Stroudsburg, Pennsylvania

KAHLUA CHEESECAKE

1 1/2 cups graham cracker crumbs	3 eggs
	1 teaspoon lemon juice
1/2 cup (1 stick) butter, melted	1/4 to 1/2 cup plus 2 tablespoons Kahlúa
16 ounces cream cheese, softened	1 cup sour cream
	3 tablespoons confectioners' sugar
1 cup sugar	

Mix the graham cracker crumbs and melted butter together. Pat into an 8-inch springform pan. Combine the cream cheese, sugar, eggs, lemon juice and the 1/4 to 1/2 cup Kahlúa in a mixing bowl and beat until smooth. Pour into the prepared pan. Bake at 300 degrees for 1 hour and 15 minutes. Combine the 2 tablespoons Kahlúa, sour cream and confectioners' sugar in a small bowl and blend well. Spread over the top of the warm cheesecake. Bake for 10 minutes longer. Chill, covered, for 6 to 10 hours.
Yield: 12 to 16 servings.

Bernice Akaki, Preceptor Alpha Pi
Everett, Washington

TOASTED ALMOND CHEESECAKE

1 1/4 cups cold milk	8 ounces whipped topping
1/4 teaspoon almond extract	1/2 cup sliced almonds, toasted
2 (4-ounce) packages cheesecake flavor pudding mix	1 (6-ounce) shortbread pie shell

Combine the milk, almond extract, pudding mix and half the whipped topping in a medium bowl and whisk for about 1 minute; mixture will be thick. Sprinkle 1/4 cup of the almonds in the pie shell. Fill the shell with the pudding mixture. Sprinkle with the remaining almonds. Serve immediately; or chill, covered, until ready to serve. Yield: 8 to 12 servings.

Beverly Sells, Preceptor Beta Phi
Columbia, California

CARAMEL PECAN CHEESECAKE

16 ounces cream cheese, softened	**25 caramels**
1/2 cup sugar	**2 tablespoons milk**
1/2 teaspoon vanilla extract	**1/2 cup chopped pecans**
2 eggs	**1 ready-to-use (9-inch) chocolate cookie shell**

Beat the cream cheese, sugar and vanilla in a mixing bowl at medium speed until well blended. Add the eggs 1 at a time, beating well after each addition. Melt the caramels with the milk in a small saucepan over low heat, stirring frequently until smooth. Stir in the pecans. Pour the caramel mixture into the pie shell. Pour the cream cheese mixture over the caramel layer. Bake at 350 degrees for 40 minutes or until center is almost set. Cool. Chill, covered, in the refrigerator for 3 to 10 hours. Drizzle chocolate syrup and caramel topping over each slice just before serving. Yield: 6 to 8 servings.

Susan Harmon, Alpha Pi
Cherryvale, Kansas

SOPAPILLA CHEESECAKE

The original sopapilla is a deep-fried pastry often served with honey.

16 ounces cream cheese, softened	**2 (8-count) cans crescent rolls**
1 teaspoon vanilla extract	**1/2 cup (1 stick) butter, melted**
1 1/2 cups sugar	**1 teaspoon cinnamon**

Combine the cream cheese, vanilla and 1 cup of the sugar in a mixing bowl and mix until smooth. Unroll 1 can of dough, pressing the perforations to seal; fit into an unbuttered 9×13-inch baking dish. Spread the cream cheese mixture evenly over the dough. Unroll the other can of dough, pressing perforations to seal; fit over the cream cheese mixture. Combine the butter with the remaining 1/2 cup sugar and cinnamon in a small bowl and mix well; spread evenly over the top dough layer. Bake at 350 degrees for 30 minutes. Best when served chilled. Yield: 10 servings.

Tina Bateman, Delta Zeta
Weatherford, Texas

HOLIDAY EGGNOG CHEESECAKE

1 cup graham cracker crumbs	**1 envelope unflavored gelatin**
1/2 cup sugar	**8 ounces cream cheese, softened**
1/4 teaspoon nutmeg	**1 cup eggnog**
1/4 cup (1/2 stick) margarine, melted	**1 cup whipping cream, whipped**

Mix the crumbs, 1/4 cup of the sugar, nutmeg and margarine together; press the mixture into a 9-inch springform pan. Soften the gelatin in 1/4 cup cold water in a small saucepan. Place over low heat and cook until dissolved, stirring constantly. Combine the cream cheese and remaining 1/4 cup sugar in a mixing bowl and beat at medium speed until well blended. Add the gelatin mixture and eggnog gradually, beating well after each addition. Chill for 30 minutes or until slightly thickened. Fold in the whipped cream. Pour over the crumb layer. Chill, covered, until firm. Garnish with additional whipped cream and nutmeg if desired. Yield: 10 to 12 servings.

Loretta West, Preceptor Alpha Kappa
Fogelsville, Pennsylvania

❖ FROZEN PEPPERMINT CHEESECAKE

1 1/2 cups chocolate wafer crumbs	**1 (14-ounce) can sweetened condensed milk**
1/4 cup sugar	**1 cup crushed hard peppermint candy**
1/4 cup (1/2 stick) butter, melted	**2 cups whipped topping**
8 ounces cream cheese, softened	

Mix the wafer crumbs, sugar and butter together; press the mixture over the bottom and 1 inch up the side of a 9-inch springform pan. Chill for at least 30 minutes. Place the cream cheese in a mixing bowl and beat at high speed until fluffy. Add the condensed milk and peppermint candy; beat well. Fold in the whipped topping. Pour into the prepared pan. Cover and freeze until firm. Yield: 12 to 16 servings.

Cindy Layton, Xi Epsilon Nu
Cape Girardeau, Mississippi

DAYS-AHEAD CHEESECAKE

1 cup cream cheese, at room temperature	**1 cup flour**
1 1/3 cups sugar	**1 teaspoon baking powder**
1/2 cup sour cream	**1/2 teaspoon salt**
4 eggs, well beaten	**1/2 cup (1 stick) butter, at room temperature**
2 teaspoons vanilla extract	**1 tablespoon milk**

Combine the cream cheese and 2/3 cup of the sugar in a mixing bowl and beat until smooth. Mix in the sour cream, 2 of the eggs and 1 teaspoon of the vanilla. Sift the flour, baking powder and salt into a separate bowl. Stir in the remaining 2/3 cup sugar. Mix in the butter, the remaining 2 eggs, milk and the remaining 1 teaspoon vanilla. Spread over the bottom and up the side of a 9-inch pie plate. Pour the cream cheese mixture into the shell. Bake at 350 degrees for

50 minutes or until edge is browned and center is springy to the touch. Cool completely. Chill, covered, for 24 hours. Top with sliced strawberries. Yield: 6 to 8 servings.

Madelyn Ward, Laureate Delta
Wilmington, Delaware

SUGAR-FREE CHEESECAKE

1 cup crushed low-sodium Triscuits	16 ounces cream cheese, softened
1/4 cup (1/2 stick) butter or margarine, softened	2 teaspoons vanilla extract
6 1/2 teaspoons granulated artificial sweetener	3 eggs
	2 cups sour cream

Combine the Triscuits, butter and 1 1/2 teaspoons of the artificial sweetener in a bowl and mix well. Pat into a lightly buttered 9-inch pie plate. Place the cream cheese in a mixing bowl and beat at medium speed for 2 to 3 minutes. Beat in 1 teaspoon of the vanilla and 3 teaspoons of the artificial sweetener gradually. Add the eggs 1 at a time, beating well after each addition. Pour into the Triscuit shell. Bake at 375 degrees for 20 minutes. Remove from oven and let stand for 15 minutes. Raise oven temperature to 475 degrees. Combine the sour cream, the remaining 1 teaspoon vanilla and the remaining 2 teaspoons artificial sweetener in a mixing bowl and beat until smooth. Spread over the top of the cheesecake and bake for 10 minutes longer. Let stand until cool. Yield: 8 to 10 servings.

Betty Sopp, Xi Epsilon Pi
Fayetteville, Georgia

CREME BRULEE

2 cups heavy cream	1 tablespoon vanilla extract
2 cups light cream	
8 egg yolks	1/4 cup raspberries (optional)
1/2 cup packed dark brown sugar	Light brown sugar for the topping
1/4 teaspoon salt	

Combine the heavy cream and light cream in a heavy saucepan over medium heat and scald. Combine the egg yolks, brown sugar and salt in a mixing bowl and beat until smooth. Pour the hot cream slowly into the egg yolk mixture, beating constantly with a wire whisk. Beat in the vanilla and stir in the raspberries. Pour into a 2-quart baking dish. Place the baking dish in a larger baking pan. Add hot water to the larger pan to a depth of 1 inch. Bake at 300 degrees for 1 hour or until a knife inserted in the center comes out clean. Let stand until cool. Chill, covered, until set. Cover top with a 1/4-inch layer of sifted light brown sugar. Place in a pan of ice and broil 6 inches from the heat source to caramelize the sugar, or use a baker's torch. Serve immediately. Yield: 12 to 16 servings.

Cynthia Kuykendall, Preceptor Alpha Kappa
Ozark, Arkansas

STRAWBERRY BRULEE

6 ounces cream cheese, softened	1 cup sour cream
4 tablespoons brown sugar	6 cups fresh strawberries

Place the cream cheese in a small mixing bowl and beat until fluffy. Add 2 tablespoons of the brown sugar and sour cream; beat until smooth. Halve the strawberries and arrange in an 8-inch-round baking dish. Spoon the cream cheese mixture over the berries. Sprinkle the remaining 2 tablespoons brown sugar evenly over the cream cheese layer. Bake in a preheated 450-degree oven for 3 to 4 minutes or until sugar is caramelized. Serve immediately. Yield: 8 servings.

Daryl Rodway, Xi Alpha
Los Lunas, New Mexico

❖ WHITE CHOCOLATE CREME BRULEE

1 1/2 cups heavy cream	3 egg yolks
1 teaspoon vanilla extract	3 tablespoons plus 4 teaspoons sugar
4 ounces white chocolate, chopped	

Position a rack in the center of the oven and preheat to 325 degrees. Line a large baking pan with a kitchen towel. Have a kettle of boiling water ready. Warm the cream and vanilla in a saucepan over medium heat for 2 to 3 minutes or until small bubbles form around the edge. Remove from heat. Add the white chocolate and stir until melted and blended; cool slightly. Place the egg yolks and 3 tablespoons of the sugar in a bowl and whisk for about 5 minutes or until thick ribbons fall from the whisk. Stir in the warm chocolate mixture slowly. Place four 4-ounce ramekins in the towel-lined pan. Strain the chocolate mixture through a fine mesh strainer into the ramekins. Cover pan loosely with aluminum foil. Bake at 325 degrees for 25 to 30 minutes or just until custards are set around the edges. Remove the ramekins from the pan to a wire rack to cool. Chill, covered, in the refrigerator for at least 4 hours. Sprinkle 1 teaspoon sugar evenly over the surface of each custard just before serving. Use a kitchen torch to melt the sugar. Serve immediately. Yield: 4 servings.

Kim Dillow, Gamma
Louisville, Kentucky

BREAD PUDDING WITH WHISKEY SAUCE

1 (1-pound) loaf French bread	4 teaspoons vanilla extract
2 cups half-and-half	1/2 teaspoon orange extract
2 cups milk	
3 eggs, lightly beaten	1 1/2 teaspoons cinnamon
2 cups sugar	2 tablespoons butter, melted
1 cup chopped pecans	
1/2 cup raisins	Whiskey Sauce
3/4 cup shredded coconut	

Break the bread into small pieces and place in a shallow bowl. Add the half-and-half and milk and let stand for 10 minutes. Crush the mixture with the hands until blended. Add the eggs, sugar, 1/2 cup of the chopped pecans, raisins, 1/4 cup of the coconut, vanilla, orange extract and cinnamon, stirring well. Pour the melted butter into a 9×13-inch baking dish and tilt to coat the bottom of the dish. Spoon the bread mixture into the dish. Bake at 325 degrees for 40 to 45 minutes or until firm. Let stand until cool. Mix the remaining 1/2 cup coconut and the remaining 1/2 cup pecans together; sprinkle evenly over the pudding. Drizzle with hot Whiskey Sauce.
Yield: 15 servings.

WHISKEY SAUCE

1 cup (2 sticks) butter	3 tablespoons whiskey
2 cups sifted confectioners' sugar	2 eggs, beaten

Melt the butter in the top of a double boiler over simmering water. Add the confectioners' sugar and whiskey and stir to dissolve. Beat half the hot mixture into the eggs. Stir the egg mixture into the hot mixture. Cook for 5 minutes, stirring constantly.

Kathy Tolliver, Laureate Alpha Zeta
Pineville, West Virginia

CRANBERRY BREAD PUDDING

1 loaf French bread	2 cups milk
1 cup chopped walnuts	1/2 cup (1 stick) butter
1 cup raisins	1 cup honey
1/2 cup dried cranberries	4 large eggs
1 cup fresh or frozen cranberries	1 teaspoon cinnamon
	1/2 teaspoon nutmeg

Cut the bread into 1-inch pieces and spread in a 9×13-inch baking dish that has been sprayed with nonstick cooking spray. Sprinkle the walnuts, raisins, dried cranberries and fresh cranberries over the bread. Combine the milk, butter and honey in a saucepan and bring to a simmer. Place the eggs, cinnamon and nutmeg in a bowl and whisk to combine. Whisk the egg mixture into the simmering honey mixture. Drizzle evenly over the cranberries. Bake at 350 degrees for 30 minutes or until golden brown. Serve with whipped cream. Yield: 12 servings.

Carol Franssen, Tau Master
North Bend, Oregon

FRUIT BREAD PUDDING

If you use peach pie filling, chop the peaches.

4 cups cubed French bread	2 tablespoons brown sugar
3 large eggs, beaten	1/2 teaspoon cinnamon
2 cups milk	2 tablespoons sliced almonds
1/2 cup sugar	
1/2 teaspoon almond extract	1 1/2 teaspoons butter, chopped
1 (21-ounce) can peach, pineapple or blueberry pie filling	

Spread the bread in a 7×11-inch baking dish that has been sprayed with nonstick cooking spray. Combine the eggs, milk, sugar and almond extract in a bowl and whisk until smooth. Stir in the pie filling. Pour the egg mixture evenly over the bread layer. Press down the bread with the back of a spoon to absorb the liquid. Sprinkle with a mixture of the brown sugar and cinnamon. Sprinkle with almonds and dot with butter. Bake at 350 degrees for 50 to 55 minutes or until a knife inserted in the center comes out clean. Yield: 9 to 12 servings.

Candace R. M. Promowicz, Laureate Alpha Iota
Niagara Falls, New York

COFFEE BREAD AND BUTTER PUDDING

6 thin slices raisin bread	1/2 cup sugar
1 cup strong coffee	1/2 teaspoon salt
1 cup light cream	1 teaspoon vanilla extract
2 cups milk	
2 eggs, slightly beaten	Dash of nutmeg

Butter each slice of bread lightly with butter; do not trim the crusts. Cut into 1/4-inch cubes and place in a bowl. Combine the coffee, cream and milk in a saucepan and bring to the scalding point. Add the bread cubes and stir. Combine the eggs, sugar and salt in a bowl and mix well; stir into the bread mixture. Pour into a buttered 1 1/2-quart baking dish and sprinkle with nutmeg. Place the baking dish in a larger baking pan. Add warm water to the larger pan to a depth of 1 inch. Bake at 325 degrees for 1 hour and 15 minutes or until a knife inserted near the edge of the baking dish comes out clean. Chill until serving time. Yield: 8 servings.

Pauline Lockwood, Laureate Delta Phi
St. Augustine, Florida

WHITE CHOCOLATE BREAD PUDDING

The people at the Plaza Café in New Orleans were kind enough to share the recipe for this pudding.

1 loaf French bread	1/2 cup sugar
3 cups heavy cream	2 eggs
10 ounces white chocolate	8 egg yolks
1 cup milk	2 tablespoons chocolate shavings

Cut the bread into small cubes and dry out in a slow oven. Combine the cream and white chocolate in the top of a double boiler over simmering water; heat until melted. Remove from heat and pour into a large bowl. Combine the milk, sugar, eggs and egg yolks in the top of a double boiler over simmering water; heat until warm. Pour the egg mixture into the chocolate mixture and blend well. Spread the dried bread pieces in a buttered 9×13-inch baking dish. Drizzle half the chocolate mixture over the bread and let stand for 15 minutes. Pour the rest of the chocolate mixture evenly over the top. Cover with foil and bake at 275 degrees for 1 hour. Remove the foil and bake for 15 minutes longer or until golden brown. Spoon the hot pudding into serving bowls, or cool in the pan to room temperature and then chill for about 45 minutes and cut into squares. Drizzle with a mixture of 8 ounces melted white chocolate and 3/8 cup heavy cream. Top with chocolate shavings. Yield: 15 servings.

Sara Howell, Xi Alpha Xi
Columbus, Mississippi

RICE PUDDING

1 1/2 cups sugar	3 eggs
10 cups milk	1 1/2 teaspoons cornstarch
4 tablespoons butter, chopped	1/2 teaspoon vanilla extract
3/4 cup long grain rice	
1/2 cinnamon stick (optional)	

Combine the sugar, milk and butter in a large saucepan; bring to a boil, stirring frequently. Add the rice and cinnamon stick and simmer for about 1 hour or until cooked completely, stirring occasionally. Discard the cinnamon stick. Combine the eggs, cornstarch and vanilla in a mixing bowl and beat until smooth. Pour a little hot milk mixture slowly into the eggs to temper and prevent curdling, stirring con-

stantly. Stir the egg mixture into the rice mixture and cook over medium heat until thickened, stirring constantly. Add raisins if desired. Serve warm or cold. Garnish with ground cinnamon if desired. Yield: 15 servings.

Eleanor Herzog, Alpha Lambda Master
Perry, Ohio

ORANGE RICE PUDDING

1 cup boiling water	2 teaspoons cinnamon
1 cup short grain white rice	1/2 cup yellow raisins (optional)
1/3 cup sugar	Grated zest of 1 large orange
1 tablespoon cornstarch	1 teaspoon butter or margarine
3 1/2 cups whole or skim milk	2 teaspoons vanilla extract
1 (12-ounce) can evaporated milk	
2 teaspoons nutmeg	

Combine the boiling water and rice in a large saucepan and return to a boil. Boil gently until water is almost evaporated, stirring frequently. Reduce heat. Stir in a mixture of the sugar and cornstarch. Whisk in 1 cup of the milk. Stir in the remaining milk and evaporated milk and bring to a full boil. Reduce heat and stir in the nutmeg, cinnamon, raisins, orange zest and butter. Cover tightly and cook for 1 1/2 to 2 hours or until desired thickness. Stir in the vanilla toward the end of the cooking time. Add additional nutmeg if desired. Serve hot or cold. Yield: 6 to 8 servings.

Jo Agnew, Xi Theta Alpha
Grimsby, Ontario, Canada

NORWEGIAN RICE DESSERT

2/3 cup quick-cooking rice	1 medium banana, sliced
1/2 cup water	1 tablespoon sugar
1/4 cup pineapple juice	1 cup whipped cream
1/2 teaspoon salt	6 maraschino cherries, chopped
3/4 to 1 cup miniature marshmallows	
3/4 cup crushed pineapple, drained	

Combine the rice, water, pineapple juice and salt in a saucepan. Cook using the rice package directions. Remove from heat and let stand for 10 minutes. Stir in the marshmallows, pineapple and banana. Let stand until cool. Blend the sugar and whipped cream and fold into the rice mixture. Fold in the cherries, or use as decoration. Chill if desired. Yield: 6 servings.

Diane McAlpin, Theta Master
Olympia, Washington

FLAN

3/4 cup sugar	1 (14-ounce) can
4 eggs	sweetened condensed
1 teaspoon vanilla	milk
extract	
1 (12-ounce) can	
evaporated milk	

Place the sugar in a heavy skillet over medium-high heat and cook until melted, stirring constantly. Pour into an 8-inch cake pan immediately. Spread in the pan very quickly, as it will harden and crack. Combine the eggs, vanilla, evaporated milk and condensed milk in a blender container and process until smooth. Pour evenly over the sugar layer. Place the cake pan in a larger baking pan. Add water to the larger pan to a depth of 3/4 inch. Bake at 350 degrees for 50 minutes or until firm but jiggly; let stand until cool. Chill, covered, in the refrigerator until cold. Run a knife around the edge and invert onto a serving plate. Sugar will be liquid. Cut into wedges. Serve on dessert plates; decorate the plates with swirls of caramel topping if desired. Yield: 8 servings.

Marilyn Harder, Preceptor Beta Beta
Palouse, Washington

BAKED CUSTARD

2 eggs	Pinch of salt
1/2 scant cup sugar	1 teaspoon vanilla
2 cups milk, scalded	extract

Place the eggs and sugar in a mixing bowl and beat until smooth. Beat in the milk gradually. Beat in the salt and vanilla. Pour into a 6-inch glass baking dish. Sprinkle with nutmeg. Place the baking dish in a larger baking pan. Add warm water to the larger pan to a depth of 1 inch. Bake at 325 degrees for 1 hour. Cool and serve. Yield: 6 servings.

Lois Hinton, Preceptor Zeta Sigma
Chillicothe, Ohio

OZARK PUDDING

1 egg	1/8 teaspoon salt
3/4 cup sugar	1/2 cup chopped pecans
2 rounded tablespoons	1/2 cup chopped peeled
flour	apple
1 1/4 teaspoons baking	1 teaspoon vanilla
powder	extract

Combine the egg and sugar in a mixing bowl and beat until smooth. Stir in a mixture of the flour, baking powder and salt. Stir in the pecans, apple and vanilla. Spoon into a buttered 8×8-inch baking pan.

Bake at 350 degrees for 35 minutes or until lightly browned. Serve with whipped topping.
Yield: 4 servings.

Connie Aguilera, Preceptor Eta
Wichita, Kansas

BANANA PUDDING WITH MERINGUE

1/3 cup flour	3 cups sliced ripe
Dash of salt	bananas
2 1/2 cups low-fat milk	45 reduced-fat vanilla
1 (14-ounce) can fat-free	wafers
sweetened condensed	4 egg whites
milk	4 tablespoons sugar
2 egg yolks	
2 teaspoons vanilla	
extract	

Combine the flour and salt in a medium saucepan. Place over medium heat and add the milk, condensed milk and egg yolks, stirring constantly for 8 minutes or until thickened. Remove from heat and add the vanilla. Arrange 1 cup of the banana slices in a 2-quart baking dish. Spoon 1/3 of the pudding over the bananas and top with 15 vanilla wafers. Repeat the layers. Arrange the remaining cup of banana slices over the top and spoon remaining pudding over the bananas. Place the remaining wafers around the edge of the dish, pressing gently into the pudding. Beat the egg whites in a mixing bowl until foamy. Add the sugar 1 tablespoon at a time, beating at high speed until stiff peaks form. Spread the meringue over the pudding. Bake at 325 degrees for 25 minutes. Cool and serve. Yield: 10 servings.

Shelly Thrash, Gamma Theta
Palestine, Arkansas

BLUEBERRY PUDDING

4 cups fresh blueberries	1 rounded teaspoon
1 1/2 cups sugar	baking powder
2 tablespoons butter	1 cup milk
1 cup flour	Pinch of salt

Combine the blueberries and 1/2 cup of the sugar in a bowl and stir gently. Melt the butter in an ovenproof bowl. Add the flour, the remaining 1 cup sugar, baking powder, milk and salt and mix well. Press the sweetened blueberries into the center of the flour mixture. Bake at 350 degrees for about 1 hour or until a knife inserted in the batter comes out clean. Serve warm or cold, with cream if desired.
Yield: 4 to 6 servings.

Jean Chapple, Xi Beta Epsilon
Berlin, Maryland

CHERRY PUDDING

2 cups flour
2 cups sugar
1/2 teaspoon salt
1 (20-ounce) can red
 cherries
2 eggs, beaten

2 tablespoons butter,
 melted
2 teaspoons baking soda
2 teaspoons water
1 cup chopped walnuts
 or pecans

Combine the flour, sugar and salt in a bowl and mix well. Drain the cherries and add the cherry juice to the flour mixture. Add the eggs and butter and blend well. Stir in a mixture of the baking soda and water. Fold in the cherries and chopped nuts. Spoon into a buttered 9×13-inch baking dish. Bake at 350 degrees for 30 minutes or until lightly browned.
Yield: 8 to 12 servings.

Lucylee Lively, Preceptor Iota Sigma
Dallas, Texas

STEAMED PERSIMMON PUDDING WITH LEMON HARD SAUCE

3 peeled ripe
 persimmons
2 teaspoons baking soda
1/2 cup (1 stick) butter,
 softened
11/2 cups sugar
1 tablespoon fresh
 lemon juice

2 eggs
1 cup flour
1 teaspoon cinnamon
1/2 teaspoon salt
2 tablespoons rum
 (optional)
2/3 cup chopped pecans

Mash the persimmons in a bowl and mix in the baking soda; let stand for 5 minutes. Combine the butter, sugar, lemon juice, eggs, flour, cinnamon, salt and rum in a separate bowl and mix well. Fold in the pecans. Add the persimmon mixture and mix well. Spoon into 2 clean 1-pound coffee cans and cover tightly with foil. Place the coffee cans in a large kettle. Add water to the kettle to a depth of several inches. Place over medium-high heat and bring to a boil. Reduce heat and simmer for 2 hours. Cool slightly in the coffee cans and unmold. Serve warm with Lemon Hard Sauce. Freezes well.
Yield: 8 servings.

LEMON HARD SAUCE

2 cups confectioners'
 sugar
1/2 cup (1 stick) butter,
 melted

2 teaspoons fresh lemon
 juice

Combine the confectioners' sugar, butter and lemon juice in a mixing bowl and beat until smooth.

Barbara Boggs, Kappa Master
Las Vegas, Nevada

POOR MAN'S PUDDING

2 cups flour
1 teaspoon baking soda
1 teaspoon salt
1 teaspoon cinnamon
1 teaspoon ground
 cloves

1 teaspoon nutmeg
1 cup raisins
1 cup currants
1 cup suet
1 cup molasses
1 cup milk

Sift the flour, baking soda, salt, cinnamon, cloves and nutmeg together. Toss the raisins and currants in 1/2 cup of the flour mixture and set aside. Combine the suet and molasses in a large bowl and mix well. Add the dry ingredients alternately with the milk, mixing well after each addition. Stir in the raisin mixture. Spoon into a round 7- or 8-inch baking pan and cover tightly with foil. Place the pan in a large kettle. Add water to the kettle to a depth of halfway up the side of the pan. Place over medium-high heat and bring to a boil. Reduce heat and simmer for 3 hours, adding water as necessary. Cool slightly in the pan and unmold. Serve with hot caramel sauce or other sauce of your choice. Yield: 10 servings.

Carol Mulcahy, Delta Master
Dartmouth, Nova Scotia, Canada

BUTTERSCOTCH TAPIOCA

1/4 cup (1/2 stick) butter
3/4 cup packed brown
 sugar
21/2 cups milk
5 tablespoons tapioca

11/2 teaspoons vanilla
 extract
1/2 teaspoon maple
 extract

Melt the butter in a 2-quart saucepan over medium heat. Stir in the brown sugar. Add the milk to the sugar mixture, stirring constantly until mixture comes to a full rolling boil. Boil for about 3 minutes, stirring constantly. Remove from heat and add the vanilla and maple extract; mix well. Pour into small dessert dishes. Let stand for 20 minutes. Serve warm or cold. Yield: 4 to 5 servings.

Marie Hass, Beta Epsilon
Madison, Wisconsin

*Joanne Trumbull, Preceptor Psi, Chapin, South Carolina, makes **Microwave Bread Pudding** by layering 4 cups bread cubes in a glass baking dish and sprinkling with 1/2 to 3/4 cup brown sugar, 1/2 teaspoon cinnamon, 1/4 teaspoon salt and 1/2 cup raisins. Microwave 2 cups milk and 1/4 cup butter on High for 4 minutes until butter melts. Stir in 2 beaten eggs with a fork, pour over the bread, and microwave on High for 10 minutes. Let stand for 10 minutes to cool and set up before serving.*

CARAMEL APPLE STREUSEL DESSERT

10 caramels	1 cup sugar
3 tablespoons milk	1 cup chopped pecans
2¼ cups flour	1 egg
1 cup (2 sticks) butter, softened	1 (21-ounce) can apple pie filling

Unwrap the caramels and place in a small saucepan over low heat; add the milk. Cook until melted, stirring until smooth. Remove from heat and cool for 5 minutes. Combine the flour, butter, sugar, pecans and egg in a large mixing bowl; beat at low speed for 2 to 3 minutes or until crumbly, scraping bowl often. Remove 1½ cups of the flour mixture and set aside. Press the remaining flour mixture over the bottom and ¾ up the side of a buttered 9-inch springform pan. Fill with the pie filling. Drizzle with the cooled caramel mixture and sprinkle with the reserved flour mixture. Bake at 350 degrees for 40 to 45 minutes or until lightly browned and bubbly. Cool before slicing. Yield: 12 servings.

Elaine Goving, Xi Beta Tau
London, Ontario, Canada

CHERRY COCONUT DELIGHT

1¾ cups flaked coconut	2 tablespoons
1 cup sugar	cornstarch
1½ cups sifted flour	½ cup chopped pecans
½ cup (1 stick) butter	
1 (16-ounce) package frozen cherries, thawed	

Combine the coconut, ½ cup of the sugar and flour in a bowl. Cut in the butter until mixture resembles coarse crumbs. Press half the mixture into a buttered 9-inch cake pan. Drain the cherries, reserving the juice. Combine the cherry juice, cornstarch and the remaining ½ cup sugar in a saucepan over medium-low heat and cook until thickened, stirring constantly. Pour evenly over the crumb layer. Top with the remaining crumbs and the pecans. Bake at 400 degrees for 30 minutes or until bubbly. Yield: 12 servings.

Betty R. Dannels, Xi Upsilon
Pensacola, Florida

CHERRY SLICES

1 cup (2 sticks) butter, softened	2½ cups flour
1¾ cups sugar	½ teaspoon baking powder
4 eggs	⅛ teaspoon salt
1 teaspoon vanilla extract	1 (21-ounce) can cherry pie filling

Combine the butter, sugar, eggs and vanilla in a mixing bowl and beat at medium speed for 2 minutes. Beat in a mixture of the flour, baking powder and salt. Remove 1½ cups of the flour mixture and set aside. Pat the remaining flour mixture in a buttered 10×15-inch cake pan. Spread the cherry pie filling over the flour mixture layer. Drop the remaining flour mixture by spoonfuls over the top. Bake at 350 degrees for 35 to 40 minutes or until browned and bubbly. Drizzle with confectioners' sugar icing while still warm. Yield: 20 servings.

Mary L. Reardon, Omicron Master
Maryville, Missouri

VANILLA CREAM CHEESE DESSERT

½ cup (1 stick) butter	8 ounces cream cheese, softened
1 cup water	16 ounces whipped topping
1 cup flour	
4 eggs	
2 (3-ounce) packages vanilla instant pudding mix	

Combine the butter and water in a saucepan and bring to a boil. Reduce heat to low and add the flour, beating constantly with an electric mixer. Remove from heat and cool for 5 minutes. Add the eggs 1 at a time, beating well after each addition. Spread in an ungreased 11×15-inch baking pan. Bake at 400 degrees for 28 to 30 minutes or until lightly browned. Cool. Prepare the pudding using the directions on the package; beat in the cream cheese. Spread the cream cheese mixture over the cooled crust. Chill for 20 minutes. Spread whipped topping over the top. Drizzle with chocolate syrup if desired.
Yield: 24 servings.

Lori Boyle, Xi Zeta Sigma
Ackley, Iowa

CHOCOLATE MINT DESSERT

1 cup flour	2 cups confectioners' sugar
1 cup sugar	2 tablespoons crème de menthe
1 cup (2 sticks) plus 6 tablespoons butter or margarine, softened	1 cup semisweet chocolate chips
4 eggs	
1 (16-ounce) can chocolate syrup	

Combine the flour, sugar, ½ cup of the butter, eggs and chocolate syrup in a large mixing bowl and beat until smooth. Pour into a buttered 9×13-inch baking dish. Bake at 350 degrees for 25 to 30 minutes or until top springs back when lightly pressed. Cool in the pan completely. Combine the confectioners' sugar,

½ cup of the butter and crème de menthe in a small mixing bowl and beat until smooth. Spread over the cooled dessert. Chill for at least 1 hour. Melt the remaining 6 tablespoons butter and chocolate chips in a small saucepan over very low heat. Remove from heat and stir until smooth; cool slightly. Spread over the chilled dessert. Cover and chill for at least 1 hour before serving. Yield: 12 servings.

Lila L. Wolfe, Laureate Alpha Omega
Wakeman, Ohio

PEANUT S'MORE DESSERT

8 to 10 whole graham crackers	1 cup semisweet chocolate chips
1 (20-ounce) package brownie mix	⅔ cup chopped peanuts
2 cups miniature marshmallows	

Place the graham crackers in a single layer in a 9×13-inch baking pan. Prepare the brownie mix using the package directions and pour evenly over the graham crackers. Bake at 350 degrees for 25 to 30 minutes or until a wooden pick inserted in the center comes out clean. Sprinkle evenly with the marshmallows, chocolate chips and peanuts. Return to the oven and bake for 5 minutes longer or until marshmallows are slightly puffy and light brown. Yield: 2 dozen.

Evelyn Chelesvig, Laureate Alpha Alpha
Eagle Grove, Iowa

COCONUT CREAM DESSERT

2 cups flour	2 (4-ounce) packages coconut instant pudding mix
2 cups shredded coconut	
½ cup sugar	
1 cup (2 sticks) margarine, melted	5 cups milk
1 (6-ounce) package vanilla instant pudding mix	8 ounces whipped topping

Combine the flour, coconut, sugar and margarine in a bowl and mix well. Press firmly into a 9×13-inch baking pan. Bake at 300 degrees for 1 hour, stirring every 15 minutes. Remove ½ to 1 cup of the coconut mixture and set aside. Press the remaining mixture firmly in the pan. Let stand until cool. Combine the dry pudding mixes with the milk in a mixing bowl and beat until smooth. Pour evenly over the cooled crust. Top with whipped topping and sprinkle with the reserved coconut mixture. Chill and serve. Yield: 15 to 20 servings.

Sherri Tharp, Xi Nu Iota
St. Elmo, Illinois

CREAM PUFF DESSERT

1 cup cold water	3 (4-ounce) packages vanilla instant pudding mix
½ cup (1 stick) margarine	
1 cup flour	8 ounces cream cheese, softened
4 eggs	
4 cups whole milk	8 ounces whipped topping

Combine the water and margarine in a saucepan and bring to a boil. Remove from heat. Add the flour, stirring until a ball is formed. Let stand until cool. Add the eggs to the cooled flour mixture 1 at a time, beating well after each addition. Spread over the bottom and up the sides of a buttered 9×13-inch baking dish. Bake in a preheated 400-degree oven for 30 to 35 minutes or until lightly browned. Combine the milk and pudding mix in a mixing bowl and beat until smooth and thickened. Mix in the cream cheese and pour evenly over the cooled crust. Spread the whipped topping over the top. Chill, covered, for at least 1 hour before serving. Yield: 12 servings.

Michaelene Campana, Laureate Epsilon Eta
Monessen, Pennsylvania

FOOD FOR THE GODS

6 egg yolks	8 ounces chopped dates
2 cups sugar	1 pound pecans or walnuts, chopped
12 rounded tablespoons saltine cracker crumbs	
2 teaspoons baking powder	6 egg whites

Combine the egg yolks and sugar in a mixing bowl and beat until smooth. Add a mixture of the cracker crumbs and baking powder and blend well. Add a mixture of the dates and pecans; blend well. Beat the egg whites in a separate mixing bowl until stiff peaks form. Fold into the date mixture. Spread in a well-buttered 9×13-inch baking dish. Bake at 350 degrees for 40 to 45 minutes or until golden brown. Yield: 24 servings.

Mattie D. Buller, Alpha Upsilon
Ville Platte, Louisiana

*Janice Duke, Alpha Eta Master, Victoria, British Columbia, Canada, makes a **Hot Peach Melba** by bringing a package of frozen raspberries to a boil in a saucepan and stirring in 1½ teaspoons cornstarch dissolved in 1 tablespoon cold water then cooking until thickened, stirring constantly. Remove from the heat and blend in 2 tablespoons orange liqueur. Place peach halves in dessert dishes. Add scoops of vanilla ice cream and spoon the raspberry sauce over the top.*

HEAVENLY CHEESE BREAD

2 (8-count) package
  crescent rolls
16 ounces cream cheese,
  softened
1 cup sugar
1 egg, separated

1 teaspoon vanilla
  extract
1/2 cup confectioners'
  sugar
1 tablespoon milk

Unroll the dough into 9×13-inch rectangles, pressing perforations to seal. Fit one rectangle in an unbuttered 9×13-inch baking pan. Blend the cream cheese, sugar, egg yolk and vanilla in a mixing bowl. Spread in the dough-lined pan. Layer the second dough rectangle over the cream cheese layer. Beat the egg white lightly and brush over the top. Bake at 350 degrees for 30 minutes or until lightly browned. Whisk the confectioners' sugar and milk in a bowl until smooth; drizzle over the warm dessert bread. Cool completely before cutting. Yield: 15 servings.

Beverly Binder, Laureate Gamma Epsilon
Toledo, Ohio

LAYERED PEACH DESSERT

2 cups flour
2 cups sugar
1 1/2 cups butter
8 ounces cream cheese,
  softened
8 ounces whipped
  topping

1 teaspoon vanilla
  extract
2 tablespoons
  unflavored gelatin
5 cups sliced fresh
  peaches
1/4 cup fresh lemon juice

Combine the flour and 1/2 cup of the sugar in a bowl. Cut in the butter until crumbly. Press into a buttered 9×13-inch baking dish. Bake at 350 degrees for 25 minutes or until edges begin to brown. Beat the cream cheese and 1/2 cup sugar in a mixing bowl until smooth; fold in the whipped topping and vanilla. Spread the cream cheese mixture over the crust; chill for 1 hour. Soften the gelatin in 1 cup cold water; add 1 cup boiling water and the remaining sugar and stir to dissolve. Toss the peach slices with the lemon juice. Stir into the gelatin mixture. Spread the peach mixture over the cream cheese layer. Chill until firm. Yield: 15 servings.

Andrea Snoke, Laureate Epsilon Nu
Shippensburg, Pennsylvania

---

*Wanda Dutch, Xi Epsilon Sigma, Temple City, California, likes to serve her **Spectacular Cherry Surprise** by slicing a brick of vanilla ice cream and an angel food cake and layering ice cream, cake and hot cherry pie filling on dessert plates and topping each with a sugar cube dipped in lemon extract. Ignite each sugar cube just before serving.*

PEACH CUSTARD DESSERT

1 1/2 cups flour
1/2 teaspoon salt
1/2 cup (1 stick)
  margarine, softened
1 (30-ounce) can sliced
  peaches

1/2 cup sugar
1/2 teaspoon cinnamon
1 egg, slightly beaten
1 cup evaporated milk

Combine the flour and salt in a bowl; cut in the margarine until mixture resembles coarse crumbs. Press firmly over the bottom and halfway up the sides of a buttered 8×8-inch baking pan. Drain the peaches well, reserving 1/2 cup of the syrup. Arrange the peach slices in the crumb-lined pan. Sprinkle a mixture of the sugar and cinnamon over the peaches. Bake at 375 degrees for 20 minutes. Combine the reserved peach syrup, egg and evaporated milk in a mixing bowl and mix until smooth. Pour evenly over the baked peaches; bake for 30 minutes longer or until custard is firm except for the center (center will firm upon standing). Serve warm or cold. Yield: 9 servings.

Roxanne Lerach, Xi Alpha Beta
Oakdale, Minnesota

PEANUT PUDDING TORTE

1 cup flour
1 cup chopped dry-
  roasted peanuts
1/2 cup (1 stick)
  margarine
1/3 cup peanut butter
8 ounces cream cheese,
  softened
1 cup confectioners'
  sugar

1 cup whipped topping
1 (4-ounce) package
  vanilla instant
  pudding mix
1 (4-ounce) package
  chocolate instant
  pudding mix
2 3/4 cups milk
1 (7-ounce) chocolate
  candy bar

Combine the flour and 2/3 cup of the peanuts in a bowl; cut in the margarine until crumbly. Pat evenly into an unbuttered 9×13-inch baking pan. Bake at 350 degrees for 20 minutes. Cool completely. Combine the peanut butter and cream cheese in a mixing bowl and beat until smooth. Mix in the confectioners' sugar. Blend in the whipped topping. Spread over the cooled peanut layer. Combine the pudding mixes and milk in a separate mixing bowl and mix well; let stand for 5 minutes. Spread over the cream cheese layer. Top with additional whipped topping. Shred the candy bar evenly over the top and sprinkle with the remaining 1/3 cup peanuts. Refrigerate leftovers. Yield: 15 servings.

Sherryl Cobb, Preceptor Phi
Oregon, Wisconsin

PECAN PUDDING DREAM

Use instant pudding mix of any flavor . . . butterscotch is particularly good.

1 cup flour	8 ounces whipped
1/2 cup chopped pecans	topping
1/2 cup (1 stick) butter or	2 (4-ounce) packages
margarine	instant pudding mix
8 ounces cream cheese,	2 1/2 cups milk
softened	
1/2 cup confectioners'	
sugar	

Combine the flour and pecans in a bowl and cut in the butter until crumbly. Press into a 9×13-inch baking pan. Bake at 375 degrees for 15 minutes. Cool. Combine the cream cheese, confectioners' sugar and 1 cup of the whipped topping in a mixing bowl; mix well. Spread the cream cheese mixture over the crust. Blend the pudding mix and milk in a bowl; let stand for a few minutes. Spread the pudding over the cream cheese layer. Spread additional whipped topping over the top. Sprinkle with a few chopped pecans. Chill, covered, for at least 1 hour. Yield: 10 to 12 servings.

Nancy Pflughoeft, Zeta Iota
Loveland, Colorado

PINEAPPLE TORTE

1 1/2 cups plus 2 to 3	2 or 3 egg yolks, slightly
tablespoons flour	beaten
1 1/4 cups sugar	2 cups whipped cream
1/2 cup (1 stick) butter	1 teaspoon vanilla
2 cups crushed pineapple	extract
in heavy syrup	

Combine the 1 1/2 cups flour and 1/2 cup of the sugar in a bowl; cut in the butter until crumbly. Roll into a ball. Roll into an 11×14-inch rectangle and fit into an unbuttered 9×12-inch baking dish. Bake at 350 degrees for 12 to 15 minutes or until light brown. Cool. Combine the undrained pineapple, another 1/2 cup of the sugar and the 2 to 3 tablespoons flour in a saucepan. Stir in the egg yolks and bring to a slow boil. Boil gently until thickened, stirring constantly. Cool. Pour into the cooled crust. Chill for at least 1 hour. Combine the whipped cream, the remaining 1/4 cup (or to taste) sugar and vanilla; spread evenly over the chilled pineapple layer. Chill for at least 1 hour before serving. Yield: 10 to 12 servings.

Marge Hefty, Alpha Gamma Master
Tucson, Arizona

PISTACHIO DESSERT

1 cup flour	8 ounces whipped
1/2 cup chopped pecans	topping
or walnuts	2 (4-ounce) packages
1/2 cup (1 stick) butter	pistachio pudding
8 ounces cream cheese,	mix
softened	2 2/3 cups cold milk
1 cup confectioners'	
sugar	

Combine the flour and chopped nuts in a bowl and cut in the butter until crumbly; press into a 9×13-inch baking dish. Bake at 350 degrees for 15 minutes; let stand until cool. Combine the cream cheese, confectioners' sugar and 1 cup of the whipped topping in a bowl and blend well. Spread over the cooled crust. Combine the pudding mix and milk in a mixing bowl and beat until smooth; spread over the cream cheese layer. Spread the remaining whipped topping over the top and sprinkle with additional chopped nuts. Chill, covered, until serving time. Yield: 12 servings.

Judi Tippin, Laureate Delta
Las Vegas, Nevada

BUTTERSCOTCH PUMPKIN DESSERT

2 cups flour	2 (4-ounce) packages
1 cup chopped walnuts	butterscotch instant
or pecans	pudding mix
1 cup (2 sticks) butter	1 3/4 cups milk
8 ounces cream cheese,	2 cups canned pumpkin
softened	1/8 teaspoon cinnamon
1 cup confectioners'	1/8 teaspoon nutmeg
sugar	
2 1/2 cups whipped	
topping	

Combine the flour and chopped nuts in a bowl and cut in the butter until crumbly; press into a 9×13-inch baking dish. Bake at 350 degrees for 30 minutes or until lightly browned; let stand until cool. Combine the cream cheese, confectioners' sugar and 1 cup of the whipped topping in a bowl and blend well. Spread over the cooled crust. Combine the pudding mix and milk in a mixing bowl and beat at medium speed for 2 minutes. Beat in the pumpkin, cinnamon and nutmeg. Spread over the cream cheese layer. Top with the remaining whipped topping. Chill, covered, until serving time. Yield: 12 to 15 servings.

Patricia A. Main, Laureate Zeta
Fremont, Nebraska

STRAWBERRY FLUFF

1¼ cups graham cracker crumbs	18 ounces whipped topping
3 tablespoons sugar	3 (3-ounce) packages strawberry gelatin
⅓ cup butter, melted	
1 (10-ounce) package large marshmallows	2 (5-ounce) packages frozen strawberries
½ cup milk	

Combine the graham cracker crumbs, sugar and melted butter in a bowl and mix well. Reserve ½ cup of the graham cracker mixture for the garnish; press the remaining mixture into a 9×13-inch baking pan. Bake in a preheated 350-degree oven for 8 minutes. Melt the marshmallows with the milk in a saucepan over medium-low heat, stirring occasionally. Remove from heat and let stand until cool. Beat in the whipped topping with a wooden spoon. Combine the dry gelatin mix and 3 cups boiling water in a large bowl and mix well. Stir in the frozen strawberries. Chill, in the refrigerator, until thickened. Spread half the marshmallow mixture over the cooled crust. Spread the strawberry mixture over the marshmallow layer. Spread the remaining marshmallow mixture over the top. Sprinkle with the reserved ½ cup crumb mixture. Sprinkle with chopped walnuts or pecans if desired. Chill, covered, until serving time. Yield: 18 servings.

Terrie L. Hatch, Preceptor Beta Delta
Niles, Michigan

BEST APPLE CRISP

4 to 5 cups sliced peeled apples	¾ cup (1½ sticks) margarine, melted
1 cup granulated sugar	½ teaspoon salt
2 tablespoons plus 1½ cups flour	1 teaspoon baking powder
1 tablespoon cinnamon	½ teaspoon baking soda
1½ cups rolled oats	¾ cup chopped walnuts (optional)
1½ cups packed brown sugar	

Combine the apples, granulated sugar, the 2 tablespoons flour and cinnamon in a bowl and mix well. Spread the apple mixture in a buttered 9×13-inch baking dish. Combine the oats, brown sugar, the 1½ cups flour, melted margarine, salt, baking powder, baking soda and walnuts in a bowl and mix until crumbly. Sprinkle evenly over the apples. Bake at 350 degrees for 45 to 50 minutes or until bubbly. Serve warm or cold with whipped cream or ice cream. Yield: 12 servings.

DeeDee Patrick, Xi Alpha Phi
Yorktown, Virginia

APPLE DUMPLINGS

2 cups sugar	2 teaspoons baking powder
¼ teaspoon cinnamon	
¼ teaspoon nutmeg	1 teaspoon salt
2 cups water	¾ cup shortening
¼ cup (½ stick) butter or margarine	½ cup milk
2 cups flour	6 cooking apples, peeled and cored

Combine the sugar, cinnamon, nutmeg and water in a saucepan over medium-low heat. Cook for 5 minutes, stirring occasionally; stir in the butter. Remove from heat. Sift the flour, baking powder and salt together; cut in the shortening until mixture resembles coarse crumbs. Add the milk all at once; stir just until moistened. Roll into a ¼-inch-thick rectangle. Cut out six 5-inch squares. Place an apple in the center of each square. Sprinkle generously with additional sugar, cinnamon and nutmeg; dot with butter. Fold up the corners of each square and pinch the edges to enclose the apple. Arrange 1 inch apart in a buttered 9×13-inch baking dish. Drizzle the cinnamon sauce over the dumplings. Bake at 375 degrees for 35 minutes. Serve hot with ice cream. Yield: 6 servings.

Lillie Dittfurth, Xi Rho Alpha
Athens, Texas

BLUEBERRY BUCKLE

3 (16-ounce) cans blueberries in syrup	16 ounces whipped topping
Juice of 2 lemons	1 (15-ounce) package graham cracker crumbs
2 cups sugar	
¼ cup cornstarch	
16 ounces cream cheese, softened	¾ cup (1½ sticks) butter, melted
2 teaspoons vanilla extract	

Drain the blueberries. Rinse half the blueberries; do not rinse the other half. Combine the blueberries, lemon juice, ½ cup of the sugar and cornstarch in a saucepan over low heat and cook until thickened, stirring frequently. Let stand until cool. Combine the cream cheese, the remaining 1½ cups sugar, vanilla and whipped topping in a mixing bowl and mix well. Combine the graham cracker crumbs and butter in a bowl and mix well. Pat half the crumb mixture into a 9×13-inch baking dish. Layer half the cream cheese mixture, all the blueberry mixture, the rest of the cream cheese mixture and the rest of the crumb mixture in the dish. Chill, covered, for 8 to 10 hours. Yield: 12 servings.

Jeanna C. Payne, Kappa Sigma
Duncan, Oklahoma

EASY BLUEBERRY COBBLER

3 cups fresh blueberries
1 tablespoon lemon juice
1 cup flour
1 cup sugar

1 egg, beaten
1/4 cup plus
   2 tablespoons butter,
   melted

Spread the blueberries in a 6×10-inch baking dish. Sprinkle with the lemon juice. Combine the flour, sugar, egg and the 1/4 cup melted butter in a bowl and stir until mixture resembles coarse crumbs. Spread evenly over the berries and drizzle with the 2 tablespoons melted butter. Bake at 375 degrees for 30 minutes. Serve warm. Yield: 6 to 8 servings.

Donna Farrell, Laureate Delta Mu
Cincinnati, Ohio

BLUEBERRY DUMPLINGS

2 1/2 cups fresh
   blueberries
1/3 cup plus
   2 tablespoons sugar
Dash of salt plus
   1/4 teaspoon salt
1 cup water

1 tablespoon lemon
   juice
1 cup flour
2 teaspoons baking
   powder
1 tablespoon butter
1/2 cup milk

Combine the blueberries, 1/3 cup sugar, dash of salt and water in a saucepan and bring to a boil. Reduce heat; simmer, covered, for 5 minutes. Stir in the lemon juice. Sift the flour, the 2 tablespoons sugar, baking powder and the 1/4 teaspoon salt together. Cut in the butter until mixture resembles coarse cornmeal. Add the milk all at once and stir just until mixed. Divide the batter into 6 portions and drop in the bubbling blueberry sauce. Cover pan tightly and cook over low heat for 10 minutes without removing the cover. Serve warm. Yield: 6 servings.

G. Arlene Knipe, Kappa Master
Staten Island, New York

BLACKBERRY COBBLER

2 1/2 cups blackberries
1 tablespoon orange
   liqueur
1 cup flour
3/4 cup granulated sugar
1/2 cup milk
1 teaspoon baking
   powder

1/2 teaspoon salt
4 teaspoons margarine,
   melted
1 tablespoon cornstarch
3/4 cup packed brown
   sugar
3/4 cup boiling water

Spread the blackberries in a unbuttered 8×8-inch baking pan. Drizzle with the orange liqueur. Combine the next 6 ingredients in a bowl and mix well. Spoon over the blackberries, sealing to the edges. Sprinkle a mixture of the cornstarch and brown sugar over the top. Pour the boiling water slowly over the top, covering the surface. Bake at 350 degrees for 1 hour and 10 minutes or until golden brown. Serve with whipped topping or ice cream. Yield: 6 to 8 servings.

Mary E. McGriff, Xi Beta Kappa
Columbia, South Carolina

FRESH PEACH COBBLER

2 cups flour
1 cup shortening
1/2 cup water
1/2 teaspoon salt
3 cups sugar

3 tablespoons
   cornstarch
1 quart fresh peaches,
   sliced

Place the flour in a bowl and cut in the shortening until mixture resembles pea-size crumbs. Add the water and salt, stirring until the mixture forms a ball. Roll out 2/3 of the dough on a floured surface into a rectangle that will fit over the bottom and up the sides of a 7×12-inch or 9×9-inch baking dish; fit into the dish. Roll out the rest of the dough to fit over the top. Combine the sugar, cornstarch and peaches in a saucepan over medium-low heat; cook until thickened, stirring frequently. Pour into the pastry-lined baking dish and cover with the remaining pastry. Dot with butter and sprinkle with sugar. Bake at 350 degrees for 35 to 45 minutes or until lightly browned. Yield: 8 to 12 servings.

Janet Walker, Xi Beta Epsilon
Woodward, Oklahoma

QUICK PEACH COBBLER

2 (21-ounce) cans peach
   pie filling
1 (2-layer) package
   yellow cake mix

1/2 cup (1 stick)
   margarine, melted
1 cup chopped pecans
   (optional)

Spread the peach pie filling in a 9×13-inch baking dish. Sprinkle the dry cake mix evenly over the filling and drizzle with the melted margarine. Sprinkle with chopped pecans. Bake at 350 degrees for 45 minutes or until top is golden brown. Serve warm with vanilla ice cream. Yield: 8 servings.

Connie Duhon, Kappa Zeta
Maurice, Louisiana

---

*Maggie Zelk, Alpha Gamma, Fort Saskatchewan, Alberta, Canada, prepares **Apple Snow** to serve as a sauce on muffins, cake, or fruit. She beats an egg until foamy and then beats in a cup of sugar gradually. Stir in a grated apple gradually and store in an airtight container in the refrigerator. Stir before serving.*

PECAN COBBLER

1 cup oat flour	3 cups granulated sugar
1 cup unbleached flour	1/3 cup melted margarine
1/4 teaspoon salt	1 tablespoon vanilla
1/2 cup (1 stick)	extract
margarine	6 eggs
1/2 cup cold water	3 cups pecans, coarsely
3 cups corn syrup	chopped

Combine the oat flour, unbleached flour and salt in a bowl. Cut in the margarine until crumbly. Mix in the cold water with a fork until the mixture forms a ball. Roll into a 9×13-inch rectangle on a lightly floured surface. Combine the corn syrup, granulated sugar, melted margarine, vanilla and eggs in a large bowl and mix well. Pour 1/3 of the mixture into a 9×13-inch baking dish that has been sprayed with nonstick cooking spray. Place the prepared pastry over the top. Stir the pecans into the remaining egg mixture and spread evenly over the pastry. Bake at 350 degrees for 50 to 60 minutes or until center is nearly set. Serve with a spoon. Yield: 12 to 18 servings.

Marcella L. Bell, Xi Iota Delta
Denver City, Texas

RHUBARB CRUNCH

1 cup flour	1 cup sugar
1 cup rolled oats	2 tablespoons
1 cup brown sugar	cornstarch
1/2 cup (1 stick) butter,	1 cup boiling water
melted	1 teaspoon vanilla
4 cups chopped rhubarb	extract

Combine the flour, oats and brown sugar in a bowl. Stir in the melted butter and blend well. Pour 2/3 of the oats mixture into a well-buttered 8×8-inch baking pan. Spread the rhubarb over the oats mixture. Combine the sugar and cornstarch in a saucepan and add the boiling water. Boil until thick and glossy, stirring frequently. Remove from heat and add the vanilla. Pour evenly over the rhubarb. Sprinkle with the remaining oats mixture. Bake at 350 degrees for 1 hour. Yield: about 6 servings.

Kathleen A. Secora, Xi Lambda Mu
Hoffman Estates, Illinois

*Kim Yonda, Delta Omicron, Lake Havasu, Arizona, prepares a **Hot Berry Fondue** to serve with cookies, shortbread, cake, and fruit. Cook a mixture of a pound of summer fruit with 1/2 cup sugar and 2/3 cup water until tender. Mash slightly, stir in 2 tablespoons cornstarch dissolved in a small amount of cold water, and cook until thickened, stirring constantly.*

RHUBARB CHERRY CRISP

1 cup rolled oats	2 tablespoons
1 cup packed brown	cornstarch
sugar	2 or 3 drops red food
1/8 teaspoon salt	coloring
1 cup flour	1 teaspoon vanilla
1/3 cup margarine,	extract
melted	1 (21-ounce) can cherry
4 cups chopped rhubarb	pie filling
1 cup granulated sugar	

Combine the oats, brown sugar, salt and flour in a bowl. Add the melted margarine and blend until crumbly. Pat 2/3 of the flour mixture over the bottom of a buttered 9×13-inch baking dish. Spread the rhubarb over the flour mixture. Combine the granulated sugar, cornstarch and 1 cup water in a saucepan over medium-high heat. Boil gently until thickened, stirring constantly. Stir in the red food coloring and vanilla. Remove from heat. Stir in the cherry pie filling. Spoon evenly over the rhubarb. Sprinkle the remaining flour mixture over the top. Bake at 350 degrees for 45 minutes. Serve warm or cold.
Yield: 15 servings.

Kathy Pemberton, Xi Alpha Beta
Sidney, Montana

BISCUIT STRAWBERRY SHORTCAKE

2 cups flour	1 cup cold milk
2 tablespoons sugar	2 cups sliced
1 teaspoon salt	strawberries, lightly
4 teaspoons baking	sugared
powder	1 teaspoon almond
1/2 teaspoon cream of	extract
tartar	1 cup whipping cream,
1/2 cup cold butter	whipped

Combine the flour, sugar, salt, baking powder and cream of tartar in a bowl and mix well. Cut in the butter until mixture resembles pea-size crumbs. Pour in the milk all at once and combine quickly. Knead gently 8 to 10 strokes on a floured surface. Roll or pat 1/2 to 3/4 inch thick and cut with a small round cookie cutter. Arrange on a buttered baking sheet, close together for soft sides. Bake at 450 degrees for 12 to 15 minutes; cool slightly. Toss the strawberries with the almond extract. Split the shortcakes and place on individual serving plates. Top with the strawberries and whipped cream. Yield: 12 servings.

Carolyn Venus, Upsilon Alpha Master
Mississauga, Ontario, Canada

HEAVENLY AMBROSIA

6 large navel oranges
2 cups grated coconut
¹/₄ cup confectioners'
    sugar

¹/₃ cup orange juice
6 maraschino cherries

Peel the oranges and remove the pith (white part of peel). Cut oranges into thin slices. Layer the orange slices, coconut and powdered sugar ¹/₃ at a time in a serving dish. Drizzle with the orange juice. Chill, covered, for at least 1 hour before serving. Decorate with cherries and serve. Yield: 6 servings.

Louise Sledge, Xi Beta Kappa
Lexington, South Carolina

PINEAPPLE AMBROSIA

2 (17-ounce) cans fruit
    cocktail
2 (20-ounce) cans
    pineapple chunks
2 (11-ounce) cans
    mandarin oranges

4 (4-ounce) packages
    pistachio instant
    pudding mix
2 cups sour cream
12 ounces whipped
    topping

Drain the fruit cocktail, pineapple chunks and mandarin oranges, reserving a total of 3 cups of the juice. Pour the juice into a 4-quart mixing bowl. Add the pudding mix and mix until smooth. Stir in the sour cream. Add the whipped topping and mix until smooth. Fold in the drained fruit. Chill, covered, for at least 2 hours. Sprinkle with chopped pecans just before serving. Yield: 16 to 20 servings.

Sharlene Heinselman, Laureate Mu
Mineral Wells, West Virginia

NEW ORLEANS BANANAS FOSTER

¹/₃ cup light brown sugar
¹/₂ teaspoon grated
    nutmeg
¹/₂ teaspoon cinnamon
¹/₄ cup butter
4 tablespoons banana
    liqueur

5 tablespoons dark rum
4 firm bananas, peeled,
    halved lengthwise
Scoops of vanilla ice
    cream

Combine the brown sugar, nutmeg and cinnamon in a small bowl and mix well. Melt the butter in a heavy skillet over medium-low heat; stir in the brown sugar mixture. Add the banana liqueur and rum and cook until syrupy, stirring constantly. Add the bananas and heat through, turning to coat with the sauce. If cooking over a gas stove, tilt the skillet to set the flame to the sauce; if cooking on an electric stove, light the sauce with a match held at arm's length. Once flames have subsided, place the bananas on serving plates with scoops of ice cream and pour the brown sugar mixture over the top. Serve immediately. Yield: 2 to 4 servings.

Pat Fraser, Beta Zeta Master
London, Ontario, Canada

BANANA CINNAMON SAUCE

¹/₂ cup (1 stick) butter
¹/₂ cup packed brown
    sugar
¹/₂ cup Grand Marnier
¹/₄ teaspoon cinnamon

3 bananas, sliced
¹/₂ cup chopped walnuts
    or pecans
¹/₄ cup raisins
Vanilla ice cream

Melt the butter with the brown sugar in a saucepan or microwave oven. Stir in the Grand Marnier, cinnamon, bananas, chopped nuts and raisins; heat until warm. Serve over ice cream. Yield: 6 servings.

Joyce Snutch, Xi Lambda Lambda
Brechin, Ontario, Canada

BASQUE FRUIT COMPOTE

3 cups dry white wine
1¹/₂ cups sugar
1 teaspoon cinnamon
1 tart apple, peeled,
    cored, sliced

1 ripe pear, peeled,
    cored, sliced
1 cup dried apricots
1 cup pitted prunes
¹/₂ cup currants

Combine the wine and sugar in a large saucepan and bring to a simmer. Add the cinnamon and apple; simmer for 10 minutes, stirring occasionally. Add the pear, apricots, prunes and currants and simmer for 10 minutes longer. Remove from heat. Let stand at room temperature, covered, for 8 to 10 hours. Refrigerate leftovers. Yield: 6 to 8 servings.

Jo Steffanic, Xi Alpha Alpha
Reno, Nevada

FRESH SUMMER FRUIT FLING

1 cup seedless grapes
1 cup whole blueberries
1 cup halved
    strawberries

1 cup sliced peaches
1 cup firmly packed
    brown sugar
2 cups sour cream

Combine the grapes, blueberries, strawberries and peaches in a bowl and mix gently. Spread in a shallow 9×13-inch baking dish. Sprinkle the brown sugar evenly over the top. Cover with sour cream. Cover with plastic wrap. Chill for 3 to 10 hours. Stir gently and serve in individual sherbet glasses.
Yield: 10 to 12 servings.

Dorothy Baker, Laureate Alpha Chi
Pittsburg, Kansas

FRUIT FIESTA

1 cantaloupe, halved and seeded	1 tablespoon orange liqueur (optional)
1/2 honeydew melon, halved and seeded	11/2 teaspoons grated lime zest
1/4 cup superfine sugar	1 cup sliced strawberries
1/4 cup fresh lime juice	1 cup green or red seedless grapes
2 tablespoons fresh lemon juice	

Scoop the flesh from the cantaloupe and honeydew with a melon baller. Combine the sugar, lime juice, lemon juice, orange liqueur and lime zest in a large glass bowl; stir to dissolve the sugar. Add the cantaloupe balls, honeydew balls, strawberries and grapes and mix well. Cover with plastic wrap. Chill for 1 hour, stirring once or twice. Serve with cocktail forks and a fruit dip made from chocolate or sour cream or yogurt. Yield: 10 or more servings.

Kathleen Callery, Preceptor Nu
Kingston, Ontario, Canada

CHRISTMAS FRUIT DESSERT

You may use fresh or canned pears.

4 medium bananas	8 currants
4 large pear halves	8 ounces cream cheese, softened
8 medium strawberries	

Peel the bananas and cut into halves lengthwise; cut off the ends to make 4-inch lengths. Arrange on serving dishes flat side down to form "runners," two on each dish. Scoop out the pear halves a little to make the cavities a little larger and place each over a pair of runners. Trim off the pointed end of each of 4 of the strawberries before placing in a pear cavity. Slice off the large end of each of the remaining 4 strawberries; place "eyes" on the cut end by attaching currants with 1-inch wooden picks. Place each on a strawberry in a pear. Cream the cream cheese with a spoon and use to fill in the joints of the strawberries and spread around the eyes to form beard and hair. Place a dot of cream cheese on the top.
Yield: 4 servings.

Maxine Houser, Preceptor Eta Omicron
West Sacramento, California

WINE PEACHES AND ICE CREAM

8 firm ripe peaches, peeled	1 cup port
2 tablespoons sugar	1 tablespoon red currant jelly
1 cup sherry	1 gallon ice cream

Cut the peaches into halves and remove the pits. Combine the peach pits, sugar, sherry, port and jelly in a saucepan and bring to a simmer. Add the peach halves carefully and simmer for 30 minutes. Remove the peach pits. Remove the peaches to a shallow dish. Cook the liquid over medium-high heat until reduced to a thick syrup. Add sugar to taste if desired. Pour over the peaches. Chill, covered, until serving time. Serve over ice cream and sprinkle with chopped pecans. Yield: 4 to 8 servings.

KK LeBlanc, Xi Rho
Carlyss, Louisiana

❖ BUTTERSCOTCH POACHED PEARS

You can serve this dish at the beginning of a meal or use it for dessert. I would call it the "Beginnings and Endings" recipe . . . and you can drink the wine that was used to poach the pears!

1 cup packed light brown sugar	1 (2-inch) strip lemon peel
1/4 cup unsalted butter	2 tablespoons lemon juice
1/4 cup light corn syrup	1 whole cinnamon stick
1/4 teaspoon salt	6 whole cloves
1/2 cup heavy cream	6 firm ripe Bosc pears with stems
2 teaspoons vanilla extract	
1 (75-milliliter) bottle white wine	
11/2 cups granulated sugar	

Combine the brown sugar, butter, corn syrup and salt in a small saucepan over medium-low heat. Cook for 3 minutes, stirring constantly. Bring to a boil over medium-high heat and boil gently for 2 minutes without stirring. Remove from heat and stir in the cream and vanilla. Cool. Chill, covered, for 1 hour. Combine the wine, sugar, lemon peel, lemon juice, cinnamon stick and cloves in a large saucepan and bring to a boil; boil for 5 minutes, or until sugar is dissolved. Peel the pears, leaving on the stems. Core from the bottom. Add the pears to the saucepan and simmer for 10 to 15 minutes or until tender. Remove to a bowl. Chill, covered, for 4 hours. Spoon a little sauce onto each individual serving plate and place the pear in the sauce. Pass additional sauce.
Yield: 6 servings.

Margie Kelarek, Laureate Eta Beta
Hilltop Lakes, Texas

BRAISED PEARS

Use pears that are not too ripe.

6 medium pears (Anjou, Bosc, Comice)	4 teaspoons unsalted butter
3 to 4 tablespoons sugar	11/2 cups heavy cream

Peel the pears and cut into halves lengthwise. Remove seeds and core. Arrange the pear halves flat side down in a gratin dish large enough that pears do not overlap. Sprinkle the sugar over the top and dot with the butter. Bake at 425 degrees for 35 minutes or until sugar has caramelized and pears feel tender when pierced with the point of a knife. Bake for another 5 to 10 minutes if pears are not yet tender; if liquid turns to caramel before pears are done, add 1 cup water. Add the cream and return to the oven. Bake for 10 to 15 minutes longer, basting every 5 minutes. The sauce should be reduced and thickened and a nice ivory color. If it reduces too much and it appears to be breaking down, add 3 or 4 tablespoons water. Serve lukewarm. Yield: 6 servings.

Rose Cook, Preceptor Xi Sigma
Cypress, Texas

STRAWBERRIES AND CREAM WITH CHOCOLATE

Artificial sweetener or sugar to taste	*1 pint strawberries, rinsed and drained*
8 ounces cream cheese, softened	*4 ounces dark chocolate, grated*

Blend sweetener into the cream cheese. Place the cream cheese, strawberries and dark chocolate in each of 3 serving bowls. Guests will dip strawberries in cream cheese and sprinkle with chocolate. Ingredients may be placed in individual serving bowls for the guests if desired. Yield: about 6 servings.

Aleksandra Stolley, Delta Gamma
Corpus Christi, Texas

SWEET DESSERT CHEESE BALL

4 ounces cream cheese, softened	*2 tablespoons fruit juice of choice (not lemon or lime)*
1 (4-ounce) package vanilla instant pudding mix	*1/2 cup chopped pecans*

Combine the cream cheese, dry pudding mix and fruit juice in a mixing bowl and mix until smooth. Roll into a ball and roll in chopped pecans. Chill, wrapped in plastic wrap, for at least 2 hours. Serve with shortbread cookies. Yield: 6 to 8 servings.

Imelda E. Sears, Laureate Epsilon Alpha
Panama City Beach, Florida

FRUIT FONDUE WITH RUM

3 cups firmly packed brown sugar	*1/3 cup butter*
1 cup evaporated milk	*1/4 cup rum*

Combine the brown sugar, evaporated milk and butter in the top of a double boiler over boiling water. Bring to a boil, stirring constantly. Boil for 3 minutes, stirring constantly. Remove from heat and let stand for 3 minutes. Stir in the rum. Serve warm or cool as a dip for chunks of Red Delicious apples, or use as a sauce for ice cream or pound cake. Yield: 4 to 6 servings.

Neva S. Ashmore, Xi Lambda
Steens, Mississippi

CHOCOLATE FONDUE

1 cup semisweet chocolate chips	*Pound cake cubes, banana slices, apple chunks, peach chunks, melon balls, orange slices, strawberries, cherries, ladyfinger pieces*
1/2 cup chocolate milk	
1 teaspoon butter	
1/4 teaspoon vanilla extract	
1 tablespoon liqueur of choice (optional)	

Combine the chocolate chips and chocolate milk in a small heavy saucepan over medium heat. Cook until chocolate melts and mixture is smooth, stirring constantly. Remove from heat. Stir in the butter. Stir in the vanilla and liqueur. Pour into a fondue pot and light the candle to keep warm. Serve with cake cubes and pieces of fruit for dipping. Yield: about 1 cup.

Arlene M. Hamilton, Xi Delta Alpha
Hamilton, Ontario, Canada

CHOCO-MALLOW FONDUE

2 cups semisweet chocolate chips	*Banana chunks, pineapple chunks, marshmallows, strawberries, apple slices, cubes of angel food or pound cake, amaretti (Italian almond cookies)*
1 (14-ounce) can sweetened condensed milk	
1 (7-ounce) jar marshmallow creme	
1/2 cup milk	
1 teaspoon vanilla extract	*1/2 cup slivered almonds or chopped walnuts*

Heat the chocolate chips with the condensed milk, marshmallow creme, milk and vanilla in a saucepan or microwave oven just until melted and smooth, whisking occasionally. Remove to a fondue pot and keep warm. Serve with pieces of cake, fruit and cookies. Spear with fondue forks and dip in the chocolate marshmallow sauce. Allow excess sauce to drip off; dip in the slivered almonds.
Yield: 8 (1/2-cup) servings.

Melody Malek, Beta Chi
Independence, Iowa

Metric Equivalents

*A*lthough the United States has opted to postpone converting to metric
measurements, most other countries, including England and Canada,
use the metric system. The following chart provides convenient approximate
equivalents for allowing use of regular kitchen measures when cooking from
foreign recipes.

Volume

*These metric measures are approximate benchmarks for purposes
of home food preparation.*
1 milliliter = 1 cubic centimeter = 1 gram

Liquid	Dry
1 teaspoon = 5 milliliters	1 quart = 1 liter
1 tablespoon = 15 milliliters	1 ounce = 30 grams
1 fluid ounce = 30 milliliters	1 pound = 450 grams
1 cup = 250 milliliters	2.2 pounds = 1 kilogram
1 pint = 500 milliliters	

Weight

1 ounce = 28 grams
1 pound = 450 grams

Length

1 inch = $2\frac{1}{2}$ centimeters
$1/16$ inch = 1 millimeter

Formulas Using Conversion Factors

*When approximate conversions are not accurate enough, use these
formulas to convert measures from one system to another.*

Measurements	Formulas
ounces to grams:	# ounces x 28.3 = # grams
grams to ounces:	# grams x 0.035 = # ounces
pounds to grams:	# pounds x 453.6 = # grams
pounds to kilograms	# pounds x 0.45 = # kilograms
ounces to milliliters:	# ounces x 30 = # milliliters
cups to liters:	# cups x 0.24 = # liters
inches to centimeters	# inches x 2.54 = # centimeters
centimeters to inches:	# centimeters x 0.39 = # inches

Approximate Weight to Volume

Some ingredients which we commonly measure by volume are measured by weight in foreign recipes. Here are a few examples for easy reference.

flour, all-purpose, unsifted	1 pound = 450 grams = 3½ cups
flour, all-purpose, sifted	1 pound = 450 grams = 4 cups
sugar, granulated	1 pound = 450 grams = 2 cups
sugar, brown, packed	1 pound = 450 grams = 2¼ cups
sugar, confectioners'	1 pound = 450 grams = 4 cups
sugar, confectioners', sifted	1 pound = 450 grams = 4½ cups
butter	1 pound = 450 grams = 2 cups

Temperature

Remember that foreign recipes frequently express temperatures in Centigrade rather than Fahrenheit.

Temperatures	Fahrenheit	Centigrade
room temperature	68°	20°
water boils	212°	100°
baking temperature	350°	177°
baking temperature	375°	190.5°
baking temperature	400°	204.4°
baking temperature	425°	218.3°
baking temperature	450°	232°

Use the following formulas when temperature conversions are necessary.

Centigrade degrees x $9/5$ + 32 = Fahrenheit degrees
Fahrenheit degrees - 32 x $5/9$ = Centigrade degrees

American Measurement Equivalents

1 tablespoon = 3 teaspoons	12 tablespoons = ¾ cup
2 tablespoons = 1 ounce	16 tablespoons = 1 cup
4 tablespoons = ¼ cup	1 cup = 8 ounces
5 tablespoons + 1 teaspoon = ⅓ cup	2 cups = 1 pint
8 tablespoons = ½ cup	4 cups = 1 quart
	4 quarts = 1 gallon

Merit Winners

Hayworth, LaVern, page 105
Jones, Dorothy, page 86
Keatley, Lorraine, page 92
McDaniel, Lynda, page 92
Piper, E. Irene, page 102
Powell, Cheryl, page 99
Renville, Roberta, page 101
Saveraid, Jean, page 98
Schlarb, Sheila, page 101
Shockey, Delona, page 91
Sisnetsky, Olga, page 107
Steinbeck, Michelle,
    page 105

PIES & PASTRIES
First Place
Burken, Arlene, page 116
Second Place
Conway, Cheryl L., page 136
Third Place
Wallace, Eugenia, page 127
Honorable Mention
Aleo, Diana T., page 114
Allen, Sylvia, page 126
Botkins, Dodie, page 120
Boutilier, Anne, page 123
Caimano, Jeanne, page 121
Cook, Lillian, page 113
Courten, Mary A., page 125
Daily, Mary L., page 124
Foster, Kathy, page 119
Graber, Julie A., page 125
Greer, Irene, page 128
Harding, Candace, page 123
Henderson, Barbara,
    page 115
Herbst, Judie M., page 129
Hornsby, Jayne, page 126
Housteau, Wanda, page 133
Lockwood, Millie, page 131
McGuire, Jean, page 113
McKeehan, Judy, page 132
McPherson, Valerie,
    page 117
Mogk, Edna, page 135
Orme, Betty J., page 122
Patterson, Jeri, page 124
Pickell, Sue, page 127
Roth, Janice, page 118
Scoggins, Ruth M., page 122
Zuidhof-Knoop, Edith,
    page 131

BARS & BROWNIES
First Place
Reiter, Sally, page 145
Second Place
McDaniel, Beverly, page 139
Third Place
Soard, Patricia R., page 155
Honorable Mention
Dickson, Rhoda, page 143
Emig, Sharmis, page 154
Fenter, Gloria, page 148
Fogle, Rhonda, page 151
Gwynn, Debbi, page 144
Hebblethwaite, Anita,
    page 152
Kerouac, Sue, page 153
Leidy, Rebecca, page 141
Muhleman, Betty L., page 142
Petersen, Jeanette, page 147
Prescott, Anita, page 147
Rayner, Sharon, page 140
Sharp, Mildred, page 140
Shurb, Phyllis, page 149
Van Etten, Julie, page 150

COOKIES & CANDY
First Place
Montgomery, Rita, page 161
Second Place
Williams, Mary Ann, page 175
Third Place
Nelson, Jan C., page 175
Honorable Mention
Center, Laurie, page 174
Cibuzar, Ardyce, page 165
DeMarinis, Kristine, page 158
Gumfory, Darlene, page 163
Hannan, Laura, page 165
Hersey, Diana, page 157
McHone, Sara, page 171
Milligan, Anita, page 171
Minor, Lillian, page 160
New, Sharon, page 164
Richards, Phoebe, page 160
Sansone, Mary Ellen,
    page 170
Steinle, Kim, page 163
Trantham, Pat, page 162

REFRIGERATOR DESSERTS
First Place
Hill, Diane, page 188

Second Place
Stewart, Dena, page 177
Third Place
Looney, Vickie, page 180
Honorable Mention
Anderson, Berlita, page 183
Baldwin, Terri K., page 189
Dix, Cindy, page 178
Donay, Dorothy M., page 177
Erickson, Shirley M., page 188
Ingman, Nancy, page 183
Jordan, Denise, page 190
Kelly, Jennifer, page 186
Lawson, Viktoria, page 178
Lipps, Ann, page 181
Myers, Millie, page 187
Rau, Irene E., page 186
Register, Cookie, page 188
Romagnoli, Rita, page 186
Stephens, Diane, page 188
Tasler, Mary Ruth, page 184

MORE DESSERTS
First Place
Dillow, Kim, page 197
Second Place
Layton, Cindy, page 196
Third Place
Kelarek, Margie, page 210
Honorable Mention
Agnew, Jo, page 199
Baker, Dorothy, page 209
Bell, Marcella L., page 208
Chelesvig, Evelyn, page 203
Dittfurth, Lillie, page 206
Dodson, Connie, page 193
Duhon, Connie, page 207
Duke, Janice, page 203
Dutch, Wanda, page 204
Hass, Marie, page 201
Hill, Eileen, page 195
Knipe, G. Arlene, page 207
Lerach, Roxanne, page 204
Malek, Melody, page 211
McAlpin, Diane, page 199
Pemberton, Kathy, page 208
Promowicz, Candace R. M.,
    page 198
Snoke, Andrea, page 204
Snutch, Joyce, page 209
Trumbull, Joanne,
    page 201

Index of Beginnings

Index of Endings

Beta Sigma Phi Cookbooks

available from *Favorite Recipes® Press* are chock-full of
home-tested recipes from Beta Sigma Phi members that earn you
the best compliment of all… "More Please!"

Every cookbook includes:

☆ delicious, family-
   pleasing recipes

☆ lay-flat binding

☆ wipe-clean color covers

☆ easy-to-read format

☆ comprehensive index

☆ almost 1,000 recipes

To place your order,
call our toll-free number
1-800-251-1520
or clip and mail the
convenient form below.

BETA SIGMA PHI COOKBOOKS	Item #	Qty.	U.S. Retail Price	Canadian Retail Price	Total
Memories of Home	1015581		$9.95	$12.95	
Beginnings & Endings	1018683		$9.95	$12.95	
Shipping and Handling		1	$1.95	$ 2.95	
TOTAL AMOUNT					

☐ Payment Enclosed   ☐ Please Charge My
        ☐ American Express ☐ Discover
        ☐ MasterCard ☐ Visa

Canadian orders: checks or money orders only

Signature _____

Account Number _____

Name _____

Address _____

City _____ State _____ Zip _____

No COD orders please.

Call our toll-free number for
faster ordering.

Please allow 30 days for delivery.

Mail completed order form to:

Favorite Recipes® Press
P.O. Box 305147
Nashville, TN 37230

Photocopies will be accepted.